BUTCHER, BAKER, CANDLESTICK MAKER

Occupations
in
Newburyport, Massachusetts
from the 1850 Census

WITH A COMPILATION OF INFORMATION LISTING
RESIDENTS WHO CAME TO THE CITY FROM
OTHER STATES AND COUNTRIES

CELEBRATING THE 150ᵀᴴ
ANNIVERSARY OF THE CITY OF
NEWBURYPORT, MASSACHUSETTS

Abstracted by
Margaret Peckham Motes

HERITAGE BOOKS
2012

HERITAGE BOOKS
AN IMPRINT OF HERITAGE BOOKS, INC.

Books, CDs, and more—Worldwide

For our listing of thousands of titles see our website at
www.HeritageBooks.com

Published 2012 by
HERITAGE BOOKS, INC.
Publishing Division
100 Railroad Ave. #104
Westminster, Maryland 21157

Copyright © 2001 Margaret Peckham Motes

All rights reserved. No part of this book may be reproduced or transmitted in any form or by any means, electronic or mechanical, including photocopying, recording or by any information storage and retrieval system without written permission from the author, except for the inclusion of brief quotations in a review.

International Standard Book Numbers
Paperbound: 978-0-7884-1823-5
Clothbound: 978-0-7884-9464-2

CONTENTS

Preface   v

Microcopy Records and   ix
Abstract Format

Abbreviations   ix

Surnames
Alphabetically listed   1 - 179

Appendix
In California   180

Index
Name   183
Occupation   191
Place of Birth   198

PREFACE

On June 24, 1851 Newburyport, Massachusetts was incorporated as a city and Caleb Cushing became the city's first Major. In the 1850's Newburyport was a bustling area with the building of the merchant ships in the boat yards along the Merrimac River and with the arrival of ships at the custom House from foreign ports bringing their goods from China, the West Indies and Europe.

Many books have been written about the history of the area and the important people who helped shape the area, but little is known about the workers in the city - where they came from and what they did in helping the city to grow and change.

This book has been prepared as a part of the celebration of the Sesquicentennial of the City of Newburyport. Using data from the 1850 Federal Census for Newburyport, two subjects were examined; 1) the place of birth of all residents born outside of Massachusetts, including foreign born, to demonstrate migration patterns, and 2) all occupations of Newburyport residents to demonstrate diversity of skills.

The abstracted information for this book was entered into a database and included: name, age, sex, occupation, color, place of birth, household and dwelling number, and the area within Newburyport. The names are listed alphabetically, then by age. Persons who are not found alphabetically are listed in the Surname Index.

The Federal Census for Newburyport shows the population was 9,572 residents, comprised of 4,158 white males, 5,374 white females, 23 colored males, and 16 colored females. There were 1,927 families and 1,431 dwellings in the city; and 1,362 residents who were of foreign birth.

There are over 4,800 individuals listed in this book between the age of one month to ninety two years of age. The oldest person listed is Abraham Wheelwright, Merchant, age 92, born in Massachusetts.

The largest number of immigrants came from Ireland and many are listed as laborers and fishermen. Many of the famine-stricken Irish left for England, then removed to Nova Scotia, New Brunswick and Maine before they settled in Newburyport. This pattern of movement is shown in the birth order and the places of birth for these children. Other immigrants came from England and Scotland and they brought with them their skills in weaving, many working in the fabric mills, with others listed as mariners and master mariners. This migration brought with it new growth, development, and socioeconomic changes to the area.

There was movement into Newburyport from the New England states, from Delaware, Maryland, Pennsylvania and some southern states.

The census data shows the following ranking for places of birth of persons born outside Massachusetts - New Hampshire (826), Maine (718), Ireland (687), England (192), Nova Scotia (150), Vermont (64), Rhode Island (62), New York (35), and Scotland (16). (See the Place of Birth Index for the full data).

The data for occupation lists over 2,172 people in the work force. The largest groups in order are: mariners, master mariners, laborers, shoemakers, operatives, carpenters, merchants, clerks, blacksmiths, painters. There were many involved in ship building who are listed by their trade, such as ship joiners, sail makers, and mast makers.

The census enumerator listed few occupations for woman. The women who were listed ran boarding houses. However, occupations for woman can be found in the *1850 Newburyport City Directory*.

The ship yards, shoe factories, fabric mills and tanneries which once dominated the skyline are gone now, only a few of the old factory buildings survive. These buildings now provide office space for the new high tech businesses, and apartments for those who work in the area or who commute to Boston and surrounding area towns.

Today the job market is constantly changing as more residents are working at home as graphic designers, computer and software developers, consultants, free lance writers and artists.

Looking at the occupations held by city residents 150 years ago, many of these positions can still be found today, e.g., bankers, butchers, bakers, grocers, boat builders (though on a smaller scale), physicians, dentists, merchants, fishermen, farmers, clerks, auctioneers, laborers, lawyers, bridge attendants, artists, gold and silversmiths, jewelers, house keepers, editors, publishers, dance teachers, school teachers, clergymen, masons, and many others.

Occupations which have disappeared are: mast makers, sail makers, tanners, cordwainers, mule spinners, math instruments makers, livery stable keepers, stage coach drivers, wheelwrights, soap boilers, stage drivers, and hatters.

In the Appendix there is a list of men who went to California, which was found in the 1850 Newburyport City Directory.

Suggested reading for further reading on the development of *Newburyport: History of Newburyport; From the Earliest Settlement of the Country to the Present Time* with a Biographical Appendix by Mrs. E. Vale Smith, Newburyport, 1854. Boston: Press of Damrell and Moore.

Margaret Peckham Motes
Newburyport, Massachusetts

MICROCOPY RECORDS:

1850 Massachusetts Federal Census

M432-313 Newburyport, Massachusetts

Abstracted Format:

> Last name, first name, age, sex, occupation {if indicated}, color, birthplace, dwelling houses numbered in the order of visitation, family numbered in the order of visitation, area. Notes if any apply (In HH of....)

Examples:

> BARTLETT, Joseph, 46, M, Mariner, W, MA, 559, 832, NBPT.
>
> BARTON, Betsy, 15, F, -, W, Canada, 536, 802, NBPT. In HH of Francis Barton, age 40, Laborer, born in Canada.

Spelling of names is always difficult, and many variations appear for the same names. Every effort has been made to keep the spelling of first and last name as they appeared in the census record.

Abbreviations:

Place:

AL	Alabama		
CT	Connecticut	NY	New York
D.C.	District of Columbia	PA	Pennsylvania
GA	Georgia	RI	Rhode Island
ILL	Illinois	VA	Virginia
LA	Louisiana	VT	Vermont
MA	Massachusetts	B	Black
MD	Maryland	M	Mulatto
MO	Missouri	In HH	In Household
NC	North Carolina	NBPT	Newburyport
N.B.	New Brunswick	NBPT*	Newburyport and North of Green Street
N.S.	Nova Scotia		
NH	New Hampshire		
NJ	New Jersey		

Dedicated

to

J.H. Motes, III

Whose Interest and Encouragement
Have Made This Work Possible

- A-

ABBOT, JOSEPH, 65, M, Blacksmith, W, NH, 441, 584, NBPT*. In HH of Moses Butts, age 44, Mariner, born in Newfoundland.
ABBOTT, DORCAS, 45, F, -, W, Maine, 736,1041, NBPT. In HH of John L. Grindal, age 48, Grocer, born in Maine.
ABBOTT, MARGARET, 12, F, -, W, Maine, 676, 968, NBPT. In HH of Sarah Hooke, age 75, born in MA.
ADAMS HANNAH, 80, F, -, W, NH, 131, 193, NBPT. In HH of Ebenezer Plumer, age 73, Merchant, born in MA.
ADAMS, Aaron B., 55, M, Merchant, W, MA, 130, 192, NBPT.
ADAMS, ANNETTA, 7, F, -, W, NH, 145, 213, NBPT. In HH of Joseph C. Adams, age 34, Blacksmith, born in NH.
ADAMS, CALEB C., 17, M, Clerk, W, MA, 363, 535, NBPT. In HH of Harriet Adams, age 51, born in MA.
ADAMS, CHARLES, 44, M, Cooper, W, MA, 73, 106, NBPT.
ADAMS, CHARLES, 30, M, Overseer, W, NH, 271, 398, NBPT. In HH of Horace Brown, age 52, Stage Agent, born in MA.
ADAMS, CHARLES A., 16, M, None, W, MA, 73, 106, NBPT. In HH of Charles Adams, age 44, Cooper, born in MA.
ADAMS, EDGAR E., 7, M, -, W, Maine, 79, 88, NBPT*. In HH of Paul S. Adams, age 38, Baptist Clergyman, born Maine.
ADAMS, ELIZA C., 44, F, -, W, Maine, 104, 124, NBPT*. In HH or Mary Coffin, age 82, born MA.
ADAMS, GEORGE F., 17, M, None, W, MA, 52, 77, NBPT. In HH of Joel Adams, age 40, Carpenter, born in MA.
ADAMS, JOEL, 40, M, Carpenter, W, MA, 52, 77, NBPT.
ADAMS, JOHN L., 15, M, -, W, NH, 8, 8, NBPT. In HH of Charles H. Hale, age 30, Carpenter, born in MA.
ADAMS, JOHN T., 25, M, Butcher, W, MA, 504, 752, NBPT.
ADAMS, JOSEPH C., 34, M, Blacksmith, W, NH, 145, 213, NBPT.
ADAMS, NANCY, 25, F, -, W, NH, 271, 398, NBPT. In HH of Horace Brown, age 52, Stage Agent, born in MA.
ADAMS, PAUL S., 38, M, Baptist Clergyman, W, Maine, 79, 88, NBPT*.
ADAMS, RICHARD, 28, M, Carpenter, W, MA, 791, 1119, NBPT.
ADAMS, SARAH B., 29, F, -, W, NH, 145, 213, NBPT. In HH of Joseph C. Adams, age 34, Blacksmith, born in NH.
ADAMS, SARAH F., 9, F, -, W, NH, 145, 213, NBPT. In HH of Joseph C. Adams, age 34, Blacksmith, born in NH.
ADAMS, SELWYN P., 18, M, Painter, W, MA, 187, 229, NBPT*. In HH of William J. Creasey, age

28, Painter, born in MA.
ADAMS, SMITH, 37, M, Cooper, W, MA, 111, 164, NBPT. In HH of Sarah Hougue, age 60, born in NH.
ADAMS, SUSAN J., 28, F, -, W, Maine, 79, 88, NBPT*. In HH of Paul S. Adams, age 38, Baptist Clergymen, born Maine.
ADAMS, THOMAS H., 33, M, Teamster, W, MA, 84, 122, NBPT.
ADAMS, WASHINGTON, 34, M, Merchant, W, MA, 555, 828, NBPT.
ADAMS, WILLIAM, 75, M, Merchant, W, MA, 315, 408, NBPT*.
ADAMS, WILLIAM H, 22, M, Rope Maker, W, MA, 74, 108, NBPT. In HH of Ann A. Adams, age 51, born in MA.
ADDISON, MARY D.G., 24, F, -, W, NH, 461, 609, NBPT*. In HH of Timothy Hilliard, age 46, Shoe Store, born in NH.
AIKEN, JOHN, 40, M, Mariner, W, MA, 471, 625, NBPT*.
AIKEN, THOMAS, 40, M, Shoemaker, W, MA, 471, 625, NBPT*. In HH of John Aiken, age 40, Mariner, born in MA.
AIKEN, THOMAS, 27, M, Stage Driver, W, NH, 306, 452, NBPT.
AKERMAN, JOHN, 53, M, Deputy Sheriff, W, MA, 78, 87, NBPT*.
AKERMAN, JOSEPH, 40, M, Victualer, W, MA, 571, 757, NBPT*.
AKERMAN, OLIVER M., 47, M, Victualer, W, MA, 569, 755, NBPT*.
ALDOM, EDGAR, 40, M, Tailor, W, MA, 246, 309, NBPT*.

ALEXANDER, CHARLES L., 19, M, Carpenter, W, MA, 356, 519, NBPT. In HH of Hannah Alexander, age 62, born in MA.
ALEXANDER, CORNELIUS, 24, M, Grocer, W, MA, 356, 519, NBPT. In HH of Hannah Alexander, age 62, born in MA.
ALEXANDER, WILLIAM, 26, M, Carpenter, W, MA, 356, 519, NBPT. In HH of Hannah Alexander, age 62, born in MA.
ALLEN, CHARLES H., 33, M, Laborer, W, England, 458, 605, NBPT*.
ALLEN, GEORGE E., 21, M, Baker, W, Maine, 591, 868, NBPT. In HH of Samuel T. Payson, age 34, Baker, born in MA.
ALLEY, CHARLES, 19, M, Shoemaker, W, MA, 156, 186, NBPT*. In HH of Joseph Alley, age 47, Organ Builder, born in MA.
ALLEY, GEORGE, 16, M, Shoemaker, W, MA, 156, 186, NBPT*. In HH of Joseph Alley, age 47, Organ Builder, born in MA.
ALLEY, HENRY, 15, M, Shoemaker, W, MA, 156, 186, NBPT*. In HH of Joseph Alley, age 47, Organ Builder, born in MA.
ALLEY, JOSEPH, 47, M, Organ Builder, W, MA, 156, 186, NBPT*.
ALLEY, JOSEPH, 18, M, Organ Builder, W, MA, 156, 186, NBPT*. In HH of Joseph Alley, age 47, Organ Builder, born in MA.
AMBROSE, ANN N., 2, F, -, W, NH, 296, 432, NBPT. In HH of David N. Ambrose, age 28, School Teacher, born in NH.
AMBROSE, DAVID N., 28, M, School teacher, W, NH, 296, 432,

NBPT.
AMBROSE, JUDITH W., 28, F, -, W, NH, 296, 432, NBPT. In HH of David N. Ambrose, age 28, School Teacher, born in NH.
AMES, DRUSSILLA, 59, F, -, W, Maine, 116, 172, NBPT. In HH of Ebenezer Ames, age 45, Pilot, born in Maine.
AMES, EBENEZER, 45, M, Pilot, W, Maine, 116, 172, NBPT.
ANDERSON, ADELAIDE M., 3, F, -, W, Nova Scotia, 375, 492, NBPT* In HH of Thomas Anderson, age 37, Cooper, born in Nova Scotia.
ANDERSON, ANNA S., 5, F, -, W, Nova Scotia, 375, 492, NBPT*. In HH of Thomas Anderson, age 37, Cooper, born in Nova Scotia.
ANDERSON, FRANK, 1, M, -, W, Nova Scotia, 375, 492, NBPT*. In HH of Thomas Anderson, age 37, Cooper, born in Nova Scotia.
ANDERSON, HANNAH, 27, F, -, W, Nova Scotia, 375, 492, NBPT*. In HH of Thomas Anderson, age 37, Cooper, born in Nova Scotia.
ANDERSON, MARY, 40, F, -, W, Ireland, 329, 485, NBPT. In HH of Henry Johnson, age 54, Merchant, born in MA.
ANDERSON, SARAH E., 7, F, -, W, Nova Scotia, 375, 492, NBPT*. In HH of Thomas Anderson, age 37, Cooper, born in Nova Scotia.
ANDERSON, THOMAS, 37, M, Cooper, W, Nova Scotia, 375, 492, NBPT*.
ANDREW, Aaron, 50, M, Cooper, W, N.S., 495, 738, NBPT. .
ANDREW, AMELIA, 46, F, -, W, N.S., 495, 738, NBPT. In HH of Aaron Andrews, age 50, Cooper, born in N.S. {Nova Scotia}.
ANDREW, GEORGE, 21, M, Cooper, W, N.S., 495, 738, NBPT. In HH of Aaron Andrews, age 50, Cooper, born in N.S. {Nova Scotia}.
ANDREW, GEORGE, 18, M, Operative, W, NH, 514, 685, NBPT*. In HH of Aaron Gardner, age 30, Carpenter, born in NH.
ANDREW, JOHN H., 13, M, -, W, N.S., 495, 738, NBPT. In HH of Aaron Andrews, age 50, Cooper, born in N.S. {Nova Scotia}.
ANDREW, LYDIA J., 16, F, -, W, N.S., 495, 738, NBPT. In HH of Aaron Andrews, age 50, Cooper, born in N.S. {Nova Scotia}.
ANDREW, MARTHA, 27, F, -, W, N.S., 495, 739, NBPT. In HH of Thomas N. Andrews, age 22, Cooper, born in N.S. {Nova Scotia}.
ANDREW, SAMUEL, 10, M, -, W, N.S., 495, 738, NBPT. In HH of Aaron Andrews, age 50, Cooper, born in N.S. {Nova Scotia}.
ANDREW, THOMAS N., 22, M, Cooper, W, N.S., 495, 739, NBPT.
ANDREW, WILLIAM, 26, M, Mason, W, MA, 41, 59, NBPT.
ANDREWS, JOHN, 50, M, Cashier, W, MA, 120, 143,NBPT*.
ANDREWS, WILLIAM H., 24, M, Clerk, W, NH, 782,1108, NBPT. In HH of Enoch Tilton, age 45, Hotel Keeper, born in NH. In Hotel.
ANNIS, ELIZA. M., 25, F, -, W, Maine, 177, 214, NBPT*. In HH of John W. Annis, age 45, Shoemaker, born in VT.
ANNIS, JOHN W., 45, M,

Shoemaker, W, VT, 177, 214, NBPT*.

ANRIGHT, CORNELIUS, 14, M, -, W, Ireland, 539, 806, NBPT. In HH of James Anright, age 70, Laborer, born in Ireland.

ANRIGHT, JAMES, 70, M, Laborer, W, Ireland, 539, 806, NBPT.

ANRIGHT, JOHN N., 24, M, Laborer, W, Ireland, 539, 806, NBPT. In HH of James Anright, age 70, Laborer, born in Ireland.

ANRIGHT, JULIA A., 10, F, -, W, Ireland, 539, 806, NBPT. In HH of James Anright, age 70, Laborer, born in Ireland.

ANRIGHT, MARGARET, 21, F, -, W, Ireland, 539, 806, NBPT. In HH of James Anright, age 70, Laborer, born in Ireland.

ANRIGHT, MARY C., 50, F, -, W, Ireland, 539, 806, NBPT. In HH of James Anright, age 70, Laborer, born in Ireland.

APPLETON, BENJN., 46, M, Hatter, W, MA, 432, 642, NBPT.

APPLETON, NATHL., 18, M, Grocer, W, MA, 302, 443, NBPT. In HH of Ann Appleton, age 52, born in MA.

ARAFTEN?, CATHERINE, 60, F, -, W, Ireland, 528, 787, NBPT. In HH of John Araften?, age 60, Laborer, born in Ireland.

ARAFTEN?, JOHN, 60, M, Laborer, W, Ireland, 528, 787, NBPT.

ARAFTEN?, MARGARET, 23, F, -, W, Ireland, 528, 787, NBPT. In HH of John Araften?, age 60, Laborer, born in Ireland.

ARMITAGE, GEORGE, 47, M,

Shoemaker, W, MA, 36, 50, NBPT.

ARMITAGE, GEORGE, 25, M, Merchant, W, MA, 309, 456, NBPT. In HH of Charles H. Hudson, age 28, Merchant, born in MA.

ARMITAGE, JAMES W., 18, M, Spinner, W, MA, 36, 50, NBPT. In HH of George Armitage, age 47, Shoemaker, born in MA.

ARMSTRONG, GEORGE, 42, M, Mason, W, England, 227, 281, NBPT*.

ARMSTRONG, LUCY, 41, F, -, W, England, 227, 281, NBPT*. In HH of George Armstrong, age 42, Mason, born in England.

ASBY, MARK T., 24, M, Farmer, W, MA, 671, 963, NBPT. In HH of William Asby, age 29, Farmer, born in MA.

ASBY, WILLIAM, 29, M, Farmer, W, MA, 671, 963, NBPT.

ASH, DAVID, 41, M, Shoemaker, W, MA, 403, 527, NBPT*.

ASH, GEORGE, 36, M, Harness Maker, W, MA, 552, 825, NBPT.

ASH, HARRIET B., 24, F, -, W, Maine, 382, 504, NBPT*.

ASHBY, ANN, 54, F, -, W, England, 10, 10, NBPT*. In HH of William Ashby, 63, trader, born in England.

ASHBY, WILLIAM, 63, M, Trader, W, England, 10, 10, NBPT*.

ATKINSON, JAMES W., 17, M, Seaman, W, MA, 314, 407, NBPT*. In HH of John Atkinson, age 51, Physician, born in Maine.

ATKINSON, JOHN, 55, M, Laborer, W, MA, 648, 938, NBPT. In HH of Anthony Cogger, age 37,

Laborer, born in Ireland.
ATKINSON, JOHN, 51, M, Physician, W, Maine, 314, 407, NBPT*.
ATKINSON, JOHN, 17, M, Mariner, W, England, 648, 938, NBPT. In HH of Anthony Cogger, age 37, Laborer, born in Ireland.
ATKINSON, JOHN JR., 22, M, Clerk, W, MA, 314, 407, NBPT*. In HH of John Atkinson, age 51, Physician, born in Maine.
ATKINSON, MICHAEL, 37, M, Shoemaker, W, MA, 215, 268, NBPT*.
ATWATER, CONSTANT, 19, M, Mariner, W, MA, 358, 472, NBPT*. In HH of William Atwater, age 64, Master Mariner, born in CT.
ATWATER, WILLIAM, 64, M, Master Mariner, W, CT, 358, 472, NBPT*.
ATWOOD, FANNY M., 37, F, -, W, NH, 505, 673, NBPT*. In HH of John B. Atwood, age 40, Ship Carpenter, born in MA.
ATWOOD, JOHN B., 40, M, Ship Carpenter, W, MA, 505, 673, NBPT*.
ATWOOD, REBECCA, 26, F, -, W, VT, 733,1035, NBPT. In HH of Stephen Downs, age 31, Mariner, born in MA.
ATWOOD, THOMAS, 37, M, Ship Joiner, W, MA, 497, 660, NBPT*.
AUBIN, CHARLES, 29, M, Laborer, W, MA, 439, 652, NBPT. In HH of Jane Aubin, age 68, born in NH.
AUBIN, JANE, 68, F, -, W, NH, 439, 652, NBPT.

AUBIN, JOHN, 27, M, Book Agent, W, MA, 439, 652, NBPT.
AVERY, ALICE, 20, F, -, W, Maine, 243, 306, NBPT*. In HH of Rebekah Carpenter, age 58, born in MA.
AVERY, BETHANY, 16, F, -, W, Maine, 427, 633, NBPT. In HH of Walter Gould, age 49, Carpenter, born in Maine.
AYNWANT?, MARY, 50, F, -, W, Newfoundland, 758,1070, NBPT. In HH of Michael Aynwant, age 56, Mariner, born in Ireland.
AYNWANT, MICHAEL, 56, M, Mariner, W, Ireland, 758,1070, NBPT.

-B-

BABSON, JOSEPH E., 20, M, Periodical Book Store, W, MA, 580, 768, NBPT*. In HH of Sarah E. Babson, age 42, born in MA.
BACKMAN, SOLOMON, 24, M, Merchant, W, Germany, 782,1108, NBPT. In HH of Enoch Tilton, age 45, Hotel Keeper, born in NH. In Hotel.
BADGER, CHARLES F., 27, M, Trader, W, NH, 256, 321, NBPT*.
BADGER, GEORGE W., 30, M, Coach Driver, W, NH, 406, 606, NBPT.
BADGER, JOHN P., 31, M, Coach Driver, W, NH, 321, 473, NBPT.
BADGER, MARY A., 31, M, -, W, Maine, 406, 606, NBPT. In HH of George W. Badger, age 30, Coach Driver, born in NH.
BADGER, WILLIAM J., 39, M, Stage Agent, W, NH, 259, 327,

NBPT*.
BAGLEY, ABNER, 84, M, None, W, Maine, 568, 754, NBPT*.
BAGLEY, JOHN A., 16, M, Student, W, NY, 568, 754, NBPT*. In HH of Abner Bagley, age 84, None, born in Maine.
BAGLEY, MARY, 43, F, -, W, Maine, 568, 754, NBPT*. In HH of Abner Bagley, age 84, None, born in Maine.
BAGLEY, SARAH, 42, F, -, W, Maine, 568, 754, NBPT*. In HH of Abner Bagley, age 84, None, born in Maine.
BAILEY, ABIGAIL M., 28, F, -, W, MA, 788,1114, NBPT. In Poor House..
BAILEY, JOHN JR., 37, M, House Carpenter, W, MA, 395, 518, NBPT*.
BAILEY, JOSEPH S., 36, M, Blacksmith, W, NH, 328, 425, NBPT*.
BAILEY, MICHAEL L., 58, M, Laborer, W, VT, 785,1111, NBPT. In HH of John Hill, age 38, Farmer, born in Maine.
BAILEY, STEPHEN S., 18, M, Mariner, W, MA, 343, 450, NBPT*. In HH of George W. Norman, age 33, Mariner, born in MA.
BAIRD, ELLEN, 23, F, -, W, Canada, 661, 952, NBPT. In HH of Dorothy Chute, age 66, born in MA.
BAIRD, MARY, 30, F, -, W, Canada, 661, 952, NBPT. In HH of Dorothy Chute, age 66, born in MA.
BAKER, JOHN, 17, M, Machinist, W, MA, 561, 834, NBPT. In HH of Mary Dorr, age 65, born in MA.

BALCH, BENJAMIN B., 52, M, Farmer, W, MA, 129, 154, NBPT*. In HH of Henry Shoof, age 48, Ship Master, born in Denmark.
BALCH, BENJN., 45, M, Broker, W, MA, 782,1108, NBPT. In HH of Enoch Tilton, age 45, Hotel Keeper, born in NH. In Hotel.
BALCH, CHARLES, 61, M, None, W, MA, 42, 49, NBPT*.
BALCH, DANIEL, 60, M, Watchmaker, W, MA, 734,1037, NBPT.
BALCH, EBENEZER G., 31, F, Clerk, W, MA, 734,1037, NBPT. In HH of Daniel Balch, age 60, Watchmaker, born in MA.
BALCH, ELIZABETH A., 24, F, -, W, Maine, 677, 969, NBPT. In HH of William C. Balch, age 30, Agent NBPT* Mills, born in MA.
BALCH, HULDAH J., 47, F, -, W, VT, 68, 77, NBPT*. In HH of Jacob A. Balch, age 49, Trader, born VT.
BALCH, ISAAC D., 15, M, Student, W, MA, 309, 402, NBPT*. In HH of John Balch, age 47, Factory Agent, born in MA.
BALCH, JACOB A., 49, M, Trader, W, VT, 68, 77, NBPT*.
BALCH, JOHN, 47, M, Factory Agent, W, MA, 309, 402, NBPT*.
BALCH, JOHN H., 24, M, Trader, W, NH, 306, 398, NBPT*. In HH of George W. Fogg, age 22, Shoemaker, born in NH.
BALCH, JULIA N., 24, F, -, W, Maine, 309, 402, NBPT*. In HH of John Balch, age 47, Factory Agent, born in MA.
BALCH, LAURA A., 42, F, -, W, VT, 309, 402, NBPT*. In HH of

John Balch, age 47, Factory Agent, born in MA.
BALCH, LEORDAS, 25, M, Trader, MA, W, 41, 48, NBPT*. In HH of William Balch, age 54, Merchant, born in MA.
BALCH, WILLIAM, 54, M, Merchant, W, MA, 41, 48, NBPT*.
BALCH, WILLIAM C., 30, M, Agent Mills, W, MA, 677, 969, NBPT.
BALLOU, CHARLES N., 27, M, Merchant, W, MA, 271, 398,
BALLOU, HENRY W., 23, M, Mason, W, MA, 774,1095, NBPT.
BALLOU, JOSEPH W., 30, M, Clothing Store, W, MA, 158, 189, NBPT*.
BALLOU, LIBERTY C., 32, M, Overseer, W, MA, 775,1096, NBPT.
BALLOU, MARY, 28, F, -, W, Maine, 775,1096, NBPT. In HH of Liberty C. Ballou, age 32, Overseer, born in MA.
BALSTON, MARY A., 23, F, -, W, N.S., 721,1020, NBPT. In HH of John Coombs, age 37, Congregational Clergyman, born in MA.
BAMFORD, BANJN. M., 17, M, Mariner, W, MA, 539, 805, NBPT. In HH of Joseph Banford, age 46, Dealer in Fish, born in MA.
BAMFORD, JOSEPH, 46, M, Dealer in Fish, W, MA, 539, 805, NBPT.
BAMFORD, JOSEPH, 25, M, Mariner, W, MA, 790,1118, NBPT. In HH of Benjamin Noble, age 28, Tailor, born in England.
BAMFORD, JOSEPH, 23, M, Fisherman, 0, MA, 412, 539, NBPT*. In HH of John Gaskill, age 52, Shipwright, born in Nova Scotia.
BAMFORD, JOSEPH JR., 23, M, Fisherman, W, MA, 264, 334, NBPT*.
BAMFORD, SUSAN, 22, F, W, 0, Nova Scotia, 412, 539, NBPT*. In HH of John Gaskill, age 52, Shipwright, born in Nova Scotia.
BANNISTER, DELPHIA P.G., 56, F, -, W, CT, 662, 953, NBPT. In HH of William B. Bannister, age 76, Gentleman, born in MA.
BANNISTER, FRANCES B., 45, F, -, W, VT, 662, 953, NBPT. In HH of William B. Bannister, age 76, Gentleman, born in MA.
BANNISTER, WILLIAM B., 76, M, Gentleman, W, MA, 662, 953, NBPT.
BARKEN?, ELISHA C., 23, M, Hackman, W, MA, 782,1108, NBPT. In HH of Enoch Tilton, age 45, Hotel Keeper, born in NH. In Hotel.
BARKER, GEORGE, 20, M, Harness Maker, W, MA, 622, 906, NBPT. In HH of John B. Seward, age 34, Harness Maker, born in MA.
BARKER, JANE, 74, F, -, W, England, 160, 230, NBPT. In HH of Thomas Taylor, age 46, Weaver, born in England.
BARLOW, JAMES R., 47, M, Stevedore, W, MA, 396, 519, NBPT*.
BARLOW, JOSEPH, 16, M, Laborer, W, MA, 396, 519, NBPT*. In HH of James R. Barlow, age 47, Stevedore, born in MA.
BARRETT, CATHARINE, 40, F,

-, W, Ireland, 377, 496, NBPT*. In HH of James Barrett, age 42, Laborer, born in Ireland.
BARRETT, ELLEN, 13, F, -, W, Ireland, 377, 496, NBPT*. In HH of James Barrett, age 42, Laborer, born in Ireland.
BARRETT, JAMES, 42, M, Laborer, W, Ireland, 377, 496, NBPT*.
BARRETT, JOHN, 9, M, -, W, Ireland, 377, 496, NBPT*. In HH of James Barrett, age 42, Laborer, born in Ireland.
BARRETT, MATTHEW, 7, M, -, W, Ireland, 377, 496, NBPT*. In HH of James Barrett, age 42, Laborer, born in Ireland.
BARRY, BRIDGET, 35, F, -, W, Ireland, 93, 110, NBPT*. In HH of John Barry, age 40, Laborer, born in Ireland.
BARRY, JOHN, 40, M, Laborer, W, Ireland, 93, 110, NBPT*.
BARSTON, ANGELINA, 20, F, -, W, Maine, 15, 18, NBPT*. In HH of Milton Smart, age 47, Blacksmith, born Maine.
BARTLET, EDMUND, 75, M, Machinist, W, MA, 204, 255, NBPT*.
BARTLET, EDWIN B., 40, M, Shoemaker, W, NH, 200, 248, NBPT*.
BARTLET, FRANCES, 17, F, -, W, NH, 346, 455, NBPT*. In HH of Patience Bartlet, age 55, born in NH.
BARTLET, GEORGE S., 18, M, Wheelwright, W, MA, 709,1004, NBPT. In HH of Jonathan C. Richardson, age 33, Carriage Maker, born in MA.

BARTLET, HENRY, 25, M, Chaise Maker, W, MA, 517, 688, NBPT*. In HH of John Bartlet, age 48, Chaise Maker, born in MA.
BARTLET, HENRY A., 47, M, Truck man, W, NH, 362, 478, NBPT*.
BARTLET, HENRY S., 39, M, Shoe Manufacturer, W, MA, 102, 120, NBPT*.
BARTLET, ISAAC, 65, M, Gardener, W, MA, 85, 99, NBPT*.
BARTLET, ISAAC, JR., 32, M, Shoemaker, W, MA, 104, 123, NBPT*.
BARTLET, JOHN, 48, M, Chaise Maker, W, MA, 517, 688, NBPT*.
BARTLET, JOSIAH, 74, M, School Teacher, W, MA, 44, 51, NBPT*.
BARTLET, MARY, 27, F, -, W, NH, 200, 248, NBPT*. In HH of Edwin B. Bartlet, age 40, Shoemaker, born in NH.
BARTLET, MARY A., 33, F, -, W, NH, 104, 123, NBPT*. In HH of Isaac Bartlet, Jr., age 32, Shoemaker, born in MA.
BARTLET, PATIENCE, 55, F, -, W, NH, 346, 455, NBPT*.
BARTLET, WILLIAM H., 20, M, Shoemaker, W, MA, 102, 120, NBPT*. In HH of Henry S. Bartlet, age 38, Shoe Manufacturer, born in MA.
BARTLETT, ACHSUH, 58, F, -, W, VT, 80, 116, NBPT. In HH of David Bartlett, age 71, Shoemaker, born in NH.
BARTLETT, ALBERT W., 18, M, Clerk, W, MA, 559, 832, NBPT. In HH of Joseph Bartlett, age 46, Mariner, born in MA.

BARTLETT, ALMA C., 26, F, -, W, Maine, 459, 685, NBPT. In HH of George W. Bartlett, age 26, Shoemaker, born in MA.
BARTLETT, DAVID, 71, M, Shoemaker, W, NH, 80, 116, NBPT.
BARTLETT, DEAN, 35, M, Carpenter, W, MA, 593, 870, NBPT. In HH of Hannah P. Elliot, age 55, born in MA.
BARTLETT, EDWARD F., 16, M, Clerk, W, MA, 559, 832, NBPT. In HH of Joseph Bartlett, age 46, Mariner, born in MA.
BARTLETT, FRANCES N., 27, F, -, W, Maine, 258, 375, NBPT. In HH of Nathl. S. Bartlett, age 23, Mariner, born in MA.
BARTLETT, FRANKLIN, 41, M, Gardner, W, MA, 707,1002, NBPT.
BARTLETT, GEORGE N., 29, M, Carpenter, W, NH, 363, 534, NBPT.
BARTLETT, GEORGE W., 26, M, Shoemaker, W, MA, 459, 685, NBPT.
BARTLETT, JOSEPH, 46, M, Mariner, W, MA, 559, 832, NBPT.
BARTLETT, JUDITH, 36, F, -, W, NH, 707,1002, NBPT. In HH of Franklin Bartlett, age 41, Gardner, born in MA.
BARTLETT, NATHL S., 23, M, Mariner, W, MA, 258, 375, NBPT.
BARTLETT, NICHOLAS, 22, M, Truck man, W, MA, 733,1035, NBPT. In HH of Stephen Downs, age 31, Mariner, born in MA.
BARTLETT, STEPHEN, 30, M, Carpenter, W, MA, 113, 169, NBPT.
BARTLETT, WILLIAM G., 36, M, Master Mariner, W, MA, 444, 660, NBPT.
BARTON, ALFRED, 17, M, None, W, Canada, 536, 802, NBPT. In HH of Francis Barton, age 40, Laborer, born in Canada.
BARTON, BETSY, 15, F, -, W, Canada, 536, 802, NBPT. In HH of Francis Barton, age 40, Laborer, born in Canada.
BARTON, CEMENTHA, 18, F, -, W, VT, 733,1035, NBPT. In HH of Stephen Downs, age 31, Mariner, born in MA.
BARTON, ELIZA, 18, F, -, W, VT, 733,1035, NBPT. In HH of Stephen Downs, age 31, Mariner, born in MA.
BARTON, FRANCIS, 40, M, Laborer, W, Canada, 536, 802, NBPT.
BARTON, HOTTY?, 5, M, -, W, VT, 536, 802, NBPT. In HH of Francis Barton, age 40, Laborer, born in Canada.
BARTON, MARY, 8, F, -, W, VT, 536, 802, NBPT. In HH of Francis Barton, age 40, Laborer, born in Canada.
BARTON, PETER, 10, M, -, W, VT, 536, 802, NBPT. In HH of Francis Barton, age 40, Laborer, born in Canada.
BARTON, ROSETTA, 48, F, -, W, Canada, 536, 802, NBPT. In HH of Francis Barton, age 40, Laborer, born in Canada.
BARTON, THOMAS, 12, M, -, W, VT, 536, 802, NBPT. In HH of Francis Barton, age 40, Laborer, born in Canada.
BARTY, JOHN, 38, M, Carder, W, England, 771,1091, NBPT. In

HH of George Pentland, age 46, Stretcher in Mill, born in England.
BASS, EDWARD, 51, M, Jeweler, W, MA, 234, 292, NBPT*. In HH of Jonathan Bickford, age 30, Trader, born in NH.
BASS, EDWARD, 16, M, Operative, W, MA, 775,1099, NBPT. In HH of Rhoda Bass, age 37, born in MA.
BASSETT, NATHANIEL G., 35, M, Crockery Dealer, W, MA, 215, 269, NBPT*.
BATCHEDER, DANIEL C., 35, M, Coach Driver, W, NH, 637, 924, NBPT.
BATCHELDER, HARRISON, 24, M, Joiner, W, MA, 363, 479, NBPT*. In HH of Sarah Batchelder, age 68, born in MA.
BATCHELDER, JOHN B., 34, M, Laborer, W, NH, 532, 792, NBPT.
BATCHELDER, JOHN W., 8, M, -, W, NH, 532, 792, NBPT. In HH of John B. Batchelder, age 34, Laborer, born in NH.
BATCHELDER, LOUISA, 24, F, -, W, NH, 632, 919, NBPT. In HH of Amos C. Clement, age 60, Clerk, born in NH.
BATCHELDER, RHODA, 37, F, -, W, NH, 532, 792, NBPT. In HH of John B. Batchelder, age 34, Laborer, born in NH.
BATCHELDER, THOMAS L., 39, M, Carpenter, W, NH, 365, 482, NBPT*.
BATCHELDER, WILLIAM, 30, M, House Joiner, W, MA, 363, 479, NBPT*. In HH of Sarah Batchelder, age 68, born in MA.
BATCHELDER, WILLIAM, 27, M, Shoemaker, W, MA, 632, 919,

NBPT. In HH of Amos C. Clement, age 60, Clerk, born in NH.
BATES, CHARITY, 20, F, -, W, Maine, 431, 640, NBPT. In HH of Oliver P. Wiggin, age 44, Cooper, born in NH.
BATES, CHARLOTTE, 17, F, -, W, Maine, 431, 640, NBPT. In HH of Oliver P. Wiggin, age 44, Cooper, born in NH.
BATES, SILVIA, 22, F, -, W, Maine, 431, 640, NBPT. In HH of Oliver P. Wiggin, age 44, Cooper, born in NH.
BATISS, GEORGE W., 26, M, Shoemaker, W, MA, 491, 733, NBPT.
BATISS, GEORGIANA H., 1, F, -, W, Maine, 491, 733, NBPT. In HH of George W. Batiss, age 26, Shoemaker, born in MA.
BATISS, SARAH, 24, F, -, W, Maine, 491, 733, NBPT. In HH of George W. Batiss, age 26, Shoemaker, born in MA.
BATTELLE, ELBRIDGE, 38, M, Farmer, W, MA, 594, 784, NBPT*.
BATTELLE, ELIZABETH, 42, F, -, W, NH, 594, 784, NBPT*. In HH of Elbridge Battelle, age 38, Farmer, born in MA.
BATTELLE, GEORGE, 15, M, -, W, RI, 594, 784, NBPT*. In HH of Elbridge Battelle, age 38, Farmer, born in MA.
BAYLE, BRIDGET, 47, F, -, W, Ireland, 198, 291, NBPT.
BAYLE, GEORGE, 46, M, Mariner, W, England, 205, 302, NBPT.
BAYLE, GEORGE, 46, M, Mariner, W, England, 205, 302, NBPT.

BAYLE, HENRY, 14, M, W, 0, Ireland, 198, 291, NBPT. In HH of Bridget Bayle, age 47, born in Ireland.
BAYLE, JAMES, 19, M, Operative, W, Ireland, 198, 291, NBPT. In HH of Bridget Bayle, age 47, born in Ireland.
BAYLE, JOANNA, 40, F, W, 0, Ireland, 205, 302, NBPT. In HH of George Bayle, age 46, Mariner, born in England.
BAYLE, JOHN, 17, M, Operative, 0, Ireland, 198, 291, NBPT. In HH of Bridget Bayle, age 47, born in Ireland.
BAYLEY, CHARLES M., 35, M, Master Mariner, W, MA, 68, 98, NBPT.
BAYLEY, DANIEL W., 40, M, Trader, W, MA, 113, 136, NBPT*.
BAYLEY, JOHN Y., 23, M, Master Mariner, W, MA, 247, 357, NBPT. In HH of Robert Bayley, age 64, Merchant, born in MA.
BAYLEY, LUCY, 81, F, -, W, MA, 788,1114, NBPT. In Poor House. .
BAYLEY, MARGARET L., 24, F, -, W, Ireland, 58, 85, NBPT. In HH of Robert Bayley, Jr. age 40, Merchant, born in MA.
BAYLEY, RAFAIL A., 39, M, Mariner, W, MA, 58, 85, NBPT. In HH of Robert Bayley, Jr. age 40, Merchant, born in MA.
BAYLEY, RICHARD N., 20, M, Weaver, W, MA, 255, 371, NBPT. In HH of Betsy Stevens, age 72, born in MA.
BAYLEY, ROBERT, 64, M, Merchant, W, MA, 247, 357, NBPT.
BAYLEY, ROBERT JR., 40, M, Merchant, W, MA, 58, 85, NBPT.
BAYLEY, SARAH S., 33, F, -, W, VT, 503, 671, NBPT*. In HH of True Choate, age 44, Ship Joiner, born in MA.
BAYLEY, THOMAS S., 31, M, Cabinet Maker, W, MA, 105, 125, NBPT*.
BAYLEY, WILLIAM H., 16, M, None, W, MA, 58, 85, NBPT. In HH of Robert Bayley, Jr. age 40, Merchant, born in MA.
BEALS, ASA W., 20, M, Operative, W, MA, 162, 195, NBPT*. In Boarding House run by Hannah S. Davidson, 47, born in MA.
BEAN, ALONSO A., 16, M, None, W, NH, 766,1081, NBPT. In HH of Hiram Bean, age 42, Machinist, born in NH.
BEAN, ALONZO, 40, M, Machinist, W, MA, 616, 808, NBPT*.
BEAN, ELIZABETH, 42, F, -, W, NH, 766,1081, NBPT. In HH of Hiram Bean, age 42, Machinist, born in NH.
BEAN, ELIZABETH, 19, F, -, W, NH, 615, 897, NBPT. In HH of Eunice W. Welch, age 48, born in Maine.
BEAN, EURINA? S., 6, F, -, W, NH, 766,1081, NBPT. In HH of Hiram Bean, age 42, Machinist, born in NH.
BEAN, FRANK H., 10, M, -, W, NH, 766,1081, NBPT. In HH of Hiram Bean, age 42, Machinist, born in NH.
BEAN, HARRIET A., 11, F, -, W, NH, 766,1081, NBPT. In HH of

Hiram Bean, age 42, Machinist, born in NH.
BEAN, HIRAM, 42, M, Machinist, W, NH, 766,1081, NBPT.
BEAN, JONATHAN, 32, M, Shoemaker, W, VT, 733,1035, NBPT. In HH of Stephen Downs, age 31, Mariner, born in MA.
BEAN, REBECCA J., 13, F, -, W, NH, 766,1081, NBPT. In HH of Hiram Bean, age 42, Machinist, born in NH.
BEARDSLEY, ELIZA, 32, F, W, -, England, 216, 319, NBPT. In HH of Robert Beardsley, age 35, Weaver, born in England.
BEARDSLEY, HENRY, 9, M, W, -, England, 216, 319, NBPT. In HH of Robert Beardsley, age 35, Weaver, born in England.
BEARDSLEY, ROBERT, 35, M, Weaver, W, England, 216, 319, NBPT.
BEARDSLEY, WILLIAM E., 11, M, _ ,W, England, 216, 319, NBPT. In HH of Robert Beardsley, age 35, Weaver, born in England. {Name also spelled Bardsley}.
BEARS, NATHANIEL, 4, M, -, W, Maine, 788,1114, NBPT. In Poor House. .
BEARSON, EMMA E., 24, F, -,_ W, NH, 212, 313, NBPT. In HH of Theodore C. Bearson, age 31, Baker, born in NH.
BEARSON, THEODORE C., 31, M, Baker, W, NH, 212, 313, NBPT.
BELKNAP, ROSINA, 20, F, -, W, NH, 427, 633, NBPT. In HH of Walter Gould, age 49, Carpenter, born in Maine.
BELKNAP, ROSWINA, 18, F, -,

W, NH, 427, 633, NBPT. In HH of Walter Gould, age 49, Carpenter, born in Maine.
BELL, JOHN, 30, M, Operative, W, England, 757,1067, NBPT. In HH of William Bell age 42, Operative, born in England.
BELL, WILLIAM, 42, M, Operative, W, England, 757,1067, NBPT.
BELL, WILLIAM, 14, M, -, W, England, 757,1067, NBPT. In HH of William Bell age 42, Operative, born in England.
BELTON, ELIZABETH P., 37, F, -, W, NH, 211, 262, NBPT*. In Boarding House.
BEMIS, GEORGE, 18, M, Shoemaker, W, MA, 372, 548, NBPT. In HH of Elizabeth A. Bemis, age 43, born in MA.
BENNER, HULDAH, 21, F, -, W, Maine, 518, 689, NBPT*. In HH of Charles Coffin, age 48, Ship Carpenter, born in MA.
BENNET, ANDREW, 22, M, None, W, NH, 615, 897, NBPT. In HH of Eunice W. Welch, age 48, born in Maine.
BENNET, ELIZA J., 24, F, -, W, NH, 615, 897, NBPT. In HH of Eunice W. Welch, age 48, born in Maine.
BENNET, LYDIA, 13, F, -, W, NH, 615, 897, NBPT. In HH of Eunice W. Welch, age 48, born in Maine.
BENNET, MARY, 53, F, -, W, NH, 615, 897, NBPT. In HH of Eunice W. Welch, age 48, born in Maine.
BENNET, MARY, 16, F, -, W, VT, 615, 897, NBPT. In HH of

Eunice W. Welch, age 48, born in Maine.
BENNET, REUBEN, 62, M, Laborer, W, NH, 615, 897, NBPT. In HH of Eunice W. Welch, age 48, born in Maine.
BENNETT, ABBY, 18, F, -, W, NH, 517, 771, NBPT. In HH of Josiah Hadley, age 28, Operative, born in NH.
BENT, AMANDA A., 14, F, -, W, Nova Scotia, 175, 254, NBPT. In HH of Dennis Bent, age 36, Blacksmith, born in Nova Scotia.
BENT, AMY, 35, F, W, 0, Nova Scotia, 175, 254, NBPT. In HH of Dennis Bent, age 36, Blacksmith, born in Nova Scotia.
BENT, CATHERINE R., 8, F, - ,W, Nova Scotia, 175, 254, NBPT. In HH of Dennis Bent, age 36, Blacksmith, born in Nova Scotia.
BENT, DENNIS, 36, M, Blacksmith, W, Nova Scotia, 175, 254, NBPT.
BENT, ISRAEL, 23, M, Daguerrotypist, W, Nova Scotia, 461, 609, NBPT*. In HH of Timothy Hilliard, age 46, Shoe Store, born in NH.
BENT, MARY E., 3, F, W, 0, Nova Scotia, 175, 254, NBPT. In HH of Dennis Bent, age 36, Blacksmith, born in Nova Scotia.
BENT, SOPHANA A., 12, F, -, W, Nova Scotia, 175, 254, NBPT. In HH of Dennis Bent, age 36, Blacksmith, born in Nova Scotia.
BENT, WILLIAM H., 10, M, -, W, Nova Scotia, 175, 254, NBPT. In HH of Dennis Bent, age 36, Blacksmith, born in Nova Scotia.
BEODY, MARY, 23, F, W, 0, Ireland, 177, 256, NBPT. In HH of James N. Canney, age 41, Teamster, born in NH.
BERDGE, EDWARD A., 20, M, Shoemaker, W, MA, 545, 725, NBPT*. In HH of Rhoda Berdge, age 57, born MA.
BERDGE, JOSEPH P., 30, M, Shoemaker, W, MA, 544, 724, NBPT*.
BERDGE, MARY A., 27, F, -, W, NH, 544, 724, NBPT*. In HH of Joseph P. Berdge, age 30, Shoemaker, born in MA.
BERNHARD, BLANCHARD, 24, M, Merchant, W, Germany, 782,1108, NBPT. In HH of Enoch Tilton, age 45, Hotel Keeper, born in NH. In Hotel.
BERNY, FRANCIS, 20, M, Baker, W, NH, 494, 737, NBPT. In HH of John Pearson, age 61, Baker, born in MA.
BERRY, LANRY M., 24, F, -, W, Maine, 133, 197, NBPT. In HH of John Townsend, age 50, Shoemaker, born in Maine.
BERRY, LUDIA, 28, F, -, W, NH, 177, 256, NBPT. In HH of James N. Canney, age 41, Teamster, born in NH.
BEVAN, CHARLES H., 25, M, Carpenter, W, MA, 438, 651, NBPT. In HH of Mary Bevan, age 60, born in MA.
BICKFORD, ELIZABETH, 31, F, -, W, Maine, 16, 20, NBPT*. In HH of Horace Bickford, age 33, Counselor and Attorney, born NH.
BICKFORD, ELIZABETH A., 5, F, -, W, NH, 234, 292, NBPT*. In HH of Jonathan Bickford, age 30, Trader, born in NH.

BICKFORD, EMILY, 21, F, -, W, Maine, 282, 361, NBPT*. In HH of Mary N. Talbot, age 41, born in Maine.
BICKFORD, HORACE, 33, M, Counselor & Attorney, W, NH, 16, 20, NBPT*.
BICKFORD, JONATHAN, 30, M, Trader, W, NH, 234, 292, NBPT*.
BICKFORD, MARY, 70, F, -, W, Maine, 282, 361, NBPT*. In HH of Mary N. Talbot, age 41, born in Maine.
BICKFORD, MEHETABLE H., 32, F, -, W, NH, 234, 292, NBPT*. In HH of Jonathan Bickford, age 30, Trader, born in NH.
BLACK, JOHN, 22, M, Shoemaker, W, NH, 431, 641, NBPT. In HH of Mary L. Rains, age 48, born in Maine.
BLACK, NATHAN, 20, M, Merchant, W, Germany, 450, 673, NBPT. In HH of Elizabeth Garland, age 53, born in NH.
BLACKSTONE, ADELINE, 18, F, -, W, Maine, 514, 685, NBPT*. In HH of Aaron Gardner, age 30, Carpenter, born in NH.
BLACKWELL, JULIA, 17, F, -, W, Ireland, 382, 563, NBPT. In HH of Jacob Noyes, age 85, Teacher of Navigation, born in MA.
BLAIDSDELL, CHARLES H., 34, M, Carpenter, W, MA, 136, 201, NBPT.
BLAIDSDELL, HARRIET A., 27, F, -, W, Maine, 136, 201, NBPT. In HH of Charles H. Blaisdell, age 34, Carpenter, born in MA.
BLAIN, NANCY, 29, F, -, W, Maine, 254, 368, NBPT. In HH of Samuel Cook, Jr., age 43, Shoemaker, born in MA.
BLAISDELL, JUDITH, 30, F, -, W, NH, 782,1108, NBPT. In HH of Enoch Tilton, age 45, Hotel Keeper, born in NH. In Hotel.
BLAKE, JEREMIAH, 33, M, House Carpenter, W, NH, 450, 596, NBPT*.
BLAKE, JOHN, 18, M, -, W, NH, 479, 719, NBPT. In HH of Moses Hodgdon, age 28, Teamster, born in Maine.
BLAKE, NATHAN B., 42, M, Victualer, W, NH, 575, 761, NBPT*.
BLAKE, NATHAN B., 17, M, Student, W, MA, 575, 761, NBPT*. In HH of Nathan B. Blake, age 42, Victualer, born in NH.
BLAKE, SAMUEL S., 30, M, Painter, W, NH, 276, 353, NBPT*.
BLAKE, SUSAN C., 30, F, -, W, NH, 276, 353, NBPT*. In HH of Samuel S. Blake, age 30, Painter, born in NH.
BLANEY, Aaron, 36, M, Master Mariner, W, Maine, 675, 967, NBPT. In HH of Moses P. Case, age 34, School Teacher, born in VT.
BLISS, BRIDGET, 25, F, -, W, Ireland, 547, 727, NBPT*. In HH of Terence Bliss, age 30, Laborer, born in Ireland.
BLISS, HUGH, 23, M, Laborer, W, Ireland, 547, 727, NBPT*. In HH of Terence Bliss, age 30, Laborer, born in Ireland.
BLISS, JAMES, 5, M, -, W, Ireland, 547, 727, NBPT*. In HH of Terence Bliss, age 30, Laborer, born in Ireland.
BLISS, TERENCE, 30, M, Laborer, W, Ireland, 547, 727,

NBPT*.
BLISS, THOMAS, 8, M, -, W, Ireland, 547, 727, NBPT*. In HH of Terence Bliss, age 30, Laborer, born in Ireland.
BLOCK, NATHAN, 21, M, Merchant, W, Germany, 782,1108, NBPT. In HH of Enoch Tilton, age 45, Hotel Keeper, born in NH. In Hotel.
BLOOD, JAMES, 56, M, None, W, NH, 487, 649, NBPT*.
BLOOMFIELD, MATHIAS, 14, M, None, W, MA, 788,1114, NBPT. In Poor House.
BLOOMFIELD, STEPHEN, 5, M, -, W, Maine, 788,1114, NBPT. In Poor House. .
BLUMPEY, PHILIP, 75, M, Rigger, W, England, 715,1011, NBPT.
BLUMPEY, PHILIP H., 31, M, Grocer, W, MA, 629, 915, NBPT.
BLUMPEY, SAMUEL, 41, M, Mariner, W, MA, 715,1011, NBPT. In HH of Philip Blumpey, age 75, Rigger, born in England.
BOARDMAN, GREEN-LEAF, 34, M, Livery Stable, W, MA, 332, 432, NBPT*.
BOARDMAN, HANNAH, 17, F, -, W, England, 660, 950, NBPT. In HH of Rebecca Boardman, age 48, born in England.
BOARDMAN, ISAAC H., 39, M, Merchant, W, MA, 580, 855, NBPT.
BOARDMAN, MARGARET, 19, F, -, W, England, 660, 950, NBPT. In HH of Rebecca Boardman, age 48, born in England.
BOARDMAN, MARY, 71, F, -, W, NH, 213, 264, NBPT*. In HH of Samuel Boardman, age 78, Ship Chandler, born in NH.
BOARDMAN, REBECCA, 48, F, -, W, England, 660, 950, NBPT.
BOARDMAN, SAMUEL, 78, M, Ship Chandler, W, NH, 213, 264, NBPT*.
BOARDMAN, WILLIAM, 30, M, Ship Chandler, W, NH, 213, 264, NBPT*. In HH of Samuel Boardman, age 78, Ship Chandler, born in NH.
BOARDMAN, WILLIAM, 17, M, Student Putnam School, W, MA, 99, 116, NBPT*. In HH of Hannah Sargent, age 50, born in MA.
BODEN, CHARLOTTE, 36, F, -, W, Maine, 339, 443, NBPT*. In HH of Stephen Boden, age 42, Laborer, born in Maine.
BODEN, ELLEN S., 14, F, -, W, Maine, 339, 443, NBPT*. In HH of Stephen Boden, age 42, Laborer, born in Maine.
BODEN, FRANCES E., 16, F, -, W, Maine, 339, 443, NBPT*. In HH of Stephen Boden, age 42, Laborer, born in Maine.
BODEN, STEPHEN, 42, M, Laborer, W, Maine, 339, 443, NBPT*.
BOLLS, LUCY M., 15, F, -, W, NB, 153, 222, NBPT. In HH of Martha A. Whright, age 86, born in England. {Most likely New Brunswick}.
BOLLS, MARY., 25, F, -, W, England, 153, 222, NBPT. In HH of Martha A. Whright, age 86, born in England.
BOLT, STACY R., 30, M, Merchant Tailor, W, MA, 782,1108, NBPT. In HH of Enoch Tilton, age

45, Hotel Keeper, born in NH. In Hotel.
BOND, DANIEL, 19, M, Clerk, W, MA, 715,1011, NBPT. In HH of Philip Blumpey, age 75, Rigger, born in England.
BOOTH, MARY, 15, F, -, W, New Brunswick, 603, 793, NBPT*. In HH of John McPhee, age 52, Ship Carpenter, born in Halifax.
BORDMAN, PAMELIA A., 21, F, -, W, Maine, 529, 788, NBPT. In Boarding House.
BOTTES, ANN, 5, F, -, W, Newfoundland, 762,1076, NBPT. In HH of William Bottes, age 35, Laborer, born in Newfoundland.
BOTTES, ELLEN, 12, F, -, W, Newfoundland, 762,1076, NBPT. In HH of William Bottes, age 35, Laborer, born in Newfoundland.
BOTTES, JAMES, 10, M, -, W, Newfoundland, 762,1076, NBPT. In HH of William Bottes, age 35, Laborer, born in Newfoundland.
BOTTES, MARGARET, 30, F, -, W, Newfoundland, 762,1076, NBPT. In HH of William Bottes, age 35, Laborer, born in Newfoundland.
BOTTES, MARY, 3, F, -, W, Newfoundland, 762,1076, NBPT. In HH of William Bottes, age 35, Laborer, born in Newfoundland.
BOTTES, MICHAEL, 12, M, -, W, Newfoundland, 762,1076, NBPT. In HH of William Bottes, age 35, Laborer, born in Newfoundland.
BOTTES, PATRICK, 7, M, -, W, Newfoundland, 762,1076, NBPT. In HH of William Bottes, age 35, Laborer, born in Newfoundland.

BOTTES, WILLIAM, 35, M, Laborer, W, Newfoundland, 762,1076, NBPT.
BOW, BROGH, 26, M, Mariner, W, MA, 201, 250, NBPT*. In HH of John Kavanagh, age 26, Mariner, born in MA.
BOWKER, MADISON, 25, M, Shoemaker, W, MA, 431, 641, NBPT. In HH of Mary L. Rains, age 48, born in Maine.
BOWLES, CATHERINE, 39, F, -, W, N.B., 768,1085, NBPT. In IIII of Patrick Bowles, age 50, Mariner, born in Ireland.
BOWLES, PATRICK, 50, M, Mariner, W, Ireland, 768,1085, NBPT.
BOWMAN, JANE T., 22, F, -, W, England, 750,1058, NBPT. In HH of John Bowman, age 22, Mule Spinner, born in England.
BOWMAN, JOHN, 22, M, Mule Spinner, W, England, 750,1058, NBPT.
BRACKETT, EXPERIENCE, 19, F, -, W, Maine, 200, 247, NBPT*. In HH of Adriel H. Hodgdon, age 37, Drayman, born in NH.
BRADBURY, APPHIA E., 21, F, -, W, Maine, 544, 723, NBPT*. In HH of William H. Bradbury, age 21, Operative, born in Maine.
BRADBURY, GEORGE F., 18, M, Fisherman, W, MA, 439, 581, NBPT*. In HH of William Jameson, age 48, Sailmaker, born in RI.
BRADBURY, WILLIAM H., 21, M, Laborer, W, Maine, 544, 723, NBPT*.
BRADBURY, WILLIAM R., 20, M, Painter, W, MA, 439, 581,

NBPT*. In HH of William Jameson, age 48, Sailmaker, born in RI.
BRADLEE, JAMES H., 17, M, Trader, W, MA, 313, 406, NBPT*. In HH of Josiah Bradlee, age 49, Merchant, born in MA.
BRADLEE, JOSIAH, 49, M, Merchant, W, MA, 313, 406, NBPT*.
BRADLEY, ELIZABETH P., 27, F, -, W, NH, 158, 191, NBPT*. In HH of Isaac Bradley, age 40, "Telaphonemaker", born in NH.
BRADLEY, ISAAC, 40, M, Telaphonemaker, W, NH, 158, 191, NBPT*.
BRADSTREET, CHARLES W., 16, M, Clerk, W, MA, 456, 679, NBPT. In HH of Sarah Bradstreet, age 42, born in MA.
BRADSTREET, WILLIAM, 48, M, Notary Public, W, MA, 157, 187, NBPT*.
BRADY, JAMES, 35, M, Laborer, W, Ireland, 532, 795, NBPT. In HH of Walter Joy, age 27, Mariner, born in Newfoundland.
BRAGDON, DANIEL S., 19, M, Mariner, W, MA, 617, 900, NBPT. In HH of Samuel Bragdon, age 55, Merchant, born in MA.
BRAGDON, JOSEPH H., 26, M, Printer, W, MA, 480, 720, NBPT.
BRAGDON, LYDIA, 63, F, -, W, Maine, 368, 542, NBPT. In HH of William Huse, age 27, Taboconest, born in MA.
BRAGDON, PHEBE A., 50, F,-, W, NH, 221, 327, NBPT. In HH of William Bragdon, age 48, Overseer in Mill, born in Maine.
BRAGDON, SAMUEL, 55, M, Merchant, W, MA, 617, 900, NBPT.
BRAGDON, SARAH, 18, F, -, W, Maine, 450, 673, NBPT. In HH of Elizabeth Garland, age 53, born in NH.
BRAGDON, SARAH W., 18, F, -, W, Maine, 16, 20, NBPT*. In HH of Horace Bickford, age 33, Counselor and Attorney, born NH.
BRAGDON, WILLIAM, 48, M, Overseer in Mill, W, Maine, 221, 327, NBPT.
BRAGG, ALEXANDER, 24, M, Machinist, W, VT, 254, 369, NBPT.
BRAGG, LUCY A., 35, F, -, W, VT, 383, 566, NBPT. In HH of Timothy Bragg, age 42, Operative, born in VT.
BRAGG, MARY A., 9, F, -, W, VT, 383, 566, NBPT. In HH of Timothy Bragg, age 42, Operative, born in VT.
BRAGG, SARAH E., 6, F, -, W, VT, 383, 566, NBPT. In HH of Timothy Bragg, age 42, Operative, born in VT.
BRAGG, TIMOTHY, 42, M, Operative, W, VT, 383, 566, NBPT.
BRAY, ISAAC, 40, M, Master Mariner, W, MA, 407, 607, NBPT.
BRAY, NEHEMIAH A., 45, M, Master Mariner, W, MA, 452, 599, NBPT*.
BRAY, RHODA, 67, F, -, W, Maine, 81, 118, NBPT.
BRENEN, MARY, 30, F, -, W, Ireland, 464, 693, NBPT. In HH of Owen Kelley, age 32, Laborer, born in Ireland.
BRENT, EMMIE, 24, F, -, W,

N.S., 493, 735, NBPT. In HH of John Post, age 24, Farmer, born in N.S. {Nova Scotia}.

BRETON, ELIZABETH J., 24, F, -, W, N.B., 598, 876, NBPT. In HH of Tristram Chase, age 76, Merchant, born in MA.

BREWSTER, WILLIAM H., 37, M, Printer & Publisher, W, NH, 263, 332, NBPT*.

BRICKETT, JOSEPH, 51, M, None, W, MA, 542, 722, NBPT*.

BRICKETT, JOSEPH, 17, M, Laborer, W, MA, 542, 722, NBPT*. In HH of Joseph Brickett, age 51, None, born in MA.

BRIER, MARY A., 17, F, -, W, VT, 615, 897, NBPT. In HH of Eunice W. Welch, age 48, born in Maine.

BRIGGS, JOSEPHINE, 7, F, -, W, RI, 93, 136, NBPT. In HH of Mary Pettingell, age 58, born in MA.

BRIGGS, MARY, 5, F, -, W, Maine, 93, 136, NBPT. In HH of Mary Pettingell, age 58, born in MA.

BRILEY, JOHN, 63, M, House Joiner, W, MA, 484, 645, NBPT*. In HH of Hannah Merrill, age 55, born in Maine.

BRITCHARD, WILLIAM T., 21, M, Rigger, W, MA, 605, 884, NBPT. In HH of Ann G. Woodman, age 61, born in MA.

BRITTON, BRIDGET, 28, F, -, W, Ireland, 521, 692, NBPT*. In HH of Patrick Dennean, age 24, Laborer, born in Ireland.

BROCKWAY, PARDON, 89, M, Cooper, W, CT, 63, 91, NBPT.

BRODERICK, ANN, 18, F, -, W, Newfoundland, 462, 612, NBPT*. In HH of Samuel Broderick, age 54, Mariner, born in Newfoundland.

BRODERICK, ELLEN, 50, F, -, W, Newfoundland, 462, 612, NBPT*. In HH of Samuel Broderick, age 54, Mariner, born in Newfoundland.

BRODERICK, MARY, 22, F, -, W, Newfoundland, 462, 612, NBPT*. In HH of Samuel Broderick, age 54, Mariner, born in Newfoundland.

BRODERICK, SAMUEL, 54, M, Mariner, W, Newfoundland, 462, 612, NBPT*.

BRODRICK, JOANNA, 20, F, -, W, N.S., 561, 834, NBPT. In HH of Mary Dorr, age 65, born in MA.

BROMBECK, DANIEL A., 17, M, None, W, MA, 11, 13, NBPT. In HH of Tallack Brombeck, age 49, Rigger, born in Norway.

BROMBECK, TALLACK, 49, M, Rigger, W, Norway, 11, 13, NBPT.

BROOK, ELLEN, 20, F, -, W, Ireland, 591, 868, NBPT. In HH of Samuel T. Payson, age 34, Baker, born in MA.

BROWN, ABEL D., 28, M, Shoemaker, W, NH, 737, 1043, NBPT.

BROWN, ABIGAIL, 67, F, W, -, NH, 186, 272, NBPT. In HH of David Brown, age 58, Watchman, born in NH.

BROWN, ALBAN, 40, M, Watchman, W, MA, 412, 538, NBPT*.

BROWN, ALEXANDER, 27, M, Paymaster in Mill, W, MA, 405, 603, NBPT.

BROWN, CHARLES, 49, M, Bow Manufacturer, W, MA, 539, 716,

NBPT*.
BROWN, CHARLES, 25, M, Farmer, W, NH, 509, 679, NBPT*. In HH of Nutter Brown, age 60, Farmer, born in NH.
BROWN, CHARLES, 20, M, Grocer, W, MA, 496, 740, NBPT. In HH of Mercy Brown, age 52, born in MA.
BROWN, CHARLES G., 20, M, Clerk, W, MA, 346, 507, NBPT. In HH of Nathan. B. Brown, age 43, Grocer, born in MA.
BROWN, CHARLES H., 47, M, House Joiner, W, MA, 270, 346, NBPT*.
BROWN, CHARLES M., 26, M, Trader, W, MA, 787,1113, NBPT. In HH of Elizabeth P. Currier, age 41, born in MA.
BROWN, CHARLES N., 21, M, Machinist, W, MA, 270, 346, NBPT*. In HH of Charles H. Brown, age 47, House Joiner, born in MA.
BROWN, DAVID, 58, M, Watchman, 0, NH, 186, 272, NBPT.
BROWN, DAVID, 28, M, Cigar Manufacturer, W, MA, 270, 346, NBPT*. In HH of Charles H. Brown, age 47, House Joiner, born in MA.
BROWN, DAVID, 23, M, Ship Carpenter, W, NH, 306, 398, NBPT*. In HH of George W. Fogg, age 22, Shoemaker, born in NH.
BROWN, DEBORAH, 20, F, -, W, Maine, 450, 673, NBPT. In HH of Elizabeth Garland, age 53, born in NH.
BROWN, EDWARD W., 31, M, Engineer, W, NH, 53, 59, NBPT*.

In HH of Thomas Goodhue, age 70, Clerk, born in MA.
BROWN, EDWARD W., 31, M, Lab. Factory, W, NH, 610, 800, NBPT*.
BROWN, EDWIN S., 17, M, Clerk, W, RI, 331, 430, NBPT*. In HH of Lyman Brown, age 48, Overseer, born in NH.
BROWN, ELVIA, 23, F, -, W, Maine, 501, 669, NBPT*. In HH of John Brown, age 30, Master Mariner, born in MA.
BROWN, ELIZABETH, 53, F, -, W, NH, 450, 573, NBPT.
BROWN, GEORGE, 19, M, Mariner, -, MA, 186, 272, NBPT. In HH of David Brown, age 58, Watchman, born in NH.
BROWN, GREEN L., 41, M, Blacksmith, -, NH, 221, 327, NBPT. In HH of William Bragdon, age 48, Overseer in Mill, born in Maine.
BROWN, HANNAH, 57, F, -, W, NH, 108, 161, NBPT.
BROWN, HANNAH, 45, F, -, W, NH, 26, 35, NBPT. In HH of Hector C. Brown, age 47, Watchman, born in MA.
BROWN, HANNAH, 20, F, -, W, NH, 351, 463, NBPT*. In HH of John O.W. Brown, age 58, Trader, born in NH.
BROWN, HECTOR C., 47, M, Watchman, W, MA, 26, 35, NBPT.
BROWN, HELLEN P., 26, F, -, W, Maine, 405, 603, NBPT. In HH of Alexander Brown, age 27, Paymaster in Mill, born in MA.
BROWN, HORACE, 52, M, Stage Agent, W, MA, 271, 398, NBPT.
BROWN, JACOB B., 15, M,

Mariner, W, MA, 791,1119, NBPT. In HH of Richard Adams, age 28, Carpenter, born in MA.
BROWN, JACOB G., 19, M, Clerk, W, MA, 346, 507, NBPT. In HH of Nathan. B. Brown, age 43, Grocer, born in MA.
BROWN, JAMES, 73, M, Cabinet Maker, W, MA, 81, 90, NBPT*. In HH of John Devereau, age 27, Mariner, born Nova Scotia.
BROWN, JAMES, 35, M, Master Mariner, W, MA, 501, 669, NBPT*. In HH of John Brown, age 30, Master Mariner, born in MA.
BROWN, JANE, 40, F, -, W, NH, 373, 490, NBPT*. In HH of A.W. Mooney, age 27, born in NH.
BROWN, JENNESS, 42, M, Merchant, W, NH, 544, 814, NBPT.
BROWN, JOHN, 30, M, Master Mariner, W, MA, 501, 669, NBPT*.
BROWN, JOHN L., 5, F, -, W, NH, 351, 463, NBPT*. In HH of John O.W. Brown, age 58, Trader, born in NH.
BROWN, JOHN L., 5, M, -, W, NH, 351, 463, NBPT*. In HH of John O.W. Brown, age 58, Trader, born in NH.
BROWN, JOHN O.W., 58, M, Trader, W, NH, 351, 463, NBPT*.
BROWN, JOHN R., 17, M, Mariner, W, MA, 374, 553, NBPT. In HH of Mary L. Brown, age 49, born in MA.
BROWN, JOHN T., 18, M, Clerk, W, MA, 634, 921, NBPT. In HH of Sarah Brown, age 48, born in MA.
BROWN, JONATHAN, 68, M, Operative in Mill, W, NH, 98, 143, NBPT.

BROWN, JOSEPH A., 15, M, Bow Manufacturer, W, MA, 539, 716, NBPT*. In HH of Charles Brown, age 49, Bow Manufacturer, born in MA.
BROWN, JOSHUA, 33, M, Ship Carpenter, W, NH, 509, 679, NBPT*. In HH of Nutter Brown, age 60, Farmer, born in NH.
BROWN, JULIA, 48, F, -, W, NH, 233, 291, NBPT*.
BROWN, JULIA, 26, F, -, W, Maine, 265, 388, NBPT. In HH of George R. Tarbox, age 31, Overseer in Mill, born in Maine.
BROWN, JULIA A., 25, F, -, W, Maine, 501, 669, NBPT*. In HH of John Brown, age 30, Master Mariner, born in MA.
BROWN, JULIA D., 52, F, -, W, NH, 331, 430, NBPT*. In HH of Lyman Brown, age 48, Overseer, born in NH.
BROWN, LAWRANCE, 19, M, Mariner, W, MA, 374, 553, NBPT. In HH of Mary L. Brown, age 49, born in MA.
BROWN, LUCY A., 23, F, -, W, CT, 331, 430, NBPT*. In HH of Lyman Brown, age 48, Overseer, born in NH.
BROWN, LYDIA, 33, F, -, W, NH, 544, 814, NBPT. In HH of Jenness Brown, age 42, Merchant, born in NH.
BROWN, LYMAN, 49, M, Overseer, W, NH, 331, 430, NBPT*.
BROWN, MAHETABLE, 27, F, -, W, NH, 249, 360, NBPT. In HH of John Porter, age 66, Merchant, born in MA.
BROWN, MARGARET, 59, F, -,

W, NH, 509, 679, NBPT*. In HH of Nutter Brown, age 60, Farmer, born in NH.
BROWN, MARY, 57, F, -, W, NH, 351, 463, NBPT*. In HH of John O.W. Brown, age 58, Trader, born in NH.
BROWN, MARY, 17, F, -, W, NH, 351, 463, NBPT*. In HH of John O.W. Brown, age 58, Trader, born in NH.
BROWN, MARY, 17, F, -, W, NH, 770,1090, NBPT. In HH of Levi Pearson, age 37, Watchman, born in MA.
BROWN, MARY A., 19, F, -, W, NH, 737,1043, NBPT. In HH of Abel D. Brown, age 28, Shoemaker, born in NH.
BROWN, MARY C., 23, F, -, W, NH, 737,1043, NBPT. In HH of Abel D. Brown, age 28, Shoemaker, born in NH.
BROWN, MARY E., 5, F, -, W, NH, 544, 814, NBPT. In HH of Jenness Brown, age 42, Merchant, born in NH.
BROWN, MOSES, 42, M, Master Mariner, W, MA, 596, 874, NBPT.
BROWN, NATHAN W., 22, M, Operative, W, NH, 354, 468, NBPT*. In HH of Caroline H. Frothingham, age 37, born in NH.
BROWN, NATHAN W., 22, M, Operative, W, MA, 634, 921, NBPT. In HH of Sarah Brown, age 48, born in MA.
BROWN, NATHLL. P., 16, M, Clerk, W, MA, 346, 507, NBPT. In HH of Nathan. B. Brown, age 43, Grocer, born in MA.
BROWN, NATHN. B., 43, M, Grocer, W, MA, 346, 507, NBPT.
BROWN, NEWMAN, 49, M, Dealer in Coal, W, NH, 653, 943, NBPT.
BROWN, NICHOLAS R., 31, M, Overseer in Mill, W, MA, 42, 62, NBPT.
BROWN, NUTTER, 60, M, Farmer, W, NH, 509, 679, NBPT*.
BROWN, ORLANDO, 60, M, Ship Carpenter, W, MA, 583, 772, NBPT*.
BROWN, PRISCILLA, 18, F, -, W, Maine, 450, 673, NBPT. In HH of Elizabeth Garland, age 53, born in NH.
BROWN, SAMUEL, 48, M, Machinist, 0, NH, 30, 36, NBPT*.
BROWN, SAMUEL, 38, M, Master Mariner, W, Maine, 120, 177, NBPT.
BROWN, SARAH, 84, F, -, W, Maine, 463, 691, NBPT.
BROWN, SARAH, 78, F, -, W, NH, 351, 463, NBPT*. In HH of John O.W. Brown, age 58, Trader, born in NH.
BROWN, SARAH M.A., 36, F, -, W, NH, 736,1041, NBPT. In HH of John L. Grindal, age 48, Grocer, born in Maine.
BROWN, THOMAS, 49, M, Innholder (Hotel), W, MA, 166, 199, NBPT*.
BROWN, WILLIAM, 30, M, Painter, W, NH, 284, 369, NBPT*.
BROWN, WILLIAM, 17, M, Operative, W, MA, 496, 740, NBPT. In HH of Mercy Brown, age 52, born in MA.

BROWN, WILLIAM W., 18, M, Mariner, W, MA, 472, 708, NBPT. In HH of John Dodge, age 67, Soap Boiler, born in Maine.
BROWN, WOODBURY, 27, M, Mariner, W, NH, 509, 679, NBPT*. In HH of Nutter Brown, age 60, Farmer, born in NH.
BRUCE, BETHANE, 24, F, -, W, Maine, 499, 663, NBPT*. In HH of Frederick J. Bruce, age 29, Ship Joiner, born in Nova Scotia.
BRUCE, FREDERICK J., 29, M, Ship Joiner, W, Nova Scotia, 499, 663, NBPT*.
BRYON, GEORGE, 26, M, Merchant, W, MA, 442, 658, NBPT. In HH of Simeon Jordan, age 39, Shoemaker, born in MA.
BUCK, CHARLES, 16, M, Ostler, W, MA, 332, 432, NBPT*. In HH of Greenleaf Boardman, age 34, Livery Stable, born in MA.
BUCKLAND, DORCAS, 67, F, -, W, Maine, 337, 439, NBPT*. In HH of George W. Ward, age 24, Wheelwright, born in Maine.
BUMS, SARAH, 22, F, -, W, Maine, 488, 730, NBPT. In HH of Lucinda G. Peabody, age 39, born in NH.
BUNTIN, CHARLES, 44, M, Master Mariner, W, MA, 679, 971, NBPT.
BUNTIN, ELIZABETH, 24, F, -, W, Ireland, 679, 971, NBPT. In HH of Charles Buntin, age, 44, Master Mariner, born in MA.
BUNTIN, JOHN L., 40, M, Dry Goods Dealer, W, MA, 211, 262, NBPT*. In Boarding House.
BUNTIN, THOMAS, 74, M, Merchant, W, MA, 700, 992, NBPT.
BUNTIN, WILLIAM, 22, M, Mariner, W, MA, 700, 992, NBPT. In HH of Thomas Buntin, age 74, Merchant, born in MA.
BURBANK, GARDNER, 30, M, Painter, W, MA, 126, 150, NBPT*.
BURBANK, HENRY, 27, M, Painter, W, MA, 522, 693, NBPT*. In HH of Nathan Burbank, age 59, Painter, born in MA.
BURBANK, JANE, 27, F, -, W, NH, 126, 150, NBPT*. In HH of Gardner Burbank, age 30, Painter, born in MA.
BURBANK, MARINDA, 25, F, -, W, Maine, 782,1108, NBPT. In HH of Enoch Tilton, age 45, Hotel Keeper, born in NH. In Hotel.
BURBANK, MARTHA, 20, F, -, W, VT, 392, 515, NBPT*. In HH of Moses Flanders, age 36, Blacksmith, born in NH.
BURBANK, MIRANDA M., 26, F, -, W, VT, 568, 843, NBPT. In HH of Moody Burbank, age 42, Restorator, born in NH.
BURBANK, MOODY, 42, M, Restorator, W, NH, 568, 843, NBPT.
BURBANK, NATHAN, 29, M, Painter, W, MA, 522, 693, NBPT*.
BURD, ELIZA, 25, F, -, W, Ireland, 532, 794, NBPT. In HH of John Burd, age 19, Operative, born in Ireland.
BURD, JOHN, 19, M, Operative, W, Ireland, 532, 794, NBPT. .
BURETT, HANNAH, 20, F, -, W, Ireland, 247, 357, NBPT. In HH of Robert Bayley, age 64, Merchant, born in MA.
BURK, CATHERINE, 26, F, W,

0, Ireland, 178, 257, NBPT. In HH of Patrick Holland, age 26, Laborer, born in Ireland.

BURKE, ANN, 13, F, -, W, Ireland, 507, 757, NBPT. In HH of Patrick G. Burke, age 60, Weaver, born in Ireland.

BURKE, BRIDGET, 55, F, -, W, Ireland, 507, 757, NBPT. In HH of Patrick G. Burke, age 60, Weaver, born in Ireland.

BURKE, BRIDGET, 15, F, -, W, Ireland, 507, 757, NBPT. In HH of Patrick G. Burke, age 60, Weaver, born in Ireland.

BURKE, PATRICK F., 17, M, Weaver, W, Ireland, 507, 757, NBPT. In HH of Patrick G. Burke, age 60, Weaver, born in Ireland.

BURKE, PATRICK G., 60, M, Weaver, W, Ireland, 507, 757, NBPT.

BURKE, WINNEFORD, 34, F, -, W, Ireland, 679, 971, NBPT. In HH of Charles Buntin, age, 44, Master Mariner, born in MA.

BURKE, WINNEFORD, 26, F, -, W, Ireland, 507, 757, NBPT. In HH of Patrick G. Burke, age 60, Weaver, born in Ireland.

BURNET, GEORGE E., 6, M, -, W, N.S., 520, 774, NBPT. In HH of John Burnet, age 54, Laborer, born in N.S. {Nova Scotia}.

BURNET, HANNAH N., 14, F, -, W, N.S., 520, 774, NBPT. In HH of John Burnet, age 54, Laborer, born in N.S. {Nova Scotia}.

BURNET, JAMES A., 9, M, -, W, N.S., 520, 774, NBPT. In HH of John Burnet, age 54, Laborer, born in N.S. {Nova Scotia}.

BURNET, JOHN, 54, M, Laborer, W, N.S., 520, 774, NBPT.

BURNET, JOHN F., 16, M, Laborer, W, N.S., 520, 774, NBPT. In HH of John Burnet, age 54, Laborer, born in N.S. {Nova Scotia}.

BURNET, LAURETHA, 43, F, -, W, N.S., 520, 774, NBPT. In HH of John Burnet, age 54, Laborer, born in N.S. {Nova Scotia}.

BURNET, PHEBE A., 19, F, -, W, N.S., 520, 774, NBPT. In HH of John Burnet, age 54, Laborer, born in N.S. {Nova Scotia}.

BURNET, WILLIAM T., 11, M, -, W, N.S., 520, 774, NBPT. In HH of John Burnet, age 54, Laborer, born in N.S. {Nova Scotia}.

BURNHAM, JOHN, 25, M, Ship Carpenter, W, Maine, 531, 705, NBPT*. In HH of James Litch, age 41, Farmer, born in Nova Scotia.

BURNHAM, THOMAS W., 44, M, Dept. Collector, W, MA, 653, 944, NBPT.

BURNS, BRIDGETT, 20, F, -, W, Ireland, 308, 454, NBPT. In HH of Daniel Smith, age 62, Druggist, born in CT.

BURNS, HANNAH, 20, F, -, W, Maine, 615, 807, NBPT*. In HH of Dexter Hildreth, age 23, Blacksmith, born in Maine.

BURNS, MARY, 22, F, -, W, Ireland, 126, 151, NBPT*. In HH of Richard Stone, age 50, Clerk Savings Inst., born in MA.

BURRILL, EDWARD, 40, M, Clerk, Bartlet Mills, 0, MA, 32, 39, NBPT*.

BURRILL, HENRY M., 24, M, Painter, W, MA, 277, 354, NBPT*. In HH of John Burrill, age 50,

Painter, born in MA.
BURRILL, JOHN, 50, M, Painter, W, MA, 277, 354, NBPT*.
BURRILL, JOHN T., 16, M, Painter, W, MA, 277, 354, NBPT*. In HH of John Burrill, age 50, Painter, born in MA.
BURRILL, JOSEPH R., 17, M, Butcher, -, MA, 32, 39, NBPT*. In HH of Edward Burrill, age 40, Clerk Bartlet Mills, born in MA.
BURTON, ALLEXANDER F., 25, M, Mariner, W, England, 4, 4, NBPT. In HH of Mary Y. Huse, age 50, born in MA.
BUSHY, ABRAHAM, 29, M, Mariner, W, Nova Scotia, 231, 288, NBPT*. In HH of Julia Bush, age 22, born in Ireland.
BUSHY, ALEXANDER, 4, M, -, W, Pr. Edward Island, 231, 288, NBPT*. In HH of Julia Bush, age 22, born in Ireland.
BUSHY, DEBORAH, 52, F, -, W, Maine, 500, 665, NBPT*. In HH of Joseph Bushy, age 63, Ship Carpenter, born in Canada.
BUSHY, EDWIN, 14, M, -, W, Maine, 500, 665, NBPT*. In HH of Joseph Bushy, age 63, Ship Carpenter, born in Canada.
BUSHY, GEORGE, 18, M, Shoemaker, W, Maine, 500, 665, NBPT*. In HH of Joseph Bushy, age 63, Ship Carpenter, born in Canada.
BUSHY, JOSEPH, 63, M, Ship Carpenter, W, Canada, 500, 665, NBPT*.
BUSHY, JOSEPH, 6, M, -, W, Pr. Edward Island, 231, 288, NBPT*. In HH of Julia Bush, age 22, born in Ireland.

BUSHY, JULIA, 22, F, -, W, Pr. Edward Island, 231, 288, NBPT*.
BUSHY, MARY, 23, F, -, W, Maine, 500, 665, NBPT*. In HH of Joseph Bushy, age 63, Ship Carpenter, born in Canada.
BUSHY, WILLIAM N., 10, M, -, W, Maine, 500, 665, NBPT*. In HH of Joseph Bushy, age 63, Ship Carpenter, born in Canada.
BUTLER, CHARLES, 58, M, Baker, W, MA, 206, 257, NBPT*.
BUTLER, JOSEPH W., 31, M, Baker, W, MA, 207, 258, NBPT*.
BUTLER, THOMAS, 28, M, Baker, W, MA, 163, 196, NBPT*.
BUTMAN, JOHN W., 23, M, Painter, W, MA, 243, 306, NBPT*. In HH of Rebekah Carpenter, age 58, born in MA.
BUTTERFIELD, RUTH A., 15, F, -, W, NH, 200, 247, NBPT*. In HH of Adriel H. Hodgdon, age 37, Drayman, born in NH.
BUTTERFIELD, SAMUEL, 23, M, Shoemaker, W, NH, 200, 247, NBPT*. In HH of Adriel H. Hodgdon, age 37, Drayman, born in NH.
BUTTS, CHARLES T., 16, M, None, W, MA, 441, 584, NBPT*. In HH of Moses Butts, age 44, Mariner, born in Newfoundland.
BUTTS, MOSES, 44, M, Mariner, W, Newfoundland, 441, 584, NBPT*.
BYLE, CATHARINE, 21, F, -, W, Ireland, 231, 287, NBPT*. In HH of Margaret Sullivan, age 28, born in Ireland.
BYLE, JAMES, 20, M, Laborer in Mill, W, Ireland, 231, 287, NBPT*. In HH of Margaret Sullivan, age 28,

born in Ireland.

- C -

CALDWELL, ABNER, 63, M, Hermetical Sealer, W, MA, 185, 269, NBPT.
CALDWELL, ALEXANDER, 25, M, Distiller, W, MA, 469, 622, NBPT*.
CALDWELL, ALONZO B., 32, M, Daguerrotypist, W, MA, 465, 616, NBPT*.
CALDWELL, ANN, 33, F, -, W, NH, 465, 616, NBPT*. In HH of Alonzo B. Cadwell, age 32, Daguerrotypist, born in MA.
CALDWELL, CHARLES H., 34, M, None, W, MA, 185, 269, NBPT. In HH of Abner Caldwell, age 63, Hermetical Sealer, born in MA.
CALDWELL, ELIZABETH A., 24, F, -, W, NH, 469, 622, NBPT*. In HH of Alexander Caldwell, age 25, Distiller, born in MA.
CALDWELL, GEORGE, 16, M, Clerk, W, MA, 464, 615, NBPT*. In HH of John Caldwell, age 64, Distiller, born in MA.
CALDWELL, JAMES, 63, M, Dry Goods Dealer, W, MA, 463, 614, NBPT*.
CALDWELL, JOHN, 64, M, Distiller, W, MA, 464, 615, NBPT*.
CALDWELL, STEPHEN, 53, M, Superintendent, W, MA, 788,1114, NBPT. Stephen Caldwell, Superintendent of Poor House.
CALDWELL, WILLIAM, 58, M, Merchant, W, MA, 171, 249, NBPT.
CALDWELL, WILLIAM, 36, M, None, W, MA, 185, 269, NBPT. In HH of Abner Caldwell, age 63, Hermetical Sealer, born in MA.
CALDWELL, WILLIAM W., 25, M, Apothecary, W, MA, 672, 964, NBPT.
CALL, ABRAHAM A., 53, M, Bookseller, W, MA, 562, 835, NBPT.
CAMERON, ELIZA, 18, F, -, W, Maine, 271, 398, NBPT. In HH of Horace Brown, age 52, Stage Agent, born in MA.
CAMPBELL, CATHARINE, 28, F, -, W, Ireland, 237, 298, NBPT*. In HH of Felix Campbell, age 40, Fireman, born in Ireland.
CAMPBELL, FELIX, 40, M, Fireman, W, Ireland, 237, 298, NBPT*.
CAMPBELL, GEORGE W., 26, M, Merchant, W, MA, 341, 500, NBPT. In HH of Anna Campbell, age 70, born in MA.
CAMPBELL, JOHN, 5, M, -, W, Ireland, 237, 298, NBPT*. In HH of Felix Campbell, age 40, Fireman, born in Ireland.
CAMPBELL, MARGARET, 28, F, -, W, Ireland, 249, 360, NBPT. In HH of John Porter, age 66, Merchant, born in MA.
CAMPBELL, PATRICK, 6, M, -, W, Ireland, 237, 298, NBPT*. In HH of Felix Campbell, age 40, Fireman, born in Ireland.
CAMPBELL, RANDLOPH, 40, M, Clergyman, Congregational., W, NJ, 655, 945, NBPT.
CANDAGE, MARY L., 20, F, -, W, Maine, 247, 357, NBPT. In HH of Robert Bayley, age 64, Merchant,

born in MA.
CANEY, JOANNA, 36, F, -, W, Ireland, 359, 526, NBPT. In HH of Michael Caney, age 26, Laborer, born in Ireland.
CANEY, MICHAEL, 26, M, Laborer, W, Ireland, 359, 526, NBPT.
CANN, ANN, 68, F, -, W, Scotland, 592, 781, NBPT*. In HH of Samuel Cann, age 70, Ship Carpenter, born in Nova Scotia.
CANN, CHARLES, 14, M, -, W, Nova Scotia, 592, 781, NBPT*. In HH of Samuel Cann, age 70, Ship Carpenter, born in Nova Scotia.
CANN, JOHN, 24, M, Mariner, W, Nova Scotia, 592, 781, NBPT*. In HH of Samuel Cann, age 70, Ship Carpenter, born in Nova Scotia.
CANN, MARTHA, 7, F, -, W, Nova Scotia, 592, 781, NBPT*. In HH of Samuel Cann, age 70, Ship Carpenter, born in Nova Scotia.
CANN, MARY, 21, F, -, W, Nova Scotia, 7, 7, NBPT*. In HH of Hervey Wilbur, age 64, Congragational. Clergyman, born MA.
CANN, MARY, 20, F, -, W, Nova Scotia, 592, 781, NBPT*. In HH of Samuel Cann, age 70, Ship Carpenter, born in Nova Scotia.
CANN, SAMUEL, 70, M, Shop Carpenter, W, Nova Scotia, 592, 781, NBPT*.
CANN, SAMUEL, 5, M, -, W, Nova Scotia, 592, 781, NBPT*. In HH of Samuel Cann, age 70, Ship Carpenter, born in Nova Scotia.
CANN, SARAH, 12, F, -, W, Nova Scotia, 592, 781, NBPT*. In HH of Samuel Cann, age 70, Ship Carpenter, born in Nova Scotia.
CANN, WILLIAM, 18, M, Mariner, W, Nova Scotia, 592, 781, NBPT*. In HH of Samuel Cann, age 70, Ship Carpenter, born in Nova Scotia.
CANNERY, BRIDGET, 32, F, -, W, Ireland, 236, 297, NBPT*. In HH of Thomas F. Cannery, age 35, Mariner, born in Ireland.
CANNERY, THOMAS F., 35, M, Mariner, W, Ireland, 236, 297, NBPT*.
CANNEY, GEORGE, 16, M, Laborer, W, MA, 208, 308, NBPT. In HH of Catherine Canney, age 49, born in MA.
CANNEY, HIRAM, 42, M, Blacksmith, W, NH, 145, 173, NBPT*.
CANNEY, JAMES, 60, M, None, W, Ireland, 263, 385, NBPT.
CANNEY, JAMES M., 41, M, Teamster, W, NH, 177, 256, NBPT.
CANNEY, JOHN, 22, M, Carpenter, W, MA, 208, 308, NBPT. In HH of Catherine Canney, age 49, born in MA.
CANNEY, MARY, 25, F, -, W, Ireland, 263, 385, NBPT. In HH of James Canney, age 60, None, born in Ireland.
CANNEY, SOPHIA, 41, F, W, 0, NH, 177, 256, NBPT. In HH of James N. Canney, age 41, Teamster, born in NH.
CANNING, ELIRA B., 38, F, -, W, NH, 128, 189, NBPT. In HH of Samuel C. Canning, age 36, Sailmaker, born in MA.
CANNING, SAMUEL C., 36, M, Sail Maker, W, MA, 128, 189,

CARAGAN, HANNAH, 24, F, -, W, Ireland, 403, 597, NBPT. In HH of James Caragan, age 36, Laborer, born in Ireland.

CARAGAN, JAMES, 36, M, Laborer, W, Ireland, 403, 597, NBPT.

CAREY, ANGELIA N., 15, F, -, W, Maine, 77, 86, NBPT*. In HH of Harriet A. Carey, age 24, born Maine.

CAREY, CATHERINE, 58, F, -, W, Ireland, 624, 908, NBPT. In HH of Patrick Carey, age 60, Laborer, born in Ireland.

CAREY, DENNIS, 27, M, Laborer, W, Ireland, 624, 908, NBPT. In HH of Patrick Carey, age 60, Laborer, born in Ireland.

CAREY, ELIZABETH R., 22, F, -, W, Maine, 77, 86, NBPT*. In HH of Harriet A. Carey, age 24, born Maine.

CAREY, HARRIET A., 24, F, -, W, Maine, 77, 86, NBPT*.

CAREY, HARRIET A., 24, F, -, W, Maine, 77, 86, NBPT*.

CAREY, HARVEY, 22, M, Operative, W, MA, 412, 538, NBPT*. In HH of Alban Brown, age 40, Watchman, born in MA.

CAREY, JOHN, 30, M, Laborer, W, Ireland, 624, 908, NBPT. In HH of Patrick Carey, age 60, Laborer, born in Ireland.

CAREY, JULIA, 24, F, -, W, Ireland, 624, 908, NBPT. In HH of Patrick Carey, age 60, Laborer, born in Ireland.

CAREY, MARTHA A., 21, F, -, W, Maine, 412, 538, NBPT*. In HH of Alban Brown, age 40, Watchman, born in MA.

CAREY, MARY, 19, F, -, W, Ireland, 464, 615, NBPT*. In HH of John Caldwell, age 64, Distiller, born in MA.

CAREY, MARY C., 17, F, -, W, Maine, 77, 86, NBPT*. In HH of Harriet A. Carey, age 24, born Maine.

CAREY, MICHAEL, 18, M, Laborer, W, Ireland, 624, 908, NBPT. In HH of Patrick Carey, age 60, Laborer, born in Ireland.

CAREY, PATRICK, 60, M, Laborer, W, Ireland, 624, 908, NBPT.

CARHILL, DANIEL, 31, M, Fireman, W, MA, 616, 808, NBPT*. In HH of Alonzo Bean, age 40, Machinist, born in MA.

CARHILL, DANIEL, 26, M, Laborer, W, Ireland, 748,1054, NBPT.

CARHILL, MARY, 26, F, -, W, Ireland, 748,1054, NBPT. In HH of Daniel Carhill, age 26, Laborer, born in Ireland.

CARLTON, FRANCIS, 39, M, Overseer, W, MA, 254, 318, NBPT*.

CARLTON, MARY, 74, F, -, W, NH, 245, 308, NBPT*.

CARLTON, MARY, 70, F, -, W, NH, 647, 937, NBPT.

CARNES, BRIDGET, 23, F, -, W, Ireland, 78, 87, NBPT*. In Jail.

CARPENTER, PAMELIA, 32, F, -, W, Maine, 736,1041, NBPT. In HH of John L. Grindal, age 48, Grocer, born in Maine.

CARR, HENRY, 43, M, Trader, W, MA, 621, 904, NBPT. In HH of Hannah Carr, age 70, born in MA.

CARR, JOSEPH F., 44, M, Merchant, W, MA, 267, 391, NBPT.

CARR, OSGOOD, 37, M, Shoemaker, W, MA, 380, 561, NBPT. In HH of Samuel Lunt, age 42, Operative, born in MA.

CARRON, JOHN, 2, M, -, W, N.S., 754,1063, NBPT. In HH of Clarissa Turner, age 36, born in N.B. {New Brunswick}.

CARRY, JAMES, 30, M, Constable, W, MA, 636, 923, NBPT.

CARTER, CHARLES W., 24, M, Confectioner, W, MA, 710,1005, NBPT.

CARTER, JEREMIAH, 46, M, Victualer, W, NH, 578, 766, NBPT*.

CARTER, LUTHER, 21, M, Laborer, W, NH, 119, 142, NBPT*. In HH of Edward S. Rand, age 65, Merchant, born in MA.

CARTER, MARY M., 47, F, -, W, NH, 578, 766, NBPT*. In HH of Jeremiah Carter, age 46, Victualler, born in NH.

CARTER, NATHAN, 43, M, R.R. Conductor, W, NH, 590, 867, NBPT.

CARTER, NATHAN, 17, M, Mariner, W, MA, 578, 766, NBPT*. In HH of Jeremiah Carter, age 46, Victualler, born in NH.

CARTER, SEWALL, 24, M, Operative, W, Maine, 770,1090, NBPT. In HH of Levi Pearson, age 37, Watchman, born in MA.

CARTER, SHERMAN J., 18, M, Apr. Victualer, W, MA, 578, 766, NBPT*. In HH of Jeremiah Carter, age 46, Victualler, born in NH.

CARTER, SUSAN, 24, F, -, W, VT, 200, 247, NBPT*. In HH of Adriel H. Hodgdon, age 37, Drayman, born in NH.

CARTER, THEODOLIA, 23, F, -, W, Maine, 770,1090, NBPT. In HH of Levi Pearson, age 37, Watchman, born in MA.

CARTER, WILLIAM, 21, M, Victualer, W, MA, 570, 756, NBPT*. In HH of Joseph Merrill, age 32, Victualler, born in MA.

CASE, MOSES P., 34, M, School Teacher, W, VT, 675, 967, NBPT.

CASEY, BRIDGET, 27, F, -, W, Ireland, 418, 622, NBPT. In HH of Isaac S. Coffin, age 50, Merchant, born in MA.

CASEY, JAMES, 25, M, Laborer, W, Ireland, 178, 257, NBPT. In HH of Patrick Holland, age 26, Laborer, born in Ireland.

CASEY, JANTHA, 22, F, -, W, Maine, 736,1041, NBPT. In HH of John L. Grindal, age 48, Grocer, born in Maine.

CASHMAN, JEREMIAH, 33, M, Laborer, W, Ireland, 595, 785, NBPT*.

CASHMAN, MARY, 30, F, -, W, Ireland, 595, 785, NBPT*. In HH of Jeremiah Cashman, age 33, Laborer, born in Ireland.

CASSMAN, JAMES, 21, M, -, W, Ireland, 229, 283, NBPT*.

CASSON, GEORGE L., 10, M, Barber, W, England, 748,1055, NBPT. In HH of John W. Casson, age 60, Barber, born in England.

CASSON, JOHN W., 60, M, Barber, W, England, 748,1055, NBPT.

CASWELL, CHARLES, 19, M,

Shoemaker, W, NH, 323, 477, NBPT. In HH of Lewis Foote, age 34, Shoemaker, born in MA.

CASWELL, HENRIETTA, 29, F, -, W, Maine, 515, 686, NBPT*. In HH of George P. Garland, age 65, Boarding House, born in NJ.

CASWIN, DANIEL, 26, M, Laborer Dye House, W, Ireland, 84, 93, NBPT*.

CASWIN, MARY, 26, F, -, W, Ireland, 84, 93, NBPT*. In HH of Daniel Caswin, age 26, Laborer, Dye House, born in Ireland.

CATE, HANNAH N., 15, F, -, W, Maine, 299, 391, NBPT*. In HH of William Cate, age 56, Master Mariner, born in MA.

CATE, MARY, 51, F, -, W, NH, 299, 391, NBPT*. In HH of William Cate, age 56, Master Mariner, born in MA.

CATE, MARY A., 21, F, -, W, Maine, 299, 391, NBPT*. In HH of William Cate, age 56, Master Mariner, born in MA.

CATE, SARAH W., 19, F, -, W, Maine, 299, 391, NBPT*. In HH of William Cate, age 56, Master Mariner, born in MA.

CATE, WILLIAM, 56, M, Master Mariner, W, MA, 299, 391, NBPT*.

CAULKS, WILLIAM, 14, M, -, W, Montividon, 337, 496, NBPT. In HH of Paul Simpson, age 76, Master Mariner, born in Maine.

CAVENAUGH, DENNIS, 17, M, Operative, W, Ireland, 538, 804, NBPT. In HH of Daniel O. Lory, age 49, Mariner, born in Ireland.

CHAS, JOHN, 19, M, Mariner, W, MA, 107, 159, NBPT. In HH of Henry Lunt, age 34, Mariner, born in MA.

CHAMBERLANE, CHARLES P., 25, M, Tin Plate Worker, W, MA, 85, 124, NBPT.

CHAMBERLIN, ASA W., 32, M, Machinist, W, MA, 268, 393, NBPT.

CHAMBERLIN, GILMAN, 36, M, Stove Dealer, W, MA, 582, 858, NBPT.

CHAMBERLIN, HENRY, 17, M, Clerk, W, MA, 269, 395, NBPT. In HH of Albert Wise, age 38, Tin Plate Worker, born in MA.

CHAMBERLIN, JOHN, 30, M, Tin Plate Worker, W, MA, 670, 962, NBPT.

CHANDLER, CHARLOTTA, 18, F, -, W, NH, 720,1019, NBPT. In HH of Dana Dodge, age 33, Broker, born in MA.

CHANDLER, JOSEPH, 22, M, Machinist, W, Maine, 431, 640, NBPT. In HH of Oliver P. Wiggin, age 44, Cooper, born in NH.

CHAPMAN, ABIGAIL, 54, F, -, W, Maine, 148, 176, NBPT*.

CHAPMAN, GEORGE W., 15, M, None, W, MA, 148, 176, NBPT*. In HH of Abigail Chapman, age 54, born in Maine.

CHAPMAN, HENRY W., 27, M, School Teacher, W, MA, 148, 176, NBPT*. In HH of Abigail Chapman, age 54, born in Maine.

CHAPMAN, JOHN K., 39, M, Shoemaker, W, MA, 358, 522, NBPT.

CHAPMAN, WILLIAM, 26, M,

Shoemaker, W, Maine, 405, 529, NBPT*. In HH of Miriam James, age 50, born in NH.
CHASE, BAILEY, 50, M, Master Mariner, W, MA, 317, 411, NBPT*.
CHASE, EDWARD, 18, M, Painter, W, MA, 534, 710, NBPT*. In HH of Moses Chase, age 58, Shoemaker, born in MA.
CHASE, EDWIN B., 17, M, Clerk, W, MA, 317, 411, NBPT*. In HH of Bailey Chase, age 50, Master Mariner, born in MA.
CHASE, GEORGE W., 22, M, Painter, W, MA, 626, 912, NBPT. In HH of Luther R. Chase, age 30, Carriage Maker, born in MA.
CHASE, JANE M., 34, F, W, 0, NH, 414, 541, NBPT*. In HH of Joseph R. Chase, age 37, Shoemaker, born in MA.
CHASE, JERMIAH, 28, M, Mariner, W, MA, 163, 234, NBPT.
CHASE, JOSEPH R., 37, M, Shoemaker, W, MA, 414, 541, NBPT*.
CHASE, LESLIE, 8, M, -, W, CT, 130, 155, NBPT*. In HH of C.S. Merchant, age 54, U.S. Army, born in NY.
CHASE, LUTHER R., 30, M, Carriage Maker, W, MA, 626, 912, NBPT.
CHASE, MARY A., 24, F, -, W, Maine, 163, 234, NBPT. In HH of Jermiah Chase, age 28, Mariner, born in MA.
CHASE, MOSES, 58, M, Shoemaker, W, MA, 534, 710, NBPT*.
CHASE, MOSES, 40, M, Mariner, W, MA, 789,1115, NBPT. In HH of John M. Smith, age 34, Brick maker, born in MA.
CHASE, NATHAN, 67, M, Laborer, W, MA, 430, 560, NBPT*.
CHASE, ROBERT G., 14, M, None listed, W, NH, 494, 657, NBPT*. In HH of Hannah Chase, age 83, born in MA.
CHASE, ROBET? F., 19, M, Clerk, W, MA, 317, 411, NBPT*. In HH of Bailey Chase, age 50, Master Mariner, born in MA.
CHASE, SAMUEL W., 35, M, Mate, W, NH, 612, 803, NBPT*.
CHASE, SARAH E.G., 26, F, -, W, NY, 130, 155, NBPT*. In HH of C.S. Merchant, age 54, U.S. Army, born in NY.
CHASE, TRISTRAM, 76, M, Merchant, W, MA, 598, 876, NBPT.
CHAWSE, MARY J., 16, F, -, W, Maine, 70, 100, NBPT. In HH of Elisa A. Atkinson, age 45, born in MA.
CHEENEY, ALLIA, 16, F, -,W, England, 216, 320, NBPT. In HH of John Cheeney, age 36, Master Mariner, born in MA.
CHEENEY, JAMES W., 24, M, Goldsmith, W, MA, 716,1012, NBPT. In HH of Benjamin Pratt, age 65, None, born in Maine.
CHEENEY, JOHN, 36, M, Master Mariner, W, MA, 216, 320, NBPT.
CHEENEY, SARAH L., 25, F, -, W, Maine, 716,1012, NBPT. In HH of Benjamin Pratt, age 65, None, born in Maine.
CHEEVER, ALBERT, 31, M, Master Mariner, W, Maine, 127, 186, NBPT.
CHEEVER, BENJ. H., 24, M,

Carpenter, W, MA, 130, 192, NBPT. In HH of Aaron B. Adams, age 55 Merchant, born in MA.
CHEEVER, EDWIN A., 29, M, Iron Moulder, W, Maine, 184, 267, NBPT.
CHEEVER, ELIZA G., 23, F, -, W, NY, 184, 267, NBPT. In HH of Edwin A. Cheever, age 29, Iron Moulder, born in Maine.
CHEEVER, PHILLIP, 63, M, Cooper, W, MA, 91, 132, NBPT.
CHENEY, ABBY, 25, F, W, 0, Maine, 204, 300, NBPT. In HH of WILLIAM B. Cheney, age 35, Laborer, born in MA.
CHENEY, CHARLES, 47, M, Merchant Tailor, W, MA, 143, 170, NBPT*.
CHENEY, GEORGE A., 18, M, Machinist, W, MA, 83, 92, NBPT*. In HH of James Cheney, age 52, Operative, born Maine.
CHENEY, JAMES, 52, M, Operative, W, Maine, 83, 92, NBPT*.
CHENEY, MARTHA D., 29, F, -, W, Maine, 560, 743, NBPT*. In HH of Samuel C. Cheney, age 35, Blacksmith, born in NH.
CHENEY, SAMUEL C., 35, M, Blacksmith, W, NH, 560, 743, NBPT*.
CHENEY, SARAH, 54, F, -, W, NH, 535, 711, NBPT*.
CHENEY, SARAH T., 24, F, -, W, NH, 535, 711, NBPT*. In HH of Sarah Cheney, age 54, born in NH.
CHENEY, WILLIAM A., 53, M, Master Mariner, W, MA, 572, 758, NBPT*.
CHENEY, WILLIAM A., 22, M, Mariner, W, NH, 535, 711, NBPT*. In HH of Sarah Cheney, age 54, born in NH.
CHENEY, WILLIAM A., 18, M, Printer, W, MA, 263, 332, NBPT*. In HH of William H. Brewster, age 37, Printer and Publisher, born in NH.
CHENEY, WILLIAM B., 35, M, Laborer, W, MA, 204, 300, NBPT.
CHESLEY, MARIAH, 23, F, -, W, NH, 588, 865, NBPT. In HH of Stilman Simonds, age 43, Shoemaker, born in MA.
CHICKEN, ELIZABETH, 19, F, -, W, NH, 778,1103, NBPT. In HH of William Chicken, age 40, Overseer, born in England.
CHICKEN, JOHN, 13, M, -, W, NH, 778,1103, NBPT. In HH of William Chicken, age 40, Overseer, born in England.
CHICKEN, NANCY, 40, F, -, W, Scotland, 778,1103, NBPT. In HH of William Chicken, age 40, Overseer, born in England.
CHICKEN, NANCY, 17, F, -, W, NH, 778,1103, NBPT. In HH of William Chicken, age 40, Overseer, born in England.
CHICKEN, WILLIAM, 40, M, Overseer, W, England, 778,1103, NBPT.
CHOATE, BENJAMIN, 79, M, Ship Joiner, W, MA, 499, 662, NBPT*.
CHOATE, EZEKIEL, 40, M, Ship Joiner, W, MA, 493, 656, NBPT*.
CHOATE, GEORGE A., 18, M, Ship Joiner, W, MA, 503, 671, NBPT*. In HH of True Choate, age 44, Ship Joiner, born in MA.
CHOATE, JAMES, 35, M, Ship Carpenter, W, MA, 559, 742, NBPT*.
CHOATE, JOSEPH, 17, M, None, W, MA, 409, 534, NBPT*. In HH

of Thomas Choate, age 37, Ship Joiner, born in MA.
CHOATE, MAHALA K., 28, F, -, W, NH, 582, 770, NBPT*. In HH of Stephen P. Chaote, age 30, Ship Joiner, born in MA.
CHOATE, STEPHEN P., 30, M, Ship Joiner, W, MA, 582, 770, NBPT*.
CHOATE, THOMAS, 37, M, Ship Joiner, W, MA, 409, 534, NBPT*.
CHOATE, TRUE, 44, M, Ship Joiner, W, MA, 503, 671, NBPT*.
CHOATE, WILLIAM, 33, M, Ship Joiner, W, MA, 561, 744, NBPT*.
CHRISTIAN, JAMES, 36, M, Shoemaker, W, Maine, 776,1100, NBPT. In HH of Moses Winn, age 62, Laborer, born in MA.
CHRISTIAN, SARAH, 24, F, -, W, Maine, 776,1100, NBPT. In HH of Moses Winn, age 62, Laborer, born in MA.
CHURCH, PHEBE, 29, F, -, W, Maine, 645, 933, NBPT.
CHURN, JAMES, 21, M, Fisherman, W, VA, 264, 333, NBPT*. In HH of Joseph Greenleaf, age 62, Sailmaker, born in MA.
CILLEY, ELIZABETH, 38, F, -, W, Maine, 503, 750, NBPT. In HH of James Cilley Jr., age 28, Mariner, born in NH.
CILLEY, JAMES JR., 28, M, Mariner, W, NH, 503, 750, NBPT.
CLANIN, SAMUEL M., 19, M, Shoemaker, W, MA, 188, 273, NBPT. In HH of Mary Clanin, age 76, born in MA.
CLARA, JULIA, 20, F, -, W, Maine, 164, 197, NBPT*. In HH of Nathaniel Coffin, age 66, Farmer, born in MA.
CLARENDON, ALICE, 16, F, 0-, W, RI, 78, 87, NBPT*. In Jail. Convict.
CLARK, ABRAHAM, 20, M, Mariner, W, MA, 92, 134, NBPT. In HH of Amos Clark, age 60, Baker, born in MA.
CLARK, AMOS, 60, M, Baker, W, MA, 92, 134, NBPT.
CLARK, ANN M., 13, F, -, W, Maine, 439, 580, NBPT*.
CLARK, GREENLEAF, 33, M, Printer, W, MA, 621, 905, NBPT.
CLARK, HELEN, 27, F, - ,W, Maine, 424, 552, NBPT*. In HH of Benjamin Smith, age 46, Painter, born in VT.
CLARK, JOHN D., 25, M, Cooper, W, MA, 468, 701, NBPT. In HH of Grating Martin, age 65, Rigger, born in Italy.
CLARK, NANCY, 27, F, W, 0, Maine, 424, 552, NBPT*. In HH of Benjamin Smith, age 46, Painter, born in VT.
CLARK, SAMUEL, 68, M, Cabinet Maker, W, MA, 12, 14, NBPT. In HH of Hosea Y. Crofoot, age 29, Bookbinder, born in CT.
CLARK, WILLIAM E., 18, M, Mariner, W, MA, 92, 134, NBPT. In HH of Amos Clark, age 60, Baker, born in MA.
CLARKSON, FREDERICK J., 21, M, Painter, W, MA, 94, 111, NBPT*. In HH of Samuel Fennimore, age 48, Shoemaker, born in MA.
CLARKSON, JOHN, 21, M, Machinist, W, MA, 350, 461, NBPT*. In HH of Sophia Clarkson, age 65, born in MA.

CLEARY, MARY, 21, F, -, W, Ireland, 10, 10, NBPT*. In HH of William Ashby, 63, trader, born in England.
CLEAVLAND, JOHN, 24, M, Book Agent, W, Canada, 275, 405, NBPT. In HH of Harriet N. Kimball, age 18, born in NJ.
CLEAVLAND, MARY E., 20, F, -, W, NY, 275, 405, NBPT. In HH of Harriet N. Kimball, age 18, born in NJ.
CLEMENT, AMOS C., 60, M, Clerk, W, NH, 632, 919, NBPT.
CLEMENT, CELINDA M., 14, F, -, W, NH, 632, 919, NBPT. In HH of Amos C. Clement, age 60, Clerk, born in NH.
CLEMENT, EMELINE, 9, F, -, W, NH, 632, 919, NBPT. In HH of Amos C. Clement, age 60, Clerk, born in NH.
CLEMENT, HIRAM H., 17, M, Machinist, W, NH, 588, 865, NBPT. In HH of Stilman Simonds, age 43, Shoemaker, born in MA.
CLEMENT, ISAAC, 26, M, Fruit Seller, W, NH, 458, 683, NBPT.
CLEMENT, JOHN M., 12, M, -, W, NH, 632, 919, NBPT. In HH of Amos C. Clement, age 60, Clerk, born in NH.
CLEMENT, LUCY M., 25, F, -, W, NH, 458, 683, NBPT. In HH of Isaac Clement, age 26, Fruit Seller, born in NH.
CLEMENT, MEHITABLE, 33, F, -, W, NH, 632, 919, NBPT. In HH of Amos C. Clement, age 60, Clerk, born in NH.
CLEMENT, SARAH, 51, F, -, W, NH, 632, 919, NBPT. In HH of Amos C. Clement, age 60, Clerk, born in NH.
CLEMENT, WILLIAM H., 16, M, Shoemaker, W, NH, 632, 919, NBPT. In HH of Amos C. Clement, age 60, Clerk, born in NH.
CLIFFORD, ANN E., 13, F, -, W, NH, 137, 202, NBPT. In HH of James F. Clifford, age 40, Laborer, born in NH.
CLIFFORD, ELIZABETH F., 40, F, -, W, NH, 137, 202, NBPT. In HH of James F. Clifford, age 40, Laborer, born in NH.
CLIFFORD, GEORGEANNAH, 8, F, -, W, NH, 137, 202, NBPT. In HH of James F. Clifford, age 40, Laborer, born in NH.
CLIFFORD, JAMES F., 40, M, Laborer, W, NH, 137, 202, NBPT.
CLIFFORD, JAMES W., 11, M, -, W, NH, 137, 202, NBPT. In HH of James F. Clifford, age 40, Laborer, born in NH.
CLIFFORD, JOHN, 15, M, Servant/Attends School, W, Maine, 118, 141, NBPT*. In HH of Ebenezer Moseley, age 68, Counselor, born in Ct.
CLIFFORD, JOHN J., 15, M, -, W, NH, 137, 202, NBPT. In HH of James F. Clifford, age 40, Laborer, born in NH.
CLIFFORD, LAURA F., 4, F, -, W, NH, 137, 202, NBPT. In HH of James F. Clifford, age 40, Laborer, born in NH.
CLIFFORD, MARY M., 17, F, -, W, NH, 137, 202, NBPT. In HH of James F. Clifford, age 40, Laborer, born in NH.
CLINTON, MARY, 25, F, -, W, Ireland, 581, 856, NBPT. In HH of George Rolfe, age 38, Boat Builder,

born in MA.
CLOTHIER, SAMUEL, 21, M, Mariner, W, MA, 163, 236, NBPT. In HH of William Davis, age 49, Confectioner, born in MA.
CLOUDMAN, DAVID P., 30, M, Ship Carpenter, W, MA, 586, 775, NBPT*.
COBB, SAMUEL H., 31, M, Mariner, W, Maine, 408, 533, NBPT*.
COFFIN, AMOS, 38, M, Ship Carpenter, W, MA, 475, 631, NBPT*. In HH of Sarah Newman, age 55, born in MA.
COFFIN, BRIDGET, 18, F, -, W, Ireland, 6, 6, NBPT*. In HH of Edward S. Moseley age 37, merchant, born MA.
COFFIN, CATHERINE, 57, F, -, W, MA, 788,1114, NBPT. In Poor House.
COFFIN, CHARLES, 48, M, Ship Carpenter, W, MA, 518, 689, NBPT*.
COFFIN, CHARLES H., 40, M, Merchant, W, MA, 682, 974, NBPT. In HH of Philip Coombs, age 70, Merchant, born in MA.
COFFIN, EMERY, 47, M, Joiner, W, MA, 566, 752, NBPT*.
COFFIN, ENNILE, 16, F, -, W, Maine, 711,1006, NBPT. In HH of Luther Davis, age 30, Engineer, born in MA.
COFFIN, ENOCH, 60, M, Sailmaker, W, MA, 381, 501, NBPT*.
COFFIN, FRANCES, 21, F, -, W, Maine, 418, 622, NBPT. In HH of Isaac S. Coffin, age 50, Merchant, born in MA.
COFFIN, FRANCIS E., 21, M, Joiner, W, MA, 566, 752, NBPT*. In HH of Emery Coffin, age 47, Joiner, born in MA.
COFFIN, FREDERICK G., 42, M, Architect & Builder, W, MA, 268, 343, NBPT*.
COFFIN, GEORGE, 52, M, Master Mariner, W, MA, 412, 614, NBPT.
COFFIN, GEORGE R., 18, M, Clerk, W, Maine, 412, 614, NBPT. In HH of George Coffin, age 52, Master Mariner, born in MA.
COFFIN, HEZIAH H., 43, F, -, W, NH, 339, 442, NBPT*. In HH of Theodore A. Coffin, age 79, Farmer, born in NH.
COFFIN, ISAAC, 28, M, Merchant, W, Maine, 418, 622, NBPT. In HH of Isaac S. Coffin, age 50, Merchant, born in MA.
COFFIN, ISAAC S., 50, M, Merchant, W, MA, 418, 622, NBPT.
COFFIN, JOHN, 55, M, Ship Carpenter, W, MA, 788,1114, NBPT. In Poor House.
COFFIN, JOHN M., 37, M, Master Mariner, W, MA, 122, 145, NBPT*. In HH of Enoch S. Williams, age 48, Merchant, born in MA.
COFFIN, LUCRETIA, 50, F, -, W, NH, 518, 689, NBPT*. In HH of Charles Coffin, age 48, Ship Carpenter, born in MA.
COFFIN, MARY, 21, F, -, W, VT, 354, 468, NBPT*. In HH of Caroline H. Frothingham, age 37,

born in NH.
COFFIN, MARY E., 18, F, -, W, Maine, 418, 622, NBPT. In HH of Isaac S. Coffin, age 50, Merchant, born in MA.
COFFIN, MOSES, 77, M, None, W, MA, 566, 752, NBPT*. In HH of Emery Coffin, age 47, Joiner, born in MA.
COFFIN, NATHANIEL, 66, M, Farmer, W, MA, 164, 197, NBPT*.
COFFIN, SOPPRONIA, 19, F, -, W, Maine, 412, 614, NBPT. In HH of George Coffin, age 52, Master Mariner, born in MA.
COFFIN, SUSAN E., 48, F, -, W, Maine, 418, 622, NBPT. In HH of Isaac S. Coffin, age 50, Merchant, born in MA.
COFFIN, THEODORE A., 79, M, Farmer, W, NH, 339, 442, NBPT*.
COFFIN, TRISTRAM, 82, M, Math Inst. Maker, W, MA, 528, 700, NBPT*.
COFFIN, TRISTRAM JR., 56, F, Merchant, W, MA, 528, 700, NBPT*. In HH of Tristram Coffin, age 82, Math Instrument Maker, born in MA.
COFFIN, WILLIAM, 46, M, Dealer in Coal, W, MA, 528, 701, NBPT*.
COFFIN, WILLIAM, 32, M, Fisherman, W, MA, 381, 502, NBPT*.
COFFIN, WILLIAM L., 16, M, Clerk, W, MA, 418, 622, NBPT. In HH of Isaac S. Coffin, age 50, Merchant, born in MA.
COFFIN, SUSAN, 62, F, -, W, NH, 164, 197, NBPT*. In HH of Nathaniel Coffin, age 66, Farmer, born in MA.
COFRAIN, EMILY, 25, F, -, W, Nova Scotia, 239, 347, NBPT. In HH of Elizabeth Currier, age 46, born in Nova Scotia.
COFRAIN, MARIA, 27, F, -, W, Nova Scotia, 239, 347, NBPT. In HH of Elizabeth Currier, age 46, born in Nova Scotia.
COGGER, ANN, 32, F, -, W, Ireland, 648, 938, NBPT. In HH of Anthony Cogger, age 37, Laborer, born in Ireland.
COGGER, ANTHONY, 37, M, Laborer, W, Ireland, 648, 938, NBPT.
COGGER, ANTHONY, 7, M, -, W, Ireland, 181, 262, NBPT. In HH of John Cogger, age 85?, Laborer, born in Ireland.
COGGER, ANTHONY, 6, M, -, W, England, 648, 938, NBPT. In HH of Anthony Cogger, age 37, Laborer, born in Ireland.
COGGER, DANIEL, 42, M, Laborer, W, Ireland, 506, 754, NBPT.
COGGER, JANE, 31, F, -, W, Ireland, 506, 754, NBPT. In HH of Daniel Cogger, age 42, Laborer, born in Ireland.
COGGER, JOHN, 85, M, W, 0, Ireland, 181, 262, NBPT. Note: Age overwritten, could be younger.
COGGER, JOHN, 15, M, -, W, England, 648, 938, NBPT. In HH of Anthony Cogger, age 37, Laborer, born in Ireland.
COGGER, MARY, 9, F, -, W, Ireland, 181, 262, NBPT. In HH of

John Cogger, age 85?, Laborer, born in Ireland.
COGGER, NANCY, 46, F, -, W, Ireland, 181, 262, NBPT. In HH of John Cogger, age 85?, Laborer, born in Ireland.
COLLINS, SAMUEL, 25, M, Operative, W, MA, 446, 591, NBPT*. In HH of Sarah Collins, age 60, born in MA.
COLBY, ABRAHAM D., 25, M, Mariner, W, MA, 442, 585, NBPT*.
COLBY, GEORGE A., 16, M, Shoemaker, W, MA, 245, 354, NBPT. In HH of Robert Colby, age 55, Shoemaker, born in MA.
COLBY, GEORGE W., 49, M, Truck man, W, NH, 448, 669, NBPT.
COLBY, JOSEPH, 21, M, Shoemaker, W, NH, 245, 354, NBPT. In HH of Robert Colby, age 55, Shoemaker, born in MA.
COLBY, OLIVE, 22, F, -, W, NH, 185, 226, NBPT*. In HH of William Colby, age 54, Blacksmith, born in Maine.
COLBY, ROBERT, 55, M, Shoemaker, W, MA, 245, 354, NBPT.
COLBY, RUFUS, 46, M, Truck man, W, NH, 448, 669, NBPT. In HH of George W. Colby, age 49, Truck man, born in NH.
COLBY, SARAH, 53, F, -, W, Maine, 185, 226, NBPT*. In HH of William Colby, age 54, Blacksmith, born in Maine.
COLBY, WILLIAM, 54, M, Blacksmith, W, Maine, 185, 226, NBPT*.
COLBY, WILLIAM C., 20, M, House Carpenter, W, Maine, 185, 226, NBPT*. In HH of William Colby, age 54, Blacksmith, born in Maine.
COLE, ALONZO, 38, M, 2 Overseer Card, W, NH, 20, 24, NBPT*.
COLE, CATHERINE M., 8, F, -, W, Maine, 21, 26, NBPT. In HH of Lois Currier, age 65, born in Maine.
COLE, ERASTUS, 25, M, Laborer, W, Maine, 789,1115, NBPT. In HH of John M. Smith, age 34, Brick maker, born in MA.
COLE, FRANCES, 11, F, -, W, Maine, 21, 26, NBPT. In HH of Lois Currier, age 65, born in Maine.
COLE, JOHN, 16, M, Mariner, W, Maine, 214, 317, NBPT. In HH of Sarah Cole, age 65, born in Maine.
COLE, LOUISA H., 14, F, -, W, Maine, 21, 26, NBPT. In HH of Lois Currier, age 65, born in Maine.
COLE, SARAH, 65, F, W, 0, Maine, 214, 317, NBPT.
COLEMAN, ALFRED, 27, M, Dealer in Junk, W, NH, 306, 451, NBPT.
COLES, MARTHA G., 18, F, -, W, NH, 15, 18, NBPT*. In HH of Milton Smart, age 47, Blacksmith, born Maine.
COLESON, ENOCH, 26, M, Carpenter, W, Maine, 452, 675, NBPT. In HH of Eveline Gunnison, age 46, born in Maine.
COLLEY, FREDERICK, 4, M, -, W, CT, 472, 708, NBPT. In HH of John Dodge, age 67, Soap Boiler,

born in Maine.

COLLEY, JOHN D., 7, M, -, W, CT, 472, 708, NBPT. In HH of John Dodge, age 67, Soap Boiler, born in Maine.

COLLIER, ISAAC J.B., 36, M, Clergyman, Methodist, W, RI, 483, 724, NBPT.

COLLINS, CHARLOTTA, 16, F, -, W, NH, 706,1001, NBPT. In HH of Alfred Trefether, age 36, Keeps Bowling Alley, born in NH.

COLLINS, ELIZA, 50, F, -, W, Ireland, 197, 288, NBPT.

COLLINS, MARY, 26, F, -, W, N.S., 493, 735, NBPT. In HH of John Post, age 24, Farmer, born in N.S. {Nova Scotia}.

COLLINS, MOORE, 34, M, None listed, W, Maine, 605, 884, NBPT. In HH of Ann G.

COLLINS, STEPHEN, 34, M, Stair Builder, W, MA, 31, 44, NBPT.

COLLINS, THOMAS, 60, M, Mariner, W, Ireland, 788,1114, NBPT. In Poor House.

COLLINS, THOMAS C., 37, M, Laborer, W, Ireland, 227, 333, NBPT. In HH of Morris Welch, age 27, Laborer, born in Ireland.

COLLINS, TIMOTHY, 33, M, -, W, Ireland, 78, 87, NBPT*. In Jail. Convict.

COLMAN, DAVID E., 35, M, Farmer, W, MA, 36, 43, NBPT*.

COLMAN, JAMES C., 24, M, Clerk, W, MA, 727,1026, NBPT. In HH of Jeremiah Colman, age 67, Farmer, born in MA.

COLMAN, JEREMIAH, 67, M, Farmer, W, MA, 727,1026, NBPT.

COLMAN, MOSES, 33, M, Stable Keeper, W, MA, 719,1017, NBPT.

COLTON, MARY, 23, F, -, W, Maine, 569, 844, NBPT. In HH of Abby F. Downs, age 41, born in MA.

COMERFORD, DAVID, 63, M, Sailmaker, W, MA, 207, 307, NBPT.

COMWELL, FRANCES N., 6, F, -, W, CT, 341, 501, NBPT. In HH of Rhodis G. Comwell, age 38, Overseer in Mill, born in RI.

COMWELL, GEORGE H., 16, M, None, W, CT, 341, 501, NBPT. In HH of Rhodis G. Comwell, age 38, Overseer in Mill, born in RI.

COMWELL, RHODIS, 38, M, Overseer in Mill, W, RI, 341, 501, NBPT.

COMWELL, SARAH, 36, F, -, W, RI, 341, 501, NBPT. In HH of Rhodis G. Comwell, age 38, Overseer in Mill, born in RI.

CONANT, WILLIAM, 52, M, Express Agent, W, MA, 100, 117, NBPT*.

CONANT, WILLIAM H., 26, M, Express Agent, W, MA, 100, 117, NBPT*. In HH of William Conant, age 62, Express Agent, born in MA.

CONLEY, JOHN S., 23, M, Merchant, W, MA, 782,1108, NBPT. In HH of Enoch Tilton, age 45, Hotel Keeper, born in NH. In Hotel.

CONNER, ANN, 17, F, -, W, Maine, 222, 276, NBPT*. In HH of Stephen Fowle, age 33, Laborer, born in MA.

CONNER, ELLEN, 17, F, -, W, Ireland, 528, 787, NBPT. In HH of John Araften?, age 60, Laborer, born in Ireland.
CONNER, HANNAH S., 16, F, -, W, Ireland, 236, 296, NBPT*. In HH of John Conner, age 29, Laborer, born in Ireland.
CONNER, JOHN, 29, M, Mariner, W, Ireland, 236, 296, NBPT*.
CONNER, MARY, 78, F, -, W, MA, 788,1114, NBPT. In Poor House..
CONNER, WILLIAM, 47, M, Truck man, W, MA, 321, 474, NBPT.
CONNERS, CATHERINE, 24, F, -, W, Ireland, 449, 671, NBPT. In HH of Patrick Conners, age 30, Laborer, born in Ireland.
CONNERS, CATHERINE, 7, F, -, W, Ireland, 263, 383, NBPT. In HH of Ellen Conners, age 35, born in Ireland.
CONNERS, DENNIS, 5, M, -, W, Ireland, 263, 383, NBPT. In HH of Ellen Conners, age 35, born in Ireland.
CONNERS, ELLEN, 35, F, -, W, Ireland, 263, 383, NBPT.
CONNERS, JOHN, 30, M, Laborer, W, Ireland, 288, 421, NBPT.
CONNERS, JULIA, 10, F, -, W, Ireland, 288, 421, NBPT. In HH of John Conners, age 30, Laborer, born in Ireland.
CONNERS, MARGARET, 30, F, -, W, Ireland, 288, 421, NBPT. In HH of John Conners, age 30, Laborer, born in Ireland.
CONNERS, MARY, 7, F, -, W, Ireland, 288, 421, NBPT. In HH of John Conners, age 30, Laborer, born in Ireland.
CONNERS, PATRICK, 30, M, Laborer, W, Ireland, 449, 671, NBPT.
CONNERS, PATRICK, 14, M, -, W, Ireland, 288, 421, NBPT. In HH of John Conners, age 30, Laborer, born in Ireland.
CONNERS, STEPHEN, 12, M, -, W, Ireland, 288, 421, NBPT. In HH of John Conners, age 30, Laborer, born in Ireland.
CONOGER, ELLEN, 21, F, -, W, Ireland, 617, 900, NBPT. In HH of Samuel Bragdon, age 55, Merchant, born in MA.
CONWAY, DANIEL, 25, M, Mariner, W, Ireland, 758,1070, NBPT. In HH of Michael Aynwant, age 56, Mariner, born in Ireland.
CONWAY, THOMAS, 26, M, Mariner, W, Newfoundland, 767,1084, NBPT.
COOB, DANIEL B., 27, M, Carpenter, W, NH, 506, 755, NBPT. In HH of George W. Young, age 35, Ropemaker, born in MA.
COOK, CHARLES, 32, M, Mariner, W, MA, 486, 647, NBPT*. In HH of Hannah Cook, age 56, born in MA.
COOK, CHARLES L., 17, M, Painter, W, Maine, 267, 341, NBPT*. In HH of Otis Hayden, age 36, Mariner, born in MA.
COOK, EDWIN, 18, M, Mariner, W, MA, 254, 368, NBPT. In HH of Samuel Cook, Jr., age 43, Shoemaker, born in MA.
COOK, ELIAS D., 29, M, Mariner, W, MA, 65, 94, NBPT. In HH of Abigail Cook, age 71, born MA.
COOK, EVELINE, 20, F, W, 0, NH, 200, 294, NBPT. In HH of Jeremiah Cook, age 23, Shoemaker, born in MA.
COOK, FULLER G., 36, M,

Grocer, W, MA, 114, 170, NBPT. In HH of Moody D. Cook, age 39, Grocer, born in MA.
COOK, HANNAH T., 22, F, -, W, NH, 65, 94, NBPT. In HH of Abigail Cook, age 71, born MA.
COOK, HENRY, 35, M, Master Mariner, W, MA, 61, 88, NBPT.
COOK, JAMES, 42, M, Master Mariner, W, MA, 344, 504, NBPT.
COOK, JEREMIAH, 23, M, Shoemaker, W, MA, 200, 294, NBPT.
COOK, JEREMIAH, 18, M, Clerk, W, MA, 498, 743, NBPT. In HH of William Cook, age 52, Mastmaker, born in MA.
COOK, JOEL, 11, M, None, W, MA, 498, 743, NBPT. In HH of William Cook, age 52, Mastmaker, born in MA.
COOK, JOHN, 64, M, Notary Public, W, MA, 500, 746, NBPT.
COOK, MOODY D., 39, M, Grocer, W, MA, 114, 170, NBPT.
COOK, RUFUS, 33, M, Tailor, W, MA, 162, 233, NBPT. In HH of Harriet Foote, age 54, born in MA.
COOK, SAMUEL, 72, M, Tin Plate Worker, W, MA, 193, 282, NBPT.
COOK, SAMUEL JR., 43, M, Shoemaker, W, MA, 254, 368, NBPT.
COOK, THOMAS, 64, M, Carpenter, W, MA, 7, 7, NBPT.
COOK, WILLIAM, 52, M, Mastmaker, W, MA, 498, 743, NBPT.
COOKER, CHARLES E., 20, M, Mariner, W, Maine, 148, 217, NBPT. In HH of Stephen Cooker, age 43, Grocer, born in NH.
COOKER, CHARLOTTA P., 14, F, -, W, Maine, 148, 217, NBPT. In HH of Stephen Cooker, age 43, Grocer, born in NH.

COOKER, FRANCES E., 16, F, -, W, Maine, 148, 217, NBPT. In HH of Stephen Cooker, age 43, Grocer, born in NH.
COOKER, STEPHEN, 43, M, Grocer, W, NH, 148, 217, NBPT.
COOLERSON, KATE, 26, F, -, W, Ireland, 68, 98, NBPT. In HH of Charles M. Bayley, age 35, Master Mariner, born in MA.
COOLIDGE, JONATHAN, 62, M, Collector of Taxes, W, MA, 290, 378, NBPT*.
COOMBS, JOHN, 37, M, Clergyman, Cong., W, MA, 721,1020, NBPT.
COOMBS, PHILIP, 70, M, Merchant, W, MA, 682, 974, NBPT.
COON, NANCY, 67, F, -, W, MA, 788,1114, NBPT. In Poor House. .
COOPER, CHARLES, 31, M, House Joiner, W, MA, 323, 418, NBPT*.
COOPER, ELIZA W., 34, F, -, W, NH, 323, 418, NBPT*. In HH of Charles Cooper, age 31, House Joiner, born in MA.
COOPER, FRANCES L., 38, F, -, W, NH, 303, 395, NBPT*. In HH of James M. Cooper, age 39, House Joiner, born in MA.
COOPER, HENRY W., 29, M, Laborer, W, MA, 386, 509, NBPT*. In HH of Harriet Cooper, age 29, born in MA.
COOPER, JAMES M., 39, M, House Joiner, W, MA, 303, 395, NBPT*.
COOPER, JOHN, 69, M, House Carpenter, W, MA, 97, 114, NBPT*.
COOPER, JOHN, 24, M, Joiner, W, MA, 359, 474, NBPT*.
COOPER, JOHN C., 16, M, Student Putnam School, W, MA, 289, 376, NBPT*. In HH of

Elizabeth Butman, age 48, born in MA.
COOPER, JOHN M., 42, M, Merchant, W, MA, 289, 376, NBPT*. In HH of Elizabeth Butman, age 48, born in MA.
COOPER, JOSEPH, 64, M, House Carpenter, W, MA, 329, 426, NBPT*.
COOPER, JOSEPH W., 26, M, House Carpenter, W, MA, 329, 426, NBPT*. In HH of Joseph Cooper, age 64, House Carpenter, born in MA.
COOPER, LYNDIA, 42, F, -, W, NH, 97, 114, NBPT*. In HH of John Cooper, age 69, House Carpenter, born in MA.
COOPER, MARY, 19, F, -, W, NH, 359, 474, NBPT*. In HH of John Cooper, age 24, Joiner, born in MA.
CORAN, ELLEN N., 32, F, -, W, Ireland, 391, 577, NBPT. In HH of Martin Coran, age 35, Laborer, born in Ireland.
CORAN, MARTIN, 35, M, Laborer, W, Ireland, 391, 577, NBPT.
CORDEN, DANIEL, 22, M, Carpenter, W, N.S., 520, 774, NBPT. In HH of John Burnet, age 54, Laborer, born in N.S. {Nova Scotia}.
COREY, HANNAH, 25, F, -, W, Maine, 278, 356, NBPT*. In HH of Robert Corey, age 23, Operative, born in Maine.
COREY, ROBERT, 23, M, Operative, W, Maine, 278, 356, NBPT*.
COREY, ROBERT JR., 0, M, -, W, Maine, 278, 356, NBPT*. In HH of Robert Corey, age 23, Operative, born in Maine. Robert Corey, Jr. age 5 months.
CORMACK, MARY R., 16, F, -, W, Ireland, 10, 12, NBPT. In HH of William Graves, Jr., age 38, Master

Mariner, born in MA.
CORNER, CATHERINE, 15, F, -, W, Ireland, 528, 786, NBPT. In HH of Dennis Corner, age 40, Laborer, born in Ireland.
CORNER, DANIEL, 17, M, -, W, Ireland, 528, 786, NBPT. In HH of Dennis Corner, age 40, Laborer, born in Ireland.
CORNER, DENNIS, 40, M, Laborer, W, Ireland, 528, 786, NBPT.
CORNER, EDWARD, 13, M, -, W, Ireland, 528, 786, NBPT. In HH of Dennis Corner, age 40, Laborer, born in Ireland.
CORNER, ELLEN, 40, F, -, W, Ireland, 528, 786, NBPT. In HH of Dennis Corner, age 40, Laborer, born in Ireland.
CORNER, HANNAH, 8, F, -, W, Ireland, 528, 786, NBPT. In HH of Dennis Corner, age 40, Laborer, born in Ireland.
CORNER, JOHN, 3, M, -, W, Ireland, 528, 786, NBPT. In HH of Dennis Corner, age 40, Laborer, born in Ireland.
CORNER, MICHAEL, 6, M, -, W, Ireland, 528, 786, NBPT. In HH of Dennis Corner, age 40, Laborer, born in Ireland.
COSTELOW, THOMAS, 14, M, -, W, Ireland, 101, 118, NBPT*. In HH of Stephen Packer, age 49, Laborer, born in MA.
COSTON, IRENE, 35, F, -, B, NH, 599, 789, NBPT*. In HH of William Coston, age 36, Mariner, Black, born in PA.
COSTON, WILLIAM, 36, M, Mariner, B, PA, 599, 789, NBPT*.
COSWELL, JOHANNA, 21, F, -, W, Ireland, 264, 387, NBPT. In HH of Michael Coswell, age 43, Laborer, born in Ireland.
COSWELL, JULIA, 14, F, -, W, Ireland, 264, 387, NBPT. In HH of Michael Coswell, age 43, Laborer,

born in Ireland.
COSWELL, MICHAEL, 43, M, Laborer, W, Ireland, 264, 387, NBPT.
COUCH, CATHERINE, 25, F, -, W, NH, 293, 428, NBPT. In HH of Robert Couch, age 31, Master Mariner, born in MA.
COUCH, JOHN H., 40, M, Ship Master, W, MA, 212, 263, NBPT*.
COUCH, ROBERT, 31, M, Master Mariner, W, MA, 293, 428, NBPT.
COUILLARD, RICHARD, 36, M, Coaster, W, Maine, 283, 366, NBPT*.
COUNER, BRIDGET, 21, F, -, W, Ireland, 483, 643, NBPT*. In HH of Catharine Goodwin, age 38, born in Ireland.
COVEN, HENRY, 39, M, Laborer, W, England, 284, 367, NBPT*. In HH of Horace Sargent, age 28, Stove Dealer, born in NH.
COVEY, AMELIA J., 9, F, -, W, New Brunswick, 67, 97, NBPT. In HH of Sarah E. Covey, age 50, born in New Brunswick.
COVEY, ESTHER Y., 17, F, -, W, New Brunswick, 67, 97, NBPT. In HH of Sarah E. Covey, age 50, born in New Brunswick.
COVEY, HANNAH E., 21, F, -, W, New Brunswick, 67, 97, NBPT. In HH of Sarah E. Covey, age 50, born in New Brunswick.
COVEY, SARAH E., 50, F, -, W, New Brunswick, 67, 97, NBPT.
COVEY, STEPHEN A., 19, M, Spinner, W, New Brunswick, 67, 97, NBPT. In HH of Sarah E. Covey, age 50, born in New Brunswick.
COVEY, SYLVANIA B., 14, M, -, W, New Brunswick, 67, 97, NBPT. In HH of Sarah E. Covey, age 50, born in New Brunswick.
COWERLY, MARGARET, 25, F, -, W, Nova Scotia, 423, 628, NBPT. In HH of Lois Fullington, age 41, Mariner, born in NH.
COX, HENERITTA, 19, F, -, W, Maine, 573, 848, NBPT. In HH of Thomas Noyes, age 70, Shoemaker, born in MA.
CRAFT, JOSEPH, 48, M, Sportsman, W, MA, 330, 427, NBPT*.
CRAFT, REBEKAH W., 47, F, -, W, Nova Scotia, 330, 427, NBPT*. In HH of Joseph Craft, age 48, Sportsman, born in MA.
CRAIN, JACOB, 48, M, Shoe Dealer, W, NH, 342, 446, NBPT*.
CRAIN, JACOB W., 14, M, -, W, NH, 342, 446, NBPT*. In HH of Jacob Crain, age 48, Shoe Dealer, born in NH.
CRAIN, JAMES A., 10, M, -, W, NH, 342, 446, NBPT*. In HH of Jacob Crain, age 48, Shoe Dealer, born in NH.
CRAIN, MOSES, 15, M, Fisherman, W, NH, 342, 446, NBPT*. In HH of Jacob Crain, age 48, Shoe Dealer, born in NH.
CRANE, CHESTER F., 31, M, Clerk, W, VT, 211, 262, NBPT*. In Boarding House.
CREASEY, CHARLES, 20, M, Carpenter, W, MA, 361, 477, NBPT*. In HH of Phebe A. Creasey, age 51, born in MA.
CREASEY, CHARLES H., 17, M, None, W, MA, 546, 726, NBPT*. In HH of William Creasey, age 56, Shoemaker, born in MA.
CREASEY, ENOCH P., 24, M, Carpenter, W, MA, 361, 477, NBPT*. In HH of Phebe A. Creasey, age 51, born in MA.
CREASEY, GEORGE, 32, M, Shoemaker, W, MA, 557, 740, NBPT*.
CREASEY, JOSEPH B., 30, M, Painter, W, MA, 556, 739, NBPT*.

CREASEY, SAMUEL, 67, M, Clerk, W, MA, 367, 484, NBPT*.
CREASEY, WILLIAM, 56, M, Shoemaker, W, MA, 546, 726, NBPT*.
CREASEY, WILLIAM J., 28, M, Painter, W, MA, 187, 229, NBPT*.
CREENY, EMILY, 22, F, -, W, Maine, 573, 848, NBPT. In HH of Thomas Noyes, age 70, Shoemaker, born in MA.
CREENY, HANNAH, 19, F, -, W, Maine, 573, 848, NBPT. In HH of Thomas Noyes, age 70, Shoemaker, born in MA.
CRESEY, {CREASY} EBENEZER, 33, M, Shoemaker, W, MA, 337, 440, NBPT*.
CROCKER, CHARLES, 20, M, None, W, NH, 770,1090, NBPT. In HH of Levi Pearson, age 37, Watchman, born in MA.
CROCKER, ELIZABETH, 29, F, -, W, NH, 740,1046, NBPT. In HH of Israel Crocker age 39, Corder in Mill, born in MA.
CROCKER, ISRAEL, 39, M, Corder in Mill, W, MA, 740,1046, NBPT.
CROFOOT, HOSEA Y., 29, M, Bookbinder, W, CT, 12, 14, NBPT.
CROSEFORD, PEGGY, 77, F, -, W, NH, 424, 552, NBPT*. In HH of Benjamin Smith, age 46, Painter, born in VT.
CROSOLEY, CATHERINE, 17, F, -, W, Ireland, 209, 310, NBPT. In HH of Timothy Crosoley, age 44, Laborer, born in Ireland.
CROSOLEY, DANIEL, 12, M, -, W, Ireland, 209, 310, NBPT. In HH of Timothy Crosoley, age 44, Laborer, born in Ireland.
CROSOLEY, ELLEN, 10, F, -, W, Ireland, 209, 310, NBPT. In HH of Timothy Crosoley, age 44, Laborer, born in Ireland.
CROSOLEY, JOANNA, 36, F, -, W, Ireland, 209, 310, NBPT. In HH of Timothy Crosoley, age 44, Laborer, born in Ireland.
CROSOLEY, JOHN, 15, M, -, W, Ireland, 209, 310, NBPT. In HH of Timothy Crosoley, age 44, Laborer, born in Ireland.
CROSOLEY, MARGARET, 7, F, -, W, Ireland, 209, 310, NBPT. In HH of Timothy Crosoley, age 44, Laborer, born in Ireland.
CROSOLEY, MARY, 9, F, -, W, Ireland, 209, 310, NBPT. In HH of Timothy Crosoley, age 44, Laborer, born in Ireland.
CROSOLEY, TIMOTHY, 44, M, Laborer, W, Ireland, 209, 310, NBPT.
CROSOLEY, TIMOTHY, 14, M, -, W, Ireland, 209, 310, NBPT. In HH of Timothy Crosoley, age 44, Laborer, born in Ireland.
CROSOLEY, WILLIAM, 5, M, -, W, Ireland, 209, 310, NBPT. In HH of Timothy Crosoley, age 44, Laborer, born in Ireland.
CROSS, BENJAMIN, 79, M, Shoemaker, W, MA, 75, 84, NBPT*.
CROSS, ENOCH, 48, M, Physician, W, MA, 557, 830, NBPT.
CROSS, HENRY, 7, M, -, W, Maine, 557, 830, NBPT. In HH of Enoch Cross, age 48, Physician, born in MA.
CROSS, JOHN S., 11, M, -, W, ILL, 557, 830, NBPT. In HH of Enoch Cross, age 48, Physician, born in MA.
CROSS, MARGARET, 37, F, -, W, NY, 557, 830, NBPT. In HH of Enoch Cross, age 48, Physician, born in MA.
CROSS, MARY E.P., 9, F, -, W, ILL, 557, 830, NBPT. In HH of Enoch Cross, age 48, Physician, born in MA.

CROW, CATHERINE, 9, F, -, W, N.B., 263, 381, NBPT. In HH of William Crow, age 50, None, born in N.B.
CROW, ELLEN, 15, F, -, W, N.B., 263, 381, NBPT. In HH of William Crow, age 50, None, born in N.B.
CROW, ELVIA, 13, F, -, W, N.B., 263, 381, NBPT. In HH of William Crow, age 50, None, born in N.B.
CROW, JOHANNA, 4, F, -, W, N.B., 263, 381, NBPT. In HH of William Crow, age 50, None, born in N.B.
CROW, NANCY, 11, F, -, W, N.B., 263, 381, NBPT. In HH of William Crow, age 50, None, born in N.B.
CROW, RACHEL, 6, F, -, W, N.B., 263, 381, NBPT. In HH of William Crow, age 50, None, born in N.B.
CROW, RACHEL S., 50, F, -, W, N.B., 263, 381, NBPT. In HH of William Crow, age 50, None, born in N.B.
CROW, WILLIAM, 50, M, None, W, N.B., 263, 381, NBPT.
CROWL, PINDENN?, 72, F, -, W, NH, 694, 986, NBPT. In HH of Thomas Davis, age 56, Treasurer Rail Road, born in MA.
CROWLEY, ALIN W., 25, F, -, W, Ireland, 303, 446, NBPT. In HH of Patrick Crowley, age 26, Mariner, born in Ireland.
CROWLEY, FRANCES, 20, F, -, W, England, 166, 240, NBPT. In HH of Timothy Crowley, age 58, Spinner, born in England.
CROWLEY, JANE, 18, F, -, W, England, 166, 240, NBPT. In HH of Timothy Crowley, age 58, Spinner, born in England.
CROWLEY, JANE E., 25, F, -, W, England, 132, 194, NBPT. In HH of John Crowley, age 29, Weaver, born in England.
CROWLEY, JOHN, 29, M, Weaver, W, England, 132, 194, NBPT.
CROWLEY, MARY, 22, F, -, W, England, 166, 240, NBPT. In HH of Timothy Crowley, age 58, Spinner, born in England.
CROWLEY, PATRICK, 26, M, Mariner, W, Ireland, 303, 446, NBPT.
CROWLEY, TIMOTHY, 58, M, Spinner, W, England, 166, 240, NBPT.
CUMMINGS, ELLEN, 25, F, -, W, Ireland, 142, 169, NBPT*. In HH of William C. Williams, age 53, Dealer in Lumber, born in MA.
CURIVER?, AMOS, 25, M, Shoemaker, W, MA, 77, 112, NBPT. In HH of Jane Curiver?, age 46, born in MA.
CURRIER, ALBERT, 31, M, Mason, W, MA, 384, 507, NBPT*.
CURRIER, AMOS, 13, M, -, W, Nova Scotia, 239, 347, NBPT. In HH of Elizabeth Currier, age 46, born in Nova Scotia.
CURRIER, BENJN. C., 27, M, Mason, W, MA, 454, 677, NBPT. In HH of Samuel Currier, age 62, Mason, born in MA.
CURRIER, CHARLES, 49, M, Sailmaker, 0, MA, 180, 260, NBPT.
CURRIER, CHARLES, 24, M, Tailor, W, MA, 454, 677, NBPT. In HH of Samuel Currier, age 62, Mason, born in MA.
CURRIER, CHARLES, 22, M, Block Maker, W, Nova Scotia, 239, 347, NBPT. In HH of Elizabeth Currier, age 46, born in Nova Scotia.
CURRIER, DAVID, 47, M, Shoemaker, W, MA, 445, 664, NBPT.
CURRIER, EDWARD, 44, M, Master Mariner, W, MA, 23, 28,

NBPT. In HH of Jane Young, age 79, born in MA.

CURRIER, EDWIN, 29, M, Overseer, W, MA, 214, 265, NBPT*.

CURRIER, ELIZABETH, 46, F, -, W, Nova Scotia, 239, 347, NBPT.

CURRIER, ENOCH, G., 44, M, Overseer, W, MA, 136, 162, NBPT*.

CURRIER, GEORGE, 43, M, Mason, W, MA, 18, 21, NBPT.

CURRIER, GEORGE, 20, M, Carpenter, W, MA, 363, 534, NBPT. In HH of George N. Bartlett, age 29, Carpenter, born in NH.

CURRIER, GEORGE, 16, M, Hostler, W, MA, 166, 199, NBPT*. In Hotel run by Thomas Brown, age 49, born in MA.

CURRIER, GEORGE, 11, M, -, W, Nova Scotia, 239, 347, NBPT. In HH of Elizabeth Currier, age 46, born in Nova Scotia.

CURRIER, JAMES M., 27, M, Bootmaker, W, NH, 703, 997, NBPT.

CURRIER, JANE, 39, F, -, W, NH, 136, 162, NBPT*. In HH of Enoch G. Currier, age 44, Overseer, born in MA.

CURRIER, JOHN, 54, M, None listed, W, MA, 788,1114, NBPT. In Poor House.

CURRIER, JOSEPH H., 28, M, Mason, W, MA, 406, 530, NBPT*.

CURRIER, LOIS, 65, F, -, W, Maine, 21, 26, NBPT.

CURRIER, MARY A., 17, F, -, W, NH, 136, 162, NBPT*. In HH of Enoch G. Currier, age 44, Overseer, born in MA.

CURRIER, MARY A., 7, F, -, W, Nova Scotia, 239, 347, NBPT. In HH of Elizabeth Currier, age 46, born in Nova Scotia.

CURRIER, MATHEW, 72, M, Shoemaker, W, MA, 194, 284, NBPT.

CURRIER, MELISSA, 15, F, -, W, Nova Scotia, 239, 347, NBPT. In HH of Elizabeth Currier, age 46, born in Nova Scotia.

CURRIER, NATHANIEL, 54, M, Block Maker, W, MA, 239, 347, NBPT. In HH of Elizabeth Currier, age 46, born in Nova Scotia.

CURRIER, NATHANIEL, 17, M, None, W, Nova Scotia, 239, 347, NBPT. In HH of Elizabeth Currier, age 46, born in Nova Scotia.

CURRIER, SALLY, 90, F, -, W, MA, 788,1114, NBPT. In Poor House. .

CURRIER, SAMUEL, 62, M, Mason, W, MA, 454, 677, NBPT.

CURRIER, SAMUEL, 26, M, Mason, W, MA, 454, 677, NBPT. In HH of Samuel Currier, age 62, Mason, born in MA.

CURRIER, SOLOMAN, 66, M, Merchant, W, MA, 427, 632, NBPT.

CURRIER, THOMAS, 43, M, Shoemaker, W, MA, 144, 212, NBPT.

CURRIER, THOMAS E., 36, M, Mason, W, MA, 46, 68, NBPT.

CURRIER, WILLIAM, 66, M, Baker, W, MA, 177, 216, NBPT*.

CURRIER, WILLIAM E., 37, M, Merchant, W, MA, 462, 690, NBPT.

CURTIS, FRANCIS, 22, M, Druggist, W, MA, 742,1048, NBPT. In HH of George Curtis, age 62, Painter, born in MA.

CURTIS, GEORGE, 62, M, Painter, W, MA, 742,1048, NBPT.

CURTIS, PHILIP, 19, M, Operative, W, England, 769,1089, NBPT. In HH of Susan Curtis, age 50, born in England.

CURTIS, REUBEN, 40, M, None listed, W, Maine, 605, 885, NBPT.

CURTIS, SUSAN, 50, F, -, W, England, 769,1089, NBPT.
CUSHING, CHARLOTTA A., 25, F, -, W, RI, 630, 916, NBPT. In HH of Sophia Richardson, age 50, born in MA.
CUSHING, JOHN N., 30, M, Merchant, W, MA, 668, 959, NBPT.
CUSHING, MARY A., 19, F, -, W, Maine, 770,1090, NBPT. In HH of Levi Pearson, age 37, Watchman, born in MA.
CUSHING, WILLIAM, 27, M, Merchant, W, MA, 668, 960, NBPT.
CUSHMAN, ELLEN, 20, F, W, 0, Ireland, 206, 304, NBPT. In HH of Thomas McGray, age 45, Laborer, born in Ireland.
CUSHMAN, ELLEN, 20, F, -, W, Ireland, 206, 304, NBPT. In HH of Thomas McGray, age 45, Laborer, born in Ireland.
CUSHMAN, JEREMIAH, 26, M, Laborer, 0, Ireland, 206, 304, NBPT. In HH of Thomas McGray, age 45, Laborer, born in Ireland.
CUSHMAN, KATE, 19, F, -, W, Ireland, 128, 153, NBPT*. In HH of Jacob Horton, age 52, Merchant, born in MA.
CUSHMAN, THANKFUL, 40, F, -, W, Maine, 276, 406, NBPT. In HH of Jacob Stickney, age 76, Cabinetmaker, born in MA.
CUTTER, DANIEL H., 39, M, Mason, W, MA, 155, 185, NBPT*.
CUTTER, DAVID E., 49, M, Sexton, W, MA, 69, 78, NBPT*.
CUTTER, HENRY T., 19, M, Clerk, W, NH, 193, 237, NBPT*. In HH of Stephen E. Cutter, age 47, Sexton, born in MA.
CUTTER, MARY L.B., 0, F, -, W, NH, 525, 697, NBPT*. In HH of William Stanwood, age 63, Harness Maker, born in MA. Mary L.B. Cutter, age 11 months.
CUTTER, NATHANIEL W., 15, M, Tailor, W, MA, 193, 237, NBPT*. In HH of Stephen E. Cutter, age 47, Sexton, born in MA.
CUTTER, RICHARD, 32, M, Goldsmith, W, MA, 525, 697, NBPT*. In HH of William Stanwood, age 63, Harness Maker, born in MA.
CUTTER, STEPHEN E., 47, M, Sexton, W, MA, 193, 237, NBPT*.
CUTTER, STEPHEN JR., 22, M, Painter, W, MA, 433, 568, NBPT*.
CUTTER, THOMAS H., 43, M, Painter, W, MA, 3, 3, NBPT*.
CUTTING, IVA, 30, M, Confectioner, W, NH, 515, 686, NBPT*. In HH of George P. Garland, age 65, Boarding House, born in NJ.
CUTTS, ELIZABETH, 29, F, -, W, NH, 365, 482, NBPT*. In HH of Thomas L. Batchelder, age 39, Carpenter, born in NH.

- D -

DADY, BRIDGET, 21, F, -, W, Ireland, 768,1087, NBPT. In HH of Eugene Dady, age 27, Laborer, born in Ireland.
DADY, EUGENE, 27, M, Laborer, W, Ireland, 768,1087, NBPT.
DAGGETT, DANIEL, 45, M, Machinist, W, MA, 481, 640, NBPT*.
DAGGETT, THOMAS, 29, M, Mariner, W, RI, 481, 640, NBPT*. In HH of Daniel Daggett, age 45, Machinist, born in MA.
DAIRY, BRIDGET, 23, F, -, W, Ireland, 84, 94, NBPT*. In HH of Michael Dairy, age 25, Operative, born Ireland.

DAIRY, MICHAEL, 25, M, Operative, W, Ireland, 84, 94, NBPT*.
DALEY, JANE, 6, F, -, W, Ireland, 228, 282, NBPT*. In HH of Michael Daley, age 45, Laborer in Foundry, born in Ireland.
DALEY, MARGARET, 19, F, -, W, Newfoundland, 731,1033, NBPT. In HH of Michael Daley, age 26, Mariner, born in Newfoundland.
DALEY, MARGARET, 9, F, -, W, Ireland, 228, 282, NBPT*. In HH of Michael Daley, age 45, Laborer in Foundry, born in Ireland.
DALEY, MICHAEL, 45, M, Laborer in Foundry, W, Ireland, 228, 282, NBPT*.
DALEY, MICHAEL, 26, M, Mariner, W, Newfoundland, 731,1033, NBPT.
DALEY, RACHEL, 38, F, -, W, Ireland, 228, 282, NBPT*. In HH of Michael Daley, age 45, Laborer in Foundry, born in Ireland.
DALEY, RACHEL, 0, F, -, W, Ireland, 228, 282, NBPT*. In HH of Michael Daley, age 45, Laborer in Foundry, born in Ireland. Rachel Daley age 4 months.
DALTON, MARY, 19, F, -, W, Ireland, 732,1034, NBPT. In HH of Patrick Johnson, age 40, Operative, born in Ireland.
DAME, AUGUSTIN W., 31, M, None, W, MA, 450, 597, NBPT*.
DAME, CAROLINE M., 33, F, -, W, Maine, 450, 597, NBPT*. In HH of Augustin W. Dame, age 31, None, born in MA.
DANA, ELIZABETH A., 23, F, -, W, NH, 717,1014, NBPT. In HH of Margaret Dana, age 46, born in NH.
DANA, MARGARET, 46, F, -, W, NH, 717,1014, NBPT.
DANA, WILLIAM H., 19, M, Clerk, W, NH, 717,1014, NBPT. In HH of Margaret Dana, age 46, born in NH.
DANATY, ALLIN?, 40, F, -, W, Ireland, 357, 520, NBPT. In HH of Charles Danaty, age 35, Peddler, born in Ireland.
DANATY, ALLIUE, 10, F, -, W, New Brunswick, 357, 520, NBPT. In HH of Charles Danaty, age 35, Peddler, born in Ireland.
DANATY, CHARLES, 35, M, Peddler, W, Ireland, 357, 520, NBPT.
DANATY, JOHN, 9, M, -, W, New Brunswick, 357, 520, NBPT. In HH of Charles Danaty, age 35, Peddler, born in Ireland.
DANATY, ROSANNA, 12, F, -, W, New Brunswick, 357, 520, NBPT. In HH of Charles Danaty, age 35, Peddler, born in Ireland.
DANFORTH, JOSHUA, 54, M, Shoemaker, W, NH, 577, 852, NBPT. In HH of Robert Robinson, Jr., age 44, Shoe Manufacturing, born in Maine.
DANFORTH, RUFUS, 59, M, Restorator, W, NH, 287, 373, NBPT*.
DANIELS, CHARLES, 31, M, Shoemaker, W, NH, 438, 578, NBPT*. In HH of Jacob Tilton, age 36, Machinist, born in NH.
DANIELSON, CHARLES, 18, M, Operative, W, MA, 31, 38, NBPT*. In HH of Albert Thompson, age 46, born in NH.
DANNETT, CAROLINE, 33, F, -, W, Maine, 406, 605, NBPT. In HH of Furver Felcher, age 43, Mariner, born in Maine.
DARATHY, BRIDGET R., 31, F, -, W, Ireland, 277, 407, NBPT.
DARATHY, ELLEN, 10, F, -, W, N.B., 277, 407, NBPT. In HH of Bridget R. Darathy, age 31, born in Ireland.
DARATHY, RODNGH M., 28,

M, None, W, Ireland, 277, 407, NBPT. In HH of Bridget R. Darathy, age 31, born in Ireland.
DARNLEY, ANN, 13, F, -, W, Ireland, 547, 728, NBPT*. In HH of Thomas Darnley, age 35, Laborer, born in Ireland.
DARNLEY, MARY, 16, F, -, W, Ireland, 547, 728, NBPT*. In HH of Thomas Darnley, age 35, Laborer, born in Ireland.
DARNLEY, MARY M., 40, F, -, W, Ireland, 547, 728, NBPT*. In HH of Thomas Darnley, age 35, Laborer, born in Ireland.
DARNLEY, THOMAS, 35, M, Laborer, W, Ireland, 547, 728, NBPT*.
DARNLEY, THOMAS, 9, M, -, W, Ireland, 547, 728, NBPT*. In HH of Thomas Darnley, age 35, Laborer, born in Ireland.
DARY, JANE, 24, F, -, W, Maine, 441, 656, NBPT. In HH of Polly Prince, age 76, born in MA.
DAVDING?, ELEANOR, 28, F, -, W, Newfoundland, 745,1051, NBPT. In HH of Thomas W. Dawding, age 35, born in England.
DAVDING?, THOMAS W., 35, M, Clerk, W, England, 745,1051, NBPT.
DAVENPORT, ANTHONY, 64, M, Merchant, W, MA, 518, 772, NBPT.
DAVENPORT, ANTHONY, 47, M, Math Instrument Make, W, MA, 237, 344, NBPT.
DAVENPORT, CHARLES W., 20, M, Merchant, W, MA, 667, 958, NBPT. In HH of Moses Davenport, age 44, Merchant, born in MA.
DAVENPORT, MOSES, 44, M, Merchant, W, MA, 667, 958, NBPT.
DAVENPORT, SARAH J., 48, F, -, W, NH, 237, 344, NBPT. In HH of Anthony Davenport, age 47, Math Instrument Maker, born in MA.
DAVENPORT, WILLIAM, 71, M, Mason, W, MA, 37, 53, NBPT. In HH of Charles W. Piper, age 25, Mason, born in MA.
DAVID, ELIZA. A., 28, F, -, W, Maine, 95, 112, NBPT*. In HH or Lewis B. Davis, age 30, Shoe Dealer, born in NH.
DAVID, LEWIS B., 30, M, Shoe Dealer, W, NH, 95, 112, NBPT*.
DAVID, RICHARD, 70, M, Shoemaker, W, MA, 460, 608, NBPT*.
DAVID, WOODMAN C., 21, M, Weaver, W, NH, 542, 720, NBPT*. In HH of Jeremiah W. Fogg, age 36, Boot and Shoemaker, born in NH.
DAVIDSON, ANN, 32, F, -, W, England, 258, 324, NBPT*.
DAVIDSON, BENJ. H., 42, M, Shoemaker, W, MA, 13, 15, NBPT.
DAVIDSON, HANNAH S., 47, F, Boarding House, W, MA, 162, 195, NBPT*.
DAVIDSON, NATH'L D., 19, M, Shoemaker, W, MA, 13, 15, NBPT. In HH of Benj. H. Davidson, age 42, Shoemaker, born in MA.
DAVIS, ADONIRAM, 12, M, -, W, Maine, 468, 621, NBPT*. In HH of Eliphalet Davis, age 52, Farmer, born in Maine.
DAVIS, ASA, 49, M, Gardner, W, MA, 320, 470, NBPT.
DAVIS, BENJN., 60, M, Sailmaker, W, MA, 473, 710, NBPT.
DAVIS, BENJN. JR., 32, M, Sailmaker, W, MA, 472, 709, NBPT.
DAVIS, BETSY J., 24, F, -, W, Maine, 468, 621, NBPT*. In HH of Eliphalet Davis, age 52, Farmer, born in Maine.
DAVIS, CALEB P., 38, M, Ship

Carpenter, W, NH, 604, 794, NBPT*.
DAVIS, CALVIN, 21, M, Carpenter, W, MA, 320, 472, NBPT.
DAVIS, CAROLINE, 28, F, -, W, NH, 711,1006, NBPT. In HH of Luther Davis, age 30, Engineer, born in MA.
DAVIS, CHARLES W., 25, M, Carpenter, W, MA, 320, 471, NBPT.
DAVIS, ELIPHALET, 52, M, Farmer, W, Maine, 468, 621, NBPT*.
DAVIS, ELIZA, 19, F, -, W, Maine, 468, 621, NBPT*. In HH of Eliphalet Davis, age 52, Farmer, born in Maine.
DAVIS, ELIZABETH, 40, F, -, W, Maine, 518, 689, NBPT*. In HH of Charles Coffin, age 48, Ship Carpenter, born in MA.
DAVIS, HARRIET, 22, F, -, W, Maine, 271, 398, NBPT. In HH of Horace Brown, age 52, Stage Agent, born in MA.
DAVIS, HIRAM E., 7, M, -, W, Maine, 468, 621, NBPT*. In HH of Eliphalet Davis, age 52, Farmer, born in Maine.
DAVIS, IRA L., 26, M, Marble Worker, W, MA, 372, 489, NBPT*. In HH of Nathaniel Davis, age 49, Marble Worker, born in MA.
DAVIS, JOHN, 26, M, Mariner, W, England, 499, 745, NBPT. In HH of Francis M. Kezer, age 45, Rigger, born in MA.
DAVIS, LUTHER, 30, M, Engineer, W, MA, 711,1006, NBPT.
DAVIS, LYDIA, 51, F, -, W, Maine, 468, 621, NBPT*. In HH of Eliphalet Davis, age 52, Farmer, born in Maine.
DAVIS, MARY A., 28, F, -, W, NH, 469, 704, NBPT. In HH of Orrin Davis age 29, Teamster, born in NH.
DAVIS, MATILDA, 22, F, -, W, Maine, 468, 621, NBPT*. In HH of Eliphalet Davis, age 52, Farmer, born in Maine.
DAVIS, NATHANIEL, 49, M, Marble Worker, W, MA, 372, 489, NBPT*.
DAVIS, ORRIN, 29, M, Teamster, W, NH, 469, 704, NBPT.
DAVIS, PRUDENCE, 52, F, -, W, CT, 694, 986, NBPT. In HH of Thomas Davis, age 56, Treasurer Rail Road, born in MA.
DAVIS, RICHARD H., 17, M, Shoemaker, 0, Maine, 468, 621, NBPT*. In HH of Eliphalet Davis, age 52, Farmer, born in Maine.
DAVIS, SAMUEL, 40, M, Rope Maker, W, MA, 40, 56, NBPT.
DAVIS, SAMUEL, 16, M, None, W, MA, 499, 745, NBPT. In HH of Francis M. Kezer, age 45, Rigger, born in MA.
DAVIS, SARAH J., 13, F, -, W, NH, 516, 687, NBPT*. In HH of James W. Davis, age 33, Shoemaker, born in MA.
DAVIS, SARAH J., 13, F, -, W, NH, 516, 687, NBPT*. In HH of James W. Davis, age 33, Shoemaker.
DAVIS, THOMAS, 56, M, Treasurer R.R., W, MA, 694, 986, NBPT.
DAVIS, WILLIAM, 60, M, Probate Agent, W, MA, 48, 55, NBPT*.
DAVIS, WILLIAM, 49, M, Confectioner, W, MA, 163, 236, NBPT.
DAVIS, WILLIAM A., 26, M, Sailmaker, W, MA, 461, 688, NBPT.
DAVIS, WILLIAM E., 26, M, Druggist, W, MA, 694, 986, NBPT. In HH of Thomas Davis, age 56,

Treasurer Rail Road, born in MA.
DAVIS, WILLIAM R., 16, M, Student Putnam School, W, MA, 99, 116, NBPT*. In HH of Hannah Sargent, age 50, born in MA.
DEAN, ANN, 71, F, -, W, NH, 576, 763, NBPT*. In HH of John Dean, age 79, None, born in NH.
DEAN, CATHERINE, 23, F, -, W, N.B., 775,1098, NBPT. In HH of William W. Dean, age 23, Mariner, born in MA.
DEAN, JOHN, 79, M, None, W, NH, 576, 763, NBPT*.
DEAN, WILLIAM W., 23, M, Mariner, W, MA, 775,1098, NBPT.
DEARBORN, JOHN E., 19, M, Machinist, W, Maine, 334, 435, NBPT*. In HH of Samuel Todd, age 26, Machinist, born in Maine.
DEARBORN, LOUERA M., 10, F, -, W, Maine, 158, 227, NBPT. In HH of Kesia Durham, age 54, born in Maine.
DEARBORN, LYDIA, 22, F, -, W, NH, 177, 256, NBPT. In HH of James N. Canney, age 41, Teamster, born in NH.
DEARBORN, MARY, 21, F, -, W, NH, 177, 256, NBPT. In HH of James N. Canney, age 41, Teamster, born in NH.
DEARBORN, MARY A., 35, F, -, W, Maine, 659, 949, NBPT. In HH of Rebecca Gardner, age 40, born in MA.
DEARBORN, THOMAS B., 37, M, Shoemaker, W, MA, 482, 722, NBPT.
DELAP, FANNY M., 18, F, -, W, N.S., 567, 842, NBPT. In HH of Jemmina Delap, age 40, born in N.S. {Nova Scotia}.
DELAP, JEMMINA, 40, F, -, W, N.S., 567, 842, NBPT.
DELAP, MARY E., 13, F, -, W, N.S., 567, 842, NBPT. In HH of Jemmina Delap, age 40, born in N.S. {Nova Scotia}.

DELILL, JUDITH, 65, F, -, W, NH, 575, 850, NBPT.
DENNEAN, CATHARINE, 16, F, -, W, Ireland, 521, 692, NBPT*. In HH of Patrick Dennean, age 24, Laborer, born in Ireland.
DENNEAN, ELLEN D., 30, F, -, W, Ireland, 521, 692, NBPT*. In HH of Patrick Dennean, age 24, Laborer, born in Ireland.
DENNEAN, HANNAH, 27, F, -, W, Ireland, 521, 692, NBPT*. In HH of Patrick Dennean, age 24, Laborer, born in Ireland.
DENNEAN, MARGARET, 22, F, -, W, Ireland, 521, 692, NBPT*. In HH of Patrick Dennean, age 24, Laborer, born in Ireland.
DENNEAN, PATRICK, 24, M, Laborer, W, Ireland, 521, 692, NBPT*.
DENNIS, AMOS, 40, M, Fish Monger, W, MA, 411, 537, NBPT*.
DENNIS, GEORGE W., 41, M, Master Mariner, W, MA, 255, 370, NBPT.
DERRGIN, GEORGE, 33, M, Overseer, W, Maine, 574, 849, NBPT.
DESESDERNIA, JOHN W., 18, M, Student, W, NH, 211, 262, NBPT*. In Boarding House.
DESSINETTE, SALLY, 59, F, -, W, NH, 252, 364, NBPT.
DEVIER, BRIDGET, 1, F, -, W, Ireland, 84, 96, NBPT*. In HH of John Devier, age 29, Laborer, born in Ireland.
DEVIER, ELLEN, 25, F, -, W, Ireland, 84, 96, NBPT*. In HH of John Devier, age 29, Laborer, born in Ireland.
DEVIER, JOHN, 29, M, Laborer, W, Ireland, 84, 96, NBPT*.
DEVINE, ANN, 50, F, -, W, Ireland, 403, 599, NBPT. In HH of William Devine, age 50, Operative,

born in Ireland.
DEVINE, CATHERINE, 21, F, -, W, Scotland, 403, 599, NBPT. In HH of William Devine, age 50, Operative, born in Ireland.
DEVINE, WILLIAM, 50, M, Operative, W, Ireland, 403, 599, NBPT.
DEWITT, ANNA, 20, F, W, 0, NY, 214, 316, NBPT. In HH of Ashbell G. Vermilye, age 27, O.S. Presbyterian Clergyman, born in NJ.
DEWLY, BETSY, 20, F, -, W, Maine, 265, 335, NBPT*. In HH of Chester A. Greenleaf, age 23, 2nd Overseer, born in MA.
DICKENS, JOB T., 45, M, Physician, W, England, 744,1050, NBPT.
DICKENS, JOSEPH M., 17, M, Clerk, W, MA, 744,1050, NBPT. In HH of Job T. Dickens, age 45, Physician, born in England.
DICKINSON, GEORGE W., 8, M, -, W, PA, 446, 666, NBPT. In HH of William Dickinson, age 29, Harness maker, born in England.
DICKINSON, JOHN W., 5, M, -, W, RI, 446, 666, NBPT. In HH of William Dickinson, age 29, Harness maker, born in England.
DICKINSON, MARY E., 1, F, -, W, RI, 446, 666, NBPT. In HH of William Dickinson, age 29, Harness maker, born in England.
DICKINSON, RIGHT E., 3, M, -, W, RI, 446, 666, NBPT. In HH of William Dickinson, age 29, Harness maker, born in England.
DICKINSON, RUTH, 28, F, -, W, England, 446, 666, NBPT. In HH of William Dickinson, age 29, Harness maker, born in England.
DICKINSON, WILLIAM, 29, M, Harness maker, W, England, 446, 666, NBPT.
DIE, CATHARINE, 32, F, -, W, Ireland, 84, 95, NBPT*. In HH of John Die, age 27, Laborer, born Ireland.
DIE, JOHN, 27, M, Laborer, W, Ireland, 84, 95, NBPT*.
DIMMICK, LUTHER F., 58, M, Clergyman, Cong. DD, W, VT, 65, 74, NBPT*.
DIMMICK, MARY E., 38, F, -, W, Maine, 65, 74, NBPT*. In HH of Luther F. Dimmick, age 58, Cong. Clergyman, born VT.
DISNEY, GEORGE W., 22, M, Mariner, W, MA, 487, 729, NBPT. In HH of Thomas Disney, age 52, Master Mariner, born in MA.
DISNEY, THOMAS, 52, M, Master Mariner, W, MA, 487, 729, NBPT.
DIVINE, WILLIAM, 55, M, Operative, W, Scotland, 771,1091, NBPT. In HH of George Pentland, age 46, Stretcher in Mill, born in England.
DIXON, BEN, 32, M, Laborer, W, MA, 455, 602, NBPT*. In HH of Amos Skeels, age 66, Tailor Chandler, born in VT.
DIXON, BRIDGET, 20, F, -, W, Ireland, 377, 495, NBPT*. In HH of Margaret Dixon, age 55, born in Ireland.
DIXON, CATHARINE, 28, F, -, W, Ireland, 377, 495, NBPT*. In HH of Margaret Dixon, age 55, born in Ireland.
DIXON, DAVID, 40, M, Master Mariner, W, NY, 343, 449, NBPT*.
DIXON, JOHN, 32, M, Mariner, W, England, 396, 587, NBPT.
DIXON, MARGARET, 55, F, -, W, Ireland, 377, 495, NBPT*.
DIXON, MARIA, 27, F, -, W, Maine, 396, 587, NBPT. In HH of John Dixon, age 32, Mariner, born in England.
DIXON, MARY, 24, F, -, W, Ireland, 377, 495, NBPT*. In HH of

Margaret Dixon, age 55, born in Ireland.
DIXON, PATRICK, 22, M, Laborer, W, Ireland, 377, 495, NBPT*. In HH of Margaret Dixon, age 55, born in Ireland.
DOCKHAM, STEVENS, 38, M, Constable, W, NH, 713,1008, NBPT.
DOCKUM, DAVID W., 14, M, -, W, NH, 285, 370, NBPT*. In HH of Joseph H. Dockum, age 27, Wood 7 Lumber D{ealer}, born in NH.
DOCKUM, JOHN, 68, M, Farmer, W, MA, 582, 771, NBPT*. .
DOCKUM, JOSEPH H., 27, M, Wood & Lumber Dealer, W, NH, 285, 370, NBPT*.
DOCKUM, MARY F., 10, F, -, W, Nova Scotia, 285, 370, NBPT*. In HH of Joseph H. Dockum, age 27, Wood 7 Lumber D{ealer}, born in NH.
DODD, CATHERINE, 7, F, -, W, Newfoundland, 537, 803, NBPT. In HH of Peter Dodd, age 47, Mariner, born in Newfoundland.
DODD, JOANNA, 37, F, -, W, Ireland, 537, 803, NBPT. In HH of Peter Dodd, age 47, Mariner, born in Newfoundland.
DODD, PETER, 47, M, Mariner, W, Newfoundland, 537, 803, NBPT.
DODGE, ABRAHAM, 44, M, Mason, W, MA, 179, 219, NBPT*.
DODGE, ALVIN., 40, M, Mason, W, MA, 317, 467, NBPT. In HH of Nathl. Dodge, age 71, Mason, born in MA.
DODGE, CATHERINE, 30, F, -, W, England, 747,1053, NBPT. In HH of George R. Dodge, age 38, Silk Dyer, born in MA.
DODGE, CHARLES H., 31, M, Painter, W, MA, 317, 467, NBPT. In HH of Nathl. Dodge, age 71, Mason, born in MA.
DODGE, DANA, 33, M, Broker, W, MA, 720,1019, NBPT.
DODGE, DORCAS A., 6, F, -, W, RI, 747,1053, NBPT. In HH of George R. Dodge, age 38, Silk Dyer, born in MA.
DODGE, GEORGE R., 38, M, Silk Dyer, W, MA, 747,1053, NBPT.
DODGE, GREENLEAF, 29, M, Carpenter, W, MA, 335, 494, NBPT.
DODGE, HANNAH, 71, F, -, W, NH, 317, 467, NBPT. In HH of Nathl. Dodge, age 71, Mason, born in MA.
DODGE, HANNAH, 44, F, -, W, NH, 391, 579, NBPT. In HH of Samuel Dodge, age 44, Tin Plate Worker, born in MA.
DODGE, JOHN, 67, M, Soap Boiler, W, Maine, 472, 708, NBPT.
DODGE, JOHN, 28, M, Tallow Chandler, W, MA, 455, 602, NBPT*. In HH of Amos Skeels, age 66, Tallor Chandler, born in VT.
DODGE, JOHN JR., 48, M, Mason, W, MA, 179, 218, NBPT*.
DODGE, MOSES, 51, M, Mason, W, MA, 5, 5, NBPT*.
DODGE, NANCY W., 40, F, -, W, Maine, 90, 105, NBPT*. In HH of Thomas G. Dodge, age 43, House Carpenter, born in MA.
DODGE, NATHL., 71, M, Mason, W, MA, 317, 467, NBPT.
DODGE, OLIVE, 50, F, -, W, NH, 179, 218, NBPT*. In HH of John Dodge, Jr., age 58, Mason, born in MA.
DODGE, RICHARD, 33, M, Operative, W, MA, 297, 434, NBPT.
DODGE, RUFUS, 20, M, Mason,

W, MA, 181, 222, NBPT*. In HH of Silas Dodge, age 53, Mason, born in MA.
DODGE, SAMUEL, 44, M, Tin Plate Worker, W, MA, 391, 579, NBPT.
DODGE, SILAS, 53, M, Mason, W, MA, 181, 222, NBPT*.
DODGE, THOMAS G., 43, M, House Carpenter, W, MA, 90, 105, NBPT*.
DODGE, THOMAS G., JR., 17, M, Trader, W, MA, 90, 105, NBPT*. In HH of Thomas G. Dodge, age 43, House Carpenter, born in MA.
DODGE, WILLIAM H.T., 15, M, Student, W, MA, 90, 105, NBPT*. In HH of Thomas G. Dodge, age 43, House Carpenter, born in MA.
DODGE, WILLIAM L., 42, M, House Carpenter, W, MA, 402, 526, NBPT*.
DODGE, WILLIAM S., 68, M, Carpenter, W, MA, 725,1024, NBPT.
DODGE, WILLIAM S. JR., 39, M, Carpenter, W, MA, 724,1023, NBPT.
DOHERTY, ANNE, 8, F, -, W, Ireland, 608, 798, NBPT*. In HH of Michael Doherty, age 40, Watchman, born in Ireland.
DOHERTY, BARBARA, 31, F, -, W, Ireland, 608, 798, NBPT*. In HH of Michael Doherty, age 40, Watchman, born in Ireland.
DOHERTY, CATHERINE, 23, F, -, W, Ireland, 665, 956, NBPT. In HH of William Wells, age 25, Merchant, born in MA.
DOHERTY, JOHN, 6, M, -, W, Ireland, 608, 798, NBPT*. In HH of Michael Doherty, age 40, Watchman, born in Ireland.
DOHERTY, MARIA, 9, F, -, W, Ireland, 608, 798, NBPT*. In HH of Michael Doherty, age 40,

Watchman, born in Ireland.
DOHERTY, MICHAEL, 40, M, Watchman, W, Ireland, 608, 798, NBPT*.
DOHERTY, MICHAEL, 11, M, -, W, Ireland, 608, 798, NBPT*. In HH of Michael Doherty, age 40, Watchman, born in Ireland.
DOLE, ANNA B., 27, F, -, W, Maine, 664, 955, NBPT. In HH of Hannah Dole, age 62, born in MA.
DOLE, CARLTON, 52, M, Gentleman, W, MA, 635, 922, NBPT.
DOLE, HANNAH B., 33, F, -, W, Maine, 664, 955, NBPT. In HH of Hannah Dole, age 62, born in MA.
DOLE, JOHN N., 32, M, Painter, W, MA, 278, 408, NBPT. In HH of William H. Ritching, age 41, Master Mariner, born in MA.
DOLE, MARY B., 24, F, -, W, Maine, 664, 955, NBPT. In HH of Hannah Dole, age 62, born in MA.
DOLE, PARKER, M., 65, M, Farmer, W, MA, 39, 46, NBPT*.
DONAGAN, HANNAH, 25, F, -, W, Ireland, 227, 333, NBPT. In HH of Morris Welch, age 27, Laborer, born in Ireland.
DONAGAN, HANNAH, 25, F, -, W, Ireland, 227, 333, NBPT. In HH of Morris Welch, age 27, Laborer, born in Ireland.
DONAHUE, MARGARET, 24, F, -, W, Ireland, 404, 602, NBPT. In HH of Michael Donahue, age 25, Mariner, born in Ireland.
DONAHUE, MARY, 27, F, -, W, Ireland, 249, 360, NBPT. In HH of John Porter, age 66, Merchant, born in MA.
DONAHUE, MARY, 18, F, -, W, Ireland, 330, 486, NBPT. In HH of Morris Romayne, age 58, Gentleman, born in Ireland.
DONAHUE, MICHAEL, 25, M, Mariner, W, Ireland, 404, 602,

NBPT.
DONDEY, LEWIS, 32, M, Master Mariner, W, MA, 782,1108, NBPT. In HH of Enoch Tilton, age 45, Hotel Keeper, born in NH. In Hotel.
DONNELS, FREDERICK W., 57, M, Sexton, W, Maine, 628, 914, NBPT.
DOONE, JOHN W., 18, M, Stable Keeper, W, CT, 233, 339, NBPT. In HH of William Shaw, age 39, Stable Keeper, born in MA.
DORETY, MARGARET, 30, F, -, W, Ireland, 636, 923, NBPT. In HH of James Carry, age 30, Constable, born in MA.
DORHERTY, CATHERINE, 26, F, -, W, Ireland, 339, 498, NBPT. In HH of Ann Wheelwright, age 54, born in MA.
DORMAN, JESSE, 47, M, Wheelwright, W, MA, 72, 103, NBPT.
DORMAN, JOHN, 85, M, Shoemaker, W, MA, 758,1069, NBPT.
DOTEN, LUCY, 26, F, -, W, Maine, 163, 235, NBPT. In HH of Elexzane Edgecombe, age 24, born in Maine.
DOW, BENJAMIN P., 39, M, Merchant, W, MA, 170, 204, NBPT*.
DOW, CHARLES E., 11, M, -, W, NH, 155, 224, NBPT. In HH of Levi Dow, age 44, Fish Dealer, born in NH.
DOW, ELIZA, 22, F, -, W, VT, 717,1015, NBPT.
DOW, JANE, 19, F, -, W, NH, 155, 224, NBPT. In HH of Levi Dow, age 44, Fish Dealer, born in NH.
DOW, JOSIAH H., 4, M, -, W, NH, 155, 224, NBPT. In HH of Levi Dow, age 44, Fish Dealer, born in NH.
DOW, LEVI, 44, M, Fish Dealer, W, NH, 155, 224, NBPT.
DOW, LEVI A., 8, M, -, W, NH, 155, 224, NBPT. In HH of Levi Dow, age 44, Fish Dealer, born in NH.
DOW, MARY M., 44, F, -, W, NH, 155, 224, NBPT. In HH of Levi Dow, age 44, Fish Dealer, born in NH.
DOW, SAMUEL P., 3, M, -, W, NH, 155, 224, NBPT. In HH of Levi Dow, age 44, Fish Dealer, born in NH.
DOW, SUSAN, 16, F, -, W, NH, 155, 224, NBPT. In HH of Levi Dow, age 44, Fish Dealer, born in NH.
DOW, ZAECHEUS, 14, M, -, W, NH, 155, 224, NBPT. In HH of Levi Dow, age 44, Fish Dealer, born in NH.
DOWELL, LYDIA, 59, F, -, W, MA, 788,1114, NBPT. In Poor House.
DOWNES, JOHN, 23, M, Operative, W, Ireland, 538, 804, NBPT. In HH of Daniel O. Lory, age 49, Mariner, born in Ireland.
DOWNS, ADALINE, 18, F, -, W, Maine, 770,1090, NBPT. In HH of Levi Pearson, age 37, Watchman, born in MA.
DOWNS, CORDELIA, 6, F, -, W, NH, 733,1035, NBPT. In HH of Stephen Downs, age 31, Mariner, born in MA.
DOWNS, DENNIS, 22, M, Laborer, W, Ireland, 173, 251, NBPT. In HH of Jeremiah Malchi, age 48, Laborer, born in Ireland.
DOWNS, HENRY, 23, M, Carpenter, W, NH, 770,1090, NBPT. In HH of Levi Pearson, age 37, Watchman, born in MA.
DOWNS, JUDITH, 13, F, -, W, Ireland, 173, 251, NBPT. In HH of Jeremiah Malchi, age 48, Laborer, born in Ireland.

DOWNS, MARY E., 5, F, -, W, NH, 733,1035, NBPT. In HH of Stephen Downs, age 31, Mariner, born in MA.
DOWNS, MICHAEL, 15, M, -, W, Ireland, 173, 251, NBPT. In HH of Jeremiah Malchi, age 48, Laborer, born in Ireland.
DOWNS, PATRICK, 28, M, Laborer, W, Ireland, 173, 251, NBPT. In HH of Jeremiah Malchi, age 48, Laborer, born in Ireland.
DOWNS, SARAH, 29, F, -, W, NH, 733,1035, NBPT. In HH of Stephen Downs, age 31, Mariner, born in MA.
DOWNS, STEPHEN, 31, M, Mariner, W, MA, 733,1035, NBPT.
DOYLE, INEZDOY?, 20, F, -, W, N.S., 782,1108, NBPT. In HH of Enoch Tilton, age 45, Hotel Keeper, born in NH. In Hotel.
DOYLE, SARAH, 19, F, -, W, Maine, 770,1090, NBPT. In HH of Levi Pearson, age 37, Watchman, born in MA.
DRAGON, ROBERT, 21, M, None, W, Maine, 770,1090, NBPT. In HH of Levi Pearson, age 37, Watchman, born in MA.
DRAKE, ABIGAIL, 25, F, -, W, NH, 527, 699, NBPT*. In HH of Samuel P.H. Drake, age 38, Stage man, born in NH.
DRAKE, JAMES C., 16, M, Student, W, NH, 527, 699, NBPT*. In HH of Samuel P.H. Drake, age 38, Stage man, born in NH.
DRAKE, ROBERT, 30, M, Bar Keeper, W, NH, 743,1049, NBPT. In HH of Elizabeth S. Nelson, age 51, born in MA.
DRAKE, SAMUEL P.H., 38, M, Stage man, W, NH, 527, 699, NBPT*.
DRAKE, WAREHAM, 41, M, Machinist, W, CT, 428, 556, NBPT*.

DROWN, JOHN B., 24, M, Watchmaker, W, MA, 108, 129, NBPT*. In HH of Richard W. Drown, age 54, Watchmaker, born in MA.
DROWN, PAUL, 34, M, Mariner, W, MA, 484, 725, NBPT. In HH of Thomas Drown, age 59, Painter, born in NH.
DROWN, RICHARD W., 54, M, Watchmaker, W, MA, 108, 129, NBPT*.
DROWN, THOMAS, 59, M, Painter, W, NH, 484, 725, NBPT.
DUDLEY, ELIZABETH, 25, F, -, W, Ireland, 337, 496, NBPT. In HH of Paul Simpson, age 76, Master Mariner, born in Maine.
DUFFEE, CAROLINE, 47, F, -, B, MA, 788,1114, NBPT. In Poor House. .
DUNN, EDWARD, 17, M, Operative, W, Maine, 770,1090, NBPT. In HH of Levi Pearson, age 37, Watchman, born in MA.
DUNNING, JAMES, 42, M, Express Driver, W, Maine, 548, 730, NBPT*. In HH of Sarah Dunning, age 28, born in NH.
DUNNING, SARAH, 28, F, -, W, NH, 548, 730, NBPT*.
DUNNING, TIMOTHY, 20, M, -, W, Ireland, 78, 87, NBPT*. In Jail. Convict.
DURGIN, MARY, 23, F, -, W, Ireland, 722,1021, NBPT. In HH of Thomas E. Pressey, age 37, Carpenter, born in MA.
DURHAM, CYRUS T., 29, M, -, W, Maine, 158, 227, NBPT. In HH of Kesia Durham, age 54, born in Maine.
DURHAM, HIRAM O., 24, M, Mariner, W, Maine, 158, 227, NBPT. In HH of Kesia Durham, age 54, born in Maine.
DURHAM, ISSABELLA B., 31, F, -, W, Maine, 158, 227, NBPT. In

HH of Kesia Durham, age 54, born in Maine.
DURHAM, JOHN B., 16, M, Mariner, W, Maine, 158, 227, NBPT. In HH of Kesia Durham, age 54, born in Maine.
DURHAM, KESIA, 54, F, -, W, Maine, 158, 227, NBPT.
DURHAM, LOIS A., 19, F, -, W, Maine, 158, 227, NBPT. In HH of Kesia Durham, age 54, born in Maine.
DURHAM, LOUISA, 20, F, -, W, Maine, 158, 227, NBPT. In HH of Kesia Durham, age 54, born in Maine.
DURHAM, WILLIAM B., 22, M, Mariner, W, Maine, 158, 227, NBPT. In HH of Kesia Durham, age 54, born in Maine.
DURRAH, WILLIAM, 39, M, Carpenter, W, Maine, 9, 9, NBPT. In HH of Edward Rogers, age 38, Sailor, born in MA.
DUTTON, BENJAMIN, 36, M, Ship Carpenter, W, MA, 584, 773, NBPT*.
DWRIN, SUSAN A., 18, F, -, W, Maine, 567, 842, NBPT. In HH of Jemmina Delap, age 40, born in N.S. {Nova Scotia}.
DWYER, ELIZA, 40, F, -, W, Ireland, 118, 141, NBPT*. In HH of Ebenezer Moseley, age 68, Counselor, born in Ct.
DYER, EZEKIEL H., 22, M, Confectioner, W, MA, 571, 846, NBPT. In HH of John R. Dyer, age 44, Restorator, born in MA.
DYER, JOHN R., 44, M, Restorator, W, MA, 571, 846, NBPT.
DYER, JOSIAH R., 20, M, Shoemaker, W, MA, 571, 846, NBPT. In HH of John R. Dyer, age 44, Restorator, born in MA.

- E -

EARL, JOHN, 17, M, Mariner, W, Maine, 465, 618, NBPT*. In HH of David Lurvey, age 35, Ship Carpenter, born in Maine.
EARLY, BRIDGET, 20, F, -, W, Ireland, 554, 827, NBPT. In HH of Charles L. Emerson, age 66, Hatter, born in MA.
EASTMAN, ELIZABETH E., 26, F, -, W, NH, 391, 514, NBPT*. In HH of Freeman O. Willey, age 37, Machinist, born in NH.
EASTMAN, HANNAH A., 35, F, -, W, VT, 661, 952, NBPT. In HH of Dorothy Chute, age 66, born in MA.
EATON, CHARLOTTE, 7, F, -, W, NH, 76, 111, NBPT. In HH of Jubez Eaton, age 47, Mariner, born in NH.
EATON, ELIZA, 28, F, -, W, NH, 268, 392, NBPT. In HH of Walter Osgood, age 39, Operative, born in NH.
EATON, FOREST, 47, M, Overseer in Mill, W, Maine, 412, 615, NBPT.
EATON, HANNAH, 55, F, -, W, NH, 782,1108, NBPT. In HH of Enoch Tilton, age 45, Hotel Keeper, born in NH. In Hotel.
EATON, JABEZ, 47, M, Mariner, W, NH, 76, 111, NBPT.
EATON, JABEZ M., 14, M, Mariner, W, NH, 76, 111, NBPT. In HH of Jabez Eaton, age 47, Mariner, born in NH.
EATON, LABONA T., 4, F, -, W, NH, 76, 111, NBPT. In HH of Jabez Eaton, age 47, Mariner, born in NH.
EATON, LEONARD, 18, M, Mariner, W, NH, 76, 111, NBPT. In

HH of Jubez Eaton, age 47, Mariner, born in NH.
EATON, LOUISA F., 11, F, -, W, NH, 76, 111, NBPT. In HH of Jabez Eaton, age 47, Mariner, born in NH.
EATON, OLIVE, 45, F, -, W, NH, 412, 615, NBPT. In HH of Forest Easton, age 47, Overseer in Mill, born in Maine.
EATON, RHODA, 16, F, -, W, NH, 587, 863, NBPT. In HH of Henry C. Perkins, age 45, Physician, born in MA.
EATON, RICHARD B., 31, M, Blacksmith, W, NH, 268, 392, NBPT. In HH of Walter Osgood, age 39, Operative, born in NH.
EATON, SARAH, 57, F, -, W, NH, 707,1002, NBPT. In HH of Franklin Bartlett, age 41, Gardner, born in MA.
EATON, SARAH, 32, F, -, W, NH, 708,1003, NBPT.
EATON, SARAH E., 24, F, -, W, Maine, 276, 406, NBPT. In HH of Jacob Stickney, age 76, Cabinetmaker, born in MA.
EATON, SULLEY, 43, F, -, W, NH, 76, 111, NBPT. In HH of Jabez Eaton, age 47, Mariner, born in NH.
EATON, WILLIAM, 44, M, -, W, NH, 78, 87, NBPT*. In Jail. Convict.
EDES, EDWARD, 13, M, -, W, Maine, 544, 815, NBPT. In HH of Lois P. Edes, age 42, born in MA.
EDGECOMBE, ELEXZANE, 24, F, -, W, Maine, 163, 235, NBPT.
EDWARDS, ABRAHAM, 35, M, Grocer, W, MA, 398, 591, NBPT.
EDWARDS, JOHN, 14, M, -, W, England, 132, 194, NBPT. In HH of John Crowley, age 29, Weaver, born in England.
EDWARDS, LUCY, 23, F, -, W, Maine, 515, 686, NBPT*. In HH of George P. Garland, age 65,
Boarding House, born in NJ.
EDWARDS, LYDIA, 18, F, -, W, NH, 573, 848, NBPT. In HH of Thomas Noyes, age 70, Shoemaker, born in MA.
ELLENSWORTH, RACHEAL, 23, F, -, W, England, 153, 222, NBPT. In HH of Martha A. Whright, age 86, born in England.
ELLIOT, JAMES O.W., 25, M, Mariner, W, MA, 593, 870, NBPT. In HH of Hannah P. Elliot, age 55, born in MA.
ELLIOT, JOHN O. B., 23, M, Mariner, W, MA, 593, 870, NBPT. In HH of Hannah P. Elliot, age 55, born in MA.
ELLISON, FRANCIS, 59, M, House Carpenter, W, MA, 421, 449, NBPT*.
ELLSWORTH, WILLIAM N., 49, M, Shoemaker, W, MA, 419, 623, NBPT.
ELWELL, MARY, 45, F, -, W, Maine, 197, 245, NBPT*. In HH of Joseph A. Frothingham, age 47, Dry Goods Dealer, born in MA.
EMERSON, CHARLES L., 66, M, Hatter, W, MA, 554, 827, NBPT.
EMERSON, JOHN E., 25, M, Clergyman, Congregational, W, MA, 554, 827, NBPT. In HH of Charles L. Emerson, age 66, Hatter, born in MA.
EMERSON, SARAH, 25, F, -, W, NH, 491, 733, NBPT. In HH of George W. Batiss, age 26, Shoemaker, born in MA.
EMERTON, BENJAMIN, 38, M, Mariner, W, MA, 319, 413, NBPT*.
EMERTON, JOHN, 52, M, Painter, W, MA, 346, 453, NBPT*.
EMERY, CHARLES T., 17, M, Clerk, W, MA, 52, 58, NBPT*. In HH of Mary Emery, age 41, born MA.
EMERY, DAVID, 64, M, Farmer, W, MA, 17, 21, NBPT*.

EMERY, EBENEZER, 19, M, Wheelwright, W, MA, 709,1004, NBPT. In HH of Jonathan C. Richardson, age 33, Carriage Maker, born in MA.
EMERY, EMILY, 20, F, -, W, Maine, 733,1035, NBPT. In HH of Stephen Downs, age 31, Mariner, born in MA.
EMERY, HANNAH, 22, F, -, W, Maine, 733,1035, NBPT. In HH of Stephen Downs, age 31, Mariner, born in MA.
EMERY, MARY, 54, F, -, W, England, 213, 315, NBPT.
EMERY, MARY, 23, F, -, W, England, 213, 315, NBPT. In HH of Mary Emery, age 54, born in England.
EMERY, MOSES, 77, M, Merchant, W, MA, 781,1107, NBPT.
EMERY, SARAH A., 60, F, -, W, CT, 781,1107, NBPT. In HH of Moses Emery, age 77, Merchant born in MA.
ENDRISED, ELIZABETH, 15, F, -, W, England, 160, 230, NBPT. In HH of Thomas Taylor, age 46, Weaver, born in England.
ENDRISED, THOMAS, 12, M, -, W, England, 160, 230, NBPT. In HH of Thomas Taylor, age 46, Weaver, born in England.
ENDRISED, WILLIAM, 12, M, -, W, England, 160, 230, NBPT. In HH of Thomas Taylor, age 46, Weaver, born in England.
ENGLAND, JANE, 34, F, -, W, NH, 321, 475, NBPT. In HH of Stephen England, age 44, Operative, born in MA.
ENGLAND, MARY E., 23, F, -, W, N.B., 610, 890, NBPT. In HH of Thomas English, age 26, Operative, born in Scotland.
ENGLAND, STEPHEN, 44, M, Operative, W, MA, 321, 475, NBPT.
ENGLAND, THOMAS, 26, M, Operative, W, Scotland, 610, 890, NBPT.
EOLLS?, ANN S., 3, F, -, W, NY, 627, 913, NBPT. In HH of William W. Eolls?, age 39, O.S. Presb. Clergyman, born in CT.
EOLLS?, CHRISTAIN, 39, F, -, W, NC, 627, 913, NBPT. In HH of William W. Eolls?, age 39, O.S. Presb. Clergyman, born in CT.
EOLLS?, WILLIAM W., 39, M, Cleryman, O.S. Presb, W, CT, 627, 913, NBPT.
ESTERS, SAMUEL, 21, M, Overseer, W, Maine, 702, 995, NBPT. In HH of Isiah Wiggen, age 28, Overseer, born in NH.
EURERGE?, JOSIAH, 32, M, Overseer, W, NH, 400, 593, NBPT.
EURERGE?, LOUISA, 29, F, -, W, NH, 400, 593, NBPT. In HH of Josiah Euerge? age 32, Overseer, born in NH.
EUSTIS, BRIDGET, 27, F, -, W, Ireland, 532, 793, NBPT. In HH of William Eustis, age 31, Laborer, born in Ireland.
EUSTIS, MARY, 22, F, -, W, Ireland, 532, 793, NBPT. In HH of William Eustis, age 31, Laborer, born in Ireland.
EUSTIS, WILLIAM, 31, M, Laborer, W, Ireland, 532, 793, NBPT.
EVANS, ANN C., 12, F, -, W, NH, 102, 149, NBPT. In HH of William S. Evans, age 44, Ropemaker, born in MA.
EVANS, DAVID J., 41, M, Rope Maker, W, MA, 137, 203, NBPT.
EVANS, DAVIS J., 41, M, Rope Maker, W, MA, 137, 203, NBPT.
EVANS, ELISA, 41, F, -, W, Maine, 137, 203, NBPT. In HH of David J. Evans, age 41, Rope Maker, born in MA.

EVANS, GEORGE E., 18, M, Rope Maker, W, MA, 137, 203, NBPT. In HH of David J. Evans, age 41, Rope Maker, born in MA.

EVANS, JOHN, 60, M, Cooper, W, England, 482, 641, NBPT*.

EVANS, JOHN JR., 34, M, Shoemaker, W, MA, 482, 641, NBPT*. In HH of John Evans, age 60, Cooper, born in England.

EVANS, JOHN P., 24, M, Ship Joiner, W, MA, 563, 749, NBPT*. In HH of Samuel Haines, age 45, Ship Carpenter, born in England.

EVANS, WILLIAM F., 23, M, Blacksmith, W, MA, 102, 149, NBPT. In HH of William S. Evans, age 44, Rope maker, born in MA.

EVANS, WILLIAM S.., 44, M, Rope Maker, W, MA, 102, 149, NBPT.

EVANS, WINTHROP A., 34, M, Ship Joiner, W, MA, 564, 750, NBPT*.

EVERETT, WARREN P., 16, M, Student, W, MA, 44, 51, NBPT*. In HH of Josiah Bartlet, age 74, school teacher, born in MA.

EWELL, GEORGE, 38, M, Ship Carpenter, W, MA, 495, 658, NBPT*.

- F -

FARRETY, MARY, 27, F, -, W, Ireland, 140, 206, NBPT. In HH of Patrick Farrety, age 30, Laborer, born in Ireland.

FARRETY, PATRICK, 30, M, Laborer, W, Ireland, 140, 206, NBPT.

FAGGERTY, ELIZA, 40, F, -, W, Ireland, 117, 173, NBPT.

FAGGERTY, ELIZA J., 4, F, -, W, Ireland, 117, 173, NBPT. In HH of Eliza Faggerty, age 40, born in Ireland.

FAGGERTY, MARY, 10, F, -, W, Ireland, 117, 173, NBPT. In HH of Eliza Faggerty, age 40, born in Ireland.

FAGGERTY, WILLIAM H., 7, M, -, W, Ireland, 117, 173, NBPT. In HH of Eliza Faggerty, age 40, born in Ireland.

FAIRBANKS, JAMES B., 29, M, Machinist, W, RI, 64, 72, NBPT*.

FANNALY, ELIZA, 17, F, -, W, Ireland, 537, 803, NBPT. In HH of Peter Dodd, age 47, Mariner, born in Newfoundland.

FARNHAM, JOHN, 35, M, Fireman, W, Maine, 477, 633, NBPT*.

FARNHAM, NAOMI J., 26, F, -, W, Nova Scotia, 477, 633, NBPT*. In HH of John Farnham, age 35, Fireman, born in Maine.

FARR, AMMI, 19, F, -, W, Maine, 515, 686, NBPT*. In HH of George P. Garland, age 65, Boarding House, born in NJ.

FARRELL, ANN, 35, F, -, W, Ireland, 312, 461, NBPT. In HH of John Farrell, age 40, Laborer, born in Ireland.

FARRELL, JOHN, 40, M, Laborer, W, Ireland, 312, 461, NBPT.

FARRELL, JOHN, 9, M, -, W, NY, 312, 461, NBPT. In HH of John Farrell, age 40, Laborer, born in Iceland.

FARRELL, MARGARET, 11, F, - , W, NY, 312, 461, NBPT. In HH of John Farrell, age 40, Laborer, born in Iceland.

FARWELL, GEREYLDA, 4, F, -, W, NY, 769, 1088, NBPT. In HH of Perlis? Farwell, age 24, born in VT.

FARWELL, GILBERT, 2, M, -, W, NH, 769, 1088, NBPT. In HH of Perlis? Farwell, age 24, born in VT.

FARWELL, MARY, 25, F, -, W,

VT, 769,1088, NBPT. In HH of Perlis? Farwell, age 24, born in VT.
FARWELL, PERLIS?, 24, F, -, W, VT, 769,1088, NBPT.
FELCH, DANIEL, 68, M, Late Master Mariner, W, NH, 252, 316, NBPT*.
FELCH, GEORGE W., 20, M, Harness Maker, W, MA, 252, 316, NBPT*. In HH of Daniel Felch, age 68, late Master Mariner, born in NH.
FELCH, LUCY M., 28, F, -, W, VT, 125, 182, NBPT. In HH of William Felch, age 31, Shoemaker, born in NH.
FELCH, MARY E., 25, F, -, W, NH, 457, 681, NBPT. In HH of Benjn. Lunt, 3rd, age 42, Truck man, born in MA.
FELCH, NICHOLAS A., 23, M, House Carpenter, W, MA, 252, 316, NBPT*. In HH of Daniel Felch, age 68, late Master Mariner, born in NH.
FELCH, OLIVE, 58, F, -, W, Maine, 252, 316, NBPT*. In HH of Daniel Felch, age 68, late Master Mariner, born in NH.
FELCH, WILLIAM, 40, M, Laborer, W, MA, 238, 345, NBPT.
FELCH, WILLIAM, 31, M, Shoemaker, W, NH, 125, 182, NBPT.
FELCHER, ELIZA, 38, F, -, W, Maine, 406, 605, NBPT. In HH of Furver Felcher, age 43, Mariner, born in Maine.
FELCHER, FURVER?, 43, M, Mariner, W, Maine, 406, 605, NBPT.
FELT, SIBYL, 63, F, -, W, NH, 458, 606, NBPT*.
FELT, VIOLA, 19, F, -, W, NH, 458, 606, NBPT*. In HH of Sibyl Felt, age 63, born in NH.
FENIMORE, JAMES WY., 23, M, House wright, W, MA, 197, 242, NBPT*. In HH of Moses R. Fenimore, age 50, Cordwainer, born in MA.
FENIMORE, MOSES R., 50, M, Cordwainer, W, MA, 197, 242, NBPT*.
FENNIMORE, PETER, 45, M, Shoemaker, W, MA, 326, 482, NBPT.
FENNIMORE, SAMUEL, 48, M, Shoemaker, W, MA, 94, 111, NBPT*.
FERGASON, MARY, 21, F, -, W, Ireland, 557, 830, NBPT. In HH of Enoch Cross, age 48, Physician, born in MA.
FERGUSON, ELLEN, 20, F, -, W, Ireland, 655, 945, NBPT. In HH of Randloph Campbell, age 40, Congregational. Clergyman, born in NJ.
FERGUSON, HANNAH, 22, F, -, W, Ireland, 287, 373, NBPT*. In HH of Rufus Danforth, age 59, Restorator, born in NH.
FIELD, MARIA, 20, F, -, W, Ireland, 687, 979, NBPT. In HH of Henry Frothingham, age 60, Broker, born in MA.
FIFIELD, ELIZABETH, 56, F, -, W, NH, 261, 330, NBPT*. In HH of Shadrach Fifield, age 61, No Occupation, born in NH.
FIFIELD, ELIZABETH, 56, F, -, W, NH, 261, 330, NBPT*. In HH of Shadrach Fifield, age 61, No Occupation, born in NH.
FIFIELD, ELIZABETH J., 28, F, -, W, NH, 461, 609, NBPT*. In HH of Timothy Hilliard, age 46, Shoe Store, born in NH.
FIFIELD, JOSEPH C., 23, M, Clerk, W, NH, 461, 609, NBPT*. In HH of Timothy Hilliard, age 46, Shoe Store, born in NH.
FIFIELD, SHADRICH, 67, M, None, W, NH, 261, 330, NBPT*.
FIFIELD, SHURBURN, 32, M,

Truck man, W, NH, 770,1090, NBPT. In HH of Levi Pearson, age 37, Watchman, born in MA.
FITZ, GEORGE, 49, M, Cooper, W, MA, 50, 56, NBPT*.
FITZGERALD, JOAN, 17, F, -, W, Ireland, 568, 754, NBPT*. In HH of Abner Bagley, age 84, None, born in Maine.
FLAGG, JAMES T., 26, M, Gardner, W, NH, 364, 537, NBPT.
FLANDERS, ANDREW S., 29, M, Peddler, W, NH, 575, 762, NBPT*.
FLANDERS, ENOCH, 59, M, Caulker, W, MA, 590, 779, NBPT*.
FLANDERS, JESSE, 37, M, Sexton, W, NH, 272, 399, NBPT.
FLANDERS, JOSEPH, 16, M, Clerk, W, MA, 272, 399, NBPT. In HH of Jesse Flanders, age 37, Sexton, born in NH.
FLANDERS, JOSEPH F., 44, M, Machinist, W, MA, 138, 165, NBPT*.
FLANDERS, MARY E., 10, F, -, W, NH, 392, 515, NBPT*. In HH of Moses Flanders, age 36, Blacksmith, born in NH.
FLANDERS, MOSES, 36, M, Blacksmith, W, NH, 392, 515, NBPT*.
FLANDERS, NAOMI S., 43, F, -, W, NH, 590, 779, NBPT*. In HH of Enoch Flanders, age 59, Caulker, born in MA.
FLANDERS, NEHEMIAH, 32, M, Cordwainer, W, MA, 219, 272, NBPT*.
FLANDERS, OLIVE, 34, F, -, W, NH, 575, 762, NBPT*. In HH of Andrew S. Flanders, age 29, Peddler, born in NH.
FLANDERS, SAMUEL, 38, M, Master Mariner, W, MA, 116, 139, NBPT*.
FLANDERS, SAMUEL S., 13, M, -, W, NH, 392, 515, NBPT*. In HH of Moses Flanders, age 36, Blacksmith, born in NH.
FLANDRS, ENOCH C., 18, M, Caulker, W, MA, 590, 779, NBPT*. In HH of Enoch Flanders, age 59, Caulker, born in MA.
FLANGAN, HANNAH, 40, F, -, W, Ireland, 336, 495, NBPT. In HH of Timothy Flangan, age 46, Laborer, born in Ireland.
FLANGAN, TIMOTHY, 46, M, Laborer, W, Ireland, 336, 495, NBPT.
FLEMING, ROBERT R., 43, M, Overseer, W, MA, 779,1105, NBPT.
FLINN, ALICE, 7, F, -, W, Pr. Edward Island, 373, 549, NBPT. In HH of James Flinn, age 34, Laborer, born in Ireland.
FLINN, JAMES, 34, M, Laborer, W, Ireland, 373, 549, NBPT.
FLINN, MARTIN, 4, M, -, W, Pr. Edward Island, 373, 549, NBPT. In HH of James Flinn, age 34, Laborer, born in Ireland.
FLINN, MARY, 2, F, -, W, Pr. Edward Island, 373, 549, NBPT. In HH of James Flinn, age 34, Laborer, born in Ireland.
FLINN, MARY D., 34, F, -, W, Ireland, 373, 549, NBPT. In HH of James Flinn, age 34, Laborer, born in Ireland.
FLINN, MICHAEL, 8, M, -, W, Pr. Edward Island, 373, 549, NBPT. In HH of James Flinn, age 34, Laborer, born in Ireland.
FLORA, PETER, 72, M, Mariner, W, France, 174, 253, NBPT. In HH of Moody Lunt, age 42, Mason, born in MA.
FLOY, ANN E., 19, F, -, W, NH, 681, 973, NBPT. In HH of Margaret H. Adams, age 57, born in MA.
FLOYD, SILAS G., 33, M, Laborer, W, MA, 288, 419, NBPT.
FLUKE, ANN, 29, F, -, W,

England, 602, 792, NBPT*. In HH of Jacob Fluke, age 29, Dresser, born in England.
FLUKE, JACOB, 29, M, Dresser, W, England, 602, 792, NBPT*.
FLUKE, JOHN, 10, M, -, W, England, 602, 792, NBPT*. In HH of Jacob Fluke, age 29, Dresser, born in England.
FLUKE, MARTHA, 3, F, -, W, England, 602, 792, NBPT*. In HH of Jacob Fluke, age 29, Dresser, born in England.
FLUKE, MARY, 8, F, -, W, England, 602, 792, NBPT*. In HH of Jacob Fluke, age 29, Dresser, born in England.
FLUKE, MATTHEW, 5, M, -, W, England, 602, 792, NBPT*. In HH of Jacob Fluke, age 29, Dresser, born in England.
FOGG, ELIZA A., 25, F, -, W, NH, 306, 398, NBPT*. In HH of George W. Fogg, age 22, Shoemaker, born in NH.
FOGG, GEORGE W., 22, M, Shoemaker, W, NH, 306, 398, NBPT*.
FOGG, JEREMIAH W., 36, M, Boot & Shoemaker, W, NH, 542, 720, NBPT*.
FOGG, LYDIA, 32, F, -, W, NH, 177, 256, NBPT. In HH of James N. Canney, age 41, Teamster, born in NH.
FOGG, SARAH J., 8, F, -, W, NH, 542, 720, NBPT*. In HH of Jeremiah W. Fogg, age 36, Boot and Shoemaker, born in NH.
FOGG, SUSAN C., 32, F, -, W, NH, 542, 720, NBPT*. In HH of Jeremiah W. Fogg, age 36, Boot and Shoemaker, born in NH.
FOLEY, BRIDGET, 29, F, -, W, Ireland, 250, 314, NBPT*. In HH of Michael Foley, age 36, Laborer, born in Ireland.
FOLEY, MARY, 24, F, -, W, Ireland, 377, 496, NBPT*. In HH of James Barrett, age 42, Laborer, born in Ireland.
FOLEY, MARY, 22, F, -, W, Ireland, 181, 262, NBPT. In HH of John Cogger, age 85?, Laborer, born in Ireland.
FOLEY, MARY, 13, F, -, W, Ireland, 250, 314, NBPT*. In HH of Michael Foley, age 36, Laborer, born in Ireland.
FOLEY, MICHAEL, 36, M, Laborer, W, Ireland, 250, 314, NBPT*.
FOLEY, RICHARD, 22, M, Laborer, W, Ireland, 377, 496, NBPT*. In HH of James Barrett, age 42, Laborer, born in Ireland.
FOLLANDSBEE, HENRY M., 25, M, Shoemaker, W, MA, 483, 642, NBPT*. In HH of Love Follansbee, age 66, born Maine.
FOLLANDSBEE, LOVE, 66, F, -, W, Maine, 483, 642, NBPT*. .
FOLLANSBEE, AMOS L., 45, M, Shoemaker, W, MA, 394, 583, NBPT.
FOLLANSBEE, BELENDA D., 36, F, -, W, NH, 76, 110, NBPT. In HH of William Follansbee, age 26, Mariner, born in NH.
FOLLANSBEE, FRANK, 10, M, -, W, Maine, 428, 557, NBPT*. In HH of rank Follansbee, age 40, Overseer, born in MA.
FOLLANSBEE, HANNAH, 29, F, -, W, England, 388, 511, NBPT*. In HH of James Folansbee, age 30, Operative, born in England.
FOLLANSBEE, ISABELLA, 15, F, -, W, Maine, 428, 557, NBPT*. In HH of rank Follansbee, age 40, Overseer, born in MA.
FOLLANSBEE, JAMES, 30, M, Operative, W, England, 388, 511, NBPT*.
FOLLANSBEE, JOHN N., 76, M, Shoemaker, W, MA, 228, 334,

NBPT.
FOLLANSBEE, NATHAN, 62, M, Grocer, W, NH, 696, 988, NBPT.
FOLLANSBEE, TAMZEN, 25, F, -, W, Maine, 428, 557, NBPT*. In HH of rank Follansbee, age 40, Overseer, born in MA.
FOLLANSBEE, WILLIAM, 26, M, Mariner, W, NH, 76, 110, NBPT.
FOLLANSBEE, WILLIAM A., 35, M, Carpenter, W, MA, 298, 435, NBPT.
FOLONSBY, JACOB R., 27, M, Weaver, W, NH, 396, 586, NBPT.
FOLONSBY, SOPHIA, 27, F, -, W, NH, 396, 586, NBPT. In HH of Jacob R. Folonsby, age 27, Weaver, born in NH.
FOLSOM, ALMIRA, 15, F, -, W, Maine, 612, 893, NBPT. In HH of William Hills, age 70, None, born in MA.
FOLSOM, SARAH A., 21, F, -, W, Maine, 659, 949, NBPT. In HH of Rebecca Gardner, age 40, born in MA.
FOOT, DANIEL, 35, M, Goldsmith, W, MA, 488, 650, NBPT*.
FOOTE, JAMES L., 61, M, Laborer, W, NH, 618, 901, NBPT.
FOOTE, JAMES R., 33, M, Mariner, W, MA, 618, 901, NBPT. In HH of James L. Foote, age 61, Laborer, born in NH.
FOOTE, JULIA, 31, F, -, W, Ireland, 618, 901, NBPT. In HH of James L. Foote, age 61, Laborer, born in NH.
FOOTE, LEWIS, 34, M, Shoemaker, W, MA, 323, 477, NBPT.
FOOTE, LYDIA A., 15, F, -, W, NH, 323, 477, NBPT. In HH of Lewis Foote, age 34, Shoemaker, born in MA.
FOOTE, MARTHA, 33, F, -, W, NH, 323, 477, NBPT. In HH of Lewis Foote, age 34, Shoemaker, born in MA.
FOOTE, MARY E., 4, F, -, W, NH, 323, 477, NBPT. In HH of Lewis Foote, age 34, Shoemaker, born in MA.
FORBES, WILLIAM, 58, M, Express man, W, MA, 697, 989, NBPT.
FORD, ANN, 37, F, -, W, England, 167, 200, NBPT*. In HH of Daniel Ford, age 38, Cotton Spinner, born in England.
FORD, DANIEL, 35, M, Cotton Spinner, W, England, 167, 200, NBPT*.
FORD, DANIEL, 13, M, -, W, England, 167, 200, NBPT*. In HH of Daniel Ford, age 38, Cotton Spinner, born in England.
FORD, SAMUEL D., 63, M, Hatter, W, MD, 353, 516, NBPT.
FORD, THOMAS, 16, M, Operative, W, England, 167, 200, NBPT*. In HH of Daniel Ford, age 38, Cotton Spinner, born in England.
FORD, WILLIAM, 17, M, Operative, W, England, 167, 200, NBPT*. In HH of Daniel Ford, age 38, Cotton Spinner, born in England.
FORMAY, ANN, 18, F, -, W, Ireland, 508, 759, NBPT. In HH of Samuel H. Rundlett, age 41, Truck man, born in NH.
FOSS, CAROLINE, 16, F, -, W, Maine, 284, 415, NBPT. In HH of Joseph N. Foss, age 51, Laborer, born in Maine.
FOSS, ELIAS, 21, M, Laborer, W, Maine, 284, 415, NBPT. In HH of Joseph N. Foss, age 51, Laborer, born in Maine.
FOSS, HANNAH J., 15, F, -, W, Maine, 284, 415, NBPT. In HH of Joseph N. Foss, age 51, Laborer,

born in Maine.
FOSS, JOSEPH, 24, M, Operative, W, MA, 140, 166, NBPT*. In HH of Hannah T. Marshall, age 39, Boarding House, born in MA.
FOSS, JOSEPH N., 51, M, Laborer, W, Maine, 284, 415, NBPT.
FOSS, LUCITTA, 13, F, -, W, Maine, 284, 415, NBPT. In HH of Joseph N. Foss, age 51, Laborer, born in Maine.
FOSS, LUCY, 59, F, -, W, Maine, 284, 415, NBPT. In HH of Joseph N. Foss, age 51, Laborer, born in Maine.
FOSS, MARY A., 19, F, -, W, Maine, 284, 415, NBPT. In HH of Joseph N. Foss, age 51, Laborer, born in Maine.
FOSS, MERRILL, 23, M, Mariner, W, Maine, 466, 619, NBPT*. In HH of Solomon Littlefield, age 42, Drayman, born in Maine.
FOSS, MOSES N., 24, M, Laborer, W, Maine, 284, 415, NBPT. In HH of Joseph N. Foss, age 51, Laborer, born in Maine.
FOSTER, DANIEL, 19, M, Clerk, W, MA, 199, 246, NBPT*. In HH of Thomas Foster, age 51, Jeweler & Silversmith, born in MA.
FOSTER, NATHL., 51, M, Watchmaker, W, MA, 651, 941, NBPT.
FOSTER, NATHL., 20, M, Clerk, W, MA, 651, 941, NBPT. In HH of Nathl. Foster, age 51, Watchmaker, born in MA.
FOSTER, THOMAS, 51, M, Jeweler/Silversmith, W, MA, 199, 246, NBPT*.
FOSTER, THOMAS W., 22, M, Jeweler, W, MA, 199, 246, NBPT*. In HH of Thomas Foster, age 51, Jeweler & Silversmith, born in MA.
FOSTER, WILLIAM O., 18, M, None, W, Maine, 770,1090, NBPT. In HH of Levi Pearson, age 37, Watchman, born in MA.
FOWLE, ELIZABETH, 37, F, -, W, NH, 271, 348, NBPT*.
FOWLE, JACOB, 17, M, Laborer, W, MA, 271, 348, NBPT*. In HH of Elizabeth Fowle, age 37, born in NH.
FOWLE, JOHN, 48, M, Gardener, W, MA, 271, 348, NBPT*. In HH of Elizabeth Fowle, age 37, born in NH.
FOWLE, STEPHEN, 33, M, Laborer, W, MA, 222, 276, NBPT*.
FOWLE, STEPHEN, 16, M, None, W, MA, 271, 348, NBPT*. In HH of Elizabeth Fowle, age 37, born in NH.
FOWLER, EDWIN, 22, M, Coal Dealer, W, MA, 313, 406, NBPT*. In HH of Josiah Bradlee, age 49, Merchant, born in MA.
FOWLER, EVERETT, 15, M, Student, W, MA, 217, 270, NBPT*. In HH of Nicholas Medbury, age 50, Bap. Clergyman, born in MA.
FOWLER, HANNAH, 23, F, -, W, NH, 749,1057, NBPT. In HH of Jacob Fowler, age 31, Mariner, born in NH.
FOWLER, JACOB, 31, M, Mariner, W, NH, 749,1057, NBPT.
FOWLER, MARGARET A., 1, F, -, W, NH, 749,1057, NBPT. In HH of Jacob Fowler, age 31, Mariner, born in NH.
FOWLER, MARY C., 24, F, -, W, NH, 612, 802, NBPT*. In HH of Thomas Morrison, age 79, late Ship master, born in NH.
FOWLER, MINNY J., 2, F, -, W, NH, 749,1057, NBPT. In HH of Jacob Fowler, age 31, Mariner, born in NH.
FOWLER, RICHARD, 48, M, Dealer in Coal, W, MA, 728,1027, NBPT.

FOWLER, RICHARD, 22, M, Trader, W, NH, 728,1027, NBPT. In HH of Richard Fowler, age 48, Dealer in Coal, born in MA.
FOX, ANN, 23, F, -, W, Ireland, 700, 992, NBPT. In HH of Thomas Buntin, age 74, Merchant, born in MA.
FOX, CATHERINE, 19, F, -, W, Ireland, 672, 964, NBPT. In HH of William W. Caldwill, age 25, Apothecary, born in MA.
FOX, CHARLES J., 36, M, Shoemaker, W, MA, 508, 677, NBPT*.
FOX, STEPHEN J., 26, M, Joiner, W, MA, 508, 676, NBPT*. In HH of Stephen R. Fox, age 61, Blacksmith, born in MA.
FOX, STEPHEN R., 61, M, Blacksmith, W, MA, 508, 676, NBPT*.
FRANKLIN, ENOCK, 17, M, Student Putnam School, W, MA, 99, 116, NBPT*. In HH of Hannah Sargent, age 50, born in MA.
FRAZER, JOHN, 33, M, Master Mariner, W, Newfoundland, 253, 317, NBPT*.
FREDERICK, ELIZABETH, 44, F, -, W, England, 84, 94, NBPT*. In HH of Michael Dairy, age 25, Operative, born Ireland.
FREEMAN, AMOS, 71, M, Master Mariner, W, MA, 788, 1114, NBPT. In Poor House.
FREEMAN, BENJAMIN, 25, M, Baker, W, Ireland, 591, 868, NBPT. In HH of Samuel T. Payson, age 34, Baker, born in MA.
FREEMAN, JAMES, 54, M, Mariner, W, MA, 476, 713, NBPT.
FREEMAN, LYDIA A., 21, F, -, W, Maine, 708,1003, NBPT. In HH of Sarah Easton, age 57, born in NH.
FREEMAN, MARY E., 23, F, -, W, Maine, 708,1003, NBPT. In HH of Sarah Easton, age 57, born in NH.
FREEMAN, THOMAS, 29, M, Shoemaker, W, NH, 401, 595, NBPT.
FREFRY, LYDIA A., 27, F, -, W, Nova Scotia, 239, 347, NBPT. In HH of Elizabeth Currier, age 46, born in Nova Scotia.
FRENCH, CHARLES, 52, M, Merchant, W, MA, 128, 153, NBPT*. In HH of Jacob Horton, age 52, Merchant, born in MA.
FRENCH, CLARRISSA, 38, F, -, W, Canada, 536, 801, NBPT. In HH of Lewis French, age 40, Shoemaker, born in Canada.
FRENCH, CLARRISSA, 18, F, -, W, Canada, 536, 801, NBPT. In HH of Lewis French, age 40, Shoemaker, born in Canada.
FRENCH, CURTIS, 24, M, Carpenter, W, NH, 486, 728, NBPT. In HH of Abby K. Livingston, age 53, born in MA.
FRENCH, EDSON G., 40, M, School Teacher, W, NH, 577, 764, NBPT*.
FRENCH, GILBERT, 6, M, -, W, Canada, 536, 801, NBPT. In HH of Lewis French, age 40, Shoemaker, born in Canada.
FRENCH, HARNET, 14, F, -, W, Canada, 536, 801, NBPT. In HH of Lewis French, age 40, Shoemaker, born in Canada.
FRENCH, LEWIS, 40, M, Shoemaker, W, Canada, 536, 801, NBPT.
FRENCH, LEWIS, 16, M, -, W, Canada, 536, 801, NBPT. In HH of Lewis French, age 40, Shoemaker, born in Canada.
FRENCH, LOUISA, 12, F, -, W, Canada, 536, 801, NBPT. In HH of Lewis French, age 40, Shoemaker, born in Canada.
FRENCH, MARGARET, 10, F, -,

W, Canada, 536, 801, NBPT. In HH of Lewis French, age 40, Shoemaker, born in Canada.
FRENCH, MARY, 4, F, -, W, Canada, 536, 801, NBPT. In HH of Lewis French, age 40, Shoemaker, born in Canada.
FRENCH, REBECCA, 30, F, -, W, Maine, 276, 406, NBPT. In HH of Jacob Stickney, age 76, Cabinetmaker, born in MA.
FRENCH, RELIEF W., 33, F, -, W, VT, 577, 764, NBPT*. In HH of Edson G. French, age 30, School Teacher, born in NH.
FRENCH, SAMUEL C., 24, M, House Joiner, W, MA, 17, 21, NBPT*. In HH of David Emery, age 64, Farmer, born MA.
FRENCH, STEPHEN, 21, M, Carpenter, W, MA, 626, 912, NBPT. In HH of Luther R. Chase, age 30, Carriage Maker, born in MA.
FREY, ALBERT, 23, M, Painter, W, MA, 561, 834, NBPT. In HH of Mary Dorr, age 65, born in MA.
FRIEND, CORNELIA, 17, F, -, W, NY, 318, 412, NBPT*. In HH of Maria C. Friend, age 45, born in MA.
FRIEND, LEVI, 11, M, -, W, NY, 318, 412, NBPT*. In HH of Maria C. Friend, age 45, born in MA.
FRIEND, WILLIAM C., 19, M, Carpenter, W, MA, 318, 412, NBPT*. In HH of Maria C. Friend, age 45, born in MA.
FROST, AUGUSTA A., 7, F, -, W, Maine, 393, 516, NBPT*. In HH of Samuel Frost, age 43, Beer Manufacturer, born in NH.
FROST, DAVID, 36, M, Truck man, W, Maine, 150, 219, NBPT.
FROST, ESTHUR, 22, F, -, W, Nova Scotia, 210, 311, NBPT. In HH of George Frost, age 47, Laborer, born in Nova Scotia.
FROST, GEORGE, 47, M, Laborer, W, Nova Scotia, 210, 311, NBPT.
FROST, GEORGE N., 10, M, W, W, Nova Scotia, 210, 311, NBPT. In HH of George Frost, age 47, Laborer, born in Nova Scotia.
FROST, HANNAH, 17, F, -, W, Nova Scotia, 210, 311, NBPT. In HH of George Frost, age 47, Laborer, born in Nova Scotia.
FROST, HELENA, 5, F, -, W, Maine, 393, 516, NBPT*. In HH of Samuel Frost, age 43, Beer Manufacturer, born in NH.
FROST, JAMES N., 8, M, -, W, Nova Scotia, 210, 311, NBPT. In HH of George Frost, age 47, Laborer, born in Nova Scotia.
FROST, JOHN S., 12, M, -, W, Maine, 393, 516, NBPT*. In HH of Samuel Frost, age 43, Beer Manufacturer, born in NH.
FROST, MARIA, 19, F, -, W, Nova Scotia, 210, 311, NBPT. In HH of George Frost, age 47, Laborer, born in Nova Scotia.
FROST, MARTHA, 43, F, -, W, Maine, 393, 516, NBPT*. In HH of Samuel Frost, age 43, Beer Manufacturer, born in NH.
FROST, MARY, 49, F, -, W, Nova Scotia, 210, 311, NBPT. In HH of George Frost, age 47, Laborer, born in Nova Scotia.
FROST, REBECCA, 20, F, -, W, Nova Scotia, 210, 311, NBPT. In HH of George Frost, age 47, Laborer, born in Nova Scotia.
FROST, SAMUEL, 43, M, Beer Manufacturer, W, NH, 393, 516, NBPT*.
FROST, SARAH, 32, F, -, W, NH, 150, 219, NBPT. In HH of David Frost, age 36, Truck man, born in Maine.
FROST, SOPHIA, 14, F, -, W, Nova Scotia, 210, 311, NBPT. In

HH of George Frost, age 47, Laborer, born in Nova Scotia.
FROST, WHITFIELD, 6, M, -, W, Nova Scotia, 210, 311, NBPT. In HH of George Frost, age 47, Laborer, born in Nova Scotia.
FROST, WILLIAM H., 9, M, -, W, Maine, 393, 516, NBPT*. In HH of Samuel Frost, age 43, Beer Manufacturer, born in NH.
FROST, WILLIAM L., 12, M, -, W, Nova Scotia, 210, 311, NBPT. In HH of George Frost, age 47, Laborer, born in Nova Scotia.
FROTHINGHAM, CAROLINE H., 37, F, -, W, NH, 354, 468, NBPT*.
FROTHINGHAM, HENRY, 60, M, Broker, W, MA, 687, 979, NBPT.
FROTHINGHAM, JAMES, 68, M, Trader, W, MA, 185, 227, NBPT*. In HH of Anna M. Emerson, age 49, born in MA.
FROTHINGHAM, JANE, 49, F, -, W, Maine, 687, 979, NBPT. In HH of Henry Frothingham, age 60, Broker, born in MA.
FROTHINGHAM, JOSEPH A., 47, M, Dry Goods Dealer, W, MA, 197, 245, NBPT*.
FROTHINGHAM, MARTHA B., 39, F, -, W, Maine, 197, 245, NBPT*. In HH of Joseph A. Frothingham, age 47, Dry Goods Dealer, born in MA.
FROTHINGHAM, STEPHEN, 81, M, Merchant, W, MA, 197, 244, NBPT*.
FRUMBERS, ANTHONY, 11, M, -, W, Canada, 755,1064, NBPT. In HH of William Frumbers, age 55, Machinist, born in Canada.
FRUMBERS, MARGARET, 43, F, -, W, Canada, 755,1064, NBPT. In HH of William Frumbers, age 55, Machinist, born in Canada.
FRUMBERS, MARY, 14, F, -, W, Canada, 755,1064, NBPT. In HH of William Frumbers, age 55, Machinist, born in Canada.
FRUMBERS, NANCY, 9, F, -, W, Canada, 755,1064, NBPT. In HH of William Frumbers, age 55, Machinist, born in Canada.
FRUMBERS, WILLIAM, 55, M, Machinist, W, Canada, 755,1064, NBPT.
FRUMBERS, WILLIAM, 6, M, -, W, Canada, 755,1064, NBPT. In HH of William Frumbers, age 55, Machinist, born in Canada.
FUIT?, ANN, 45, F, -, W, Ireland, 497, 742, NBPT.
FULLER, JOHN, 48, M, Sailor, W, MA, 25, 32, NBPT.
FULLER, SARAH, 31, F, -, W, Maine, 726,1025, NBPT. In HH of Giles P. Stone, age 51, Clerk, born in MA.
FULLINGTON, BENJAMIN A., 16, M, Laborer, W, MA, 789,1116, NBPT. In HH of Lois Fullington, age 40, born in MA.
FULLINGTON, LOIS, 41, F, -, W, NH, 423, 628, NBPT.
FURBUSH, ALONZO, 32, M, Mariner, W, Maine, 342, 448, NBPT*.

- G -

GADDIS, DAVID, 14, M, -, W, England, 777,1101, NBPT. In HH of Joseph Gaddis, age 38, Mule spinner, born in England.
GADDIS, JANE, 12, F, -, W, England, 777,1101, NBPT. In HH of Joseph Gaddis, age 38, Mule spinner, born in England.
GADDIS, JOSEPH, 38, M, Mule Spinner, W, England, 777,1101, NBPT.
GADDIS, LOUISA, 10, F, -, W, England, 777,1101, NBPT. In HH

of Joseph Gaddis, age 38, Mule spinner, born in England.
GADDIS, MARY, 35, F, -, W, England, 777,1101, NBPT. In HH of Joseph Gaddis, age 38, Mule spinner, born in England.
GADDIS, THOMAS, 16, M, Operative, W, England, 777,1101, NBPT. In HH of Joseph Gaddis, age 38, Mule spinner, born in England.
GALLAHU, JOANNA, 40, F, 0-, W, Ireland, 78, 87, NBPT*. In Jail. For Tr. sdire?.
GALLILAND, ALEXANDER L., 13, M, -, W, Scotland, 656, 946, NBPT. In HH of Thomas H. Galliland, age 30, Operative, born in Scotland.
GALLILAND, CAWSSWELL, 24, F, -, W, Scotland, 656, 946, NBPT. In HH of Thomas H. Galliland, age 30, Operative, born in Scotland.
GALLILAND, JANET, 22, F, -, W, Scotland, 656, 946, NBPT. In HH of Thomas H. Galliland, age 30, Operative, born in Scotland.
GALLILAND, THOMAS F., 7, M, -, W, Scotland, 656, 946, NBPT. In HH of Thomas H. Galliland, age 30, Operative, born in Scotland.
GALLILAND, THOMAS H., 30, M, Operative, W, Scotland, 656, 946, NBPT.
GARDNER, Aaron, 30, M, Carpenter, W, NH, 514, 685, NBPT*.
GARDNER, DEBORAH, 75, F, -, W, NH, 576, 763, NBPT*. In HH of John Dean, age 79, None, born in NH.
GARDNER, JOHN F., 25, M, Coach Driver, W, NH, 360, 531, NBPT.
GARDNER, LEONORA, 27, F, -, W, Maine, 514, 685, NBPT*. In HH of Aaron Gardner, age 30, Carpenter, born in NH.
GARDNER, LORENZA N., 27, F, -, W, NH, 638, 925, NBPT. In HH of Merriam D. Gardner, age 48, born in NH.
GARDNER, LOUISA, 25, F, -, W, Maine, 360, 531, NBPT. In HH of John F. Gardner, age 25, Coach Driver, born in NH.
GARDNER, MERRIAM, 48, F, -, W, NH, 638, 925, NBPT.
GARDNER, NELSON, 37, M, Operative, W, MA, 424, 552, NBPT*. In HH of Benjamin Smith, age 46, Painter, born in VT.
GARDNER, STEPHEN D., 18, M, Coach Driver, W, NH, 638, 925, NBPT. In HH of Merriam D. Gardner, age 48, born in NH.
GARDON, EUNICE A., 18, F, -, W, Maine, 445, 662, NBPT. In HH of Elizabeth C. Perkins, age 53, born in MA.
GARKIN, BRIDGET, 25, F, -, W, Ireland, 685, 977, NBPT. In HH of Joseph S. Pike, age 69, Merchant, born in MA.
GARLAND, AUGUSTA, 16, F, -, W, NH, 515, 686, NBPT*. In HH of George P. Garland, age 65, Boarding House, born in NJ.
GARLAND, CAROLINE, 15, F, -, W, NH, 515, 686, NBPT*. In HH of George P. Garland, age 65, Boarding House, born in NJ.
GARLAND, ELIZABETH, 53, F, -, W, NH, 450, 673, NBPT.
GARLAND, ELIZABETH, 51, F, -, W, Maine, 515, 686, NBPT*. In HH of George P. Garland, age 65, Boarding House, born in NJ.
GARLAND, FRANKLIN, 25, M, Operative, W, Maine, 515, 686, NBPT*. In HH of George P. Garland, age 65, Boarding House, born in NJ.
GARLAND, GEORGE P., 65, M, Boarding House, W, NJ, 515, 686,

NBPT*.
GARLAND, HARRIET, 23, F, -, W, NH, 515, 686, NBPT*. In HH of George P. Garland, age 65, Boarding House, born in NJ.
GARLAND, JAMES, 37, M, Carpenter, W, MA, 301, 441, NBPT.
GARLAND, MARTHA A., 11, F, -, W, Maine, 515, 686, NBPT*. In HH of George P. Garland, age 65, Boarding House, born in NJ.
GARLAND, MARY A., 47, F, -, W, NH, 301, 441, NBPT. In HH of James Garland, age 37, Carpenter, born in MA.
GASKILL, ELIZABETH, 52, F, W, W, Nova Scotia, 412, 539, NBPT*. In HH of John Gaskill, age 52, Shipwright, born in Nova Scotia.
GASKILL, JOHN, 52, M, Shipwright, W, Nova Scotia, 412, 539, NBPT*.
GASKIN, LORANNA, 18, F, W, W, Nova Scotia, 412, 539, NBPT*. In HH of John Gaskill, age 52, Shipwright, born in Nova Scotia.
GASKIN, MARY A., 25, F, W, 0, Nova Scotia, 412, 539, NBPT*. In HH of John Gaskill, age 52, Shipwright, born in Nova Scotia.
GASKIN, RACHEL, 19, F, W, 0, Nova Scotia, 412, 539, NBPT*. In HH of John Gaskill, age 52, Shipwright, born in Nova Scotia.
GASKIN, SARAH, 12, F, W, 0, Nova Scotia, 412, 539, NBPT*. In HH of John Gaskill, age 52, Shipwright, born in Nova Scotia.
GASKIN, SARAH, 12, F, W, 0, Nova Scotia, 412, 539, NBPT*. In HH of John Gaskill, age 52, Shipwright, born in Nova Scotia.
GASKIN, THOMAS, 20, M, Ship Master, W, Nova Scotia, 412, 539, NBPT*. In HH of John Gaskill, age 52, Shipwright, born in Nova Scotia.

GEARY, GEORGE W., 38, M, Hatter, W, N.B., 650, 940, NBPT.
GEARY, SARAH, 32, F, -, W, NH, 650, 940, NBPT. In HH of Austin? J. Hale, age 51, born in MA.
GEORGE, CHARLES, 21, M, Fisherman, W, MA, 223, 277, NBPT*. In HH of Washington Roaf, age 21, Operative, born in NH.
GEORGE, EDWARD N., 34, M, Blacksmith, W, MA, 324, 419, NBPT*.
GEORGE, GEORGE J., 33, M, Blacksmith, W, MA, 481, 721, NBPT.
GEORGE, JAMES P., 26, M, Blacksmith, W, MA, 396, 588, NBPT.
GEORGE, JOSEPH, 67, M, Blacksmith, W, MA, 54, 60, NBPT*.
GEORGE, JOSEPH M., 45, M, Blacksmith, W, MA, 452, 676, NBPT.
GEORGE, JOSEPH O., 17, M, Blacksmith, W, MA, 452, 676, NBPT. In HH of Joseph O. Gerrish, age 45, Blacksmith, born in MA.
GEORGE, MARTHA, 19, F, -, W, NH, 396, 588, NBPT. In HH of James P. George, age 26, Blacksmith, born in MA.
GERRISH, CECILIA E., 11, F, -, W, Maine, 279, 409, NBPT. In HH of Orwin B. Gerrish, age 35, Carpenter, born in Maine.
GERRISH, CHARLES, 35, M, Machinist, W, MA, 281, 411, NBPT.
GERRISH, HARRIET N., 9, F, -, W, Maine, 279, 409, NBPT. In HH of Orwin B. Gerrish, age 35, Carpenter, born in Maine.
GERRISH, JANE, 33, F, -, W, NH, 281, 411, NBPT. In HH of

Charles Gerrish, age 35, Machinist, born in MA.
GERRISH, ORWIN B., 35, M, Carpenter, W, Maine, 279, 409, NBPT.
GERRISH, SARAH W., 33, F, -, W, NH, 279, 409, NBPT. In HH of Orwin B. Gerrish, age 35, Carpenter, born in Maine.
GILBERT, JOHN C., 35, M, Mariner, W, MA, 179, 259, NBPT.
GILLAND, FRANCIS, 23, M, Laborer, W, Ireland, 376, 493, NBPT*.
GILLAND, SARAH, 25, F, -, W, Ireland, 376, 493, NBPT*. In HH of Francis Gilland, age 23, Laborer, born in Ireland.
GILLESPIE, FRANCIS, 27, F, W, W, NH, 177, 256, NBPT. In HH of James N. Canney, age 41, Teamster, born in NH.
GILMAN, ABIGAIL P., 58, F, -, W, NH, 560, 833, NBPT. In HH of John Gilman, age 72, Printer, born in NH.
GILMAN, ELIZA A., 31, F, -, W, NH, 226, 332, NBPT. In HH of John S. Gilman, age 36, Overseer in Mill, born in NH.
GILMAN, HENRY, 38, M, Overseer, W, NH, 456, 679, NBPT. In HH of Sarah Bradstreet, age 42, born in MA.
GILMAN, JOHN, 72, M, Printer, W, NH, 560, 833, NBPT.
GILMAN, JOHN S., 36, M, Overseer in Mill, W, NH, 226, 332, NBPT.
GILMAN, PRUDANCE, 28, F, -, W, NH, 456, 679, NBPT. In HH of Sarah Bradstreet, age 42, born in MA.
GILMAN, SUSAN C., 15, F, -, W, NH, 226, 332, NBPT. In HH of John S. Gilman, age 36, Overseer in Mill, born in NH.
GILSON, SAMUEL, 50, M, Joiner, W, MA, 146, 174, NBPT*. In HH of George Towles, age 38, House Carpenter, born in MA.
GLEASON, JAMES, 25, M, Laborer, W, Ireland, 178, 257, NBPT. In HH of Patrick Holland, age 26, Laborer, born in Ireland.
GLIDDEN, LYDIA, 22, F, -, W, Maine, 736,1041, NBPT. In HH of John L. Grindal, age 48, Grocer, born in Maine.
GLIDDEN, REBECCA, 24, F, -, W, Maine, 736,1041, NBPT. In HH of John L. Grindal, age 48, Grocer, born in Maine.
GODDARD, CLARA, 37, F, -, W, NH, 8, 8, NBPT*. In HH of Samuel D. Goddard, 67, born MA.
GODDARD, EMILY, 20, F, -, W, D. Cola., 8, 8, NBPT*. In HH of Samuel D. Goddard, 67, born MA.
GODDARD, SAMUEL D., 67, M, None, W, MA, 8, 8, NBPT*.
GODFREY, WILLIAM, 34, M, Mariner, W, MA, 749,1056, NBPT.
GOLDTHWAIT, GEORGE, 26, M, Baggage Master, W, MA, 782,1108, NBPT. In HH of Enoch Tilton, age 45, Hotel Keeper, born in NH. In Hotel.
GOLLAHER, ELLEN M., 23, F, -, W, Ireland, 547, 729, NBPT*. In HH of John Gollaher, age 23, No Occupation listed, born in Ireland.
GOLLAHER, JOHN, 23, M, -, W, Ireland, 547, 729, NBPT*.
GOMEZ, STEPHEN, 20, M, Mariner, W, MA, 116, 139, NBPT*. In HH of Samuel Flanders, age 38, Master Mariner, born in MA.
GOODFREY, CHARLES, 27, M, Mariner, W, MA, 754,1062, NBPT.
GOODHUE, JANE R., 26, F, -, W, NH, 471, 706, NBPT. In HH of Joseph Goodhue age 53, Grocer, born in MA.
GOODHUE, JOSEPH, 53, M, Grocer, W, MA, 471, 706, NBPT.

GOODHUE, THOMAS, 70, M, Clerk, W, MA, 53, 59, NBPT*.

GOODHUE, WILLIAM F., 29, M, Teamster, W, MA, 548, 819, NBPT.

GOODRIDGE, EDWARD, 25, M, House Carpenter, W, MA, 415, 543, NBPT*. In HH of Hannah Goodridge, age 56, born in MA.

GOODWIN, ABEL L., 40, M, Fireman in Mill, W, MA, 154, 223, NBPT.

GOODWIN, ABEL L., 16, M, Spinner, W, MA, 154, 223, NBPT. In HH of Abel L. Goodwin, 40, Fireman in Mill, born in MA.

GOODWIN, AMOS, 68, M, Cooper, W, MA, 115, 171, NBPT.

GOODWIN, BENJAMIN, 47, M, Cooper, W, MA, 202, 297, NBPT.

GOODWIN, CATHARINE, 38, F, -, W, Ireland, 483, 643, NBPT*.

GOODWIN, CYRUS, 20, M, Mason, W, MA, 107, 158, NBPT.

GOODWIN, DANIEL A., 25, M, -, W, Maine, 20, 24, NBPT.

GOODWIN, EBENEZER P., 25, M, Sailmaker, W, MA, 447, 668, NBPT.

GOODWIN, ELEAZER P., 24, M, Mason, W, MA, 380, 500, NBPT*.

GOODWIN, ELIZABETH, 18, F, -, W, Maine, 776,1100, NBPT. In HH of Moses Winn, age 62, Laborer, born in MA.

GOODWIN, ELLEN, 17, F, -, W, Newfoundland, 483, 643, NBPT*. In HH of Catharine Goodwin, age 38, born in Ireland.

GOODWIN, GEORGE W., 17, M, Clerk, W, MA, 201, 296, NBPT. In HH of John Goodwin, age 46, Cooper, born in MA.

GOODWIN, JAMES E., 19, M, Iron Founder, W, MA, 607, 797, NBPT*. In HH of Sarah B. Goodwin, age 45, born in MA.

GOODWIN, JOHN, 46, M, Cooper, W, MA, 201, 296, NBPT.

GOODWIN, JOHN B., 23, M, Merchant, W, MA, 201, 296, NBPT. In HH of John Goodwin, age 46, Cooper, born in MA.

GOODWIN, JOSEPH, 18, M, Shoemaker, W, MA, 107, 158, NBPT. In HH of Cyrus Goodwin, age 20, Mason, born in MA.

GOODWIN, MARY, 17, F, -, W, NH, 423, 628, NBPT. In HH of Lois Fullington, age 41, Mariner, born in NH.

GOODWIN, MARY, 16, F, -, W, Newfoundland, 483, 643, NBPT*. In HH of Catharine Goodwin, age 38, born in Ireland.

GOODWIN, MOSES, 76, M, Cooper, W, MA, 129, 190, NBPT.

GOODWIN, MOSES JR., 50, M, Shoemaker, W, MA, 129, 190, NBPT. In HH of Moses Goodwin, age 76, Cooper, born in MA.

GOODWIN, SALLY, 61, F, -, W, MA, 788,1114, NBPT. In Poor House. .

GOODWIN, SARAH, 15, F, -, W, NH, 423, 628, NBPT. In HH of Lois Fullington, age 41, Mariner, born in NH.

GOODWIN, SARAH A., 34, F, -, W, Maine, 731,1031, NBPT. In HH of Daniel Horton, age 38, Hatter, born in MA.

GOOVER, MATILDA J., 22, F, -, W, NH, 315, 464, NBPT. In HH of William E. Goover, age 24, Operative, born in Maine.

GOOVER, WILLIAM E., 24, M, Operative, W, Maine, 315, 464, NBPT.

GORDON, CHARLES, 59, M, Blacksmith, W, MA, 788,1114, NBPT. In Poor House.

GORDON, JOHN, 26, M, Barber, W, MA, 718,1016, NBPT.

GORMAN, ANN, 19, F, -, W, Nova Scotia, 178, 257, NBPT. In HH of Patrick Holland, age 26, Laborer, born in Ireland.
GORMAN, ELLEN, 8, F, -, W, Ireland, 240, 302, NBPT*. In HH of Morris Gorman, age 40, Painter, born in MA.
GORMAN, HELLEN, 20, F, -, W, Ireland, 257, 374, NBPT. In HH of George Greenleaf, age 59, Deputy Sheriff, born in MA.
GORMAN, JOAN, 28, F, -, W, Ireland, 240, 302, NBPT*. In HH of Morris Gorman, age 40, Painter, born in MA.
GORMAN, JOHN, 6, M, -, W, Ireland, 240, 302, NBPT*. In HH of Morris Gorman, age 40, Painter, born in MA.
GORMAN, MARGARET, 26, F, -, W, Nova Scotia, 178, 257, NBPT. In HH of Patrick Holland, age 26, Laborer, born in Ireland.
GORMAN, MORRIS, 5, M, -, W, Ireland, 240, 302, NBPT*. In HH of Morris Gorman, age 40, Painter, born in MA.
GORMAN, PATRICK, 21, M, Mariner, W, Nova Scotia, 178, 257, NBPT. In HH of Patrick Holland, age 26, Laborer, born in Ireland.
GORMANE, ANN, 35, F, -, W, Ireland, 149, 218, NBPT. In HH of Henry Lenlar, age 29, R.C. Clergyman, born in Ireland.
GORWAIZ, CHARLES, 20, M, Mariner, W, MA, 368, 485, NBPT*. In HH of Thomas Gorwaiz, age 50, Painter, born in Italy.
GORWAIZ, JOHN, 17, M, Clerk, W, MA, 368, 485, NBPT*. In HH of Thomas Gorwaiz, age 50, Painter, born in Italy.
GORWAIZ, JOSEPH, 19, M, Mariner, W, MA, 368, 485, NBPT*. In HH of Thomas Gorwaiz, age 50, Painter, born in Italy.
GORWAIZ, THOMAS, 50, M, Painter, W, Italy, 368, 485, NBPT*.
GOUD, MARY C., 27, F, -, W, Maine, 45, 67, NBPT. In HH of Michjah B. Kimball, age 27, Shoemaker, born in MA.
GOULD, SAMUEL L., 30, M, Shoemaker, W, MA, 17, 20, NBPT. In HH of Ann Gould, age 65, born in MA.
GOULD, WALTER, 49, M, Carpenter, W, Maine, 427, 633, NBPT.
GOVE, ABRAHAM D., 32, M, Carpenter, W, NH, 409, 609, NBPT.
GOVE, AMAND, 29, F, -, W, NH, 409, 609, NBPT. In HH of Abraham D. Gove, age 32, Carpenter, born in NH.
GOVE, LAZANIA, 16, F, -, W, Maine, 405, 529, NBPT*. In HH of Miriam James, age 50, born in NH.
GOVERNOR, JAMES, 21, M, Iron Foundry, W, Ireland, 224, 278, NBPT*. In HH of Ann Mahaffy, age 32, born in Ireland.
GRACE, ANDREW J., 30, M, Hackman, W, Maine, 734, 1038, NBPT.
GRACE, LAURA A., 31, F, -, W, Maine, 734, 1038, NBPT. In HH of Andrew J. Grace, age 30, Hackman, born in Maine.
GRAHAM, MARY, 20, F, -, W, Ireland, 158, 189, NBPT*. In HH of Joseph W. Ballou, age 30, Clothing Store, born in MA.
GRANGER, ANN, 18, F, -, W, Newfoundland, 352, 464, NBPT*. In HH of John B. Tuttle, age 40, Grocer, born in NH.
GRANGER, DANIEL, 43, M, Lumber Merchant, W, MA, 260, 377, NBPT.
GRANGER, GEORGE, 20, M, Clerk, W, MA, 338, 441, NBPT*. In HH of George F. Granger, age

45, Lumber Dealer, born in MA.
GRANGER, GEORGE F., 45, M, Lumber Dealer, W, MA, 338, 441, NBPT*.
GRANGER, MARY, 20, F, -, W, Newfoundland, 130, 155, NBPT*. In HH of C.S. Merchant, age 54, U.S. Army, born in NY.
GRANT, ANGUS, 25, M, Ship Carpenter, W, Nova Scotia, 465, 618, NBPT*. In HH of David Lurvey, age 35, Ship Carpenter, born in Maine.
GRAVES, ALEXANDER, 27, M, Master Mariner, W, MA, 60, 87, NBPT.
GRAVES, ANNIA, 32, F, -, W, NH, 125, 182, NBPT. In HH of William Felch, age 31, Shoemaker, born in NH.
GRAVES, EDWARD, 19, M, Mariner, W, MA, 34, 47, NBPT. In HH of William Graves, age 64, Master Mariner, born in MA.
GRAVES, JOHN, 40, M, Laborer, W, Ireland, 763,1077, NBPT.
GRAVES, JOHN, 12, M, -, W, N.B., 763,1077, NBPT. In HH of John Graves, age 40, Laborer, born in Ireland.
GRAVES, MARY, 40, F, -, W, Ireland, 763,1077, NBPT. In HH of John Graves, age 40, Laborer, born in Ireland.
GRAVES, MARY A., 3, F, -, W, N.B., 763,1077, NBPT. In HH of John Graves, age 40, Laborer, born in Ireland.
GRAVES, THOMAS, 9, M, -, W, N.B., 763,1077, NBPT. In HH of John Graves, age 40, Laborer, born in Ireland.
GRAVES, WILLIAM, 64, M, Master Mariner, W, MA, 34, 47, NBPT.
GRAVES, WILLIAM, 6, M, -, W, N.B., 763,1077, NBPT. In HH of John Graves, age 40, Laborer, born in Ireland.
GRAVES, WILLIAM JR., 38, M, Master Mariner, W, MA, 10, 12, NBPT.
GRAY, CATHERINE, 20, F, -, W, Maine, 431, 641, NBPT. In HH of Mary L. Rains, age 48, born in Maine.
GRAY, HORATIO, 21, M, Student, W, MA, 430, 639, NBPT. In HH of Frances E. Gray, age 38, born in MA.
GRAY, WILLIAM, 46, M, Master Mariner, W, Enlance?, 62, 90, NBPT.
GREELEY, DEBORAH, 50, F, -, W, NH, 714,1009, NBPT.
GREELEY, GEORGE, 22, M, Tin Plate Worker, W, MA, 714,1009, NBPT. In HH of Deborah Greeley, age 50, born in NH.
GREELEY, JAMES P., 17, M, Shoemaker, W, MA, 714,1009, NBPT. In HH of Deborah Greeley, age 50, born in NH.
GREELEY, JOSEPH, 42, M, Shoemaker, W, MA, 587, 864, NBPT.
GREELY, ERASTUS P., 13, M, -, W, Maine, 509, 678, NBPT*. In HH of Thomas Greely, age 40, Ship Carpenter, born in Maine.
GREELY, FRANCES D., 30, F, -, W, Maine, 45, 66, NBPT. In HH of John B. Greely, age 47, Shoemaker, born in MA.
GREELY, JOHN B., 47, M, Shoemaker, W, MA, 45, 66, NBPT.
GREELY, MARY, 37, F, -, W, Maine, 509, 678, NBPT*. In HH of Thomas Greely, age 40, Ship Carpenter, born in Maine.
GREELY, THOMAS, 40, M, Ship Carpenter, W, Maine, 509, 678, NBPT*.
GREELY, WILSON, 11, M, -, W, Maine, 509, 678, NBPT*. In HH of Thomas Greely, age 40, Ship

Carpenter, born in Maine.
GREEN, GEORGE L., 20, M, Carpenter, W, NH, 641, 928, NBPT. In HH of Herekiah Ripley, age 27, Carpenter, born in Maine.
GREEN, GEORGE W., 29, M, Grocer, W, MA, 252, 365, NBPT.
GREEN, JANE, 40, F, -, W, England, 314, 463, NBPT. In HH of William Green, age 40, Operative, born in England.
GREEN, MARY L., 19, F, -, W, Maine, 770,1090, NBPT. In HH of Levi Pearson, age 37, Watchman, born in MA.
GREEN, SAMUEL A., 39, M, Boot/Shoe/Clothing, W, MA, 170, 205, NBPT*.
GREEN, SARAH A., 27, F, -, W, NH, 252, 365, NBPT. In HH of George W. Green, age 29, Grocer, born in MA.
GREEN, SILAS, 30, M, Laborer, W, NH, 125, 149, NBPT*. In HH of Jeremy C. Wingate, age 47, Milkman, born in NH.
GREEN, THOMAS J., 9, M, -, W, RI, 314, 463, NBPT. In HH of William Green, age 40, Operative, born in England.
GREEN, WILLIAM, 40, M, Operative, W, England, 314, 463, NBPT.
GREEN, WILLIAM J., 11, M, -, W, RI, 314, 463, NBPT. In HH of William Green, age 40, Operative, born in England.
GREENLAW, RUTH R., 28, F, -, W, Maine, 620, 903, NBPT. In HH of William L. Greenlaw, age 34, Cooper, born in Maine.
GREENLEAF, ALBERT F., 20, M, Shoemaker, W, MA, 165, 198, NBPT*. In HH of Betsy Page, age 45, born in MA.
GREENLEAF, CAROLINE, 21, F, -, W, Maine, 265, 335, NBPT*. In HH of Chester A. Greenleaf, age 23, 2nd Overseer, born in MA.
GREENLEAF, CHARLES W., 23, M, Shoemaker, W, MA, 165, 198, NBPT*. In HH of Betsy Page, age 45, born in MA.
GREENLEAF, CHESTER A., 23, M, 2nd Overseer, W, MA, 265, 335, NBPT*.
GREENLEAF, DANIEL P., 26, M, Mariner, W, MA, 265, 335, NBPT*. In HH of Chester A. Greenleaf, age 23, 2nd Overseer, born in MA.
GREENLEAF, ENOCH D., 50, M, None, W, MA, 788,1114, NBPT. In Poor House.
GREENLEAF, GEORGE, 59, M, Deputy Sheriff, W, MA, 257, 374, NBPT.
GREENLEAF, JEREMIAH, 49, M, Caulker, W, MA, 95, 138, NBPT.
GREENLEAF, JOSEPH, 62, M, Sailmaker, W, MA, 264, 333, NBPT*.
GREENLEAF, JOSEPH, 35, M, Mason, W, MA, 89, 104, NBPT*.
GREENLEAF, JOSHUA, 83, M, None, W, MA, 239, 301, NBPT*.
GREENLEAF, LORINDA S., 24, F, -, W, Maine, 265, 335, NBPT*. In HH of Chester A. Greenleaf, age 23, 2nd Overseer, born in MA.
GREENLEAF, RUFUS, 45, M, Painter, W, MA, 239, 301, NBPT*. In HH of Joshua Greenleaf, age 83, no occupation listed, born in MA.
GREENLEAF, SUSAN, 62, F, -, W, NH, 264, 333, NBPT*. In HH of Joseph Greenleaf, age 62, Sailmaker, born in MA.
GREENLEIF, ANN, 73, F, -, W, MA, 788,1114, NBPT. In Poor House. .
GREENLIEF, RUBAN O., 22, M, Roll Coverer, W, Maine, 219, 325, NBPT. In HH of Ruth A. Kerman, age 76, born in MA.

GREENOUGH, CHARLES, 22, M, Works in Distillery, W, Maine, 467, 620, NBPT*. In HH of Freeman Greenough, age 47, Laborer, born in Maine.
GREENOUGH, EMILY, 8, F, -, W, Maine, 467, 620, NBPT*. In HH of Freeman Greenough, age 47, Laborer, born in Maine.
GREENOUGH, FREEMAN, 47, M, Laborer, W, Maine, 467, 620, NBPT*.
GREENOUGH, FREEMAN, 20, M, Operative, W, Maine, 467, 620, NBPT*. In HH of Freeman Greenough, age 47, Laborer, born in Maine.
GREENOUGH, GEORGE, 11, M, -, W, Maine, 467, 620, NBPT*. In HH of Freeman Greenough, age 47, Laborer, born in Maine.
GREENOUGH, HENRY, 17, M, Operative, W, Maine, 467, 620, NBPT*. In HH of Freeman Greenough, age 47, Laborer, born in Maine.
GREENOUGH, JOSEPH, 13, M, -, W, Maine, 467, 620, NBPT*. In HH of Freeman Greenough, age 47, Laborer, born in Maine.
GREENOUGH, MARY, 19, F, -, W, Maine, 467, 620, NBPT*. In HH of Freeman Greenough, age 47, Laborer, born in Maine.
GREENOUGH, N.C., 30, M, Watchmaker, W, NH, 40, 47, NBPT*. In HH of Frances F. Monroe, age 32, female, Boarding House, born in Maine.
GREENOUGH, SARAH, 15, F, -, W, Maine, 467, 620, NBPT*. In HH of Freeman Greenough, age 47, Laborer, born in Maine.
GREENOUGH, TRYPHENA, 49, F, -, W, Maine, 467, 620, NBPT*. In HH of Freeman Greenough, age 47, Laborer, born in Maine.
GRIFFIN, ALBERT, 36, M, Shoemaker, W, MA, 359, 473, NBPT*.
GRIFFIN, EBENEZER, 40, M, Machinist, W, MA, 144, 172, NBPT*.
GRIFFIN, ELIPHALET, 25, M, Dry Goods Dealer, W, MA, 211, 262, NBPT*. In Boarding House.
GRIFFIN, ELLAS, 18, F, Spinner, W, Nova Scotia, 37, 52, NBPT. In HH of Samuel Griffin, age 57, Laborer, born in NY.
GRIFFIN, GEORGE W., 18, M, Iron Foundry, W, MA, 144, 172, NBPT*. In HH of Ebenezer Griffin, age 40, Machinist, born in MA.
GRIFFIN, HENRY, 60, M, Master Mariner, W, MA, 301, 442, NBPT.
GRIFFIN, JACOB L., 10, M, -, W, Nova Scotia, 37, 52, NBPT. In HH of Samuel Griffin, age 57, Laborer, born in NY.
GRIFFIN, JAMES, 42, M, Engineer, W, MA, 35, 42, NBPT*.
GRIFFIN, JUSTICE, 18, M, -, W, Nova Scotia, 37, 52, NBPT. In HH of Samuel Griffin, age 57, Laborer, born in NY.
GRIFFIN, SAMUEL, 57, M, Laborer, W, NY, 37, 52, NBPT.
GRIFFIN, SAMUEL, 16, M, None, W, Nova Scotia, 37, 52, NBPT. In HH of Samuel Griffin, age 57, Laborer, born in NY.
GRIFFIN, SARAH, 53, F, -, W, Nova Scotia, 37, 52, NBPT. In HH of Samuel Griffin, age 57, Laborer, born in NY.
GRIFFIN, WILLIAM, 40, M, Mariner, W, MA, 112, 167, NBPT.
GRIFFIN, WILLIAM H., 18, M, Spinner, W, MA, 35, 42, NBPT*. In HH of James Griffin, age 42, Engineer, born in MA.
GRIFFITH, AUGUSTUS, 21, M, Clothing Store, W, MA, 541, 811, NBPT. In HH of Nancy Griffith, age 60, born in MA.

GRIFFITH, HARRIET D., 27, F, -, W, Maine, 370, 544, NBPT. In HH of Paul T. Griffith, age 28, Clothing Dealer, born in MA.
GRIFFITH, JOSEPH, 47, M, Shoemaker, W, MA, 297, 433, NBPT. In HH of Margaret F. Noyes, age 76, born in MA.
GRIFFITH, PAUL T., 28, M, Clothing Dealer, W, MA, 370, 544, NBPT.
GRIFFITH, RUFUS F., 30, M, Clothing Store, W, MA, 541, 811, NBPT. In HH of Nancy Griffith, age 60, born in MA.
GRIFFITH, THOMAS, 45, M, Clerk, W, MA, 602, 880, NBPT.
GRINDAL, JOHN L., 48, M, Grocer, W, Maine, 736,1041, NBPT.
GRINDAL, JULIA A., 27, F, -, W, NH, 736,1042, NBPT. In HH of Stover Grindal, age 25, Clerk, born in Maine.
GRINDAL, MARY E., 18, F, -, W, Maine, 736,1041, NBPT. In HH of John L. Grindal, age 48, Grocer, born in Maine.
GRINDAL, NANCY, 44, F, -, W, Maine, 736,1041, NBPT. In HH of John L. Grindal, age 48, Grocer, born in Maine.
GRINDAL, STOVER, 25, M, Clerk, W, Maine, 736,1042, NBPT.
GRINDALL, FRONA, 21, F, -, W, Maine, 441, 656, NBPT. In HH of Polly Prince, age 76, born in MA.
GROVE, ANGELINE, 27, F, -, W, NH, 416, 620, NBPT. In HH of Sarah Tappan, age 77, born in MA.
GROVE, CHARLOTTE, 22, F, -, W, NH, 416, 620, NBPT. In HH of Sarah Tappan, age 77, born in MA.
GUNNISON, EVELINE, 46, F, -, W, Maine, 452, 675, NBPT.
GUNNISON, WILLIAM, 63, M, Merchant, W, MA, 477, 714, NBPT.
GURNEY, ABRAHAM, 15, M, Operative, W, MA, 357, 471, NBPT*. In HH of Nathaniel Gurney, age 45, Coach maker, born in MA.
GURNEY, CHARLES W., 19, M, Operative, W, MA, 162, 195, NBPT*. In Boarding House run by Hannah S. Davidson, 47, born in MA.
GURNEY, EDWARD T., 11, M, -, W, NH, 366, 483, NBPT*. In HH of Nathaniel M. Gurney, age 69, Carriage Maker, born in MA.
GURNEY, JOHN G., 34, M, Harness Maker, W, MA, 366, 483, NBPT*. In HH of Nathaniel M. Gurney, age 69, Carriage Maker, born in MA.
GURNEY, NATHANIEL, 45, M, Coach Maker, W, MA, 357, 471, NBPT*.
GURNEY, NATHANIEL M., 69, M, Carriage Maker, W, MA, 366, 483, NBPT*.
GURNEY, ROBERT F., 28, M, Operative, W, NH, 162, 195, NBPT*. In Boarding House run by Hannah S. Davidson, 47, born in MA.
GURNEY, SAMUEL P., 38, M, Painter, W, MA, 524, 696, NBPT*.
GURNEY, WILLIAM F., 24, M, Operative, W, MA, 162, 195, NBPT*. In Boarding House run by Hannah S. Davidson, 47, born in MA.
GURNEY, WILLIAM F., 24, M, Carpenter, W, MA, 42, 61, NBPT.

- H -

HACKETT, JAMES, 43, M, Printer, W, MA, 186, 228, NBPT*.
HACKETT, SARAH H., 48, M, -,

W, Maine, 186, 228, NBPT*. In HH of James Hackett, age 43, Printer, born in MA.

HADLEY, ALBERT H., 4, M, -, W, NJ, 517, 771, NBPT. In HH of Josiah Hadley, age 28, Operative, born in NH.

HADLEY, JOSIAH, 28, M, Operative, W, NH, 517, 771, NBPT.

HADLEY, SARAH, 24, F, -, W, NH, 517, 771, NBPT. In HH of Josiah Hadley, age 28, Operative, born in NH.

HAGGERTY, DENNIS, 18, M, Laborer, W, Ireland, 288, 420, NBPT. In HH of William Haggerty, age 42, Laborer, born in Ireland.

HAGGERTY, JEREMIAH, 10, M, -, W, Ireland, 288, 420, NBPT. In HH of William Haggerty, age 42, Laborer, born in Ireland.

HAGGERTY, JOHN, 14, M, -, W, Ireland, 288, 420, NBPT. In HH of William Haggerty, age 42, Laborer, born in Ireland.

HAGGERTY, JULIA, 3, F, -, W, Nova Scotia, 288, 420, NBPT. In HH of William Haggerty, age 42, Laborer, born in Ireland.

HAGGERTY, MARGARET, 6, F, -, W, Ireland, 288, 420, NBPT. In HH of William Haggerty, age 42, Laborer, born in Ireland.

HAGGERTY, MARY, 16, F, -, W, Ireland, 288, 420, NBPT. In HH of William Haggerty, age 42, Laborer, born in Ireland.

HAGGERTY, MARY H., 38, F, -, W, Ireland, 288, 420, NBPT. In HH of William Haggerty, age 42, Laborer, born in Ireland.

HAGGERTY, WILLIAM, 42, M, Laborer, W, Ireland, 288, 420, NBPT.

HAGGERTY, WILLIAM, 12, M, -, W, Ireland, 288, 420, NBPT. In HH of William Haggerty, age 42, Laborer, born in Ireland.

HAINES, ABBA, 18, F, -, W, Maine, 222, 276, NBPT*. In HH of Stephen Fowle, age 33, Laborer, born in MA.

HAINES, ALBERT, 17, M, Operative, W, MA, 610, 800, NBPT*. In HH of Edward W. Brown, age 31, Lab. Factory, born in NH.

HAINES, ANDREW, 70, M, Sail Maker, W, MA, 519, 690, NBPT*.

HAINES, ANDREW, 18, M, Painter, W, Maine, 140, 166, NBPT*. In HH of Hannah T. Marshall, age 39, Boarding House, born in MA.

HAINES, DANIEL, 16, M, Apprentice Blacksmith, W, Nova Scotia, 324, 419, NBPT*. In HH of Edward N. George, age 34, Blacksmith, born in MA.

HAINES, DANIEL, 16, M, Blacksmith, W, England, 563, 749, NBPT*. In HH of Samuel Haines, age 45, Ship Carpenter, born in England.

HAINES, HANNAH, 19, F, -, W, Nova Scotia, 563, 749, NBPT*. In HH of Samuel Haines, age 45, Ship Carpenter, born in England.

HAINES, JOSEPH, 8, M, -, W, England, 563, 749, NBPT*. In HH of Samuel Haines, age 45, Ship Carpenter, born in England.

HAINES, LUCINDA, 2, F, -, W, England, 563, 749, NBPT*. In HH of Samuel Haines, age 45, Ship Carpenter, born in England.

HAINES, MAHALA, 22, F, -, W, NH, 200, 247, NBPT*. In HH of Adriel H. Hodgdon, age 37, Drayman, born in NH.

HAINES, REBEKAH, 11, F, -, W, England, 563, 749, NBPT*. In HH of Samuel Haines, age 45, Ship Carpenter, born in England.

HAINES, ROSANNA, 38, F, -, W,

England, 563, 749, NBPT*. In HH of Samuel Haines, age 45, Ship Carpenter, born in England.
HAINES, SAMUEL, 45, M, Ship Carpenter, W, England, 563, 749, NBPT*.
HAINES, SAMUEL, 10, M, -, W, England, 563, 749, NBPT*. In HH of Samuel Haines, age 45, Ship Carpenter, born in England.
HAINES, SAMUEL W., 33, M, Sail Maker, W, MA, 103, 121, NBPT*.
HAINES, SOLOMON, 19, M, Wheelwright, W, England, 563, 749, NBPT*. In HH of Samuel Haines, age 45, Ship Carpenter, born in England.
HALE, BENJAMIN, 71, M, None, W, MA, 43, 50, NBPT*.
HALE, BENJAMIN, 71, M, None, W, MA, 43, 50, NBPT*.
HALE, BENJN., 33, M, Master Mariner, W, MA, 689, 981, NBPT. In HH of William Nichols, age 69, Merchant, born in MA.
HALE, CHARLES, 22, M, Mariner, W, MA, 4, 4, NBPT. In HH of Mary Y. Huse, age 50, born in MA.
HALE, CHARLES H., 30, M, Carpenter, W, MA, 8, 8, NBPT.
HALE, EDWARD, 15, M, Student, W, MA, 301, 393, NBPT*. In HH of Jacob Hale, age 53, Stove Dealer, born in MA.
HALE, ELIPHALET C., 19, M, Mariner, W, MA, 649, 939, NBPT. In HH of Austin? J. Hale, age 51, born in MA.
HALE, GEORGE H., 19, M, Student, W, MA, 301, 393, NBPT*. In HH of Jacob Hale, age 53, Stove Dealer, born in MA.
HALE, GEORGE W., 35, M, Sail Maker, W, MA, 56, 83, NBPT.
HALE, GEORGE W., 25, M, Mariner, W, MA, 83, 92, NBPT*. In HH of James Cheney, age 52, Operative, born Maine.
HALE, GEORGE W., 23, M, Weaver, W, NH, 469, 703, NBPT.
HALE, HANNAH J., 25, F, -, W, Maine, 469, 703, NBPT. In HH of George W. Hale, age 23, Weaver, born in NH.
HALE, JACOB, 53, M, Stove dealer, W, MA, 301, 393, NBPT*.
HALE, MOSES, 35, M, Dealer in Fancy Good, W, MA, 649, 939, NBPT. In HH of Austin? J. Hale, age 51, born in MA.
HALE, MOSES E., 33, M, Merchant, W, MA, 43, 50, NBPT*. In HH of Benjamin Hale, age 71, born MA.
HALE, MOSES H., 21, M, Stove manufacturer, W, MA, 301, 393, NBPT*. In HH of Jacob Hale, age 53, Stove Dealer, born in MA.
HALE, NATHL., 27, M, Mariner, W, MA, 649, 939, NBPT. In HH of Austin? J. Hale, age 51, born in MA.
HALE, SARAH J., 27, F, -, W, NH, 8, 8, NBPT. In HH of Charles H. Hale, age 30, Carpenter, born in MA.
HALE, SELINA, 57, F, -, W, England, 43, 50, NBPT*. In HH of Benjamin Hale, age 71, no occupation, born MA.
HALE, STEPHEN, 27, M, Shoemaker, W, NH, 607, 797, NBPT*. In HH of Sarah B. Goodwin, age 45, born in MA.
HALES, MARY, 25, F, -, W, Maine, 264, 333, NBPT*. In HH of Joseph Greenleaf, age 62, Sailmaker, born in MA.
HALEY, JULIA, 24, F, -, W, Ireland, 78, 87, NBPT*. In Jail. Convict.
HALL, AUGUSTA, 22, F, -, W, NH, 753, 1061, NBPT. In HH of Martha Royers, age 57, born in MA

HALL, EVIRA, 20, F, -, W, NH, 702, 996, NBPT. In HH of James Hall, age 28, Shoemaker, born in NH.
HALL, HARRIET, 21, F, -, W, NH, 753,1061, NBPT. In HH of Martha Royers, age 57, born in MA.
HALL, JAMES, 28, M, Shoemaker, W, NH, 702, 996, NBPT.
HALL, JAMES H., 27, M, Painter, W, MA, 327, 424, NBPT*. In HH of Sarah Leighton, age 50, born in MA.
HALL, JOSEPH, 27, M, Shoemaker, W, MA, 529, 702, NBPT*.
HALL, JOSEPH, 16, M, Operative, W, MA, 360, 476, NBPT*. In HH of Nancy Hall, age 50, born in NH.
HALL, NANCY, 50, F, -, W, NH, 360, 476, NBPT*.
HALL, REBECCA, 22, F, -, W, Maine, 737,1043, NBPT. In HH of Abel D. Brown, age 28, Shoemaker, born in NH.
HAM, LUCY, 22, F, -, W, NH, 373, 490, NBPT*. In HH of A.W. Mooney, age 27, born in NH.
HAMDEN, HANNAH E., 22, F, -, W, Maine, 69, 99, NBPT. In HH of George Knight, age 38, Merchant, born in MA.
HAMEN, ABRAHAM, 20, M, Operative, W, England, 108, 161, NBPT. In HH of Hannah Brown, age 57, born in NH.
HAMEN, ROGER, 28, M, Operative, W, England, 108, 161, NBPT. In HH of Hannah Brown, age 57, born in NH.
HAMEN, SAMUEL, 30, M, Operative, W, England, 108, 161, NBPT. In HH of Hannah Brown, age 57, born in NH.
HAMILTON, ANN P., 42, F, -, W, England, 677, 969, NBPT. In HH of William C. Balch, age 30, Agent NBPT* Mills, born in MA.
HAMILTON, JOHN, 39, M, Painter, W, England, 39, 46, NBPT*. In HH of Parker M. Dole, age 65, farmer, born in MA.
HAMILTON, LYDIA A., 17, F, -, W, England, 39, 46, NBPT*. In HH of Parker M. Dole, age 65, farmer, born in MA.
HAMILTON, MARY, 39, F, W, 0, England, 39, 46, NBPT*. In HH of Parker M. Dole, age 65, farmer, born in MA.
HAMILTON, SARAH, 22, F, -, W, Ireland, 764,1078, NBPT. In HH of Jonathan Lovering, age 33, Hotel Keeper, born in NH.
HAMILTON, THOMAS A., 13, M, -, W, England, 39, 46, NBPT*. In HH of Parker M. Dole, age 65, farmer, born in MA.
HANDON, FRANCIS, 45, M, Laborer, W, Ireland, 540, 808, NBPT.
HANDON, MARY, 42, F, -, W, Ireland, 540, 808, NBPT. In HH of Francis Handon, age 45, Laborer, born in Ireland.
HANE, ANN, 19, F, -, W, Ireland, 630, 916, NBPT. In HH of Sophia Richardson, age 50, born in MA.
HANICHY, MARY A., 18, F, -, W, England, 661, 952, NBPT. In HH of Dorothy Chute, age 66, born in MA.
HANICHY, MARY A., 18, F, -, W, England, 661, 952, NBPT. In HH of Dorothy Chute, age 66, born in MA.
HARA, MARY C., 25, F, -, W, Ireland, 122, 145, NBPT*. In HH of Enoch S. Williams, age 48, Merchant, born in MA.
HARDY, DUDLEY, 77, M, Laborer, W, NH, 292, 382, NBPT*.
HARDY, EDWARD T., 38, M, -, W, NH, 122, 145, NBPT*. In HH of

Enoch S. Williams, age 48, Merchant, born in MA.

HARDY, HANNAH, 70, F, -, W, NH, 292, 382, NBPT*. In HH of Dudley Hardy, age 77, Laborer, born in NH.

HARDY, JOSEPH, 36, M, Attached to Railroad, W, MA, 296, 388, NBPT*.

HARDY, JOSEPH W., 31, M, Laborer, W, MA, 292, 382, NBPT*. In HH of Dudley Hardy, age 77, Laborer, born in NH.

HARDY, LUCINDA, 21, F, -, W, Nova Scotia, 263, 332, NBPT*. In HH of William H. Brewster, age 37, Printer and Publisher, born in NH.

HARDY, MARY A., 25, F, -, W, NH, 436, 574, NBPT*. In HH of William Hardy, age 30, Mariner, born in Maine.

HARDY, MARY A., 23, F, -, W, N.S., 765,1079, NBPT. In HH of William Hardy, age 28, Mariner, born in NY.

HARDY, MARY J., 38, F, -, W, Maine, 608, 888, NBPT.

HARDY, MOSES H., 38, M, Mariner, W, MA, 292, 383, NBPT*.

HARDY, WILLIAM, 48, M, Laborer, W, MA, 284, 368, NBPT*.

HARDY, WILLIAM, 30, M, Mariner, W, Maine, 436, 574, NBPT*.

HARDY, WILLIAM, 28, M, Mariner, W, NY, 765,1079, NBPT.

HARGIN, MARGARET, 16, F, -, W, Ireland, 80, 89, NBPT*. In HH of Charles Peabody, age 34, Shoe Dealer, born in MA.

HARMON, DANIEL, 24, M, Baker, W, Maine, 125, 183, NBPT.

HARMON, REBECCA, 21, F, -, W, Maine, 125, 183, NBPT. In HH of Daniel Harmon, age 24, Baker, born in Maine.

HARMON, WILLIAM, 18, M, None, W, Maine, 125, 183, NBPT. In HH of Daniel Harmon, age 24, Baker, born in Maine.

HARRIN, JAMES, 50, M, Laborer, W, Ireland, 373, 550, NBPT.

HARRIN, JOHN, 5, M, -, W, Newfoundland, 373, 550, NBPT. In HH of James Harrin, age 50, Laborer, born in Ireland.

HARRIN, MARGARET, 7, F, -, W, Newfoundland, 373, 550, NBPT. In HH of James Harrin, age 50, Laborer, born in Ireland.

HARRIN, MARY, 47, F, -, W, Newfoundland, 373, 550, NBPT. In HH of James Harrin, age 50, Laborer, born in Ireland.

HARRIN, MATHEW, 2, M, -, W, Newfoundland, 373, 550, NBPT. In HH of James Harrin, age 50, Laborer, born in Ireland.

HARRINGTON, ELIZABETH, 22, F, -, W, Maine, 488, 730, NBPT. In HH of Lucinda G. Peabody, age 39, born in NH.

HARRINGTON, LOUISA, 20, F, -, W, Maine, 615, 807, NBPT*. In HH of Dexter Hildreth, age 23, Blacksmith, born in Maine.

HARRINGTON, LOUISA, 19, F, -, W, Maine, 488, 730, NBPT. In HH of Lucinda G. Peabody, age 39, born in NH.

HARRINGTON, THOMAS, 23, M, Laborer, W, Ireland, 229, 283, NBPT*. In HH of James Cassman, age 21, Laborer, born in Ireland.

HARRIS, GEORGE, 15, M, Operative, W, MA, 169, 202, NBPT*. In HH of William L. Harris, age 45, Fisherman, born in MA.

HARRIS, MIRENDA, 39, F, -, W, Maine, 107, 160, NBPT. In HH of Samuel Harris, age 41, Laborer, born in MA.

HARRIS, SAMUEL, 41, M,

Laborer, W, MA, 107, 160, NBPT.
HARRIS, SAMUEL, 30, M, Fisherman, W, MA, 169, 202, NBPT*. In HH of William L. Harris, age 45, Fisherman, born in MA.
HARRIS, WILLIAM, 52, M, Grocer, W, MA, 240, 348, NBPT.
HARRIS, WILLIAM C., 23, M, Clerk, W, MA, 240, 348, NBPT. In HH of William Harris, age 52, Grocer, born in MA.
HARRIS, WILLIAM L., 45, M, Fisherman, W, MA, 169, 202, NBPT*.
HARRIS, WILLIAM S. JR., 27, M, Fisherman, W, MA, 169, 202, NBPT*. In HH of William L. Harris, age 45, Fisherman, born in MA.
HARROD, BENJN., 66, M, Farmer, W, MA, 413, 616, NBPT. In HH of John Harrod, age 73, President Savings Bank, born MA.
HARROD, BENJN., JR., 19, M, Mariner, W, MA, 413, 616, NBPT. In HH of John Harrod, age 73, President Savings Bank, born in MA.
HARROD, JOHN, 73, M, President, Saving Bank, W, MA, 413, 616, NBPT.
HARSON, MARY, 22, F, -, W, Ireland, 523, 780, NBPT. In HH of Samuel O. Johnson, age 28, Fruit Dealer, born in MA.
HART, DAVID, 70, M, Merchant, W, NH, 106, 157, NBPT.
HART, JAMES C., 21, M, Tailor, W, England, 369, 486, NBPT*. In HH of Robert McQuillen, age 66, Millwright, born in NH.
HART, SARAH, 17, F, -, W, NH, 369, 486, NBPT*. In HH of Robert McQuillen, age 66, Millwright, born in NH.
HARTH, FELIX, 30, M, Merchant, W, France, 782,1108, NBPT. In HH of Enoch Tilton, age 45, Hotel Keeper, born in NH. In Hotel.
HARVEY, ARVILLA S., 28, F, -, W, Maine, 319, 469, NBPT. In HH of William Y. Harvey, age 27, Operative, born in MA.
HARVEY, JUDITH, 24, F, -, W, NH, 782,1108, NBPT. In HH of Enoch Tilton, age 45, Hotel Keeper, born in NH. In Hotel.
HARVEY, WILLIAM T., 27, M, Operative, W, MA, 319, 469, NBPT.
HASE, THOMAS C., 52, M, Hatter, W, MA, 440, 655, NBPT.
HASE, WILLIAM, 23, M, Cabinetmaker, W, MA, 440, 655, NBPT. In HH of Thomas C. Hase, age 52, Hatter, born in MA.
HASKELL, AGNES, 62, F, -, W, Jamaica, 241, 349, NBPT.
HASKELL, ANN E., 23, F, W, 0, Maine, 190, 276, NBPT. In HH of Caleb Haskell, age 64, Carpenter, born in MA.
HASKELL, AUGUSTUS, 24, M, Truck man, W, Maine, 466, 619, NBPT*. In HH of Solomon Littlefield, age 42, Drayman, born in Maine.
HASKELL, CALEB, 64, M, Carpenter, W, MA, 190, 276, NBPT.
HASKELL, CALEB N., 34, M, Tin Plate Worker, W, MA, 190, 277, NBPT.
HASKELL, CYRUS A., 21, M, Accountant, W, MA, 190, 276, NBPT. In HH of Caleb Haskell, age 64, Carpenter, born in MA.
HASKELL, DAVID, 74, M, Master Mariner, W, MA, 43, 63, NBPT.
HASKELL, EDNAH M., 28, F, -, W, NB, 190, 276, NBPT. In HH of Caleb Haskell, age 64, Carpenter, born in MA.

HASKELL, EDWARD, 7, M, -, W, LA, 307, 453, NBPT. In HH of Elias Haskell, age 56, Trader, born in MA.
HASKELL, ELIAS, 56, M, Trader, W, MA, 307, 453, NBPT.
HASKELL, FANNY M., 62, F, -, W, NB, 190, 276, NBPT. In HH of Caleb Haskell, age 64, Carpenter, born in MA.
HASKELL, GEORGE, 30, M, Mariner, W, MA, 789,1116, NBPT. In HH of Lois Fullington, age 40, born in MA.
HASKELL, HARRIET L.L., 3, F, -, W, LA, 307, 453, NBPT. In HH of Elias Haskell, age 56, Trader, born in MA.
HASKELL, MARK, 47, M, Teamster, W, MA, 348, 509, NBPT.
HASKELL, MARY A., 37, F, -, W, NH, 348, 509, NBPT. In HH of Mark Haskell, age 47, Teamster, born in MA.
HASKELL, SAMUEL, 22, M, Mariner, W, MA, 790,1118, NBPT. In HH of Benjamin Noble, age 28, Tailor, born in England.
HASKINS, CHARLES, 20, M, Ostler, W, MA, 249, 313, NBPT*. In HH of John J. Haskins, age 48, Painter, born in France.
HASKINS, JOHN J., 48, M, Painter, W, France, 249, 313, NBPT*.
HASKINS, JOHN T., 23, M, Mariner, W, MA, 249, 313, NBPT*. In HH of John J. Haskins, age 48, Painter, born in France.
HASTINGS, JANE, 24, F, -, W, Ireland, 683, 975, NBPT. In HH of George L. Rogers, age 42, Master Mariner, born in MA.
HASTINGS, MARTHA, 18, F, -, W, Ireland, 666, 957, NBPT. In HH of Phineas Parker, age 66, Gentleman, born in MA.
HASTINGS, REBECCA, 21, F, -, W, Ireland, 378, 558, NBPT. In HH of Mary Nelson, age 50, born in MA.
HASTNETT, CORNELIUS, 26, M, Operative in Mill, W, MA, 357, 521, NBPT. In HH of Jeremiah Hastnett, age 24, Operative in Mill, born in Ireland.
HASTNETT, JEREMIAH, 24, M, Operative in Mill, W, MA, 357, 521, NBPT.
HATCH, MANUEL S., 24, M, Combmaker, W, MA, 735,1040, NBPT. In HH of Hannah Hatch, age 63, born in MA.
HAYDEN, (UNKNOWN) MR., 28, M, Telegraph Agent, W, CT, 40, 47, NBPT*. In HH of Frances F. Monroe, age 32, female, Boarding House, born in Maine.
HAYDEN, OTIS, 36, M, Mariner, W, MA, 267, 341, NBPT*.
HAYES, EBENEZER, 33, M, Wool Puller, W, MA, 409, 535, NBPT*.
HAYES, NANCY J., 17, F, -, W, NH, 271, 398, NBPT. In HH of Horace Brown, age 52, Stage Agent, born in MA.
HAYNES, HAMILTON, 33, M, Carriage Maker, W, MA, 269, 344, NBPT*.
HAYNES, SARAH, 32, F, -, W, Maine, 269, 344, NBPT*. In HH of Hamilton Haynes, age 33, Carriage Maker, born in MA.
HAYNES, SOLOMON, 19, M, Carriage Maker, W, Nova Scotia, 269, 344, NBPT*. In HH of Hamilton Haynes, age 33, Carriage Maker, born in MA.
HEATH, RICHARD, 36, M, Joiner, W, MA, 444, 588, NBPT*.
HEDDEN, JOHN, 52, M, Town Crier, W, MA, 189, 275, NBPT.
HEDDEN, MARGARET, 51, F, W, 0, NH, 189, 275, NBPT. In HH

of John Hedden, age 52, Town Crier, born in MA.
HENDERSON, BENJAMIN P., 21, M, Joiner, W, MA, 533, 708, NBPT*. In HH of Charles E. Sweet, age 28, Mason, born in MA.
HENNESY, CATHARINE, 11, F, -, W, Pr. Edward Island, 236, 295, NBPT*. In HH of James Hennesy, age 60, Ship Carpenter, born in Ireland.
HENNESY, JAMES, 60, M, Ship Carpenter, W, Ireland, 236, 295, NBPT*.
HENNESY, JAMES, 18, M, Operative, W, Pr. Edward Island, 236, 295, NBPT*. In HH of James Hennesy, age 60, Ship Carpenter, born in Ireland.
HENNESY, MARGARET, 9, F, -, W, Pr. Edward Island, 236, 295, NBPT*. In HH of James Hennesy, age 60, Ship Carpenter, born in Ireland.
HENNESY, MARY, 15, F, -, W, Pr. Edward Island, 236, 295, NBPT*. In HH of James Hennesy, age 60, Ship Carpenter, born in Ireland.
HENNESY, MARY L., 42, F, -, W, Ireland, 236, 295, NBPT*. In HH of James Hennesy, age 60, Ship Carpenter, born in Ireland.
HENNESY, PATRICK, 19, M, Ship Carpenter, W, Pr. Edward Island, 236, 295, NBPT*. In HH of James Hennesy, age 60, Ship Carpenter, born in Ireland.
HENNESY, PAUL, 13, M, -, W, Pr. Edward Island, 236, 295, NBPT*. In HH of James Hennesy, age 60, Ship Carpenter, born in Ireland.
HERBERT, CHARLES, 43, M, Porter, W, MA, 287, 374, NBPT*.
HERMAN, RUFUS, 37, M, Mariner, W, England, 437, 650, NBPT.

HERRICK, ANSON D., 29, M, Carpenter, W, Maine, 490, 732, NBPT. In HH of Davis Verrill, age 25, Carpenter, born in Maine.
HERRICK, ARBELLA V., 18, F, -, W, Maine, 490, 732, NBPT. In HH of Davis Verrill, age 25, Carpenter, born in Maine.
HERRICK, MARY P., 28, F, -, W, Maine, 490, 732, NBPT. In HH of Davis Verrill, age 25, Carpenter, born in Maine.
HERRIMAN, JEANNA, 3, F, -, W, Ireland, 465, 696, NBPT. In HH of William Herriman, age 34, Laborer, born in Ireland.
HERRIMAN, JOHN, 1, M, -, W, Ireland, 465, 696, NBPT. In HH of William Herriman, age 34, Laborer, born in Ireland.
HERRIMAN, MARY, 25, F, -, W, Ireland, 465, 696, NBPT. In HH of William Herriman, age 34, Laborer, born in Ireland.
HERRIMAN, WILLIAM, 34, M, Laborer, W, Ireland, 465, 696, NBPT.
HERVEY, STEPHEN, 18, M, Porter, W, NH, 782, 1108, NBPT. In HH of Enoch Tilton, age 45, Hotel Keeper, born in NH. In Hotel.
HERVEY, THOMAS, 71, M, House Carpenter, W, MA, 326, 423, NBPT*. In HH of Abraham Williams, age 62, Merchant, born in MA.
HERVY, ELIZABETH, 70, F, -, W, MA, 442, 657, NBPT. In HH of William Hervy, age 70, Boat Builder, born in MA.
HERVY, WILLIAM, 70, M, Boat Builder, W, MA, 442, 657, NBPT.
HERVY, WILLIAM, 25, M, Boat Builder, W, MA, 442, 657, NBPT. In HH of William Hervy, age 70, Boat Builder, born in MA.
HEWS, MARTHA, 21, F, -, W, Ireland, 635, 922, NBPT. In HH of

Carlton Dole, age 52, Gentleman, born in MA.
HEZELTINE, CHARLES, 48, M, Dry Goods Dealer, W, VT, 242, 304, NBPT*.
HEZELTINE, MARY, 43, F, -, W, NH, 242, 304, NBPT*. In HH of Charles Hezeltine, age 48, Dry Goods Dealer, born in VT.
HICKER, JOHN, 24, M, Clerk, W, MA, 219, 273, NBPT*.
HICKER, MARTHA E., 1, F, -, W, Newfoundland, 219, 273, NBPT*. In HH of John Hicker, age 24, Clerk, born in MA.
HICKER, MARY, 66, F, -, W, Newfoundland, 219, 273, NBPT*. In HH of John Hicker, age 24, Clerk, born in MA.
HICKLEY, DAVID R., 30, M, Ironfounder, W, Maine, 291, 381, NBPT*.
HIGGENSON, CATHERINE, 15, F, -, W, Ireland, 66, 96, NBPT. In HH of Owen Higgenson, age 49, Laborer, born in Ireland.
HIGGENSON, ELLEN, 11, F, -, W, Ireland, 66, 96, NBPT. In HH of Owen Higgenson, age 49, Laborer, born in Ireland.
HIGGENSON, MARY, 40, F, -, W, Ireland, 66, 96, NBPT. In HH of Owen Higgenson, age 49, Laborer, born in Ireland.
HIGGENSON, OWEN, 49, M, Laborer, W, Ireland, 66, 96, NBPT.
HIGGENSON, WILLIAM, 13, M, -, W, Ireland, 66, 96, NBPT. In HH of Owen Higgenson, age 49, Laborer, born in Ireland.
HIGGINBOTTOM, CATHERINE, 42, F, -, W, Ireland, 684, 976, NBPT. In HH of Eben F. Stone, age 28, Attorney at Law, born in MA.
HILDRETH, DEXTER, 23, M, Blacksmith, W, Maine, 615, 807, NBPT*.

HILDRETH, HARRIET, 26, F, -, W, Maine, 615, 807, NBPT*. In HH of Dexter Hildreth, age 23, Blacksmith, born in Maine.
HILL, FORDYLE? F., 18, M, Tin Plate Worker, W, Maine, 396, 589, NBPT. In HH of Louisa H. Hill, age 49, born in MA.
HILL, GEORGE W., 50, M, Shoemaker, W, MA, 304, 396, NBPT*.
HILL, GEORGE W., 20, M, Clerk, W, MA, 304, 396, NBPT*. In HH of George W. Hill, age 50, Shoemaker, born in MA.
HILL, HENRY C., 29, M, Shoemaker, W, MA, 203, 254, NBPT*.
HILL, JOHN, 38, M, Farmer, W, Maine, 785, 1111, NBPT.
HILL, LAURA A., 7, F, -, W, Maine, 785, 1111, NBPT. In HH of John Hill, age 38, Farmer, born in Maine.
HILL, MEHETABLE, 50, F, -, W, NH, 304, 396, NBPT*. In HH of George W. Hill, age 50, Shoemaker, born in MA.
HILL, OBADIAH, 17, M, Shoemaker, W, MA, 203, 254, NBPT*. In HH of Henry C. Hill, age 29, Shoemaker, born in MA.
HILL, WALDO A., 14, M, -, W, Maine, 396, 589, NBPT. In HH of Louisa H. Hill, age 49, born in MA.
HILLIARD, CHARLES E., 5, M, -, W, NH, 461, 609, NBPT*. In HH of Timothy Hilliard, age 46, Shoe Store, born in NH.
HILLIARD, FRANCES, 7, F, -, W, NH, 461, 609, NBPT*. In HH of Timothy Hilliard, age 46, Shoe Store, born in NH.
HILLIARD, LUCY, 38, F, -, W, NH, 461, 609, NBPT*. In HH of Timothy Hilliard, age 46, Shoe Store, born in NH.

HILLIARD, TIMOTHY, 46, M, Shoe Store, W, NH, 461, 609, NBPT*.
HILLS, CLARENCE A.B., 22, F, -, W, VT, 612, 893, NBPT. In HH of William Hills, age 70, None, born in MA.
HILLS, HANNAH, 38, F, -, W, Maine, 612, 893, NBPT. In HH of William Hills, age 70, None, born in MA.
HILLS, JOHN, 27, M, Shoemaker, W, MA, 342, 447, NBPT*.
HILLS, MOSES N., 22, M, Clerk, W, MA, 321, 416, NBPT*. In HH of Wid. Joshua Hills, age 55, {female}, born in MA.
HILLS, PHILIP K., 30, M, Custom House Weigher, W, MA, 58, 64, NBPT*.
HILLS, SARAH J., 34, F, -, W, VT, 612, 893, NBPT. In HH of William Hills, age 70, None, born in MA.
HILLS, WILLIAM, 70, M, None, W, MA, 612, 893, NBPT.
HILLS, WILLIAM, 28, M, Shoemaker, W, VT, 612, 893, NBPT. In HH of William Hills, age 70, None, born in MA.
HINCKLEY, BETHIAH, 65, F, -, W, Maine, 260, 328, NBPT*.
HINCKLEY, HANNAH, 27, F, -, W, Maine, 260, 328, NBPT*. In HH of Bethiah Hinckley, age 65, born in Maine.
HINCKLEY, LYDIA, 19, F, -, W, Maine, 260, 328, NBPT*. In HH of Bethiah Hinckley, age 65, born in Maine.
HIND, MARY J.R., 29, F, -, W, Maine, 57, 84, NBPT. In HH of Nath. Hind, age 31, Carpenter, born in NH.
HIND, NATH., 31, M, Carpenter, W, NH, 57, 84, NBPT.
HINKLEY, CYNTHIA, 20, F, -, W, Maine, 431, 640, NBPT. In HH of Oliver P. Wiggin, age 44, Cooper, born in NH.
HINKLEY, CYRUS, 21, M, Iron Foundry, W, Maine, 633, 920, NBPT.
HINKLEY, SUSAN J., 20, F, -, W, Maine, 633, 920, NBPT. In HH of Cyrus P. Hinkley, age 21, Iron foundry, born in Maine.
HOBBERT, JOSHUA, 20, M, Mariner, W, VA, 377, 495, NBPT*. In HH of Margaret Dixon, age 55, born in Ireland.
HODGDON, ADRIEL H., 37, M, Drayman, W, NH, 200, 247, NBPT*.
HODGDON, CHARLES, 32, M, Switchman, W, NH, 55, 61, NBPT*.
HODGDON, CHARLES A., 10, M, -, W, NH, 55, 61, NBPT*. In HH of Charles Hodgdon, age 32, Switchman, born in NH.
HODGDON, LEANDER A., 14, M, -, W, NH, 200, 247, NBPT*. In HH of Adriel H. Hodgdon, age 37, Drayman, born in NH.
HODGDON, MARY E., 18, F, -, W, NH, 476, 713, NBPT. In HH of James Freeman, age 54, Mariner, born in MA.
HODGDON, NAOMI, 32, F, -, W, NH, 55, 61, NBPT*. In HH of Charles Hodgdon, age 32, Switchman, born in NH.
HODGDON, SARAH, 14, F, -, W, NH, 200, 247, NBPT*. In HH of Adriel H. Hodgdon, age 37, Drayman, born in NH.
HODGE, CHARLES, 75, M, None, W, MA, 157, 188, NBPT*.
HODGE, CHARLES, 21, M, Apothecary, W, MA, 235, 342, NBPT. In HH of Nathaniel Hodge, age 57, Shoemaker, born in MA.
HODGE, CHARLES M., 34, M, Apothecary, W, MA, 159, 192, NBPT*.

HODGE, NATHANIEL, 57, M, Shoemaker, W, MA, 235, 342, NBPT.
HODGE, WILLIAM G., 45, M, Overseer Harness, W, MA, 567, 753, NBPT*.
HODGEDON, ABBY, 25, F, -, W, NH, 479, 719, NBPT. In HH of Moses Hodgdon, age 28, Teamster, born in Maine.
HODGEDON, MOSES, 28, M, Teamster, W, Maine, 479, 719, NBPT.
HODGEKINS, JACOB F., 32, M, Jeweler, W, MA, 241, 350, NBPT.
HODGKINS, GEORGE A., 19, M, Mariner, W, MA, 133, 158, NBPT*. In HH of Thomas Hodgkins, age 42, Painter, born in MA.
HODGKINS, HALL, 38, M, Ship Carpenter, W, Maine, 14, 16, NBPT*. In HH of Joseph Huse, age 57, Painter, born in MA.
HODGKINS, JOSEPH, 67, M, Ship Carpenter, W, NH, 316, 409, NBPT*.
HODGKINS, LYDIA, 17, F, -, W, Maine, 450, 673, NBPT. In HH of Elizabeth Garland, age 53, born in NH.
HODGKINS, MARY S., 54, F, -, W, NH, 316, 409, NBPT*. In HH of Joseph Hodgkins, age 67, Ship Carpenter, born in NH.
HODGKINS, THOMAS, 42, M, Painter, W, MA, 133, 158, NBPT*.
HOLKER, CATHERINE, 37, F, -, W, England, 757, 1068, NBPT. In HH of John Holker, age 42, Operative, born in England.
HOLKER, ELIZABETH, 11, F, -, W, England, 757,1068, NBPT. In HH of John Holker, age 42, Operative, born in England.
HOLKER, JOHN, 42, M, Operative, W, England, 757,1068, NBPT.
HOLKER, JOHN, 13, M, -, W, England, 757,1068, NBPT. In HH of John Holker, age 42, Operative, born in England.
HOLKER, MIVRAVN?, 5, M, -, W, England, 757,1068, NBPT. In HH of John Holker, age 42, Operative, born in England.
HOLLAND, EDWARD H., 46, M, Hatter, W, MA, 643, 930, NBPT.
HOLLAND, MARGARET, 1, F, -, W, Ireland, 178, 257, NBPT. In HH of Patrick Holland, age 26, Laborer, born in Ireland.
HOLLAND, MARY, 30, F, -, W, Ireland, 272, 349, NBPT*. In HH of Timothy Holland, age 33, Laborer, born in Ireland.
HOLLAND, MARY, 27, F, -, W, Ireland, 178, 257, NBPT. In HH of Patrick Holland, age 26, Laborer, born in Ireland.
HOLLAND, PATRICK, 26, M, Laborer, W, Ireland, 178, 257, NBPT.
HOLLAND, TIMOTHY, 33, M, Laborer, W, Ireland, 272, 349, NBPT*.
HOLLISTER, ELIZABETH, 47, F, -, W, England, 370, 487, NBPT*. In HH of Jacob Hollister, age 52, Hatter, born in England.
HOLLISTER, JACOB, 52, M, Hatter, W, England, 370, 487, NBPT*.
HOLLODEY, JOHN, 68, M, Merchant, W, MA, 783,1109, NBPT.
HOLMES, SHEDAH, 21, F, -, W, Maine, 132, 195, NBPT. In HH of William Holmes, age 21, Overseer in Mill, born in England.
HOLMES, WILLIAM, 21, M, Overseer in Mill, W, England, 132, 195, NBPT.
HOLT, ALTHEA, 23, F, -, W, Maine, 736,1041, NBPT. In HH of John L. Grindal, age 48, Grocer,

born in Maine.
HONAN, ALICE, 15, F, -, W, Ireland, 211, 262, NBPT*. In Boarding House.
HONAN, MARY, 17, F, -, W, Ireland, 211, 262, NBPT*. In Boarding House.
HONEST, JOHN, 67, M, Laborer, W, Holland, 445, 589, NBPT*.
HOOD, SAMUEL, 25, M, Bootmaker, W, N.S., 626, 912, NBPT. In HH of Luther R. Chase, age 30, Carriage Maker, born in MA.
HOOK, WILLIAM, 27, M, Operative, W, Maine, 62, 89, NBPT. In HH of Phebe Cook, age 64, born in MA.
HOOKE, HARRIET, 32, F, -, W, Maine, 676, 968, NBPT. In HH of Sarah Hooke, age 75, born in MA.
HOOKE, JOHN, 11, M, -, W, Maine, 676, 968, NBPT. In HH of Sarah Hooke, age 75, born in MA.
HOPKINS, ELLEN, 30, F, -, W, Ireland, 466, 698, NBPT. In HH of Patrick Hopkins, age 40, Laborer, born in Ireland.
HOPKINS, JOHN, 7, M, -, W, England, 466, 698, NBPT. In HH of Patrick Hopkins, age 40, Laborer, born in Ireland.
HOPKINS, PATRICK, 40, M, Laborer, W, Ireland, 466, 698, NBPT.
HOPKINSON, CHARLES, 16, M, Painter, W, MA, 241, 303, NBPT*. In HH of Julia A. Hopkinson, age 44, born in MA.
HOPKINSON, FRANCIS, 20, M, Shoemaker, W, NH, 241, 303, NBPT*. In HH of Julia A. Hopkinson, age 44, born in MA.
HORTELL, HENRY, 20, M, Baker, W, England, 591, 868, NBPT. In HH of Samuel T. Payson, age 34, Baker, born in MA.
HORTON, ALFRED, 24, M, Traller?, W, MA, 183, 224, NBPT*. In HH of Nathaniel Horton, age 64, Boots Shoe Dealer, born in MA.
HORTON, ANGELINE, 37, F, -, W, Maine, 731,1031, NBPT. In HH of Daniel Horton, age 38, Hatter, born in MA.
HORTON, CHARLES, 34, M, Goldsmith, W, MA, 47, 52, NBPT*
HORTON, CLARA, 22, F, -, W, RI, 196, 241, NBPT*. In HH of Samuel Horton, age 33, Tinner, born in MA.
HORTON, DANIEL, 38, M, Hatter, W, MA, 310, 403, NBPT*.
HORTON, DANIEL, 38, M, Hatter, W, MA, 731,1031, NBPT.
HORTON, EDWARD B., 22, M, Trader, W, MA, 183, 224, NBPT*. In HH of Nathaniel Horton, age 64, Boots Shoe Dealer, born in MA.
HORTON, FREDERICK W., 18, M, Assist. in Shoe Store, W, MA, 183, 224, NBPT*. In HH of Nathaniel Horton, age 64, Boots Shoe Dealer, born in MA.
HORTON, JACOB, 52, M, Merchant, W, MA, 128, 153, NBPT*.
HORTON, JAMES M., 31, M, Clerk, W, MA, 183, 224, NBPT*. In HH of Nathaniel Horton, age 64, Boots Shoe Dealer, born in MA.
HORTON, JOHN, 70, M, Cordwainer, W, MA, 197, 243, NBPT*.
HORTON, JOHN, JR., 45, M, Goldsmith, W, MA, 67, 76, NBPT*.
HORTON, NATHANIEL, 64, M, Boots Shoe Dealer, W, MA, 183, 224, NBPT*.
HORTON, SAMUEL, 33, M, Tinner, W, MA, 196, 241, NBPT*.
HORTON, SAMUEL, 26, M, Tinman, W, MA, 197, 243, NBPT*. In HH of John Horton, age 70, Cordwainer, born in MA.
HORTON, WILLIAM, 27, M, Tin

Plate Worker, W, MA, 138, 164, NBPT*.
HOUFIN, JAMES, 8, M, -, W, Ireland, 264, 386, NBPT. In HH of Thomas Houfin, age 27, None, born in Ireland.
HOUFIN, JOHANNA, 25, F, -, W, Ireland, 264, 386, NBPT. In HH of Thomas Houfin, age 27, None, born in Ireland.
HOUFIN, MARY, 6, F, -, W, Ireland, 264, 386, NBPT. In HH of Thomas Houfin, age 27, None, born in Ireland.
HOUFIN, THOMAS, 27, M, None, W, Ireland, 264, 386, NBPT.
HOUGUE, SARAH, 60, F, -, W, NH, 111, 164, NBPT.
HOUSE, LOUISA, 46, F, -, W, NH, 788,1114, NBPT. In Poor House. .
HOUSTIN, THADEUS, 24, M, Cord Stripper, 0, NH, 177, 256, NBPT. In HH of James N. Canney, age 41, Teamster, born in NH.
HOUSTINE, ELIZABETH, 30, F, -, W, Ireland, 181, 261, NBPT. In HH of Robert Houstine, age 27, Laborer, born in Ireland.
HOUSTINE, MARY A., 5, F, -, W, NY, 181, 261, NBPT. In HH of Robert Houstine, age 27, Laborer, born in Ireland.
HOUSTINE, ROBERT, 27, M, Laborer, W, Ireland, 181, 261, NBPT.
HOUSTINE, WILLIAM, 3, M, - W, W, NY, 181, 261, NBPT. In HH of Robert Houstine, age 27, Laborer, born in Ireland.
HOW, JOHN, 19, M, Operative, W, MA, 515, 686, NBPT*. In HH of George P. Garland, age 65, Boarding House, born in NJ.
HOWARD, ANN, 37, F, -, W, Maine, 99, 145, NBPT. In HH of Thomas Howard, age 41, Master Mariner, born in Maine.

HOWARD, BENJ. F., 41, M, Shoemaker, W, Maine, 644, 931, NBPT.
HOWARD, DORCAS, 34, F, -, W, Maine, 644, 931, NBPT. In HH of Benj. F. Howard, age 41, Shoemaker, born in Maine.
HOWARD, EDWARD, 76, M, Reading Room Keeper, W, MA, 180, 221, NBPT*. In HH of Nancy Pickman, age 76, born in MA.
HOWARD, HANNAH, 30, F, -, W, England, 190, 234, NBPT*.
HOWARD, JOSEPH H., 36, M, Master Mariner, W, Maine, 89, 130, NBPT. In HH of Sarah Peirce, age 63, born in MA.
HOWARD, LYDIA F., 22, F, -, W, Maine, 122, 179, NBPT. In HH of James Pentland, age 36, Overseer in Mill, born in England.
HOWARD, THOMAS, 41, M, Master Mariner, W, Maine, 99, 145, NBPT.
HOWARD, WILLIAM H., 15, M, None, W, MA, 175, 213, NBPT*. In HH of Sarah C. Howard, age 46, born in MA.
HOYT, ABEL C., 33, M, None, W, MA, 325, 422, NBPT*. In HH of Joseph C. Hoyt, age 36, Master Mariner, born in MA.
HOYT, ADALAIDE, 6, F, -, W, NH, 766,1082, NBPT. In HH of Jemima Hoyt, age 50, born in NH.
HOYT, AMBERTHA J., 8, M, -, W, RI, 757,1067, NBPT. In HH of William Bell age 42, Operative, born in England.
HOYT, DAVID W., 17, M, Student, W, MA, 217, 270, NBPT*. In HH of Nicholas Medbury, age 50, Bap. Clergyman, born in MA.
HOYT, ELBRIDGE G., 41, M, Blacksmith, W, MA, 432, 566, NBPT*.
HOYT, GEORGE, 13, M, -, W, NH, 766,1082, NBPT. In HH of

Jemima Hoyt, age 50, born in NH.
HOYT, HENRY, 18, M, Mariner, W, NH, 766,1082, NBPT. In HH of Jemima Hoyt, age 50, born in NH.
HOYT, JOSEPH, 36, M, Master Mariner, W, MA, 325, 422, NBPT*.
HOYT, MARY A., 24, F, -, W,NH, 766,1082, NBPT. In HH of Jemima Hoyt, age 50, born in NH.
HOYT, MERRISIN, 74, F, -, W, NH, 431, 640, NBPT. In HH of Oliver P. Wiggin, age 44, Cooper, born in NH.
HOYT, RHODA, 28, F, -, W, NH, 226, 280, NBPT*. In HH of Samuel D. Hoyt, age 29, Ship Master, born in MA.
HOYT, SAMUEL D., 29, M, Ship Master, W, MA, 226, 280, NBPT*.
HUBBARD, MARY, 20, F, -, W, Maine, 200, 247, NBPT*. In HH of Adriel H. Hodgdon, age 37, Drayman, born in NH.
HUBBARD, NANCY, 15, F, -, W, Maine, 200, 247, NBPT*. In HH of Adriel H. Hodgdon, age 37, Drayman, born in NH.
HUFFANY, ALICE, 35, F, -, W, England, 166, 199, NBPT*. In Hotel run by Thomas Brown, age 49, born in MA.
HUGGETT, SARAH, 79, F, -, W, Maine, 90, 131, NBPT.
HUNT, GEORGE B., 14, M, None, W, MA, 217, 322, NBPT. In HH of Nathaniel Hunt, age 51, Ship Carpenter, born in MA.
HUNT, GIDEON W., 41, M, Ship Carpenter, W, MA, 705,1000, NBPT.
HUNT, JOHN B., 17, M, Mariner, W, MA, 216, 321, NBPT. In HH of John W. Hunt, age 46, Ship Carpenter, born in MA.
HUNT, JOHN W., 46, M, Ship Carpenter, W, MA, 216, 321,NBPT.
HUNT, JOSEPH, 38, M, Painter, W, MA, 371, 545, NBPT.
HUNT, MARY W., 39, F, -, W, NH, 705,1000, NBPT. In HH of Gideon W. Hunt, age 41, Ship Carpenter, born in MA.
HUNT, NATHANIEL, 51, M, Ship Carpenter, W, MA, 217, 322, NBPT.
HUNTEE, MICHAEL, 44, M, Peddler, W, NH, 286, 372, NBPT*.
HUNTINGTON, JANE C., 25, F, -, W, Maine, 151, 181, NBPT*. In HH of Samuel B. Huntington, age 34, Wheelwright, born in Canada.
HUNTINGTON, SAMUEL B., 34, M, Wheelwright, W, Canada, 151, 181, NBPT*.
HURBISH, FRANCES, 16, F, -, W, Maine, 276, 406, NBPT. In HH of Jacob Stickney, age 76, Cabinetmaker, born in MA.
HURBISH, HENRETTA T., 16, F, -, W, Maine, 276, 406, NBPT. In HH of Jacob Stickney, age 76, Cabinetmaker, born in MA.
HURLEY, MARGARET, 2, F, -, W, Ireland, 235, 293, NBPT*. In HH of Rachel Hurley, age 31, born in Ireland.
HURLEY, RACHEL, 31, F, -, W, Ireland, 235, 293, NBPT*.
HUSE, CALEB, 16, M, Painter, W, MA, 14, 16, NBPT*. In HH of Joseph Huse, age 57, Painter, born in MA.
HUSE, CHARLES L., 32, M, Painter, W, MA, 218, 271, NBPT*.
HUSE, ENOCH, 55, M, Tobacconist, W, MA, 564, 838, NBPT.
HUSE, GEORGE A., 29, M, Painter, W, MA, 14, 16, NBPT*. In HH of Joseph Huse, age 57, Painter, born in MA.
HUSE, JOHN, 42, M, Tobacco Manufacturer, W, MA, 194, 238, NBPT*.

HUSE, JOSEPH, 57, M, Painter, W, MA, 14, 16, NBPT*.
HUSE, RALPH C., 44, M, Morocco Dresser, W, MA, 132, 157, NBPT*.
HUSE, SAMUEL, 50, M, Machinist, W, MA, 82, 91, NBPT*.
HUSE, SAMUEL, 40, M, Tanner, W, MA, 506, 674, NBPT*.
HUSE, SAMUEL JR., 18, M, Mariner, W, MA, 82, 91, NBPT*. In HH of Samuel Huse, age 50, Machinist, born in MA.
HUSE, WILLIAM, 27, M, Tobacconist, W, MA, 368, 542, NBPT.
HUSE, WILLIAM H., 26, M, Printer, W, MA, 215, 267, NBPT*.
HUTCHINS, ANN, 24, F, -, W, Maine, 222, 328, NBPT. In HH of Abigail Wilson, age 53, born in MA.
HUTCHINS, AVRALINE, 22, F, -, W, Maine, 222, 328, NBPT. In HH of Abigail Wilson, age 53, born in MA.
HUTCHINS, LACETTA, 17, F, -, W, Maine, 222, 328, NBPT. In HH of Abigail Wilson, age 53, born in MA.
HUTCHINS, MARY, 28, F, -, W, Maine, 222, 328, NBPT. In HH of Abigail Wilson, age 53, born in MA.
HUZZEY, LEONARD, 25, M, -, W, Maine, 109, 162, NBPT. In HH of Margaret Hickman, age 58, born in MA.
HUZZEY, SARAH, 24, F, -, W, Maine, 109, 162, NBPT. In HH of Margaret Hickman, age 58, born in MA.
HYNES, WILLIAM H., 26, M, Ship Carpenter, W, MA, 465, 617, NBPT*.

- I -

ILSLEY, MOSES, 20, M, Carpenter, W, MA, 151, 220, NBPT. In HH of Hannah White, age 45, born in Maine.
INGALLS, DAVID, 42, M, Merchant, W, Maine, 442, 657, NBPT. In HH of William Hervy, age 70, Boat Builder, born in MA.
INGERHAM, L.P., 20, M, Machinist, W, RI, 561, 834, NBPT. In HH of Mary Dorr, age 65, born in MA.
INGRAHAM, GEORGE L.P., 18, M, Clerk, W, MA, 678, 970, NBPT. In HH of L.P. Ingraham, age 44, Machinist, born in MA.
INGRAHAM, HERBERT, 30, M, Machinist, W, RI, 674, 966, NBPT.
INGRAHAM, L.P., 44, M, Machinist, W, MA, 678, 970, NBPT.
INGRAHAM, LEMUEL, 46, M, Machinist, W, MA, 678, 970, NBPT. In HH of L.P. Ingraham, age 44, Machinist, born in MA.
IRELAND, JEREMIAH R., 28, M, Mason, W, MA, 550, 821, NBPT.
IRELAND, NANCY, 22, F, -, W, NH, 478, 716, NBPT. In HH of Nathn. Ireland, age 26, Painter, born in MA.
IRELAND, NATHN., 26, M, Painter, W, MA, 478, 716, NBPT.
IRISH, ELIZABETH, 22, F, -, W, Ireland, 67, 76, NBPT*. In HH of John Horton, Jr., age 45, Goldsmith, born in MA.
IRVING, JOHN, 31, m, Printer, W, Maine, 25, 30, NBPT*.
ISLEY, JOSEPH, 34, M, Carpenter, W, MA, 372, 547, NBPT.
ISLEY, MARY J., 34, F, -, W, Maine, 372, 547, NBPT. In HH of Joseph Isley, age 34, Carpenter, born in MA.
IVERS, ANN, 41, F, -, W, Ireland,

169, 203, NBPT*. In HH of Benjamin Ivers, age 49, Fireman, born in Ireland.

IVERS, BENJAMIN, 49, M, Fireman, Enex., W, Ireland, 169, 203, NBPT*.

IVORY, LUCINDA, 24, F, -, W, Ireland, 472, 626, NBPT*. In HH of William Ivory, age 24, Shop Carpenter, born in New Brunswick.

IVORY, WILLIAM, 24, M, Shop Carpenter, W, New Brunswick, 472, 626, NBPT*.

- J -

JACK, ANDREW, 27, M, Painter, W, Maine, 334, 436, NBPT*.

JACK, EMILY A., 29, F, -, W, Maine, 334, 436, NBPT*. In HH of Andrew Jack, age 27, Painter, born in Maine.

JACK, MARTHA J., 2, F, -, W, RI, 334, 436, NBPT*. In HH of Andrew Jack, age 27, Painter, born in Maine.

JACKMAN, GEORGE, 46, M, Sailmaker, W, MA, 788,1114, NBPT. In Poor House.

JACKMAN, JOHN JR., 24, M, Engineer, W, MA, 383, 506, NBPT*.

JACKMAN, SAMUEL JR., 40, M, Machine Shop, W, MA, 443, 586, NBPT*.

JACKSON, CHARLES A.J., 43, M, None, B, MA, 788,1114, NBPT. In Poor House.

JACKSON, JAMES, 38, M, -, B, MA, 78, 87, NBPT*. In Jail. Discharged.

JACKSON, JOANNA, 49, F, -, W, Sweden, 12, 13, NBPT*. In HH of Nathaniel Jackson, age 68, Surveyor of the Port, born in MA.

JACKSON, NATHANIEL, 68, M, Surveyor of the Port, W, MA, 12, 13, NBPT*.

JACKSON, PHEBE, 52, F,- , B, MA, 600, 790, NBPT*. In HH of Andrew Raymond, age 50, Barber, Mulatto, born in MA.

JAMES, ELLEN, 20, F, -, W, England, 370, 487, NBPT*. In HH of Jacob Hollister, age 52, Hatter, born in England.

JAMES, LUCY, 16, F, -, W, NH, 405, 529, NBPT*. In HH of Miriam James, age 50, born in NH.

JAMES, MIRIAM, 50, F, -, W, NH, 405, 529, NBPT*.

JAMES, SARAH, 4, F, -, W, NH, 405, 529, NBPT*. In HH of Miriam James, age 50, born in NH.

JAMES, WILLIAM, 22, M, Stone Cutter, W, England, 370, 487, NBPT*. In HH of Jacob Hollister, age 52, Hatter, born in England.

JAMESON, MARY, 30, F, -, W, Canada, 150, 219, NBPT. In HH of David Frost, age 36, Truck man, born in Maine.

JAMESON, SHAW, 25, M, Laborer, W, Canada, 450, 673, NBPT. In HH of Elizabeth Garland, age 53, born in NH.

JAMESON, WILLIAM, 48, M, Sailmaker, W, RI, 439, 581, NBPT*.

JANVERIN, JOSEPH, 38, M, Master Mariner, W, MA, 165, 239, NBPT.

JAQUES, AMOS F., 27, M, Tobacconist, W, MA, 551, 734, NBPT*.

JAQUES, BENJN. H., 37, M, Mariner, W, MA, 97, 141, NBPT.

JAQUES, DAVID, 68, F, Truck man, W, MA, 85, 97, NBPT*.

JAQUES, EDMUND, 24, M, Overseer in Mill, W, MA, 144, 212, NBPT. In HH of Thomas Currier,

43, Shoemaker, born in MA.
JAQUES, HENRY, 60, M, Painter, W, MA, 270, 347, NBPT*.
JEFFERS, JAMES, 10, M, -, W, Newfoundland, 303, 445, NBPT. In HH of William Jeffers, age 50, Mariner, born in Ireland.
JEFFERS, JOSEPH, 7, M, -, W, Newfoundland, 303, 445, NBPT. In HH of William Jeffers, age 50, Mariner, born in Ireland.
JEFFERS, MARY, 15, F, -, W, Newfoundland, 303, 445, NBPT. In HH of William Jeffers, age 50, Mariner, born in Ireland.
JEFFERS, MICHAEL, 13, M, -, W, Newfoundland, 303, 445, NBPT. In HH of William Jeffers, age 50, Mariner, born in Ireland.
JEFFERS, PATRICK, 10, M, -, W, Newfoundland, 303, 445, NBPT. In HH of William Jeffers, age 50, Mariner, born in Ireland.
JEFFERS, ROXANNE, 35, F, -, W, Ireland, 303, 445, NBPT. In HH of William Jeffers, age 50, Mariner, born in Ireland.
JEFFERS, WILLIAM, 50, M, Mariner, W, Ireland, 303, 445, NBPT.
JENKINS, JONNA, 23, F, -, W, NH, 90, 131, NBPT. In HH of Sarah Huggett, age 79, born in Maine.
JENNESS, SUSAN, 28, F, -, W, NH, 445, 662, NBPT. In HH of Elizabeth C. Perkins, age 53, born in MA.
JEWETT, JOSEPH, 56, M, Mariner, W, France, 184, 268, NBPT.
JEWETT, WILLIAM, 52, M, Blacksmith, W, MA, 592, 869, NBPT.
JEWITT, EBEN, 44, M, Blacksmith, W, MA, 542, 812, NBPT.
JOHNSON, CHARLES, 30, M, Carpenter, W, MA, 608, 888, NBPT. In HH of Mary J. Hardy, age 38, born in Maine.
JOHNSON, CHARLES, 25, M, Painter, W, Sweden, 322, 417, NBPT*. In HH of Sally Woodman, age 67, born MA.
JOHNSON, DANIEL, 23, M, Grocer, W, MA, 778,1104, NBPT.
JOHNSON, EBESER, 59, M, Town Clerk, W, MA, 250, 361, NBPT.
JOHNSON, ELEAZOR, 75, M, None, W, MA, 353, 514, NBPT.
JOHNSON, ELISA J.G., 1, F, -, W, England, 387, 510, NBPT*. In HH of William Johnson, age 39, Shoemaker, born in England.
JOHNSON, ELISABETH, 9, F, -, W, England, 387, 510, NBPT*. In HH of William Johnson, age 39, Shoemaker, born in England.
JOHNSON, FRANCES W., 19, M, Clerk, W, MA, 433, 645, NBPT. In HH of Jonathan G. Johnson, age 59, Physician, born in MA.
JOHNSON, FRANCIS, 18, M, Mariner, W, MA, 732,1034, NBPT. In HH of Patrick Johnson, age 40, Operative, born in Ireland.
JOHNSON, FREDERICK W., 16, M, Clerk, W, MA, 492, 734, NBPT. In HH of Philip Johnson, age 58, Merchant, born in MA.
JOHNSON, GILMAN, 24, M, Engineer, W, MA, 433, 645, NBPT. In HH of Jonathan G. Johnson, age 59, Physician, born in MA.
JOHNSON, GRACE, 15, F, -, W, England, 750,1058, NBPT. In HH of John Bowman, age 22, Mule Spinner, born in England.
JOHNSON, HANNAH R., 50, F, -, W, NH, 698, 990, NBPT. In HH of Harrison J.O. Johnson, age 51, Grocer, born in NH.
JOHNSON, HARRISON G., 27, M, Trader, W, MA, 184, 225, NBPT*.

JOHNSON, HARRISON J.O., 51, M, Grocer, W, NH, 698, 990, NBPT.
JOHNSON, HENRY, 54, M, Merchant, W, MA, 329, 485, NBPT.
JOHNSON, ISAAC, 63, M, Painter, W, MA, 424, 629, NBPT.
JOHNSON, JACOB P., 26, M, Mariner, W, MA, 433, 645, NBPT. In HH of Jonathan G. Johnson, age 59, Physician, born in MA.
JOHNSON, JOHN, 32, M, Express man, W, MA, 424, 629, NBPT. In HH of Isaac Johnson, age 63, Painter, born in MA.
JOHNSON, JONATHAN G., 59, M, Physician, W, MA, 433, 645, NBPT.
JOHNSON, JOSEPH, 48, M, Merchant, W, MA, 141, 167, NBPT*.
JOHNSON, JOSEPH H., 19, M, Mariner, B, MA, 545, 816, NBPT. In HH of John Young, age 32, Barber, black, born in MA.
JOHNSON, LEWIS H., 17, M, Clerk, W, MA, 433, 645, NBPT. In HH of Jonathan G. Johnson, age 59, Physician, born in MA.
JOHNSON, LYDIA, 38, F, -, W, England, 387, 510, NBPT*. In HH of William Johnson, age 39, Shoemaker, born in England.
JOHNSON, MARY, 67, F, -, W, Ireland, 258, 326, NBPT*.
JOHNSON, MARY, 17, F, -, W, England, 750,1058, NBPT. In HH of John Bowman, age 22, Mule Spinner, born in England.
JOHNSON, MARY A., 45, F, -, W, MA, 788,1114, NBPT. In Poor House. .
JOHNSON, NICHOLAS, 22, M, Merchant, W, MA, 377, 557, NBPT.
JOHNSON, PATRICK, 40, M, Operative, W, Ireland, 732,1034, NBPT.
JOHNSON, PAUL, 50, M, Master Mariner, W, MA, 159, 228, NBPT.
JOHNSON, PHILIP, 58, M, Merchant, W, MA, 492, 734, NBPT.
JOHNSON, RICHARD, 38, M, Ship master, W, MA, 141, 168, NBPT*. In HH of William A. Johnson, age 42, Merchant, born in MA.
JOHNSON, SAMUEL, 30, M, Blacksmith, W, MA, 424, 629, NBPT. In HH of Isaac Johnson, age 63, Painter, born in MA.
JOHNSON, SAMUEL O., 28, M, Fruit Dealer, W, MA, 523, 780, NBPT.
JOHNSON, SUSAN, 22, F, -, W, Ireland, 39, 46, NBPT*. In HH of Parker M. Dole, age 65, farmer, born in MA.
JOHNSON, THOMAS, 30, M, Operative, W, England, 39, 46, NBPT*. In HH of Parker M. Dole, age 65, farmer, born in MA.
JOHNSON, WILLIAM, 39, M, Shoemaker, W, England, 387, 510, NBPT*.
JOHNSON, WILLIAM, 21, M, Clerk, W, MA, 424, 629, NBPT. In HH of Isaac Johnson, age 63, Painter, born in MA.
JOHNSON, WILLIAM, 16, M, Mariner, W, MA, 732,1034, NBPT. In HH of Patrick Johnson, age 40, Operative, born in Ireland.
JOHNSON, WILLIAM A., 42, M, Merchant, W, MA, 141, 168, NBPT*.
JOHNSON, WILLIAM H., 29, M, Master Mariner, W, MA, 380, 561, NBPT. In HH of Samuel Lunt, age 42, Operative, born in MA.
JOHNSTON, JOHN, 36, M, Shoemaker, W, MA, 414, 542,

NBPT*.
JOHNSTON, LAVINA, 41, F, -, W, MA, 204, 301, NBPT.
JOHNSTON, THOMAS, 78, M, Painter, W, MA, 353, 465, NBPT*.
JOHNSTON, WILLIAM, 21, M, None, MA, 204, 301, NBPT. In HH of Lavina Johnson, age 41, born in MA.
JONES, ABBY, 18, F, -, W, NH, 775,1098, NBPT. In HH of William W. Dean, age 23, Mariner, born in MA.
JONES, ANTHONEY S., 48, M, Druggist, W, NH, 376, 556, NBPT. In HH of Mary Jones, age 80, born in MA.
JONES, ELIZA, 22, F, -, W, NH, 588, 865, NBPT. In HH of Stilman Simonds, age 43, Shoemaker, born in MA.
JONES, JANE, 20, F, -, W, NH, 775,1098, NBPT. In HH of William W. Dean, age 23, Mariner, born in MA.
JONES, JOHN, 31, M, Charge of R R.Bridge, W, MA, 302, 394, NBPT*.
JONES, JOHN B., 50, M, Shoemaker, W, NH, 182, 263, NBPT.
JONES, MARY C., 27, F, -, W, NH, 45, 67, NBPT. In HH of Michjah B. Kimball, age 27, Shoemaker, born in MA.
JONES, OLIVER O., 36, M, Master Mariner, W, MA, 31, 43, NBPT.
JONES, SARAH J., 20, F, -, W, Maine, 282, 361, NBPT*. In HH of Mary N. Talbot, age 41, born in Maine.
JONES, SEWELL, 40, M, Harness maker, W, NH, 438, 577, NBPT*. In HH of Mary Tilton, age 63, born in NH.
JONES, STEPHEN, 44, M, Charge of Bridge, W, MA, 305, 397, NBPT*.
JONES, WILLIAM B., 42, M, Blacksmith, W, NH, 437, 650, NBPT.
JONES, WILLIAM P., 23, M, Silversmith, W, MA, 333, 433, NBPT*.
JORDAN, MARY J., 22, F, -, W, Ireland, 214, 316, NBPT. In HH of Ashbell G. Vermilye, age 27, O.S. Presbyterian Clergyman, born in NJ.
JORDAN, SIMEON, 39, M, Shoemaker, W, MA, 442, 658, NBPT.
JORDON, MARGARET, 20, F, -, W, Maine, 140, 166, NBPT*. In HH of Hannah T. Marshall, age 39, Boarding House, born in MA.
JOY, CATHERINE, 29, F, -, W, Newfoundland, 273, 401, NBPT. In HH of Richard Joy, age 29, Mariner, born in Newfoundland.
JOY, CATHERINE, 4, F, -, W, Newfoundland, 263, 382, NBPT. In HH of John Joy, age 39, Mariner, born in Ireland.
JOY, ELLEN, 23, F, -, W, Newfoundland, 532, 795, NBPT. In HH of Walter Joy, age 27, Mariner, born in Newfoundland.
JOY, FRANCES, 5, M, -, W, Newfoundland, 273, 401, NBPT. In HH of Richard Joy, age 29, Mariner, born in Newfoundland.
JOY, JOHN, 39, M, Mariner, W, Ireland, 263, 382, NBPT.
JOY, MARGARET, 13, F, -, W, Newfoundland, 263, 382, NBPT. In HH of John Joy, age 39, Mariner, born in Ireland.
JOY, MARY, 13, F, -, W, Newfoundland, 263, 382, NBPT. In HH of John Joy, age 39, Mariner, born in Ireland.
JOY, MARY B., 33, F, -, W, Newfoundland, 263, 382, NBPT. In HH of John Joy, age 39, Mariner,

born in Ireland.
JOY, RICHARD, 29, M, Mariner, W, Newfoundland, 273, 401, NBPT.
JOY, THOMAS, 9, M, -, W, Newfoundland, 263, 382, NBPT. In HH of John Joy, age 39, Mariner, born in Ireland.
JOY, WALTER, 27, M, Mariner, W, Newfoundland, 532, 795, NBPT.

- K -

KALLAHER, BRIDGET, 21, F, -, W, Ireland, 130, 155, NBPT*. In HH of C.S. Merchant, age 54, U.S. Army, born in NY.
KAVANAGH, DAVID, 52, M, Mariner, W, MA, 420, 548, NBPT*.
KAVANAGH, JOHN, 26, M, Mariner, W, MA, 201, 250, NBPT*.
KAVANAGH, MARY, 20, F, -, W, Ireland, 201, 250, NBPT*. In HH of John Kavanagh, age 26, Mariner, born in MA.
KAVANAGH, MICHAEL, 16, M, Mariner, W, MA, 420, 548, NBPT*. In HH of David Kavanagh, age 52, Mariner, born in MA.
KAVANAGH, THOMAS, 20, M, Operative, W, MA, 420, 548, NBPT*. In HH of David Kavanagh, age 52, Mariner, born in MA.
KEEKE, JOANNA, 18, F, -, W, Ireland, 571, 757, NBPT*. In HH of Joseph Akerman, age 40, Victualer, born in MA.
KEEP, ELLEN M.C., 25, F, -, W, Nova Scotia, 200, 295, NBPT. In HH of John Whitty, age 48, Caulker, born in Ireland.
KEEP, JOHN, 25, M, Laborer, W, Ireland, 200, 295, NBPT. In HH of John Whitty, age 48, Caulker, born in Ireland.
KELLER, MARGARET, 22, F, -, W, Ireland, 788,1114, NBPT. In Poor House. .
KELLEY, HANNAH, 54, F, W, 0, Nova Scotia, 173, 252, NBPT.
KELLEY, HONORA, 22, F, -, W, Ireland, 464, 693, NBPT. In HH of Owen Kelley, age 32, Laborer, born in Ireland.
KELLEY, JAMES, 15, M, W, 0, Nova Scotia, 173, 252, NBPT. In HH of Hannah Kelley, age 54, born Nova Scotia.
KELLEY, JOHN, 7, M, W, 0, Nova Scotia, 173, 252, NBPT. In HH of Hannah Kelley, age 54, born Nova Scotia.
KELLEY, MARY A., 10, F, -, W, Nova Scotia, 173, 252, NBPT. In HH of Hannah Kelley, age 54, born Nova Scotia.
KELLEY, MARY A., 4, F, -, W, Ireland, 464, 693, NBPT. In HH of Owen Kelley, age 32, Laborer, born in Ireland.
KELLEY, MICHAEL, 12, M, W, 0, Nova Scotia, 173, 252, NBPT. In HH of Hannah Kelley, age 54, born Nova Scotia.
KELLEY, OWEN, 32, M, Laborer, W, Ireland, 464, 693, NBPT.
KELLEY, PATRICK, 3, M, -, W, Ireland, 464, 693, NBPT. In HH of Owen Kelley, age 32, Laborer, born in Ireland.
KELLY, ANN, 19, F, -, W, Ireland, 430, 637, NBPT. In HH of Abraham Wheelwright, age 92, Merchant, born in MA.
KELLY, ARTHER, 48, M, Overseer in Mill, W, Scotland, 365, 538, NBPT.
KELLY, CATHARINE, 30, F, -, W, Ireland, 6, 6, NBPT*. In HH of Edward S. Moseley age 37, merchant, born MA.

KELLY, ELI G., 37, M, Physician, W, NH, 117, 140, NBPT*.

KELLY, ELLEN, 16, F, -, W, Ireland, 333, 434, NBPT*. In HH of Robert Piper, age 64, Rigger, born in MA.

KELLY, MARY, 23, F, -, W, Ireland, 601, 791, NBPT*. In HH of Patrick Kelly, age 23 Dealer in Wood, born in Ireland.

KELLY, MARY, 22, F, -, W, Ireland, 384, 507, NBPT*. In HH of Albert Currier, age 31, Mason, born in MA.

KELLY, PATRICK, 23, M, Dealer in Wood, W, Ireland, 601, 791, NBPT*.

KELLY, PATRICK, 23, M, Dealer in Wood, W, MA, 601, 791, NBPT*.

KELLY, ROSE, 19, F, -, W, Ireland, 116, 139, NBPT*. In HH of Samuel Flanders, age 38, Master Mariner, born in MA.

KELLY, SARAH, 26, F, -, W, Ireland, 368, 542, NBPT*. In HH of William Huse, age 27, Tobacconist, born in MA.

KELSEY, JOHN B., 46, M, Stove Dealer, W, England, 712, 1007, NBPT.

KENISON, CAROLINE, 17, F, -, W, NH, 369, 486, NBPT*. In HH of Robert McQuillen, age 66, Millwright, born in NH.

KENISON, GEORGE, 20, M, Truck man, W, NH, 533, 707, NBPT*. In HH of Nathaniel Perkins, age 51, Truck man, born in Maine.

KENISON, MARY, 17, F, -, W, NH, 369, 486, NBPT*. In HH of Robert McQuillen, age 66, Millwright, born in NH.

KENISTON, CLARK, 25, M, Laborer, W, NH, 573, 579, NBPT*. In HH of Sarah Hale, age 31, born in MA.

KENNISON, GEORGE W., 37, M, Dentist, W, Maine, 672, 964, NBPT. In HH of William W. Caldwill, age 25, Apothecary, born in MA.

KEY, ABY, 19, M, -, W, NH, 608, 888, NBPT. In HH of Mary J. Hardy, age 38, born in Maine.

KEYES, MARTHA, 74, F, -, W, MA, 554, 737, NBPT*.

KEYES, MOODY P., 16, M, Shoemaker, W, MA, 160, 193, NBPT*. In HH of William P. Keyes, age 18, Shoemaker, born in MA.

KEYES, WILLIAM P., 18, M, Shoemaker, W, MA, 160, 193, NBPT*.

KEZER, FRANCIS M., 45, M, Rigger, W, MA, 499, 745, NBPT.

KIDDEN, CATHERINE, 22, F, -, W, Maine, 566, 840, NBPT. In HH of Lydia Cooley, age 39, born in MA.

KIDDEN, KIMBALL P., 29, M, Physician, W, VT, 566, 840, NBPT. In HH of Lydia Cooley, age 39, born in MA.

KIDDEN, SARAH B., 45, F, -, W, VT, 566, 840, NBPT. In HH of Lydia Cooley, age 39, born in MA.

KILBORN, ANGELINE B., 14, F, -, W, NH, 520, 775, NBPT. In HH of John C. Kilborn, age 44, Operative, born in MA.

KILBORN, GEORGE, 63, M, Master Mariner, W, MA, 451, 674, NBPT.

KILBORN, JOHN C., 44, M, Operative, W, MA, 520, 775, NBPT.

KILBORN, MARIA, 41, F, -, W, NH, 520, 775, NBPT. In HH of John C. Kilborn, age 44, Operative, born in MA.

KILBORN, MARY N., 2, F, -, W, NH, 520, 775, NBPT. In HH of

John C. Kilborn, age 44, Operative, born in MA.
KILBORN, SAMUEL, 28, M, Shoemaker, W, MA, 202, 297, NBPT. In HH of Benjamin Goodwin, age 47, Cooper, born in MA.
KILBORN, SUSAN E., 8, F, -, W, NH, 520, 775, NBPT. In HH of John C. Kilborn, age 44, Operative, born in MA.
KILBORN, WARREN, 26, M, Carpenter, W, MA, 451, 674, NBPT. In HH of George Kilborn, age 63, Master Mariner, born in MA.
KILPATRICK, MARY J., 21, F, -, W, Maine, 404, 528, NBPT*. In HH of William Kyes, age 32, Overseer Weaving, born in NH.
KIMBALL, ALICE, 20, F, -, W, Maine, 787,1113, NBPT. In HH of Elizabeth P. Currier, age 41, born in MA.
KIMBALL, AMELIA, 12, F, -, W, NJ, 275, 405, NBPT. In HH of Harriet N. Kimball, age 18, born in NJ.
KIMBALL, EDWARD, 44, M, Lumber Dealer, W, MA, 121, 178, NBPT.
KIMBALL, EDWIN F., 11, M, -, W, Maine, 9, 11, NBPT. In HH of Joseph D. Kimball, age 40, Carpenter, born in MA.
KIMBALL, FRANCIS, 28, M, Mariner, W, Maine, 550, 822, NBPT.
KIMBALL, HANNAH E., 32, F, -, W, Maine, 550, 822, NBPT. In HH of Francis Kimball, age 28, Mariner, born in Maine.
KIMBALL, HARRIET N., 18, F, -, W, NJ, 275, 405, NBPT.
KIMBALL, HARVEY, 46, M, Lumber Dealer, W, MA, 123, 180, NBPT.
KIMBALL, ISABELLA R., 9, F, -, W, Maine, 9, 11, NBPT. In HH of Joseph D. Kimball, age 40, Carpenter, born in MA.
KIMBALL, JAMES, 20, M, Laborer, W, Maine, 159, 228, NBPT. In HH of Paul Johnson, age 50, Master Mariner, born in MA.
KIMBALL, JOHN, 30, M, Tailor, W, NH, 166, 199, NBPT*. In Hotel run by Thomas Brown, age 49, born in MA.
KIMBALL, JOHN C., 9, M, -, W, Maine, 123, 180, NBPT. In HH of Harvey Kimball, age 46, Lumber Dealer, born in MA.
KIMBALL, JOSEPH D., 40, M, Carpenter, W, MA, 9, 11, NBPT.
KIMBALL, JOSEPH H., 12, M, -, W, Maine, 123, 180, NBPT. In HH of Harvey Kimball, age 46, Lumber Dealer, born in MA.
KIMBALL, LOUISA R., 34, F, -, W, Maine, 9, 11, NBPT. In HH of Joseph D. Kimball, age 40, Carpenter, born in MA.
KIMBALL, MARTHA E., 10, F, -, W, Maine, 121, 178, NBPT. In HH of Edward Kimball, age 44, Lumber Dealer, born in MA.
KIMBALL, MARY A., 19, F, -, W, NH, 323, 477, NBPT. In HH of Lewis Foote, age 34, Shoemaker, born in MA.
KIMBALL, MARY H., 46, F, -, W, PA, 123, 180, NBPT. In HH of Hervey Kimball, age 46, Lumber Dealer, born in MA.
KIMBALL, MARY L., 8, F, -, W, Maine, 121, 178, NBPT. In HH of Edward Kimball, age 44, Lumber Dealer, born in MA.
KIMBALL, MICHJAH B., 27, M, Shoemaker, W, MA, 45, 67, NBPT.
KIMBALL, MOODY, 44, M, Stonemason, W, MA, 142, 208, NBPT.
KIMBALL, MOSES, 71, M, Merchant, W, MA, 287, 418,

NBPT.
KIMBALL, STEPHEN, 39, M, Mason, W, MA, 56, 82, NBPT.
KIMBALL, WILLIE, 7, F, -, W, Maine, 9, 11, NBPT. In HH of Joseph D. Kimball, age 40, Carpenter, born in MA.
KINCAID, CATHARINE, 38, F, -, W, Ireland, 112, 135, NBPT*.
KINCAID, JOHN, 8, M, -, W, Ireland, 112, 135, NBPT*. In HH of Catharine Kincaid, age 38, born in Ireland.
KING, FONDLEY, 45, M, Operative, W, Scotland, 752,1060, NBPT.
KING, ISABELLA, 45, F, -, W, Scotland, 752,1060, NBPT. In HH of Fondley King, age 45, Operative, born in Scotland.
KING, ISABELLA, 16, F, -, W, RI, 752,1060, NBPT. In HH of Fondley King, age 45, Operative, born in Scotland.
KING, JAMES, 30, M, Operative, W, MA, 609, 799, NBPT*.
KING, JENNET, 18, F, -, W, NY, 752,1060, NBPT. In HH of Fondley King, age 45, Operative, born in Scotland.
KING, JOHN, 25, M, Operative, W, Scotland, 752,1060, NBPT. In HH of Fondley King, age 45, Operative, born in Scotland.
KINGSLEY, ALBERT E., 11, M, -, W, Maine, 503, 750, NBPT. In HH of James Cilley Jr., age 28, Mariner, born in NH.
KINSMAN, HENRY W., 48, M, Counselor & Attorney, W, MA, 2, 2, NBPT*.
KITCHING, WILLIAM H., 41, M, Master Mariner, W, MA, 278, 408, NBPT.
KNAPP, ANTHONY, 52, F, Master Mariner, W, MA, 223, 329, NBPT.
KNAPP, ANTHONY, 22, M, Carpenter, W, MA, 15, 17, NBPT. In HH of Charles Knapp, age 49, Merchant, born in MA.
KNAPP, CHARLES, 49, M, Merchant, W, MA, 15, 17, NBPT.
KNAPP, ISAAC, 84, M, Calker, W, MA, 304, 447, NBPT.
KNAPP, SAMUEL, 46, M, Master Mariner, W, MA, 408, 608, NBPT.
KNAPP, WILLIAM, 64, M, Calker, W, MA, 422, 627, NBPT.
KNAPP, WILLIAM H., 33, M, Mariner, W, MA, 422, 627, NBPT. In HH of William Knapp, age 64, Calker, born in MA.
KNIGHT, ADAMS, 34, M, Master Mariner, W, MA, 274, 403, NBPT.
KNIGHT, ALPHUES G., 18, M, Mariner, W, MA, 105, 156, NBPT. In HH of Moses C. Knight, age 43, Shoemaker, born in MA.
KNIGHT, AUGUSTUS, 26, M, Mariner, W, MA, 789,1116, NBPT. In HH of Lois Fullington, age 40, born in MA.
KNIGHT, DANIEL, 44, M, Master Mariner, W, MA, 693, 985, NBPT.
KNIGHT, DANIEL H., 37, M, Weaver, W, MA, 19, 22, NBPT.
KNIGHT, DANIEL JR., 16, M, Mariner, W, MA, 789,1116, NBPT. In HH of Lois Fullington, age 40, born in MA.
KNIGHT, GEORGE, 38, M, Merchant, W, MA, 69, 99, NBPT.
KNIGHT, MOSES C., 43, M, Shoemaker, W, MA, 105, 156, NBPT.
KNOULES, SARAH, 17, F, -, W, Maine, 60, 87, NBPT. In HH of Alexander Graves, age 27, Master Mariner, born in MA.
KNOWELES, HENRY, 34, M, Tin-plate Worker, W, RI, 608, 888, NBPT. In HH of Mary J. Hardy, age 38, born in Maine.

KN{A}PP, CHRISTOPHER, 35, M, Laborer, W, Ireland, 273, 401, NBPT. In HH of Richard Joy, age 29, Mariner, born in Newfoundland.

KYES, ADELINE, 27, F, -, W, NH, 404, 528, NBPT*. In HH of William Kyes, age 32, Overseer Weaving, born in NH.

KYES, CHARLES W., 5, M, -, W, NH, 404, 528, NBPT*. In HH of William Kyes, age 32, Overseer Weaving, born in NH.

KYES, SARAH F., 27, F, -, W, NH, 404, 528, NBPT*. In HH of William Kyes, age 32, Overseer Weaving, born in NH.

KYES, WILLIAM, 32, M, Overseer Weaving, W, NH, 404, 528, NBPT*.

- L -

LADD, FRANK J., 23, M, Overseer in Mill, W, Maine, 151, 220, NBPT. In HH of Hannah White, age 45, born in Maine.

LADD, JOSEPH, 33, M, Boat Builder, W, MA, 405, 604, NBPT.

LADD, LOUIS, 21, M, Overseer in Mill, W, Maine, 151, 220, NBPT. In HH of Hannah White, age 45, born in Maine.

LADD, LOUISA, 34, F, -, W, Denmark, 405, 604, NBPT. In HH of Joseph Ladd, age 33, Boat Builder, born in MA.

LADD, MARY L., 47, M, Rigger, W, England, 714, 1010, NBPT.

LAKE, JOSEPH W., 55, M, Shoemaker, W, MA, 631, 918, NBPT.

LAKEMAN, DANIEL, 45, M, Harness maker, W, MA, 349, 460, NBPT*.

LAMPARY, FRANCIS, 16, F, -, W, NH, 529, 788, NBPT. In Boarding House.

LAMPERY, ELI, 21, M, Carpenter, W, NH, 551, 824, NBPT. In HH of Ann H. Shaflish, age 49, born in NH.

LAMPREY, ELIZABETH, 20, F, -, W, NH, 776, 1100, NBPT. In HH of Moses Winn, age 62, Laborer, born in MA.

LAMSON, MARTHA, 24, F, -, W, Maine, 405, 529, NBPT*. In HH of Miriam James, age 50, born in NH.

LAMSON, STEPHEN, 24, M, 2nd Overseer, W, MA, 407, 532, NBPT*.

LANCESTER, DANIEL M., 51, M, Depot Master, W, MA, 691, 983, NBPT.

LANCESTER, THOMAS, 75, M, Carpenter, W, MA, 458, 682, NBPT.

LANDFORD, JOSEPH B., 38, M, Overseer in Mill, W, MA, 141, 207, NBPT.

LANDFORD, MARY, 72, F, -, W, NH, 104, 152, NBPT. In HH of Peter Landford, age 62, Laborer, born in Prussia.

LANDFORD, PETER, 62, M, Laborer, W, Prussia, 104, 152, NBPT.

LANE, ABBY, 28, F, -, W, NH, 452, 675, NBPT. In HH of Eveline Gunnison, age 46, born in Maine.

LANE, ABNER, 49, M, Master Mariner, W, Maine, 575, 850, NBPT. In HH of Judith Delill, age 65, born in NH.

LANE, ELIZA, 17, F, -, W, Maine, 15, 18, NBPT*. In HH of Milton Smart, age 47, Blacksmith, born Maine.

LANE, JOSEPH D., 19, M, Mariner, W, MA, 80, 117, NBPT. In HH of Joseph A. Somerby, age

51, Branch Pilot, born in MA.
LANE, JOSHUA, 45, M, None, W, MA, 788,1114, NBPT. In Poor House.
LANE, REUBEN, 65, M, Carpenter, W, NH, 225, 331, NBPT.
LANG, DAVID, 40, M, Barber, W, MA, 133, 196, NBPT.
LANG, LOWELL Y., 39, M, Resturator, W, NH, 642, 929, NBPT.
LANGLEY, HANNAH, 27, M, -, W, NH, 285, 371, NBPT*. In HH of John Pearson, 4th, age 34, Clergyman, 2nd Advent., born in NH.
LANGLEY, JOHN, 35, M, Mariner, W, England, 397, 590, NBPT.
LANKESTER, WILLIAM D., 46, M, Conductor, W, MA, 275, 352, NBPT*.
LANKESTER, WILLIAM H., 16, M, Farming, W, MA, 275, 352, NBPT*. In HH of William D. Lankester, age 46, Conductor, born in MA.
LARD, ABEL C., 16, M, None, W, MA, 671, 963, NBPT. In HH of William Asby, age 29, Farmer, born in MA.
LARRY, MARY, 55, F, -, W, Ireland, 788,1114, NBPT. In Poor House. .
LARY?, ELLEN M., 40, M, -, W, Ireland, 760,1073, NBPT. In HH of Michael Lary?, age 42, Laborer, born in Ireland.
LARY?, MICHAEL, 42, M, Laborer, W, Ireland, 760,1073, NBPT.
LATTIMER, JAMES S., 42, M, Shoemaker, W, MA, 489, 652, NBPT*.
LAWRENCE, EDWIN, 36, M, Newspaper Publisher, W, MA, 14, 17, NBPT*.

LAWRENCE, MARY, 34, F, -, W, NY, 14, 17, NBPT*. In HH of Edwin Lawrence, age 36, Newspaper Publisher born in MA.
LAWRY, JAMES, 9, M, -, W, Ireland, 540, 807, NBPT. In HH of Michael Lawry, age 35, Laborer, born in Ireland.
LAWRY, MARY, 32, F, -, W, Ireland, 540, 807, NBPT. In HH of Michael Lawry, age 35, Laborer, born in Ireland.
LAWRY, MICHAEL, 35, M, Laborer, W, Ireland, 540, 807, NBPT.
LAWRY, PETER, 11, M, -, W, Ireland, 540, 807, NBPT. In HH of Michael Lawry, age 35, Laborer, born in Ireland.
LAWRY, SARAH, 13, F, -, W, Ireland, 540, 807, NBPT. In HH of Michael Lawry, age 35, Laborer, born in Ireland.
LAWS, JAMES, 50, M, Mariner, B, DEL, 546, 817, NBPT.
LAWS, LUCINDA, 46, F, -, B, NH, 546, 817, NBPT. In HH of James Laws, age 50, Mariner, Black, born in MA.
LAWS, PETER, 27, M, Mariner, B, MA, 546, 817, NBPT. In HH of James Laws, age 50, Mariner, Black, born in MA.
LAYWARD, HENRY B., 50, M, Master Mariner, W, MA, 303, 444, NBPT.
LEACH, CHANNEY B., 20, M, Laborer, W, NH, 56, 62, NBPT*. In HH of Oliver Sanborn, age 29, Laborer, born MA.
LEACH, CHARLES, 19, M, Machinist, W, Maine, 770,1090, NBPT. In HH of Levi Pearson, age 37, Watchman, born in MA.
LEACH, GEORGE, 38, M, Overseer, W, MA, 530, 790, NBPT. In HH of Almira Swap, age 42, born in MA.

99

LEACH, JANE, 20, F, -, W, CT, 612, 893, NBPT. In HH of William Hills, age 70, None, born in MA.

LEACH, SILINU, 50, M, Overseer, W, MA, 530, 790, NBPT. In HH of Almira Swap, age 42, born in MA.

LEARY, JOHN, 17, M, Laborer, W, Ireland, 756,1066, NBPT. In HH of Timothy Sennon, age 30, Laborer, born in Ireland.

LEAVITT, BENJAMIN, 25, M, Shoemaker, W, NH, 166, 199, NBPT*. In Hotel run by Thomas Brown, age 49, born in MA.

LECRAW, WILLIAM, 54, M, Master Mariner, W, MA, 16, 18, NBPT.

LECRAW, WILLIAM, 28, M, Master Mariner, W, MA, 193, 283, NBPT.

LEE, SEWARD, 56, M, Master Mariner, W, MA, 71, 101, NBPT.

LEECAW, DAVID, 25, M, Mariner, W, MA, 520, 776, NBPT.

LEGRAFF, FRANCES, 28, M, Mariner, B, Surinan, 545, 816, NBPT. In HH of John Young, age 32, Barber, black, born in MA.

LEIGHTON, ANDREW J., 16, M, Clerk, W, MA, 741,1047, NBPT. In HH of Gideon E. Leighton, age 50, Watchman, born in NH.

LEIGHTON, FRANKLIN J., 22, M, Painter, W, VT, 327, 424, NBPT*. In HH of Sarah Leighton, age 50, born in MA.

LEIGHTON, GEORGE W., 25, M, Fisherman, W, VT, 327, 424, NBPT*. In HH of Sarah Leighton, age 50, born in MA.

LEIGHTON, GIDEON E., 50, M, Watchman, W, NH, 741,1047, NBPT.

LEIGHTON, MARY J., 17, F, -, W, VT, 327, 424, NBPT*. In HH of Sarah Leighton, age 50, born in MA.

LEIGHTON, NATHAN, 15, M, Clerk, W, MA, 327, 424, NBPT*. In HH of Sarah Leighton, age 50, born in MA.

LENLAR, HENRY, 29, M, Clergyman, R.C., W, Ireland, 149, 218, NBPT.

LESLEY, EDWARD S., 45, M, Machinist, W, MA, 205, 256, NBPT*.

LEWIS, ELIZABETH A., 23, M, -, W, Maine, 244, 307, NBPT*. In HH of Susanna Marden, age 55, born in NH.

LEWIS, JOHN, 77, M, None, W, MA, 471, 624, NBPT*.

LEWIS, JOHN, 47, M, Mariner, W, Portugal, 345, 452, NBPT*.

LEWIS, JOHN A., 21, M, Operative, W, MA, 345, 452, NBPT*. In HH of John Lewis, age 47, Mariner, born in Portugal.

LEWIS, MARK S., 21, M, Clerk, W, MA, 305, 449, NBPT. In HH of Thomas Lewis, age 45, Pump and Block Maker, born in MA.

LEWIS, THOMAS, 45, M, Pump and Block Maker, W, MA, 305, 449, NBPT.

LEWIS, WILLIAM, 23, M, Clerk, W, VT, 573, 848, NBPT. In HH of Thomas Noyes, age 70, Shoemaker, born in MA.

LEWIS, WILLIAM, 21, M, Mariner, W, Maine, 173, 250, NBPT. In HH of George R. Sillez, age 28, Mariner, born in NH.

LIBBEY, DEBORAH, 61, F, -, W, MA, 788,1114, NBPT. In Poor House. .

LIBBEY, HANNAH, 63, F, -, W, MA, 788,1114, NBPT. In Poor House. .

LIBBEY, JOHN, 59, M, Laborer, W, MA, 28, 33, NBPT*

LINES, MARGARET O., 28, F, -, W, Ireland, 359, 527, NBPT. In HH of Michael Caney, age 26, Laborer, born in Ireland.
LINES, PETER, 26, M, Laborer, W, Ireland, 359, 527, NBPT.
LINKSON, MARTHA, 30, F, -, W, N.S., 782,1108, NBPT. In HH of Enoch Tilton, age 45, Hotel Keeper, born in NH. In Hotel.
LINKSON, ORINDA, 27, F, -, W, N.S., 782,1108, NBPT. In HH of Enoch Tilton, age 45, Hotel Keeper, born in NH. In Hotel.
LITCH, ARMENELLA, 15, F, -, W, Nova Scotia, 531, 705, NBPT*. In HH of James Litch, age 41, Farmer, born in Nova Scotia.
LITCH, ELIZA, 13, F, -, W, Nova Scotia, 531, 705, NBPT*. In HH of James Litch, age 41, Farmer, born in Nova Scotia.
LITCH, HANNAH, 41, F, -, W, Nova Scotia, 531, 705, NBPT*. In HH of James Litch, age 41, Farmer, born in Nova Scotia.
LITCH, HANNAH, 7, F, -, W, Nova Scotia, 531, 705, NBPT*. In HH of James Litch, age 41, Farmer, born in Nova Scotia.
LITCH, JAMES, 41, M, Farmer, W, Nova Scotia, 531, 705, NBPT*.
LITCH, JAMES, 17, M, Farmer, W, Nova Scotia, 531, 705, NBPT*. In HH of James Litch, age 41, Farmer, born in Nova Scotia.
LITCH, JOHN, 5, M, -, W, Nova Scotia, 531, 705, NBPT*. In HH of James Litch, age 41, Farmer, born in Nova Scotia.
LITCH, MAHALA, 20, F, -, W, Nova Scotia, 531, 705, NBPT*. In HH of James Litch, age 41, Farmer, born in Nova Scotia.
LITCH, REBEKAH, 8, F, -, W, Nova Scotia, 531, 705, NBPT*. In HH of James Litch, age 41, Farmer, born in Nova Scotia.
LITCH, SALINA, 10, F, -, W, Nova Scotia, 531, 705, NBPT*. In HH of James Litch, age 41, Farmer, born in Nova Scotia.
LITCH, SARAH N., 19, F, -, W, Nova Scotia, 531, 705, NBPT*. In HH of James Litch, age 41, Farmer, born in Nova Scotia.
LITCH, WILLIAM, 21, M, Ship Carpenter, W, Nova Scotia, 531, 705, NBPT*. In HH of James Litch, age 41, Farmer, born in Nova Scotia.
LITTLE, WILLIAM A., 28, M, Shoemaker, W, MA, 739,1045, NBPT.
LITTLEFIELD, ELIZA M., 20, F, -, W, Maine, 266, 339, NBPT*. In HH of Levi Littlefield, age 23, Truck man, born in Maine.
LITTLEFIELD, EMILY, 21, F, -, W, Maine, 741,1047, NBPT. In HH of Gideon E. Leighton, age 50, Watchman, born in NH.
LITTLEFIELD, HARRIET, 24, F, -, W, Maine, 741,1047, NBPT. In HH of Gideon E. Leighton, age 50, Watchman, born in NH.
LITTLEFIELD, ISAIAH L., 28, M, Brewer, W, Maine, 458, 684, NBPT.
LITTLEFIELD, JOSEPH R., 35, M, Shoemaker, W, Maine, 289, 377, NBPT*.
LITTLEFIELD, LEVI, 23, M, Truck man, W, Maine, 266, 339, NBPT*.
LITTLEFIELD, LUCY, 68, F, -, W, Maine, 326, 481, NBPT. In HH of Benjn. Robinson, age 45, Shoemaker, born in Maine.
LITTLEFIELD, MARY J., 24, F, -, W, Maine, 266, 339, NBPT*. In HH of Levi Littlefield, age 23, Truck man, born in Maine.
LITTLEFIELD, SARAH, 43, F, -, W, Maine, 466, 619, NBPT*. In HH of Solomon Littlefield, age 42,

Drayman, born in Maine.
LITTLEFIELD, SOLOMON, 42, M, Drayman, W, Maine, 466, 619, NBPT*.
LIVINGSTON, CHARLES, 26, M, Mariner, W, MA, 486, 728, NBPT. In HH of Abby K. Livingston, age 53, born in MA.
LOARD, ALFRED, 27, M, Merchant, W, MA, 338, 497, NBPT. In HH of Moses Loard, age 60, Merchant, born in MA.
LOARD, MOSES, 60, M, Merchant, W, MA, 338, 497, NBPT.
LOCKE, ELIZABETH S., 61, F, -, W, NH, 407, 531, NBPT*.
LOCKE, SARAH A., 21, F, -, W, NH, 119, 142, NBPT*. In HH of Edward S. Rand, age 65, Merchant, born in MA.
LONG, ELIZABETH, 50, F, -, W, Ireland, 201, 249, NBPT*. In HH of Jeremiah Long, age 48, Laborer, born in Ireland.
LONG, ELLEN, 11, F, -, W, Ireland, 201, 251, NBPT*. In HH of Catharine Lucy, age 55, born in Ireland.
LONG, JEREMIAH, 48, M, Laborer, W, Ireland, 201, 249, NBPT*.
LONG, JEREMIAH, 17, M, None, W, Ireland, 201, 251, NBPT*. In HH of Catharine Lucy, age 55, born in Ireland.
LONG, JOANNA, 14, F, -, W, Ireland, 201, 249, NBPT*. In HH of Jeremiah Long, age 48, Laborer, born in Ireland.
LONG, JOHN, 17, M, Mariner, W, Ireland, 201, 249, NBPT*. In HH of Jeremiah Long, age 48, Laborer, born in Ireland.
LONG, TIMOTHY, 23, M, House Carpenter, W, Ireland, 201, 251, NBPT*. In HH of Catharine Lucy, age 55, born in Ireland.

LONG, TIMOTHY, 15, M, Mariner, W, Ireland, 201, 249, NBPT*. In HH of Jeremiah Long, age 48, Laborer, born in Ireland.
LONGFELLOW, JOHN, 23, M, Painter, W, MA, 334, 436, NBPT*. In HH of Andrew Jack, age 27, Painter, born in Maine.
LONGFELLOW, MARY, 25, F, -, W, NH, 334, 436, NBPT*. In HH of Andrew Jack, age 27, Painter, born in Maine.
LORD, FREDRICK, 42, M, Mariner, W, Nova Scotia, 157, 226, NBPT.
LORD, JOHN L., 38, M, Blacksmith, W, MA, 591, 780, NBPT*.
LORD, JOHN T., 22, M, None, W, MA, 309, 455, NBPT. In HH of Philip Lord, age 36, Painter, born in MA.
LORD, KITTY, 38, F, -, W, Nova Scotia, 157, 226, NBPT. In HH of Frederick Lord, age 42, Mariner, born in Nova Scotia.
LORD, MARGARET C., 17, F, -, W, Nova Scotia, 157, 226, NBPT. In HH of Frederick Lord, age 42, Mariner, born in Nova Scotia.
LORD, MARY A., 19, F, -, W, Nova Scotia, 157, 226, NBPT. In HH of Frederick Lord, age 42, Mariner, born in Nova Scotia.
LORD, MARY H., 33, F, -, W, NH, 588, 865, NBPT. In HH of Stilman Simonds, age 43, Shoemaker, born in MA.
LORD, PHILIP, 36, M, Painter, W, MA, 309, 455, NBPT.
LORD, THOMAS H., 30, M, Upholsterer, W, MA, 470, 705, NBPT.
LORING, DOROTHY, 44, F, -, B, MA, 597, 787, NBPT*.
LORY, DANIEL O., 49, M, Mariner, W, Ireland, 538, 804, NBPT.

LORY, JANE, 49, F, -, W, Ireland, 538, 804, NBPT. In HH of Daniel O. Lory, age 49, Mariner, born in Ireland.
LOUD, ABEL C., 16, M, None, W, MA, 419, 547, NBPT*. In HH of Sarah Loud, age 46, born in MA.
LOUDS, ELIZABETH, 40, F, -, W, England, 660, 950, NBPT. In HH of Rebecca Boardman, age 48, born in England.
LOUISSON, MORRIS, 28, M, Painter, W, Germany, 566, 840, NBPT. In HH of Lydia Cooley, age 39, born in MA.
LOVERING, JOHN D., 4, M, -, W, Maine, 764,1078, NBPT. In HH of Jonathan Lovering, age 33, Hotel Keeper, born in NH.
LOVERING, JONATHAN, 33, M, Hotel Keeper, W, NH, 764,1078, NBPT.
LOVEJOY, JAMES, 20, M, Watchmaker, W, NH, 40, 47, NBPT*. In HH of Frances F. Monroe, age 32, female, Boarding House, born in Maine.
LOVELETT, WM. N., 45, M, None, W, MA, 788,1114, NBPT. In Poor House.
LOVETT, WILLIAM, 45, M, Blacksmith, W, MA, 582, 857, NBPT.
LOVETT, WILLIAM H., 19, M, Coach Driver, W, MA, 582, 857, NBPT. In HH of William Lovett, age 45, Blacksmith, born in MA.
LOWE, ANN, 31, F, -, W, Ireland, 662, 953, NBPT. In HH of William B. Bannister, age 76, Gentleman, born in MA.
LOWE, ELLEN, 19, F, -, W, Ireland, 695, 987, NBPT. In HH of Stephen W. Marston, age 62, Judge Police Court, born in NH.
LOWE, HENRY, 49, M, Master Mariner, W, Ireland, 758,1071, NBPT.
LOWE, JAMES R., 41, M, Gardner, W, England, 738,1044, NBPT.
LOWE, RHODA, 47, M, Master Mariner, W, NH, 758,1071, NBPT. In HH of Henry Lowe, age 49, Master Mariner, born in Ireland.
LOWELL, JOSEPH, 45, M, Drayman, W, MA, 171, 206, NBPT*.
LOWELL, JOSEPH JR., 25, M, Coachman, W, MA, 436, 575, NBPT*.
LOWELL, LEWIS, 23, M, Truck driver, W, MA, 171, 206, NBPT*. In HH of Joseph Lowell, age 45, Drayman, born in MA.
LOWELL, LUCILLA, 25, F, -, W, Maine, 436, 575, NBPT*. In HH of Joseph Lowell, Jr., age 25, Coachman, born in MA.
LUCY, CATHARINE, 55, F, -, W, Ireland, 201, 251, NBPT*.
LUCY, CHARLES W., 23, M, Confectioner, W, NH, 244, 307, NBPT*. In HH of Susanna Marden, age 55, born in NH.
LUCY, CORNELIUS, 31, M, Operative, W, Ireland, 431, 562, NBPT*.
LUCY, DENNIS, 12, M, -, W, Ireland, 479, 638, NBPT*. In HH of Mary Lucy, age 44, born in Ireland.
LUCY, ELLEN, 19, F, -, W, Ireland, 479, 638, NBPT*. In HH of Mary Lucy, age 44, born in Ireland.
LUCY, JEREMIAH, 22, M, Laborer, W, Ireland, 201, 251, NBPT*. In HH of Catharine Lucy, age 55, born in Ireland.
LUCY, JEREMIAH, 16, M, Mariner, W, Ireland, 479, 638, NBPT*. In HH of Mary Lucy, age 44, born in Ireland.
LUCY, JOANNA, 17, F, -, W, Ireland, 108, 129, NBPT*. In HH of Richard W. Drown, age 54, Watchmaker, born in MA.

LUCY, JOANNA, 6, F, -, W, Ireland, 479, 638, NBPT*. In HH of Mary Lucy, age 44, born in Ireland.

LUCY, JULIA, 29, F, -, W, Ireland, 431, 562, NBPT*. In HH of Cornelius Lucy, age 31, Operative, born in Ireland.

LUCY, MARGARET, 18, F, -, W, Ireland, 479, 638, NBPT*. In HH of Mary Lucy, age 44, born in Ireland.

LUCY, MARGARET, 17, F, -, W, Ireland, 201, 251, NBPT*. In HH of Catharine Lucy, age 55, born in Ireland.

LUCY, MARY, 44, F, -, W, Ireland, 479, 638, NBPT*.

LUCY, MARY, 23, F, -, W, Ireland, 201, 251, NBPT*. In HH of Catharine Lucy, age 55, born in Ireland.

LUCY, MARY, 15, F, -, W, Ireland, 479, 638, NBPT*. In HH of Mary Lucy, age 44, born in Ireland.

LUNT, ABRAHAM S., 38, M, Mariner, W, MA, 50, 74, NBPT.

LUNT, ALMIRA, 43, F, -, W, NH, 457, 681, NBPT. In HH of Benjn. Lunt, 3rd, age 42, Truck man, born in MA.

LUNT, AMOS, 28, M, Mariner, W, MA, 432, 567, NBPT*.

LUNT, BENJAMIN C., 53, M, Music Inst. Maker, W, MA, 232, 290, NBPT*.

LUNT, BENJN., 76, M, Master Mariner, W, MA, 83, 120, NBPT.

LUNT, BENJN. 3RD, 42, M, Truck man, W, MA, 457, 681, NBPT.

LUNT, CHARLES, 24, M, Mariner, W, MA, 263, 384, NBPT.

LUNT, DANIEL, 41, M, Baker/Grocer, W, MA, 86, 100, NBPT*.

LUNT, EDWARD, 17, M, Truck man, W, NH, 457, 681, NBPT. In HH of Benjn. Lunt, 3rd, age 42, Truck man, born in MA.

LUNT, EDWARD W., 25, M, Mast maker, W, MA, 33, 46, NBPT. In HH of Ezra Lunt, age 65, Mast Maker, born in MA.

LUNT, ELMIRA N., 15, F, -, W, NH, 457, 681, NBPT. In HH of Benjn. Lunt, 3rd, age 42, Truck man, born in MA.

LUNT, EZRA, 65, M, Mast Maker, W, MA, 33, 46, NBPT.

LUNT, FRANCES C., 12, F, -, W, NH, 457, 681, NBPT. In HH of Benjn. Lunt, 3rd, age 42, Truck man, born in MA.

LUNT, GEORGE, 45, M, Master Mainer, W, MA, 30, 40, NBPT.

LUNT, HENRY, 34, M, Mariner, W, MA, 107, 159, NBPT.

LUNT, HENRY P., 33, M, Grocer, W, MA, 393, 581, NBPT.

LUNT, JACOB W., 21, M, Stable Keeper, W, MA, 30, 41, NBPT. In HH of Sarah B. Lunt, age 56, born in MA.

LUNT, JOSEPH, 45, M, Branch Pilot, W, MA, 90, 131, NBPT. In HH of Sarah Huggett, age 79, born in Maine.

LUNT, JOSEPH C., 80, M, Ship master, Retired, W, MA, 123, 146, NBPT*.

LUNT, JOSEPH J., 36, M, Weaver, Bartlet, W, MA, 418, 546, NBPT*.

LUNT, MARTHA P., 19, F, -, W, NH, 86, 100, NBPT*. In HH of Daniel Lunt, age 41, Baker/Grocer, born MA.

LUNT, MOODY, 42, M, Mason, W, MA, 174, 253, NBPT.

LUNT, MOSES, 26, M, Dresser in Mill, W, MA, 365, 539, NBPT.

LUNT, SAMUEL, 42, M, Operative, W, MA, 380, 561, NBPT.

LUNT, SARAH J., 8, F, -, W, NH, 457, 681, NBPT. In HH of Benjn. Lunt, 3rd, age 42, Truck man, born

in MA.
LUNT, SARAH K., 46, F, -, W, MA, 90, 131, NBPT. In HH of Sarah Huggett, age 79, born in Maine.
LUNT, THOMAS R., 23, M, Mason, W, MA, 195, 285, NBPT. In HH of John H. White, age 39, Master Mariner, born in England.
LUNT, WILLIAM H., 31, M, Master Mariner, W, MA, 33, 46, NBPT. In HH of Ezra Lunt, age 65, Mast Maker, born in MA.
LUNT, WILLIAM P., 15, M, Student, W, MA, 86, 100, NBPT*. In HH of Daniel Lunt, age 41, Baker/Grocer, born MA.
LUNT, WYMAN B., 33, M, Mariner, W, MA, 123, 146, NBPT*. In HH of Joseph C. Lunt, age 80, Ship master, Retired, born in MA.
LURVEY, DAVID, 35, M, Ship Carpenter, W, Maine, 465, 618, NBPT*.
LURVEY, EZRA, 10, M, -, W, Maine, 465, 618, NBPT*. In HH of David Lurvey, age 35, Ship Carpenter, born in Maine.
LURVEY, JANE, 36, F, -, W, Maine, 465, 618, NBPT*. In HH of David Lurvey, age 35, Ship Carpenter, born in Maine.
LURVEY, LORENDA, 14, F, -, W, Maine, 465, 618, NBPT*. In HH of David Lurvey, age 35, Ship Carpenter, born in Maine.
LUSCOMB, GEORGE E., 25, M, Grainer, W, England, 196, 240, NBPT*.
LYDSTON, WEYMOUTH, 34, M, Barber, W, NH, 699, 991, NBPT.
LYNCH, ELLEN, 20, F, -, W, Ireland, 182, 223, NBPT*. In HH of Mary Woart, age 74, born in MA.
LYNCH, ELLEN, 20, F, -, W, Ireland, 586, 862, NBPT. In HH of Samuel Phillips, age 49, Attorney, born in MA.
LYNCH, MARGARET, 24, F, W, W, Ireland, 40, 47, NBPT*. In HH of Frances F. Monroe, age 32, female, Boarding House, born in Maine.
LYNCH, MARY, 37, F, -, W, Ireland, 112, 134, NBPT*.
LYNCH, PATRICK S., 28, M, Laborer, W, Ireland, 662, 953, NBPT. In HH of William B. Bannister, age 76, Gentleman, born in MA.
LYONS, HOWARD, 23, F, -, W, Ireland, 259, 376, NBPT. In HH of Edmund Bartlett, age 35, Merchant, born in MA.
LYONS, JOHN, 66, M, Mariner, B, West Indies, 788,1114, NBPT. In Poor House.
LYONS, JULIA, 24, F, -, W, Ireland, 570, 845, NBPT. In HH of William B. Packer, age 30, born in MA.

- M -

MACE, JOSEPH, 32, M, Engineer, W, MA, 438, 579, NBPT*.
MACE, MARY A., 19, F, -, W, NH, 708,1003, NBPT. In HH of Sarah Easton, age 57, born in NH.
MACE, THOMAS J., 17, M, Operative, W, MA, 135, 161, NBPT*. In HH of Sarah Mace, age 54, born in MA.
MACE, WILLIAM, 23, M, Baker, W, MA, 135, 161, NBPT*.
MACK, JANE, 41, F, -, W, Ireland, 39, 46, NBPT*. In HH of Parker M. Dole, age 65, farmer, born in MA.
MACKINTOSH, HANNAH D., 72, F, -, W, NH, 645, 934, NBPT.

MADIX, WILLIAM, 30, M, Laborer, W, Newfoundland, 532, 795, NBPT. In HH of Walter Joy, age 27, Mariner, born in Newfoundland.
MAGRIDGE, ELIZA A., 26, F, -, W, Maine, 382, 565, NBPT. In HH of William Magridge, age 34, Carpenter, born in NH.
MAGRIDGE, WILLIAM, 34, M, Carpenter, W, NH, 382, 565, NBPT.
MAHAFFY, ANN, 32, F, -, W, Ireland, 224, 278, NBPT*.
MAHAN, ANN, 8, F, -, W, Ireland, 258, 323, NBPT*. In HH of Susan Mahan, age 35, born in Ireland.
MAHAN, BRIDGET, 15, F, -, W, Ireland, 258, 323, NBPT*. In HH of Susan Mahan, age 35, born in Ireland.
MAHAN, JOSEPH, 3, M, -, W, Ireland, 258, 323, NBPT*. In HH of Susan Mahan, age 35, born in Ireland.
MAHAN, MARY, 6, F, -, W, Ireland, 258, 323, NBPT*. In HH of Susan Mahan, age 35, born in Ireland.
MAHAN, ROSE, 12, F, -, W, Ireland, 258, 323, NBPT*. In HH of Susan Mahan, age 35, born in Ireland.
MAHAN, SUSAN, 35, F, -, W, Ireland, 258, 323, NBPT*.
MAHONEY, MARGARET, 20, F, -, W, Ireland, 668, 960, NBPT. In HH of William Cushing, age 27, Merchant, born in MA.
MAHONEY, MICHAEL, 41, M, -, W, Ireland, 78, 87, NBPT*. In Jail. Convict.
MAHONY, ELLEN, 17, F, -, W, Ireland, 118, 141, NBPT*. In HH of Ebenezer Moseley, age 68, Counselor, born in Ct.
MAHURON, AUGUSTUS, 15, M, Operative, W, Maine, 140, 166, NBPT*. In HH of Hannah T. Marshall, age 39, Boarding House, born in MA.
MALCHI, JEREMIAH, 48, M, Laborer, W, Ireland, 173, 251, NBPT.
MALCHI, JUDITH, 50, F, -, W, Ireland, 173, 251, NBPT. In HH of Jeremiah Malchi, age 48, Laborer, born in Ireland.
MALDINE, ELLEN, 5, F, -, W, Ireland, 465, 694, NBPT. In HH of Ellen Owens, age 30, born in Ireland.
MALDINE, JOHN, 11, M, -, W, Ireland, 465, 694, NBPT. In HH of Ellen Owens, age 30, born in Ireland.
MALDINE, MARY, 8, F, -, W, Ireland, 465, 694, NBPT. In HH of Ellen Owens, age 30, born in Ireland.
MALDINE, MICHAEL, 7, M, -, W, Ireland, 465, 694, NBPT. In HH of Ellen Owens, age 30, born in Ireland.
MALDINE, PATRICK, 10, M, -, W, Ireland, 465, 694, NBPT. In HH of Ellen Owens, age 30, born in Ireland.
MALONEY, JAMES, 0, M, -, W, Maine, 788,1114, NBPT. In Poor House. James Maloney age 9 months.
MALONY, BRIDGET, 11, F, -, W, N.S., 755,1065, NBPT. In HH of Patrick Malony, age 50, Laborer, born in N.S. {Nova Scotia}.
MALONY, DANIEL, 6, M, -, W, N.S., 755,1065, NBPT. In HH of Patrick Malony, age 50, Laborer, born in N.S. {Nova Scotia}.
MALONY, ELLEN, 35, F, -, W, N.S., 755,1065, NBPT. In HH of Patrick Malony, age 50, Laborer, born in N.S. {Nova Scotia}.
MALONY, JAMES, 2, M, -, W,

N.S., 755,1065, NBPT. In HH of Patrick Malony, age 50, Laborer, born in N.S. {Nova Scotia}.
MALONY, JOHN, 7, M, -, W, N.S., 755,1065, NBPT. In HH of Patrick Malony, age 50, Laborer, born in N.S. {Nova Scotia}.
MALONY, JULIA, 9, F, -, W, N.S., 755,1065, NBPT. In HH of Patrick Malony, age 50, Laborer, born in N.S. {Nova Scotia}.
MALONY, PATRICK, 50, M, Laborer, W, N.S., 755,1065, NBPT.
MALONY, PATRICK, 15, M, -, W, N.S., 755,1065, NBPT. In HH of Patrick Malony, age 50, Laborer, born in N.S. {Nova Scotia}.
MANDURER, GEORGE, 30, M, Laborer, W, Ireland, 528, 785, NBPT.
MANDURER, JOANNA, 13, F, -, W, Maine, 528, 785, NBPT. In HH of George Mandurer, age 30, Confectioner, born in England.
MANDURER, JOHN, 5, M, -, W, Maine, 528, 785, NBPT. In HH of George Mandurer, age 30, Confectioner, born in England.
MANDURER, MARGARET, 8, F, -, W, Maine, 528, 785, NBPT. In HH of George Mandurer, age 30, Confectioner, born in England.
MANDURER, MARGARET W., 30, F, -, W, Ireland, 528, 785, NBPT. In HH of George Mandurer, age 30, Confectioner, born in England.
MANDURER, THOMAS, 11, M, -, W, Maine, 528, 785, NBPT. In HH of George Mandurer, age 30, Confectioner, born in England.
MANHOLL, ROBERT, 62, M, Painter, W, PA, 529, 788, NBPT. In Boarding House.
MANN, ALICE, 22, F, -, W, Maine, 722,1021, NBPT. In HH of Thomas E. Pressey, age 37, Carpenter, born in MA.

MANN, JAMES, 27, M, Artist, W, N.B., 722,1021, NBPT. In HH of Thomas E. Pressey, age 37, Carpenter, born in MA.
MANNIX, EDMUND, 48, M, Laborer, W, Ireland, 540, 809, NBPT.
MANNIX, ELIZABETH, 8, F, -, W, Ireland, 540, 809, NBPT. In HH of Edmunt Mannix, age 48, Laborer, born in Ireland.
MANNIX, ELIZABETH C., 45, F, -, W, Ireland, 540, 809, NBPT. In HH of Edmunt Mannix, age 48, Laborer, born in Ireland.
MANNIX, JAMES, 14, M, -, W, Ireland, 540, 809, NBPT. In HH of Edmunt Mannix, age 48, Laborer, born in Ireland.
MANNIX, JULIA, 6, F, -, W, Ireland, 540, 809, NBPT. In HH of Edmunt Mannix, age 48, Laborer, born in Ireland.
MANNIX, MARY, 16, F, -, W, Ireland, 540, 809, NBPT. In HH of Edmunt Mannix, age 48, Laborer, born in Ireland.
MANROE, CHARLOTTE, 6, F, -, W, N.S., 536, 800, NBPT. In HH of James Manroe, age 33, Shoemaker, born in N.S. {Nova Scotia}.
MANROE, JAMES, 33, M, Shoemaker, W, N.S., 536, 800, NBPT.
MANROE, JAMES O., 4, M, -, W, N.S., 536, 800, NBPT. In HH of James Manroe, age 33, Shoemaker, born in N.S. {Nova Scotia}.
MANROE, MARGARET D., 31, F, -, W, N.S., 536, 800, NBPT. In HH of James Manroe, age 33, Shoemaker, born in N.S. {Nova Scotia}.
MANSFIELD, ALBERT F., 28, M, Fallow Chandler, W, MA, 294, 386, NBPT*.
MANSFIELD, DAVID, 30, M, Mariner, W, Nova Scotia, 283, 365,

NBPT*.
MANSFIELD, HARRIET, 24, F, -, W, NH, 294, 386, NBPT*. In HH of Albert F. Mansfield, age 28, Tallow Chandler, born in MA.
MANSFIELD, HENRY F., 1, M, -, W, Maine, 283, 365, NBPT*. In HH of David Mansfield, age 30, Mariner, born in Nova Scotia.
MANSFIELD, JOHN, 21, M, Fisherman, W, MA, 265, 337, NBPT*.
MANSFIELD, MARY J., 21, F, -, W, Maine, 283, 365, NBPT*. In HH of David Mansfield, age 30, Mariner, born in Nova Scotia.
MANSFIELD, WILLIAM, 16, M, Fisherman, W, MA, 265, 337, NBPT*. In HH of John Mansfield, age 21, Fisherman, born in MA.
MANSON, JAMES, 36, M, Tallow Chandler, W, MA, 398, 521, NBPT*.
MARCH, CHARLES, 43, M, Master Mariner, W, MA, 12, 14, NBPT. In HH of Hosea Y. Crofoot, age 29, Bookbinder, born in CT.
MARCH, HANNAH C., 26, F, -, W, Maine, 378, 498, NBPT*. In HH of Enoch C. March, age 46, Shoemaker, born in MA.
MARCH, STEPHEN, 47, M, Shoemaker, W, MA, 429, 558, NBPT*.
MARCROTT, EDWARD, 30, M, Machinist, W, VT, 268, 392, NBPT. In HH of Walter Osgood, age 39, Operative, born in NH.
MARDEN, ANN, 30, F, -, W, NH, 461, 689, NBPT. In HH of Jeremiah A. Marden, age 30, Machinist, born in NH.
MARDEN, CHARLES E., 5, M, -, W, NH, 461, 689, NBPT. In HH of Jeremiah A. Marden, age 30, Machinist, born in NH.
MARDEN, ELISA B., 22, F, -, W, NH, 460, 687, NBPT. In HH of Sewall Marden, age 55, Wheelwright, born in NH.
MARDEN, ELIZABETH, 18, F, -, W, NH, 460, 687, NBPT. In HH of Sewall Marden, age 55, Wheelwright, born in NH.
MARDEN, ELSEY ANN, 27, F, -, W, NH, 460, 687, NBPT. In HH of Sewall Marden, age 55, Wheelwright, born in NH.
MARDEN, IRA, 28, M, Overseer, W, NH, 584, 860, NBPT.
MARDEN, JEREMIAH A., 30, M, Machinist, W, NH, 461, 689, NBPT.
MARDEN, LOIS J., 10, F, -, W, NH, 461, 689, NBPT. In HH of Jeremiah A. Marden, age 30, Machinist, born in NH.
MARDEN, MARY, 25, F, -, W, NH, 460, 687, NBPT. In HH of Sewall Marden, age 55, Wheelwright, born in NH.
MARDEN, MARY J., 19, F, -, W, Maine, 659, 949, NBPT. In HH of Rebecca Gardner, age 40, born in MA.
MARDEN, SALLY, 55, F, -, W, NH, 460, 687, NBPT. In HH of Sewall Marden, age 55, Wheelwright, born in NH.
MARDEN, SARAH A., 21, F, -, W, Maine, 659, 949, NBPT. In HH of Rebecca Gardner, age 40, born in MA.
MARDEN, SEWALL, 55, M, Wheelwright, W, NH, 460, 687, NBPT.
MARDEN, SUSANNA, 55, F, -, W, NH, 244, 307, NBPT*.
MARR, ANDREW, 16, M, Laborer, W, Ireland, 206, 305, NBPT. In HH of Margreat {sic} Marr, age 40, born in Ireland.
MARR, BRIDGET, 19, F, -, W, Ireland, 206, 305, NBPT. In HH of Margreat {sic} Marr, age 40, born in Ireland.

MARR, CATHERINE, 15, F, -, W, Ireland, 206, 305, NBPT. In HH of Margreat {sic} Marr, age 40, born in Ireland.

MARR, MARGREAT, 40, F, -,W, Ireland, 206, 305, NBPT.

MARR, MARY, 8, F, -, W, Ireland, 206, 305, NBPT. In HH of Margreat {sic} Marr, age 40, born in Ireland.

MARSH, JOHN J., 29, M, Mariner, W, MA, 192, 279, NBPT.

MARSH, JOSEPH, 60, M, None, W, MA, 788,1114, NBPT. In Poor House.

MARSHALL, HANNAH T., 39, F, Boarding House, W, MA, 140, 166, NBPT*.

MARSHALL, JAMES E., 25, M, Wheelwright, W, Nova Scotia, 262, 331, NBPT*. In HH of Shan Marshall age 28, Wheelwright, born in MA.

MARSHALL, MOLELY, 25, F, -, W, Nova Scotia, 262, 331, NBPT*. In HH of Shan Marshall age 28, Wheelwright, born in MA.

MARSHALL, SARAH, 15, F, -, W, NH, 532, 706, NBPT*. In HH of Henry P. Tuttle, age 32, Blacksmith, born in Ct.

MARSHALL, SHAN, 28, M, Wheelwright, W, MA, 262, 331, NBPT*.

MARSHALL, THOMAS E., 18, M, Painter, W, MA, 140, 166, NBPT*. In HH of Hannah T. Marshall, age 39, Boarding House, born in MA.

MARSLON, WILLIAM A., 29, M, Attorney at Law, 0, MA, 40, 47, NBPT*. In HH of Frances F. Monroe, age 32, female, Boarding House, born in Maine.

MARSTES, CHARLES, 64, M, Shoe Manufacturer, W, NH, 320, 415, NBPT*.

MARSTES, CHARLES A., 10, M, -, W, NY, 320, 415, NBPT*. In HH of Charles Marstes, age 64, Shoe Manufacturer, born in NH.

MARSTON, JACOB, 20, M, Shoemaker, W, MA, 577, 852, NBPT. In HH of Robert Robinson, Jr., age 44, Shoe Manufacturing, born in Maine.

MARSTON, STEPHEN W., 62, M, Judge Police Court, W, NH, 695, 987, NBPT.

MARTHIN, CAROLINE, 24, F, -, W, NH, 135, 200, NBPT. In HH of Joshua Marthin, age 27, Painter, born in NH.

MARTHIN, JOSHUA, 27, M, Painter, W, NH, 135, 200, NBPT.

MARTIN, BARTHOLOMEW, 22, M, Engineer, W, NH, 53, 78, NBPT.

MARTIN, CALVIN P., 43, M, Machinist, W, MA, 253, 366, NBPT.

MARTIN, CANDACE, 45, F, -, W, RI, 253, 366, NBPT. In HH of Calvin P. Martin, age 43, Machinist, born in MA.

MARTIN, CATHARINE, 21, F, -, W, Ireland, 127, 152, NBPT*. In HH of Samuel Stevens, Jr., age 24, Dry Goods Dealer, born in MA.

MARTIN, DEAN R., 25, M, Merchant, W, MA, 369, 543, NBPT.

MARTIN, ENOCH, 23, M, Joiner, W, MA, 424, 552, NBPT*. In HH of Benjamin Smith, age 46, Painter, born in VT.

MARTIN, GRATIN JR., 33, M, Drayman, W, MA, 257, 322, NBPT*.

MARTIN, HARRIET, 75, F, -, W, MA, 788,1114, NBPT. In Poor House. .

MARTIN, JANE, 19, F, -, W, Maine, 427, 633, NBPT. In HH of Walter Gould, age 49, Carpenter, born in Maine.

MARTIN, MARGARET, 25, F, -, W, NH, 53, 78, NBPT. In HH of Bartholomew Martin, age 22, Engineer, born in NH.

MARTON, ANN B., 21, F, -, W, Ireland, 139, 205, NBPT. In HH of Dennis Marton, age 57, Laborer, born in Ireland.

MARTON, BRIDGET, 18, F, -, W, Ireland, 139, 205, NBPT. In HH of Dennis Marton, age 57, Laborer, born in Ireland.

MARTON, DENNIS, 57, M, Laborer, W, Ireland, 139, 205, NBPT.

MARTON, DENNIS, 20, M, Laborer, W, Ireland, 139, 205, NBPT. In HH of Dennis Marton, age 57, Laborer, born in Ireland.

MARTON, ELIZABETII, 47, F, -, W, Ireland, 139, 205, NBPT. In HH of Dennis Marton, age 57, Laborer, born in Ireland.

MASON, MARGARET, 17, F, -, W, Ireland, 110, 131, NBPT*. In HH of Mary Jenkins, age 60, born in MA.

MASON, WILLIAM, 33, M, Painter, W, MA, 282, 362, NBPT*.

MAXWELL, LOANNI, 17, M, Mariner, W, MA, 435, 571, NBPT*. In HH of Dorcas Maxwell, age 40, born in MA.

MAY, PATRICK, 22, M, Mariner, W, Newfoundland, 758,1070, NBPT. In HH of Michael Aynwant, age 56, Mariner, born in Ireland.

MAY, RICHARD, 25, M, Mariner, W, Newfoundland, 758,1070, NBPT. In HH of Michael Aynwant, age 56, Mariner, born in Ireland.

MAYS, LARRON, 27, M, Operative in Mill, W, MA, 146, 215, NBPT. In HH of George Munroe, age 33, Confectioner, born in MA.

MCAFFEE, ADAMS, 31, M, Weaver, W, NH, 166, 241, NBPT.

MCAFFEE, ELIZABETH R., 26, F, -, W, VT, 166, 241, NBPT. In HH of Adams McAffee, age 31, Weaver, born in NH.

MCBRIDE, MARY, 28, F, -, W, Ireland, 277, 407, NBPT. In HH of Bridget R. Darathy, age 31, born in Ireland.

MCBRIDGE, CATHARINE, 20, F, -, W, Ireland, 41, 48, NBPT*. In HH of William Balch, age 54, Merchant, born in MA.

MCCABE, ANN, 20, F, -, W, Ireland, 640, 927, NBPT. In HH of Catherine McCoffery, age 42, born in Ireland.

MCCABES, JOHN, 25, M, Laborer, W, Ireland, 56, 62, NBPT*. In HH of Oliver Sanborn, age 29, Laborer, born MA.

MCCARTER, CORNELIUS, 13, M, -, W, Ireland, 507, 758, NBPT. In HH of John McCarter, age 38, Laborer, born in Ireland.

MCCARTER, HANNAH, 3, F, -, W, Ireland, 507, 758, NBPT. In HH of John McCarter, age 38, Laborer, born in Ireland.

MCCARTER, HANNAH C., 32, F, -, W, Ireland, 507, 758, NBPT. In HH of John McCarter, age 38, Laborer, born in Ireland.

MCCARTER, JEREMIAH, 9, M, -, W, Ireland, 507, 758, NBPT. In HH of John McCarter, age 38, Laborer, born in Ireland.

MCCARTER, JOANNA, 34, F, Dentist, W, Ireland, 597, 875, NBPT. In HH of Mayo G. Smith, age 33, Dentist, born in MA.

MCCARTER, JOANNA, 11, F, -, W, Ireland, 507, 758, NBPT. In HH of John McCarter, age 38, Laborer, born in Ireland.

MCCARTER, JOHN, 38, M, Laborer, W, Ireland, 507, 758, NBPT.

MCCARTER, JUDITH, 16, F, -, W, Ireland, 727,1026, NBPT. In HH of Jeremiah Colman, age 67, Farmer, born in MA.
MCCARTER, JULIA, 7, F, -, W, Ireland, 507, 758, NBPT. In HH of John McCarter, age 38, Laborer, born in Ireland.
MCCARTER, MARGARET, 23, F, -, W, Ireland, 640, 927, NBPT. In HH of Catherine McCoffery, age 42, born in Ireland.
MCCARTER, MARGARET, 19, F, -, W, Ireland, 719,1018, NBPT. In HH of William Thurston, age 43, Dealer in Lumber, born in Maine.
MCCARTER, MARY, 5, F, -, W, Ireland, 507, 758, NBPT. In HH of John McCarter, age 38, Laborer, born in Ireland.
MCCARTHY, JAMES, 27, M, -, W, Ireland, 413, 540, NBPT*. In HH of Jacob Souther, age 37, Mariner, born in NH.
MCCARTHY, MARY H., 27, F, -, W, Ireland, 413, 540, NBPT*. In HH of Jacob Souther, age 37, Mariner, born in NH.
MCCHASE, JOHN, 17, M, Clerk, W, MA, 658, 948, NBPT. In HH of Parker Roberts, age 45, Merchant, born in MA.
MCCOFFERY, CATHERINE, 42, M, -, W, Ireland, 640, 927, NBPT.
MCCOFFERY, CATHERINE, 13, F, -, W, Ireland, 640, 927, NBPT. In HH of Catherine McCoffery, age 42, born in Ireland.
MCCOFFERY, FELIX, 15, M, -, W, Ireland, 640, 927, NBPT. In HH of Catherine McCoffery, age 42, born in Ireland.
MCCOFFERY, JOHN, 19, M, Operative, W, Ireland, 640, 927, NBPT. In HH of Catherine McCoffery, age 42, born in Ireland.
MCCOFFERY, MARY A., 19, F, -, W, Ireland, 640, 927, NBPT. In HH of Catherine McCoffery, age 42, born in Ireland.
MCCUSKER, JOHN, 37, M, Trader, W, Ireland, 25, 29, NBPT*.
MCDONNEL, ALEXANDER, 40, M, Laborer, W, Ireland, 288, 422, NBPT.
MCDONNEL, JULIA, 42, F, -, W, Ireland, 288, 422, NBPT. In HH of Alexander McDonnel, age 40, Laborer, born in Ireland.
MCDONNEL, PATRICK, 25, M, Laborer, W, Ireland, 788,1114, NBPT. In Poor House.
MCELROY, ISABELLA, 30, F, -, W, Ireland, 411, 613, NBPT. In HH of Hannah Tappan, age 78, born in MA.
MCFEE, MARY J., 21, F, -, W, NH, 226, 332, NBPT. In HH of John S. Gilman, age 36, Overseer in Mill, born in NH.
MCGIMLEY/MCGINLEY
MCGIMLEY, CATHERINE, 15, F, -, W, N.B., 567, 841, NBPT. In HH of Edward McGimley, age 39, Artist, born in Ireland.
MCGIMLEY, EDWARD, 80, M, None, W, Ireland, 567, 841, NBPT. In HH of Edward McGimley, age 39, Artist, born in Ireland.
MCGIMLEY, EDWARD, 39, M, Artist, W, Ireland, 567, 841, NBPT.
MCGIMLEY, ELIJAH, 7, M, -, W, Maine, 567, 841, NBPT. In HH of Edward McGimley, age 39, Artist, born in Ireland.
MCGIMLEY, ELLEN, 38, F, -, W, Ireland, 567, 841, NBPT. In HH of Edward McGimley, age 39, Artist, born in Ireland.
MCGIMLEY, ISAAC, 3, M, -, W, Maine, 567, 841, NBPT. In HH of Edward McGimley, age 39, Artist, born in Ireland.
MCGIMLEY, JAMES W., 9, M, -, W, N.B., 567, 841, NBPT. In HH of Edward McGimley, age 39, Artist,

born in Ireland.
MCGIMLEY, JOHN W.F., 11, M, -, W, N.B., 567, 841, NBPT. In HH of Edward McGimley, age 39, Artist, born in Ireland.
MCGIMLEY, MARY J., 13, F, -, W, N.B., 567, 841, NBPT. In HH of Edward McGimley, age 39, Artist, born in Ireland.
MCGLELON, ALICE, 10, F, -, W, Ireland, 403, 600, NBPT. In HH of Patrick McGlelon, age 35, Blacksmith, born in Ireland.
MCGLELON, JANE, 7, F, -, W, Ireland, 403, 600, NBPT. In HH of Patrick McGlelon, age 35, Blacksmith, born in Ireland.
MCGLELON, KATE, 5, F, -, W, Ireland, 403, 600, NBPT. In HH of Patrick McGlelon, age 35, Blacksmith, born in Ireland.
MCGLELON, MARY A., 2, F, -, W, Ireland, 403, 600, NBPT. In HH of Patrick McGlelon, age 35, Blacksmith, born in Ireland.
MCGLELON, PATRICK, 35, M, Blacksmith, W, Ireland, 403, 600, NBPT.
MCGLELON, ROSE, 31, F, -, W, Ireland, 403, 600, NBPT. In HH of Patrick McGlelon, age 35, Blacksmith, born in Ireland.
MCGLEW, CATHERINE, 46, F, -, W, Ireland, 325, 479, NBPT. In HH of Hugh McGlew, age 25, Blacksmith, born in MA.
MCGLEW, HUGH, 25, M, Blacksmith, W, MA, 325, 479, NBPT.
MCGLEW, LYDIA, 24, F, -, W, Maine, 325, 479, NBPT. In HH of Hugh McGlew, age 25, Blacksmith, born in MA.
MCGLEW, MARY A., 20, F, -, W, Nova Scotia, 325, 480, NBPT. In HH of Patrick McGlew, age 29, Blacksmith, born in Ireland.
MCGLEW, PATRICK, 29, M, Blacksmith, W, Ireland, 325, 480, NBPT.
MCGLEW, WINEFORD, 26, M, Blacksmith, W, Newfoundland, 325, 480, NBPT. In HH of Patrick McGlew, age 29, Blacksmith, born in Ireland.
MCGRACE, HELLEN, 20, F, -, W, Ireland, 251, 362, NBPT. In HH of Mark Symonds, age 59, Master Mariner, born in MA.
MCGRAFF, BRIDGET, 6, F, -, W, Newfoundland, 731,1032, NBPT. In HH of Patrick McGraff, age 39, Mariner, born in Ireland.
MCGRAFF, ELLEN, 11, F, -, W, Newfoundland, 731,1032, NBPT. In HH of Patrick McGraff, age 39, Mariner, born in Ireland.
MCGRAFF, MARY, 32, M, -, W, Newfoundland, 731,1032, NBPT. In HH of Patrick McGraff, age 39, Mariner, born in Ireland.
MCGRAFF, MARY, 4, F, -, W, Newfoundland, 731,1032, NBPT. In HH of Patrick McGraff, age 39, Mariner, born in Ireland.
MCGRAFF, MICHAEL, 9, M, -, W, Newfoundland, 731,1032, NBPT. In HH of Patrick McGraff, age 39, Mariner, born in Ireland.
MCGRAFF, PATRICK, 39, M, Mariner, W, Ireland, 731,1032, NBPT.
MCGRAY, JULIA, 40, F, W, 0, Ireland, 205, 303, NBPT. In HH of Thomas McGray, age 45, Laborer, born in Ireland.
MCGRAY, THOMAS, 45, M, Laborer, W, Ireland, 205, 303, NBPT.
MCGRULL, BRIDGET, 32, F, -, W, Ireland, 466, 697, NBPT. In HH of James McGrull, age 31, Laborer, born in Ireland.
MCGRULL, JAMES, 31, M, Laborer, W, Ireland, 466, 697, NBPT.

MCGRULL, MARGARET, 4, F, -, W, England, 466, 697, NBPT. In HH of James McGrull, age 31, Laborer, born in Ireland.
MCGRULL, MICHAEL, 8, M, -, W, England, 466, 697, NBPT. In HH of James McGrull, age 31, Laborer, born in Ireland.
MCGUINN, MARY, 15, F, -, W, Ireland, 580, 855, NBPT. In HH of Isaac H. Boardman, age 39, Merchant, born in MA.
MCGUIRE, ANNA, 10, F, -, W, Ireland, 356, 470, NBPT*. In HH of John Souther, age 23, Mariner, born in NH.
MCGUIRE, BRIDGET, 18, F, -, W, Ireland, 356, 470, NBPT*. In HH of John Souther, age 23, Mariner, born in NH.
MCGUIRE, DANIEL, 20, M, Laborer, W, Ireland, 356, 470, NBPT*. In HH of John Souther, age 23, Mariner, born in NH.
MCGUIRE, ELLEN, 16, F, -, W, Ireland, 594, 871, NBPT. In HH of Sophia Todd, age 64, born in MA.
MCGUIRE, FELIX, 12, M, -, W, Ireland, 356, 470, NBPT*. In HH of John Souther, age 23, Mariner, born in NH.
MCGUIRE, HUGH, 8, M, -, W, Ireland, 356, 470, NBPT*. In HH of John Souther, age 23, Mariner, born in NH.
MCGUIRE, MARY, 50, F, -, W, Ireland, 356, 470, NBPT*. In HH of John Souther, age 23, Mariner, born in NH.
MCHENNEY, ROSONNA, 40, F, -, W, Ireland, 667, 958, NBPT. In HH of Moses Davenport, age 44, Merchant, born in MA.
MCKENNEY, MARGARET, 63, F, -, W, England, 179, 258, NBPT. In HH of Patrick McKenney, age 40, Laborer, born in Ireland.
MCKENNEY, PATRICK, 40, M, Laborer, W, Ireland, 179, 258, NBPT.
MCKENNY, THOMAS, 31, M, Master of Steamer, W, England, 382, 564, NBPT.
MCMAHON, ROSE, 17, F, -, W, Ireland, 30, 40, NBPT. In HH of George Lunt, age 45, Master Mariner, born in MA.
MCMAIN, MARY A., 22, F, -, W, Ireland, 378, 558, NBPT. In HH of Mary Nelson, age 50, born in MA.
MCMANNEY, ANNA, 11, F, -, W, Nova Scotia, 431, 565, NBPT*. In HH of Barnard McManney, age 45, Farmer, born in Ireland.
MCMANNEY, BARNARD, 45, M, Farmer, W, Ireland, 431, 565, NBPT*.
MCMANNEY, BARNARD, 15, M, Farmer, W, Nova Scotia, 431, 565, NBPT*. In HH of Barnard McManney, age 45, Farmer, born in Ireland.
MCMANNEY, BRIDGET, 13, F, -, W, Nova Scotia, 431, 565, NBPT*. In HH of Barnard McManney, age 45, Farmer, born in Ireland.
MCMANNEY, CHARLES, 4, M, -, W, Nova Scotia, 431, 565, NBPT*. In HH of Barnard McManney, age 45, Farmer, born in Ireland.
MCMANNEY, HUGH, 18, M, Farmer, W, Nova Scotia, 431, 565, NBPT*. In HH of Barnard McManney, age 45, Farmer, born in Ireland.
MCMANNEY, JOHN, 2, M, -, W, Nova Scotia, 431, 565, NBPT*. In HH of Barnard McManney, age 45, Farmer, born in Ireland.
MCMANNEY, MARGARET, 27, F, -, W, Ireland, 431, 565, NBPT*. In HH of Barnard McManney, age 45, Farmer, born in Ireland.
MCMANNEY, MARGARET, 8,

F, -, W, Nova Scotia, 431, 565, NBPT*. In HH of Barnard McManney, age 45, Farmer, born in Ireland.
MCMANNEY, EDWARD, 17, M, Farmer, W, Nova Scotia, 431, 565, NBPT*. In HH of Barnard McManney, age 45, Farmer, born in Ireland.
MCMARTIN, BRIDGET, 26, F, -, W, Ireland, 209, 309, NBPT. In HH of Sarah McMartin, age 50, born in Ireland.
MCMARTIN, MARTIN, 18, M, Laborer, M, Ireland, 209, 309, NBPT. In HH of Sarah McMartin, age 50, born in Ireland.
MCMARTIN, MARY, 16, F, -, W, Ireland, 209, 309, NBPT. In HH of Sarah McMartin, age 50, born in Ireland.
MCMARTIN, MARY H., 19, F, -, W, Ireland, 209, 309, NBPT. In HH of Sarah McMartin, age 50, born in Ireland.
MCMARTIN, PATRICK, 23, M, Laborer, W, Ireland, 209, 309, NBPT. In HH of Sarah McMartin, age 50, born in Ireland.
MCMARTIN, SARAH, 50, F, -, W, Ireland, 209, 309, NBPT.
MCMARTIN, WILLIAM, 25, M, Laborer, M, Ireland, 209, 309, NBPT. In HH of Sarah McMartin, age 50, born in Ireland.
MCMUNROW, PATRICK, 14, M, W, Ireland, 205, 303, NBPT. In HH of Thomas McGray, age 45, Laborer, born in Ireland.
MCNULTY, BRIDGET, 21, F, -, W, Ireland, 262, 380, NBPT. In HH of Joseph Shakford, age 50, Mariner, born in MA.
MCNUTY, BRIDGET, 60, F, -, W, Ireland, 261, 378, NBPT. In HH of Patrick McNuty, age 60, Laborer, born in Ireland.
MCNUTY, BRIDGET, 4, F, -, W, Ireland, 261, 378, NBPT. In HH of Patrick McNuty, age 60, Laborer, born in Ireland.
MCNUTY, FERMENA, 18, M, Laborer, W, Ireland, 261, 378, NBPT. In HH of Patrick McNuty, age 60, Laborer, born in Ireland.
MCNUTY, MATHA, 15, F, -, W, Ireland, 261, 378, NBPT. In HH of Patrick McNuty, age 60, Laborer, born in Ireland.
MCNUTY, PATRICK, 50, M, Laborer, W, Ireland, 261, 378, NBPT.
MCNUTY, PATRICK, 14, M, -, W, Ireland, 261, 378, NBPT. In HH of Patrick McNuty, age 60, Laborer, born in Ireland.
MCNUTY, WILLIAM, 30, M, Laborer, W, Ireland, 261, 378, NBPT. In HH of Patrick McNuty, age 60, Laborer, born in Ireland.
MCNUTY, WINNEFER, 16, F, -, W, Ireland, 261, 378, NBPT. In HH of Patrick McNuty, age 60, Laborer, born in Ireland.
MCPHEE, JANE, 41, F, -, W, New Brunswick, 603, 793, NBPT*. In HH of John McPhee, age 52, Ship Carpenter, born in Halifax.
MCPHEE, JOHN, 52, M, Ship Carpenter, W, Halifax, 603, 793, NBPT*.
MCQUILLEN, MEHETABLE, 56, F, -, W, NH, 369, 486, NBPT*. In HH of Robert McQuillen, age 66, Millwright, born in NH.
MCQUILLEN, ROBERT, 66, M, Millwright, W, NH, 369, 486, NBPT*.
MCRAY, WILLIAM, 25, M, None, W, Nova Scotia, 239, 347, NBPT. In HH of Elizabeth Currier, age 46, born in Nova Scotia.
MCRENSIE, WILLIAM, 25, M, Mariner, W, N.S., 493, 736, NBPT. In HH of Ann Post, age 54, born in N.S. {Nova Scotia}.

MCVAY, JAMES, 50, M, Tailor, W, MA, 87, 102, NBPT*.
MCVAY, JOHN, 18, M, Blacksmith, W, MA, 87, 102, NBPT*. In HH of James McVay, age 50, Tailor, born in MA.
MCVAY, SARAH J., 20, F, -, W, Ireland, 153, 222, NBPT. In HH of Martha A. Whright, age 86, born in England.
MEADER, CHARLES H., 16, M, None, W, MA, 701, 994, NBPT. In HH of James Meader, age 36, Machinist, born in NH.
MEADER, JAMES, 36, M, Machinist, W, NH, 701, 994, NBPT.
MEDBURY, EDWIN J., 20, M, Tin Plate Worker, W, MA, 217, 270, NBPT*. In HH of Nicholas Medbury, age 50, Bap. Clergyman, born in MA.
MEDBURY, NICHOLAS, 50, M, Baptist Clergyman, W, MA, 217, 270, NBPT*.
MEGAN, ELIZA, 50, F, -, W, Ireland, 736,1041, NBPT. In HH of John L. Grindal, age 48, Grocer, born in Maine.
MEGAN, MARY, 16, F, -, W, Ireland, 736,1041, NBPT. In HH of John L. Grindal, age 48, Grocer, born in Maine.
MELLEN, BRIDGET, 12, F, -, W, N.B., 768,1086, NBPT. In HH of Charles Mellen, age 46, Laborer, born in Ireland.
MELLEN, CATHERINE, 45, F, -, W, Ireland, 768,1086, NBPT. In HH of Charles Mellen, age 46, Laborer, born in Ireland.
MELLEN, CATHERINE, 8, F, -, W, N.B., 768,1086, NBPT. In HH of Charles Mellen, age 46, Laborer, born in Ireland.
MELLEN, CHARLES, 46, M, Laborer, W, Ireland, 768,1086, NBPT.
MELLEN, FRANCIS, 12, M, -, W, N.B., 768,1086, NBPT. In HH of Charles Mellen, age 46, Laborer, born in Ireland.
MELLEN, JOHN, 18, M, Machinist, W, Ireland, 768,1086, NBPT. In HH of Charles Mellen, age 46, Laborer, born in Ireland.
MELLEN, SARAH, 15, F, -, W, N.S., 768,1086, NBPT. In HH of Charles Mellen, age 46, Laborer, born in Ireland.
MELOUR, GEORGE B., 16, M, Carpenter, W, MA, 363, 534, NBPT. In HH of George N. Bartlett, age 29, Carpenter, born in NH.
MERCHANT, C.S., 54, M, U.S. Army, W, NY, 130, 155, NBPT*.
MERCHANT, CHARLES G., 29, M, U.S. Army, W, NH, 130, 155, NBPT*. In HH of C.S. Merchant, age 54, U.S. Army, born in NY.
MERCHANT, CLARK, 14, M, -, W, GA, 130, 155, NBPT*. In HH of C.S. Merchant, age 54, U.S. Army, born in NY.
MERCHANT, LYDIA B., 8, F, -, W, CT, 130, 155, NBPT*. In HH of C.S. Merchant, age 54, U.S. Army, born in NY.
MERCHANT, STEPHEN C., 16, M, Student, W, GA, 130, 155, NBPT*. In HH of C.S. Merchant, age 54, U.S. Army, born in NY.
MERCHANT, VALERIA, 23, F, -, W, PA, 130, 155, NBPT*. In HH of C.S. Merchant, age 54, U.S. Army, born in NY.
MERCHANT, VIRGINIA, 10, F, -, W, NY, 130, 155, NBPT*. In HH of C.S. Merchant, age 54, U.S. Army, born in NY.
MERDAN, JOHN L., 39, M, Stage Driver, W, NH, 464, 692, NBPT.
MERILL, MOSES, 39, M, Cabinetmaker, W, MA, 512, 765, NBPT.

MERILL, WILLIAM, 52, M, Tobacconist, W, MA, 246, 356, NBPT.
MERRIAN, DELIA, 21, F, -, W, NH, 39, 55, NBPT. In HH of Mathew Merrian, age 53, Grocer, born in Maine.
MERRIAN, IZETTE, 52, F, -, W, NH, 39, 55, NBPT. In HH of Mathew Merrian, age 53, Grocer, born in Maine.
MERRIAN, MATHEW, 53, M, Grocer, W, Maine, 39, 55, NBPT.
MERRIAN, MATHEW H., 26, M, Machinist, W, NH, 39, 55, NBPT. In HH of Mathew Merrian, age 53, Grocer, born in Maine.
MERRILL, ABNER L., 24, M, Trader, W, NH, 489, 651, NBPT*. In HH of Rebekah H. Toppan, age 43, born in MA.
MERRILL, AMANDA W., 19, F, -, W, NH, 474, 630, NBPT*. In HH of Elizabeth A. Merrill, age 45, born in MA.
MERRILL, AMOS B., 2, M, -, W, NH, 138, 204, NBPT. In HH of Nathaniel J. Merrill, age 32, Methodist Clergyman, born in NH.
MERRILL, AMOS C., 13, M, -, W, NH, 531, 704, NBPT*. In HH of Jacob Merrill, age 57, Ship Carpenter, born in MA.
MERRILL, ASA, 29, M, Wheelwright, W, Maine, 21, 25, NBPT.
MERRILL, CORNWELL, 9, M, -, W, Nova Scotia, 176, 255, NBPT. In HH of William H. Merrill, age 29, Engineer, born in Nova Scotia.
MERRILL, DAVID J., 43, M, Apothecary, W, MA, 459, 607, NBPT*.
MERRILL, DOROTHY, 48, F, -, W, NH, 531, 704, NBPT*. In HH of Jacob Merrill, age 57, Ship Carpenter, born in MA.
MERRILL, ELINSER?, 33, F, -, W, NH, 65, 74, NBPT*. In HH of Luther F. Dimmick, age 58, Cong. Clergyman, born VT.
MERRILL, ELIZABETH, 29, F, -, W, Nova Scotia, 176, 255, NBPT. In HH of William H. Merrill, age 29, Engineer, born in Nova Scotia.
MERRILL, ELIZABETH R., 20, F, -, W, NH, 531, 704, NBPT*. In HH of Jacob Merrill, age 57, Ship Carpenter, born in MA.
MERRILL, EUNICE D., 26, F, -, W, Maine, 124, 147, NBPT*. In HH of John Merrill, 3rd, age 29, Physician, born in MA.
MERRILL, GEORGIEANA P., 28, F, -, W, NH, 138, 204, NBPT. In HH of Nathaniel J. Merrill, age 32, Methodist Clergyman, born in NH.
MERRILL, HALEY, 10, F, W, 0, Nova Scotia, 176, 255, NBPT. In HH of William H. Merrill, age 29, Engineer, born in Nova Scotia.
MERRILL, HANNAH, 55, F, -, W, Maine, 484, 645, NBPT*.
MERRILL, HARRIET, 42, F, -, W, Maine, 192, 280, NBPT.
MERRILL, HENRY JR., 42, M, Wool Business, W, MA, 492, 655, NBPT*.
MERRILL, JACOB, 57, M, Ship Carpenter, W, MA, 531, 704, NBPT*.
MERRILL, JOHN, 57, M, Conveyances, W, MA, 74, 83, NBPT*.
MERRILL, JOHN JR., 29, M, Shoemaker, W, MA, 540, 718, NBPT*.
MERRILL, JOHN, 3RD, 29, M, Physician, W, MA, 124, 147, NBPT*.
MERRILL, JOSEPH, 32, M,

Victualler, W, MA, 570, 756, NBPT*.
MERRILL, JOSEPH W., 24, M, Shoe Cutter, W, MA, 611, 801, NBPT*.
MERRILL, LUCY M., 49, F, -, W, NH, 74, 83, NBPT*. In HH of John Merrill, age 57, Conveyances, born MA.
MERRILL, LUTHER C., 38, M, Shoemaker, W, MA, 149, 177, NBPT*.
MERRILL, MARIA S., 6, F, -, W, NH, 531, 704, NBPT*. In HH of Jacob Merrill, age 57, Ship Carpenter, born in MA.
MERRILL, MARY E., 2, F, W, 0, Nova Scotia, 176, 255, NBPT. In HH of William H. Merrill, age 29, Engineer, born in Nova Scotia.
MERRILL, MARY N., 18, F, -, W, NH, 531, 704, NBPT*. In HH of Jacob Merrill, age 57, Ship Carpenter, born in MA.
MERRILL, MOSES M., 37, M, Carpenter, W, MA, 113, 168, NBPT.
MERRILL, NANCY, 33, F, -, W, Maine, 21, 25, NBPT. In HH of Asa Merrill, age 29, Wheelwright, born in Maine.
MERRILL, NATHANIEL J., 32, M, Clergyman, Methodist, W, NH, 138, 204, NBPT.
MERRILL, RACHAEL, 11, F, -, W, Nova Scotia, 176, 255, NBPT. In HH of William H. Merrill, age 29, Engineer, born in Nova Scotia.
MERRILL, ROBERT M., 42, M, Joiner, W, MA, 579, 767, NBPT*.
MERRILL, ROSINA P., 6, F, -, W, NH, 138, 204, NBPT. In HH of Nathaniel J. Merrill, age 32, Methodist Clergyman, born in NH.
MERRILL, SARAH, 4, F, W, 0, Nova Scotia, 176, 255, NBPT. In HH of William H. Merrill, age 29, Engineer, born in Nova Scotia.
MERRILL, WARREN, 24, M, Ship Carpenter, W, NH, 531, 704, NBPT*. In HH of Jacob Merrill, age 57, Ship Carpenter, born in MA.
MERRILL, WILLIAM E., 35, M, Carpenter, W, MA, 143, 210, NBPT.
MERRILL, WILLIAM H., 29, M, Engineer, W, Nova Scotia, 176, 255, NBPT.
MERRITT, WASHINGTON, 18, M, Shoemaker, W, Pr. Edward Island, 479, 636, NBPT*. In HH of David Murphy, age 29, Shoemaker, born in Prince Edward Island.
MERRITT, WILLIAM, 71, M, None, W, MA, 241, 303, NBPT*. In HH of Julia A. Hopkinson, age 44, born in MA.
MERROW, CHARLES W., 40, M, Fisherman, W, MA, 589, 778, NBPT*. In HH of James Merrow, age 49, Ship Carpenter, born in NH.
MERROW, JAMES, 49, M, Ship Carpenter, W, NH, 589, 778, NBPT*.
MERROW, JAMES H., 18, M, Fisherman, W, MA, 589, 778, NBPT*. In HH of James Merrow, age 49, Ship Carpenter, born in NH.
MEYERS, JOHN, 22, M, Fisherman, W, VA, 264, 333, NBPT*. In HH of Joseph Greenleaf, age 62, Sailmaker, born in MA.
MIDDLETON, CHARLES W., 31, M, Shoemaker, W, MA, 222, 328, NBPT. In HH of Abigail Wilson, age 53, born in MA.
MILAN, CATHERINE, 30, F, -, W, Ireland, 507, 756, NBPT. In HH of Thomas Milan, age 30, Laborer, born in Ireland.
MILAN, THOMAS, 30, M, Laborer, W, Ireland, 507, 756, NBPT.
MILLER, BETSY, 14, F, -, W, Ireland, 449, 671, NBPT. In HH of Patrick Conners, age 30, Laborer, born in Ireland.

MILLER, ELLEN, 21, F, -, W, Maine, 641, 928, NBPT. In HH of Herekiah Ripley, age 27, Carpenter, born in Maine.

MILLER, ROSNSELL M., 33, M, Roll Coverer, W, RI, 144, 212, NBPT. In HH of Thomas Currier, 43, Shoemaker, born in MA.

MILLER, THOMAS, 60, M, Laborer, W, Ireland, 449, 671, NBPT. In HH of Patrick Conners, age 30, Laborer, born in Ireland.

MINCHAM, MARGARET, 26, F, -, W, Ireland, 403, 598, NBPT.

MITCHEL, WILLIAM, 30, M, Mariner, W, England, 789,1116, NBPT. In HH of Lois Fullington, age 40, born in MA.

MITCHELL, WILLIAM, 30, M, Painter, W, MA, 446, 590, NBPT*.

MOLAN, BARNET, 23, M, Operative, W, England, 777,1102, NBPT. In HH of Unity Molan, age 58, born in Ireland.

MOLAN, JAMES, 26, M, Operative, W, England, 777,1102, NBPT. In HH of Unity Molan, age 58, born in Ireland.

MOLAN, UNITY, 58, F, -, W, Ireland, 777,1102, NBPT.

MOLTON, WILLIAM, 46, M, Iron Foundry, W, MA, 255, 319, NBPT*.

MONKS, AMELIA, 20, F, -, W, England, 660, 951, NBPT. In HH of James Monks, age 28, Operative, born in England.

MONKS, JAMES, 28, M, Operative, W, England, 660, 951, NBPT.

MONROE, ANNA J., 12, F, W, 0, NH, 40, 47, NBPT*. In HH of Frances F. Monroe, age 32, female, Boarding House, born in Maine.

MONROE, FRANCES F., 32, F, Boarding House, W, Maine, 40, 47, NBPT*.

MONROE, GEORGIANA, 14, F, -, W, NH, 40, 47, NBPT*. In HH of Frances F. Monroe, age 32, female, Boarding House, born in Maine.

MONROE, JAMES O., 10, M, - ,W, Maine, 40, 47, NBPT*. In HH of Frances F. Monroe, age 32, female, Boarding House, born in Maine.

MONROE, LUCY, 61, F, -, W, Maine, 658, 948, NBPT. In HH of Parker Roberts, age 45, Merchant, born in MA.

MOODY, ADALAID B., 20, F, -, W, NH, 252, 364, NBPT. In HH of Sally Dessinette, age 59, born NH.

MOODY, HENRY, 46, M, Blacksmith, W, MA, 218, 323, NBPT.

MOODY, HENRY JR., 28, M, Blacksmith, W, MA, 446, 667, NBPT.

MOODY, HENRY T., 20, M, Blacksmith, W, Maine, 218, 323, NBPT. In HH of Henry Moody, age 44, Blacksmith, born in Maine.

MOODY, JAMES, 5, M, -, W, Nova Scotia, 283, 363, NBPT*. In HH of Patrick Moody, age 40, Cooper, born in Nova Scotia.

MOODY, JANE, 32, F, -, W, Nova Scotia, 283, 363, NBPT*. In HH of Patrick Moody, age 40, Cooper, born in Nova Scotia.

MOODY, MOSES, 70, M, Cabinet Maker, W, MA, 394, 517, NBPT*.

MOODY, NATHAN C., 19, M, Blacksmith, W, NH, 218, 323, NBPT. In HH of Henry Moody, age 44, Blacksmith, born in Maine.

MOODY, PATRICK, 40, M, Cooper, W, Nova Scotia, 283, 363, NBPT*.

MOODY, SARAH, 22, F, -, W, Maine, 652, 942, NBPT. In HH of Nathl. Osgood, age 49, Master Mariner, born in MA.

MOODY, SIMON, 3, M, -, W, Nova Scotia, 283, 363, NBPT*. In

HH of Patrick Moody, age 40, Cooper, born in Nova Scotia.
MOODY, THOMAS, 8, M, -, W, Nova Scotia, 283, 363, NBPT*. In HH of Patrick Moody, age 40, Cooper, born in Nova Scotia.
MOONEY, A.W., 26, M, Trader, W, NH, 373, 490, NBPT*.
MOONEY, ELLEN, 16, F, -, W, Ireland, 668, 960, NBPT. In HH of William Cushing, age 27, Merchant, born in MA.
MOONEY, JOSEPH B., 2, M, -, W, NH, 373, 490, NBPT*. In HH of A.W. Mooney, age 27, born in NH.
MOONEY, NANCY M., 27, F, -, W, NH, 373, 490, NBPT*. In HH of A.W. Mooney, age 27, born in NH.
MOORE, FREDERICK, 35, M, Master Mariner, W, MA, 266, 390, NBPT.
MOORE, LUTHER B., 17, M, Farmer, W, MA, 164, 197, NBPT*. In HH of Nathaniel Coffin, age 66, Farmer, born in MA.
MOORE, PRISCILLA, 56, F, -, W, MA, 788,1114, NBPT. In Poor House. .
MORAN, MICHAEL, 18, M, Laborer, W, Ireland, 547, 727, NBPT*. In HH of Terence Bliss, age 30, Laborer, born in Ireland.
MORETON, GILBERT, 22, M, Wheelwright, W, N.S., 493, 735, NBPT. In HH of John Post, age 24, Farmer, born in N.S. {Nova Scotia}.
MORGAN, MARY, 22, F, -, W, Ireland, 96, 113, NBPT*. In HH of John B. Swazey, age 31, Attorney at Law, born in Maine.
MORRILL, CHARLES O., 27, M, Victualler, W, MA, 587, 776, NBPT*. In HH of Rebekah Mott, age 33, born in MA.
MORRILL, RICHARD B., 29, M, Mariner, W, MA, 434, 570, NBPT*.

MORRILL, SAMUEL G., 34, M, Auctioneer, W, NH, 471, 707, NBPT.
MORRILL, WILLIAM, 30, M, Cabinet Maker, W, MA, 729,1028, NBPT. In HH of Henry Scidenberg, age 42, Cabinet Maker, born in Bremen {Germany}.
MORRIS, CATHARINE, 20, F, -, W, Ireland, 431, 563, NBPT*. In HH of Mary Morris, age 36, born in Ireland.
MORRIS, JAMES, 9, M, -, W, Ireland, 431, 563, NBPT*. In HH of Mary Morris, age 36, born in Ireland.
MORRIS, JANE, 17, F, -, W, Ireland, 431, 563, NBPT*. In HH of Mary Morris, age 36, born in Ireland.
MORRIS, JOHN, 5, M, -, W, Ireland, 431, 563, NBPT*. In HH of Mary Morris, age 36, born in Ireland.
MORRIS, MARY, 36, F, -, W, Ireland, 431, 563, NBPT*.
MORRIS, MARY, 15, F, -, W, Ireland, 431, 563, NBPT*. In HH of Mary Morris, age 36, born in Ireland.
MORRIS, SUSANNA, 13, F, -, W, Ireland, 431, 563, NBPT*. In HH of Mary Morris, age 36, born in Ireland.
MORRISON, ALBERT, 22, M, Mason, W, MA, 566, 840, NBPT. In HH of Lydia Cooley, age 39, born in MA.
MORRISON, ANTHONY, 20, M, Shoemaker, W, MA, 91, 107, NBPT*. In HH of William Morrison, age 58, Shoemaker, born MA.
MORRISON, ELENEZER, 33, M, Ship Carpenter, W, Maine, 473, 629, NBPT*.
MORRISON, HENRY, 60, M, Shoemaker, W, MA, 91, 107,

NBPT*. In HH of William Morrison, age 58, Shoemaker, born MA.

MORRISON, JOHN, 27, M, Truck man, W, Maine, 473, 628, NBPT*.

MORRISON, LUTHER, 18, M, Shoemaker, W, MA, 91, 106, NBPT*. In HH of William Morrison, age 58, Shoemaker, born MA.

MORRISON, MARY F., 23, F, -, W, Maine, 344, 451, NBPT*. In HH of Nathaniel P. Morrison, age 26, Mason, born in MA.

MORRISON, MERRY, 54, F, -, W, NH, 91, 106, NBPT*. In HH of William Morrison, age 58, Shoemaker, born MA.

MORRISON, NATHANIEL P., 26, M, Mason, W, MA, 344, 451, NBPT*.

MORRISON, RICHARD, 16, M, Shoemaker, W, MA, 91, 106, NBPT*. In HH of William Morrison, age 58, Shoemaker, born MA.

MORRISON, THOMAS, 79, M, Late Ship Master, W, NH, 612, 802, NBPT*.

MORRISON, WILLIAM, 58, M, Shoemaker, W, MA, 91, 106, NBPT*.

MORRISON, WILLIAM, 24, M, Shoemaker, W, MA, 91, 107, NBPT*. In HH of William Morrison, age 58, Shoemaker, born MA.

MORRY, HARRIET, 24, F, -, W, Maine, 222, 276, NBPT*. In HH of Stephen Fowle, age 33, Laborer, born in MA.

MORSE, ARABELLA, 48, F, -, W, Maine, 736,1041, NBPT. In HH of John L. Grindal, age 48, Grocer, born in Maine.

MORSE, CHARLES, 45, M, Caulder, W, MA, 400, 594, NBPT.

MORSE, CHARLES H., 16, M, Clerk, W, MA, 340, 444, NBPT*. In HH of Michael Morse, age 50, Carpenter, born in MA.

MORSE, CHARLES W., 18, M, Boat Builder, W, MA, 183, 266, NBPT. In HH of Joseph Morse, Jr., Sail Maker, born in MA.

MORSE, ELLEN, 22, F, -, W, England, 330, 486, NBPT. In HH of Morris Romayne, age 58, Gentleman, born in Ireland.

MORSE, JOSEPH B., 41, M, Printer, W, MA, 579, 854, NBPT.

MORSE, JOSEPH JR., 41, M, Sailmaker, W, MA, 183, 266, NBPT.

MORSE, MICHAEL, 50, M, Carpenter, W, MA, 340, 444, NBPT*.

MORSE, WILLIAM, 18, M, Shoemaker, W, MA, 340, 444, NBPT*. In HH of Michael Morse, age 50, Carpenter, born in MA.

MORSS, WILLIAM B., 46, M, Shoemaker, W, MA, 242, 305, NBPT*.

MORY, CHRISTOPHER, 48, M, Mariner, W, NH, 751,1059, NBPT.

MORY, HANNAH, 18, F, -, W, Maine, 751,1059, NBPT. In HH of Christopher Mory, age 48, Mariner, born in NH.

MOSE, DEBORAH, 64, F, -, W, NH, 300, 438, NBPT. In HH of Joseph Mose, age 66, Carpenter, born in MA.

MOSE, JAMES, 33, M, Laborer, W, MA, 300, 438, NBPT. In HH of Joseph Mose, age 66, Carpenter, born in MA.

MOSE, JOSEPH, 66, M, Carpenter, W, MA, 300, 438, NBPT.

MOSELEY, CHARLOTTE A., 32, F, -, W, Maine, 6, 6, NBPT*. In HH of Edward S. Moseley, age 37, merchant, born in MA.

MOSELEY, EBENEZER, 68, M, Counselor, W, CT, 118, 141, NBPT*.
MOSELEY, EDWARD S., 37, M, Merchant, W, MA, 6, 6, NBPT*.
MOTTRAM, JAMES, 37, M, Machinist, W, England, 135, 199, NBPT.
MOTTRAM, MARY, 35, F, -, W, England, 135, 199, NBPT. In HH of James Mottram, age 37, Machinist, born in England.
MOULTON, JOHN, 30, M, Shipbuilder, W, Maine, 37, 44, NBPT*.
MOULTON, MOSES B., 24, M, Master Mariner, W, MA, 170, 245, NBPT.
MOULTON, NATHANIEL A., 26, M, School Teacher, W, NH, 106, 127, NBPT*.
MOYLAN, PATRICK, 35, M, Laborer, W, Ireland, 24, 28, NBPT*.
MOZZILL, EDWARD M., 23, M, Mariner, W, MA, 377, 494, NBPT*. In HH of William Robinson, age 37, Mariner, born in England.
MUDD, SARAH S., 29, M, -, W, NH, 306, 398, NBPT*. In HH of George W. Fogg, age 22, Shoemaker, born in NH.
MUEKLEROY, MARY, 22, F, -, W, Ireland, 440, 654, NBPT. In HH of Richard S. Spofford, age 63, Physician, born in MA.
MULLIKEN, MOSES J., 33, M, Master Mariner, W, MA, 1, 1, NBPT. In HH of Samuel Mulliken, age 81, Cashier of Bank, born in MA.
MULLIKEN, SAMUEL, 81, M, Cashier of Bank, W, MA, 1, 1, NBPT.
MULLIKEN, SAMUEL G.P., 31, M, Sailor, W, MA, 1, 1, NBPT. In HH of Samuel Mulliken, age 81, Cashier of Bank, born in MA.
MUMFORD, MARTIN M., 26, M, Dentist, W, MA, 609, 889, NBPT. In HH of George W. Skinner, age 22, Physician, born in MA.
MUNROE, GEORGE, 33, M, Confectioner, W, MA, 146, 215, NBPT.
MURDOCK, FRANCIS B., 38, M, Operative, W, England, 199, 293, NBPT.
MURDOCK, JANE, 16, F, W, 0, England, 199, 293, NBPT. In HH of Francis B. Murdock, age 38, Operative, born in England.
MURDOCK, MARY, 37, F, -, W, England, 199, 293, NBPT. In HH of Francis B. Murdock, age 38, Operative, born in England.
MURDOCK, MARY, 13, F, -, W, England, 199, 293, NBPT. In HH of Francis B. Murdock, age 38, Operative, born in England.
MURPHY, DAVID, 29, M, Shoemaker, W, Pr. Edward Island, 479, 636, NBPT*.
MURPHY, EPHRAIM, 31, M, Laborer, W, Maine, 161, 232, NBPT.
MURPHY, ESTHER, 28, F, -, W, Maine, 177, 256, NBPT. In HH of James N. Canney, age 41, Teamster, born in NH.
MURPHY, MARGARET, 23, F, -, W, Pr. Edward Island, 479, 636, NBPT*. In HH of David Murphy, age 29, Shoemaker, born in Prince Edward Island.
MURPHY, MARGARET, 15, F, -, W, Ireland, 405, 529, NBPT*. In HH of Miriam James, age 50, born in NH.
MURPHY, MARGARET, 2, F, -, W, Ireland, 788,1114, NBPT. In Poor House.
MURPHY, MARGARET J., 24, F , -, W, Maine, 161, 232, NBPT. In

HH of Ephraim Murphy, age 31, Laborer, born in Maine.

MURPHY, MARY, 46, F, -, W, Ireland, 474, 711, NBPT. In HH of Michael Murphy, age 48, Laborer, born in Ireland.

MURPHY, MARY, 20, F, -, W, Ireland, 405, 529, NBPT*. In HH of Miriam James, age 50, born in NH.

MURPHY, MARY A., 30, F, -, W, Maine, 177, 256, NBPT. In HH of James N. Canney, age 41, Teamster, born in NH.

MURPHY, SAMUEL H., 5, M, -, W, Maine, 161, 232, NBPT. In HH of Ephraim Murphy, age 31, Laborer, born in Maine.

MURPHY, SARAH, 9, F, -, W, NH, 788,1114, NBPT. In Poor House. .

MURPHY, TIDELIA H., 0, F, -, W, Maine, 161, 232, NBPT. In HH of Ephraim Murphy, age 31, Laborer, born in Maine. Tidelia H. Murphy, age 2 months.

MURS, JOHN, 25, M, Blacksmith, W, RI, 561, 834, NBPT. In HH of Mary Dorr, age 65, born in MA.

MUSSO, JAMES, 61, M, Confectioner, W, MA, 606, 796, NBPT*.

MYRICK, FREDERICK, 35, M, Master Mariner, W, MA, 584, 860, NBPT. In HH of Ira Marden, age 28, Overseer, born in NH.

- N -

NASH, FRANCIS, 24, M, House Joiner, W, MA, 232, 289, NBPT*. In HH of Rebekah Nash, age 45, born in MA.

NASH, SAMUEL, 19, M, Mariner, W, MA, 232, 289, NBPT*. In HH of Rebekah Nash, age 45, born in MA.

NASON, DANIEL, 26, M, Farmer, W, NH, 222, 276, NBPT*. In HH of Stephen Fowle, age 33, Laborer, born in MA.

NAYLAN, MARY M., 24, F, -, W, Ireland, 404, 601, NBPT. In HH of Patrick Naylan, age 30, Laborer, born in Ireland.

NAYLAN, PATRICK, 30, M, Laborer, W, Ireland, 404, 601, NBPT.

NEAL, ALONZO, 14, M, -, W, Maine, 360, 476, NBPT*. In HH of Nancy Hall, age 50, born in NH.

NEAL, CATHARINE, 30, F, -, W, Ireland, 512, 683, NBPT*. In HH of Lawrence Neal, age 28, Ship Carpenter, born in Halifax.

NEAL, DANIEL, 24, M, Carpenter, W, NH, 612, 893, NBPT. In HH of William Hills, age 70, None, born in MA.

NEAL, DARIUS, 32, M, Overseer, W, NH, 746,1052, NBPT.

NEAL, LAWRENCE, 28, M, Ship Carpenter, W, Halifax, 512, 683, NBPT*.

NEAL, LOIS, 27, F, -, W, NH, 746,1052, NBPT. In HH of Darius Neal, age 32, Overseer, born in NH.

NEAL, NATHL., 21, M, Overseer in Mill, W, NH, 371, 546, NBPT.

NEAL, SARAH A., 20, F, -, W, NH, 371, 546, NBPT. In HH of Nathl. C. Neal, age 21, Overseer in Mill, born in NH.

NEIL, ROSELLA, 1, F, -, W, NH, 283, 366, NBPT*. In HH of Richard Couillard, age 36, born in Maine.

NELSON, CLARA, 32, F, -, W, NH, 434, 646, NBPT. In HH of John B. Nelson, age 32, Tailor, born in MA.

NELSON, DANIEL, 65, M, Shoemaker, W, MA, 533, 796, NBPT.
NELSON, JAMES, 13, M, -, W, England, 660, 950, NBPT. In HH of Rebecca Boardman, age 48, born in England.
NELSON, JOHN, 50, M, Operative, W, England, 660, 950, NBPT. In HH of Rebecca Boardman, age 48, born in England.
NELSON, JOHN B., 32, M, Tailor, W, MA, 434, 646, NBPT.
NELSON, MARY, 85, F, -, W, NH, 92, 108, NBPT*. In HH of Justarus A. Stowell, age 50, Machinist, born in MA.
NEVERS, NORAH, 28, F, -, W, Ireland, 237, 299, NBPT*. In HH of William Nevers, age 30, Blacksmith, born in Ireland.
NEVERS, WILLIAM, 30, M, Blacksmith, W, Ireland, 237, 299, NBPT*.
NEWCOMB, JAMES, 28, M, Carpenter, W, Maine, 573, 848, NBPT. In HH of Thomas Noyes, age 70, Shoemaker, born in MA.
NEWCOMB, MARY, 20, F, -, W, Maine, 573, 848, NBPT. In HH of Thomas Noyes, age 70, Shoemaker, born in MA.
NEWCOMB, SUSAN C., 20, F, -, W, Maine, 363, 534, NBPT. In HH of George N. Bartlett, age 29, Carpenter, born in NH.
NEWMAN, BENJAMIN, 54, M, Surveyor of Lumber, W, MA, 33, 40, NBPT*.
NEWMAN, JOHN, 38, M, Joiner, W, MA, 451, 598, NBPT*.
NEWMAN, MARK, 32, M, Trader, W, MA, 33, 40, NBPT*. In HH of Benjamin Newman, age 54, Surveyor of Lumber, born in MA.
NICHOLS, PRUDENCE, 28, F, -, W, Maine, 210, 261, NBPT*. In HH of Thomas Tracy, age 69, Cong. Clergyman, born in MA.
NICHOLS, SAMUEL, 65, M, Master Mariner, W, MA, 455, 677, NBPT.
NICHOLS, SUSAN, 30, F, -, W, Maine, 151, 220, NBPT. In HH of Hannah White, age 45, born in Maine.
NICHOLS, SUSAN, 25, F, -, W, Maine, 125, 182, NBPT. In HH of William Felch, age 31, Shoemaker, born in NH.
NICHOLS, WILLIAM, 69, M, Merchant, W, MA, 689, 981, NBPT.
NICKERSON, JAMES, 26, M, Caulker, W, New Brunswick, 613, 804, NBPT*.
NICKERSON, MATILDA, 20, F, -, W, New Brunswick, 613, 804, NBPT*. In HH of James Nickerson, age 26, Caulker, born in New Brunswick.
NICKERSON, WALTER, 0, M, -, W, New Brunswick, 613, 804, NBPT*. In HH of James Nickerson, age 26, Caulker, born in New Brunswick. Walter Nickerson age 6 months.
NILAN, HANNAH P., 25, F, -, W, Ireland, 311, 460, NBPT.
NILAN, HANNAH P., 25, F, -, W, Ireland, 311, 460, NBPT. In HH of David Shennon, age 23, Laborer, born in Ireland.
NILAN, JAMES, 27, M, Laborer, W, Ireland, 311, 459, NBPT. In HH of David Shennon, age 23, Laborer, born in Ireland.
NOBLE, BENJAMIN, 28, M, Tailor, W, England, 790,1118, NBPT.
NOBLE, DAVID C., 35, M, Shoemaker, W, NY, 60, 67, NBPT*.
NOBLE, GEORGE W., 6, M, -, W, England, 790,1118, NBPT. In HH of Benjamin Noble, age 28,

Tailor, born in England.
NOBLE, MARY, 28, F, -, W, England, 790,1118, NBPT. In HH of Benjamin Noble, age 28, Tailor, born in England.
NORMAN, GEORGE W., 33, M, Mariner, W, MA, 343, 450, NBPT*.
NORMAN, LOIS, 28, F, -, W, Maine, 343, 450, NBPT*. In HH of George W. Norman, age 33, Mariner, born in MA.
NORRIS, CHARLES C., 22, M, Goldsmith, W, MA, 343, 503, NBPT. In HH of Lucy Norris, age 50, born in NH.
NORRIS, LUCY, 58, F, -, W, NH, 343, 503, NBPT.
NORTON, GEORGE, 34, M, Laborer, W, MA, 270, 396, NBPT.
NORTON, JAMES, 58, M, Mariner, W, MA, 100, 147, NBPT.
NORTON, JAMES, 32, M, None, W, Ireland, 25, 33, NBPT. In HH of Rosanna Roune, age 54, born in Ireland.
NORTON, MARGARET W., 24, F, -, W, Ireland, 25, 33, NBPT. In HH of Rosanna Roune, age 54, born in Ireland.
NOWELL, GEORGE, 60, M, Mariner, W, MA, 788,1114, NBPT. In Poor House.
NOWELL, WILLIAM E., 43, M, Shoemaker, W, MA, 54, 79, NBPT.
NOYES, ALBERT, 39, M, Shoemaker, W, MA, 401, 524, NBPT*.
NOYES, CHARLES, 82, M, Machinist, W, NH, 188, 230, NBPT*.
NOYES, CHARLES, 66, M, Shoemaker, W, MA, 788,1114, NBPT. In Poor House.
NOYES, CHARLES A., 17, M, Clerk, W, MA, 686, 978, NBPT. In HH of Nathaniel Noyes, age 59, Merchant, born in MA.

NOYES, DANIEL, 70, M, Carpenter, W, Maine, 788,1114, NBPT. In Poor House.
NOYES, DANIEL D., 28, M, Operative, W, MA, 4, 4, NBPT*.
NOYES, ELIZA, 38, F, -, W, Maine, 382, 563, NBPT. In HH of Jacob Noyes, age 85, Teacher of Navigation, born in MA.
NOYES, GEORGE, 29, M, Clerk, W, MA, 686, 978, NBPT. In HH of Nathaniel Noyes, age 59, Merchant, born in MA.
NOYES, GEORGE W., 29, M, Carpenter, W, MA, 2, 2, NBPT.
NOYES, HANNAH, 35, F, -, W, NH, 188, 230, NBPT*. In HH of Charles Noyes, age 32, Machinist, born in NH.
NOYES, HARRIET, 24, F, -, W, NH, 4, 4, NBPT*. In HH of Daniel D. Noyes, age 28, operative, born MA.
NOYES, JACOB, 85, M, Teacher of Navigation, W, MA, 382, 563, NBPT.
NOYES, JOSIAH P., 50, M, Baker, W, MA, 399, 592, NBPT.
NOYES, NATHAIEL, 59, M, Merchant, W, MA, 686, 978, NBPT.
NOYES, NATHANIEL, 28, M, Carpenter, W, MA, 605, 884, NBPT. In HH of Ann G. Woodman, age 61, born in MA.
NOYES, PHILIP H., 21, M, Painter, W, MA, 449, 595, NBPT*. In HH of Lydia Rendall, age 62, born in MA.
NOYES, SAMUEL, 40, M, Laborer, W, MA, 572, 847, NBPT.
NOYES, SAMUEL, 18, M, Laborer, W, MA, 572, 847, NBPT. In HH of Samuel Noyes, age 40, Laborer, born in MA.
NOYES, SARAH, 30, F, -, W, NH, 4, 4, NBPT*. In HH of Daniel D. Noyes, age 28, operative, born

MA.
NOYES, SEWALL B., 23, M, Mason, W, MA, 218, 323, NBPT. In HH of Henry Moody, age 44, Blacksmith, born in Maine.
NOYES, THOMAS, 70, M, Shoemaker, W, MA, 573, 848, NBPT.
NOYES, WILLIAM, 17, M, Laborer, W, MA, 572, 847, NBPT. In HH of Samuel Noyes, age 40, Laborer, born in MA.
NOYES, WILLIAM P., 31, M, Baker, W, MA, 51, 76, NBPT.
NUTTER, ARIADNA, 24, F, -, W, NH, 145, 213, NBPT. In HH of Joseph C. Adams, age 34, Blacksmith, born in NH.
NUTTING, RACHELL, 19, F, -, W, Maine, 125, 184, NBPT. In HH of Soloman Nutting, age 25 Mariner, born in Maine.
NUTTING, SOLOMAN, 25, M, Mariner, W, Maine, 125, 184, NBPT.

- O -

O'BRIEN, BRIDGET, 37, F, -, W, Ireland, 767,1083, NBPT. In HH of John O'Brien, age 37, Mariner, born in Ireland.
O'BRIEN, BRIDGET, 17, F, -, W, Ireland, 403, 598, NBPT. In HH of Margaret Mincham, age 26, born in Ireland.
O'BRIEN, ELIZABETH C., 32, F, -, W, Nova Scotia, 358, 525, NBPT. In HH of James O'Brien, age 43, Laborer, born in Ireland.
O'BRIEN, ERWIN, 56, F, -, W, Nova Scotia, 299, 437, NBPT. In HH of Thomas W. O'Brien, age 56, Carpenter, born in Ireland.
O'BRIEN, GEORGE, 5, M, -, W, Newfoundland, 767,1083, NBPT. In HH of John O'Brien, age 37, Mariner, born in Ireland.
O'BRIEN, HELEN, 9, F, -, W, Newfoundland, 767,1083, NBPT. In HH of John O'Brien, age 37, Mariner, born in Ireland.
O'BRIEN, JAMES, 43, M, Laborer, W, Ireland, 358, 525, NBPT.
O'BRIEN, JAMES, 15, M, -, W, Newfoundland, 767,1083, NBPT. In HH of John O'Brien, age 37, Mariner, born in Ireland.
O'BRIEN, JOHN, 37, M, Mariner, W, Ireland, 767,1083, NBPT.
O'BRIEN, JOHN, 24, M, Laborer, W, Ireland, 377, 497, NBPT*.
O'BRIEN, MARY, 26, F, -, W, Ireland, 377, 497, NBPT*. In HH of John O'Brien, age 24, Laborer, born in Ireland.
O'BRIEN, MARY A., 17, F, -, W, Newfoundland, 767,1083, NBPT. In HH of John O'Brien, age 37, Mariner, born in Ireland.
O'BRIEN, MARY E., 4, F, -, W, Nova Scotia, 358, 525, NBPT. In HH of James O'Brien, age 43, Laborer, born in Ireland.
O'BRIEN, PORTER, 7, M, -, W, Newfoundland, 767,1083, NBPT. In HH of John O'Brien, age 37, Mariner, born in Ireland.
O'BRIEN, THOMAS W., 56, M, Carpenter, W, Ireland, 299, 437, NBPT.
O'CONNER, ELIZABETH, 22, F, -, W, Ireland, 595, 872, NBPT. In HH of William H. Wells, age 38, School Teacher, born in CT.
O'CONNER, MARY, 38, F, -, W, Ireland, 596, 786, NBPT*. In HH of Michael O'Conner, age 39, Laborer, born in Ireland.
O'CONNER, MICHAEL, 39, M, Laborer, W, Ireland, 596, 786, NBPT*.
O'CONNER, PETER, 12, M, -, W,

Ireland, 596, 786, NBPT*. In HH of Michael O'Conner, age 39, Laborer, born in Ireland.
O'CONNER, ROSE, 22, F, -, W, Ireland, 640, 927, NBPT. In HH of Catherine McCoffery, age 42, born in Ireland.
O'DONNEL, CATHARINE, 22, F, -, W, Ireland, 314, 407, NBPT*. In HH of John Atkinson, age 51, Physician, born in Maine.
O'GRADY, BRIDGET, 18, F, -, W, Ireland, 309, 402, NBPT*. In HH of John Balch, age 47, Factory Agent, born in MA.
O'NEAL, CATHERINE, 13, F, -, W, Ireland, 197, 289, NBPT. In HH of Thomas O'Neal, age 25, Mariner, born in Ireland.
O'NEAL, JOHN, 25, M, Mariner, W, Ireland, 197, 288, NBPT. In HH of Eliza Collins, age 50, born in Ireland.
O'NEAL, MARY, 24, F, -, W, Ireland, 391, 577, NBPT. In HH of Martin Coran, age 35, Laborer, born in Ireland.
O'NEAL, MARY, 22, F, W, 0, Ireland, 197, 288, NBPT. In HH of Eliza Collins, age 50, born in Ireland.
O'NEAL, MARY, 15, F, W, 0, Ireland, 197, 289, NBPT. In HH of Thomas O'Neal, age 25, Mariner, born in Ireland.
O'NEAL, THOMAS, 40, M, Laborer, W, Ireland, 197, 289, NBPT.
O'NEAL, THOMAS, 12, M, -, W, Ireland, 197, 289, NBPT. In HH of Thomas O'Neal, age 25, Mariner, born in Ireland.
OBER, ELIZABETH, 79, F, -, W, MA, 788, 1114, NBPT. In Poor House. .
OBUNN, BARNARD, 40, M, Weaver, W, Ireland, 153, 222, NBPT. In HH of Martha A. Whright, age 86, born in England.
OBUNN, MARY, 34, F, -, W, Ireland, 153, 222, NBPT. In HH of Martha A. Whright, age 86, born in England.
ODELL, BRIDGET, 12, F, -, W, Newfoundland, 161, 194, NBPT*. In HH of James Odell, age 40, Laborer, born in Ireland.
ODELL, BRIDGET P., 40, F, -, W, Ireland, 161, 194, NBPT*. In HH of James Odell, age 40, Laborer, born in Ireland.
ODELL, JAMES, 40, M, Laborer, W, Ireland, 161, 194, NBPT*.
ODELL, JEREMIAH, 8, M, -, W, Newfoundland, 161, 194, NBPT*. In HH of James Odell, age 40, Laborer, born in Ireland.
ODELL, JOHN, 10, M, -, W, Newfoundland, 161, 194, NBPT*. In HH of James Odell, age 40, Laborer, born in Ireland.
ODELL, MARY A., 17, F, -, W, Newfoundland, 161, 194, NBPT*. In HH of James Odell, age 40, Laborer, born in Ireland.
ODELL, TIMOTHY, 5, M, -, W, Newfoundland, 161, 194, NBPT*. In HH of James Odell, age 40, Laborer, born in Ireland.
OHERA, MARY, 29, F, -, W, Ireland, 277, 407, NBPT. In HH of Bridget R. Darathy, age 31, born in Ireland.
ORDWAY, LYDIA, 60, F, -, W, NH, 440, 583, NBPT*. In HH of Luther Pearson, age 45, Cordwainer, born in MA.
ORDWAY, PARSONS, 33, M, Teamster, W, MA, 581, 769, NBPT*.
ORNE, JOHN, 43, M, Boat Builder, W, MA, 531, 791, NBPT.
OSBORN, AMANDA MALVINA, 13, F, W, M, Maine, 426, 554, NBPT*. In HH of John

Osborn, age 35, black, Barber, born in MA.
OSBORN, FRANCES ELLEN, 7, F, W, M, MA, 426, 554, NBPT*. In HH of John Osborn, age 35, black, Barber, born in MA.
OSBORN, GEORGE ALBERT S., -, M, W, M, MA, 426, 554, NBPT*. In HH of John Osborn, age 35, black, Barber, born in MA. George Albert S. Osborn age 1 month.
OSBORN, GEORGE J., 48, M, Plater, W, MA, 788,1114, NBPT. In Poor House.
OSBORN, JOHN, 35, M, Barber, B, MA, 426, 554, NBPT*.
OSBORN, JOHN, 5, M, W, M, MA, 426, 554, NBPT*. In HH of John Osborn, age 35, black, Barber, born in MA.
OSBORN, MARY A., 34, F, W, M, Maine, 426, 554, NBPT*. In HH of John Osborn, age 35, black, Barber, born in MA.
OSBORN, MARY ELIZABETH, 12, F, W, M, Maine, 426, 554, NBPT*. In HH of John Osborn, age 35, black, Barber, born in MA.
OSBORN, WILLIAM HENRY, 2, M, W, M, MA, 426, 554, NBPT*. In HH of John Osborn, age 35, black, Barber, born in MA.
OSGOOD, CHARLES W., 11, M, -, W, NH, 268, 392, NBPT. In HH of Walter Osgood, age 39, Operative, born in NH.
OSGOOD, EDWARD P., 9, M, -, W, NH, 784,1110, NBPT. In HH of Wyatt Osgood, age 44, Operative, born in MA.
OSGOOD, ELIZABETH F., 49, F, -, W, Maine, 652, 942, NBPT. In HH of Nathl. Osgood, age 49, Master Mariner, born in MA.
OSGOOD, EZEKIEL, 48, M, Blacksmith, W, MA, 133, 196, NBPT. In HH of David Lang, age 40, Barber, born in MA.
OSGOOD, MARY E., 15, F, -, W, NH, 784,1110, NBPT. In HH of Wyatt Osgood, age 44, Operative, born in MA.
OSGOOD, NATHL., 49, M, Master Mariner, W, MA, 652, 942, NBPT.
OSGOOD, RHODA A., 10, M, -, W, NH, 268, 392, NBPT. In HH of Walter Osgood, age 39, Operative, born in NH.
OSGOOD, SAMUEL, 20, M, Clerk, W, MA, 294, 429, NBPT. In HH of Rebecca Osgood, age 60, born in MA.
OSGOOD, SARAH, 38, F, -, W, VT, 784,1110, NBPT. In HH of Wyatt Osgood, age 44, Operative, born in MA.
OSGOOD, SARAH D., 12, F, -, W, NH, 784,1110, NBPT. In HH of Wyatt Osgood, age 44, Operative, born in MA.
OSGOOD, SMITH, 50, M, Laborer, W, MA, 520, 691, NBPT*.
OSGOOD, WALTER, 39, M, Operative, W, NH, 268, 392, NBPT.
OSGOOD, WYATT, 44, M, Operative, W, MA, 784,1110, NBPT.
OSTERHOLD, GEORGE, 21, M, -, W, RI, 525, 782, NBPT. In HH of John Woodburn, age 37, Weaver, born in England.
OTIS, ELIZABETH N., 30, F, -, W, NH, 704, 998, NBPT. In HH of Willard Otis, age 32, Machinist, born in NH.
OTIS, LAURETTA, 8, F, -, W, NH, 704, 998, NBPT. In HH of Willard Otis, age 32, Machinist, born in NH.
OTIS, WILLARD, 32, M, Machinist, W, NH, 704, 998, NBPT.
OWENS, ALICE, 28, F, -, W,

Ireland, 3, 3, NBPT*. In HH of Thomas H. Cutter, age 43, painter born MA.

OWENS, ALICE, 14, F, -, W, Ireland, 465, 694, NBPT. In HH of Ellen Owens, age 30, born in Ireland.

OWENS, ANN, 30, F, -, W, Ireland, 465, 695, NBPT. In HH of Barney Owens, age 40, Laborer, born in Ireland.

OWENS, BARNEY, 40, M, Laborer, W, Ireland, 465, 695, NBPT.

OWENS, CATHERINE, 12, F, -, W, Ireland, 465, 694, NBPT. In HH of Ellen Owens, age 30, born in Ireland.

OWENS, CELIA, 30, F, -, B, VA, 573, 759, NBPT*. In HH of Sarah Hale, age 31, born in MA.

OWENS, ELLEN, 30, F, -, W, Ireland, 465, 694, NBPT.

OWENS, MARY, 6, F, -, W, Ireland, 465, 695, NBPT. In HH of Barney Owens, age 40, Laborer, born in Ireland.

- P -

PACKER, HANNAH B., 19, F, -, W, NH, 570, 845, NBPT. In HH of William B. Packer, age 30, born in MA.

PACKER, OLIVE, 64, F, -, W, Maine, 570, 845, NBPT. In HH of William B. Packer, age 30, born in MA.

PACKER, STEPHEN, 49, M, Laborer, W, MA, 101, 118, NBPT*.

PACKER, WILLIAM B., 30, M, Restorator, W, MA, 570, 845, NBPT.

PAGE, AMELIA K., 36, F, -, W, CT, 515, 768, NBPT. In HH of Thomas C. Page, Master Mariner, born in MA.

PAGE, CHARLES W., 17, M, None, W, MA, 453, 600, NBPT*. In HH of John T. Page, age 46, Blacksmith, born in MA.

PAGE, DANIEL, 45, M, Machinist, W, MA, 549, 820, NBPT.

PAGE, DOLLY, 35, F, -, W, NH, 234, 341, NBPT. In HH of William Page, age 36, Master Mariner, born in MA.

PAGE, HENRY, 33, M, House Carpenter, W, MA, 416, 544, NBPT*.

PAGE, JOHN H., 39, M, House Carpenter, W, MA, 348, 457, NBPT*.

PAGE, JOHN T., 46, M, Blacksmith, W, MA, 453, 600, NBPT*.

PAGE, MARGARET R., 34, F, -, W, NH, 416, 544, NBPT*. In HH of Henry Page, age 33, House Carpenter, born in MA.

PAGE, THOMAS C., 37, M, Master Mariner, W, MA, 515, 768, NBPT.

PAGE, WILLIAM, 36, M, Master Mariner, W, MA, 234, 341, NBPT.

PALMER, ELIZA A., 13, F, -, W, NH, 376, 556, NBPT. In HH of Mary Jones, age 80, born in MA.

PALMER, GEORGE C., 51, M, House Carpenter, W, MA, 221, 275, NBPT*.

PAPANTI, HANNINNIO, 1, F, W, 0, Italy, 167, 242, NBPT. In HH of Laige Papanti, age 22, Dancing Master, born in Italy.

PAPANTI, LAIGE, 22, M, Dancing Master, W, Italy, 167, 242, NBPT.

PAPANTI, QUSQUIRA, 23, F, -, W, Italy, 167, 242, NBPT. In HH of Laige Papanti, age 22, Dancing Master, born in Italy.

PARISH, MOSES P., 45, M, Agt. Ploughshuvil?, W, MA, 99, 116, NBPT*. In HH of Hannah Sargent, age 50, born in MA.
PARKER, CHARLES, 28, M, Mariner, W, NH, 266, 340, NBPT*.
PARKER, CHARLES W., 32, M, Grocer, W, Maine, 429, 636, NBPT.
PARKER, JOHN, 27, M, Hatter, W, England, 533, 709, NBPT*.
PARKER, JOHN, 25, M, Carriage Maker, W, CT, 607, 887, NBPT. In HH of Eliza Reyes, age 48, born in MA.
PARKER, LEVI, 25, M, Mariner, W, MA, 197, 242, NBPT*. In HH of Moses R. Fenimore, age 50, Cordwainer, born in MA.
PARKER, MARTHA, 27, F, -, W, NH, 266, 340, NBPT*. In HH of Charles Parker, age 28, Trader, born in NH.
PARKER, MARTHA H., 27, F, -, W, NH, 429, 636, NBPT. In HH of Charles W. Parker, age 32, Grocer, born in Maine.
PARKER, PHINEAS, 66, M, Gentleman, W, MA, 666, 957, NBPT.
PARSHLEY, HANAH, 28, F, -, W, NH, 530, 790, NBPT. In HH of Almira Swap, age 42, born in MA.
PARSONS, JOHN, 24, M, Printer, W, MA, 264, 334, NBPT*. In HH of Sarah Parsons, age 52, born in MA.
PARSONS, JOHN D., 25, M, Painter, W, MA, 607, 887, NBPT. In HH of Eliza Reyes, age 48, born in MA.
PARSONS, STEPHEN, 16, M, Clerk, W, MA, 264, 334, NBPT*. In HH of Sarah Parsons, age 52, born in MA.
PATCH, JOSEPH, 81, M, Wharfinger, W, MA, 485, 646, NBPT*.
PATCH, JOSEPH, 54, M, Mariner, W, MA, 485, 646, NBPT*. In HH of Joseph Patch, age 81, Wharfinger, born in MA.
PATE, DAVID H., 38, M, Mariner, W, MA, 256, 373, NBPT. In HH of John Page, age 64, Cabinet Maker, born in NH.
PATE, JOHN, 64, M, Cabinet Maker, W, NH, 256, 373, NBPT.
PATTEN, ALFRED, 22, M, Mariner, W, MA, 790,1118, NBPT. In HH of Benjamin Noble, age 28, Tailor, born in England.
PATTEN, GEORGE W., 35, M, Cooper, W, MA, 421, 625, NBPT.
PATTEN, HENRY, 47, M, Cooper, W, MA, 421, 626, NBPT. In HH of Thomas Patten, age 47, Cooper, born in MA.
PATTEN, HENRY, 23, M, Carpenter, W, MA, 421, 626, NBPT. In HH of Thomas Patten, age 47, Cooper born in MA.
PATTEN, JOHN, 17, M, Carpenter, W, MA, 421, 626, NBPT. In HH of Thomas Patten, age 47, Cooper, born in MA.
PATTEN, THOMAS, 47, M, Cooper, W, MA, 421, 626, NBPT.
PATTEN, THOMAS H., 24, M, Mariner, W, MA, 790,1118, NBPT. In HH of Benjamin Noble, age 28, Tailor, born in England.
PATTEN, WILLIAM C., 38, M, Cooper, W, MA, 439, 653, NBPT.
PAUL, JAMES, 20, M, Shoemaker, W, Maine, 770,1090, NBPT. In HH of Levi Pearson, age 37, Watchman, born in MA.
PAYNE, EMMEY, 26, F, -, W, NH, 482, 723, NBPT. In HH of Henry N. Payne, age 26, Operative, born in MA.
PAYNE, HENRY N., 26, M, Operative, W, MA, 482, 723, NBPT.
PAYSON, SAMUEL T., 34, M, Baker, W, MA, 591, 868, NBPT.
PEABODY, CHARLES, 34, M,

Shoe Dealer, W, MA, 80, 89, NBPT*.
PEABODY, EDWARD, 36, M, Shoemaker, W, NH, 49, 72, NBPT.
PEABODY, LUCINDA G., 39, F, -, W, NH, 488, 730, NBPT.
PEABODY, NANCY P., 18, F, -, W, Maine, 488, 730, NBPT. In HH of Lucinda G. Peabody, age 39, born in NH.
PEARL, ASA, 29, M, Master Mariner, W, NH, 170, 246, NBPT.
PEARL, JOHN, 21, M, Mariner, W, NH, 170, 246, NBPT. In HH of Asa Pearl, age 29, Master Mariner, born in NH.
PEARSON, ABNER, 23, M, Tinner, W, MA, 491, 654, NBPT*. In HH of Michael Pearson, age 58, Ships Wheel maker.
PEARSON, ABNER, 23, M, Tinner, W, MA, 491, 654, NBPT*. In HH of Michael Pearson, age 58, Ships Wheelmaker, born in MA.
PEARSON, ABNER W., 40, M, Shoemaker, W, MA, 91, 133, NBPT.
PEARSON, ALBERT S., 20, M, Painter, W, MA, 341, 445, NBPT*. In HH of Isaac Pearson, age 56, Painter, born in MA.
PEARSON, AMOS, 67, M, Carpenter, W, MA, 606, 886, NBPT.
PEARSON, AMOS, 65, M, Shoemaker, W, MA, 266, 338, NBPT*.
PEARSON, AMOS, 22, M, Operative, W, MA, 266, 338, NBPT*. In HH of Amos Pearson, age 65, Shoemaker, born in MA.
PEARSON, ANN, 59, F, -, W, MA, 788,1114, NBPT. In Poor House. .
PEARSON, ARIEL, 55, M, Ropemaker, W, NH, 64, 92, NBPT.
PEARSON, BENJAMIN, 65, M, Painter, W, MA, 788,1114, NBPT.

In Poor House.
PEARSON, CHARLES, 40, M, House Carpenter, W, MA, 400, 523, NBPT*.
PEARSON, EDWIN, 10, M, -, W, Maine, 285, 371, NBPT*. In HH of John Pearson, 4th, age 34, Clergyman, 2nd Advent., born in NH.
PEARSON, ELIZA, 24, F, -, W, NH, 64, 93, NBPT. In HH of George Pearson, age 28, Ropemaker, born in MA.
PEARSON, ELIZABETH, 34, F, -, W, Maine, 491, 654, NBPT*. In HH of Michael Pearson, age 58, Ships Wheelmaker, born in MA.
PEARSON, ELIZABETH, 25, F, -, W, England, 285, 370, NBPT*. In HH of Joseph H. Dockum, age 27, Wood 7 Lumber D{ealer}, born in NH.
PEARSON, ELIZABETH S., 16, F, -, W, NH, 494, 737, NBPT. In HH of John Pearson, age 61, Baker, born in MA.
PEARSON, GEORGE, 28, M, Ropemaker, W, MA, 64, 93, NBPT.
PEARSON, HARRIET P., 29, F, -, W, NH, 494, 737, NBPT. In HH of John Pearson, age 61, Baker, born in MA.
PEARSON, HARRIS, 33, M, Baker, W, NH, 212, 314, NBPT.
PEARSON, ISAAC, 56, M, Painter, W, MA, 341, 445, NBPT*.
PEARSON, ISABELLA, 39, F, -, W, Ireland, 639, 926, NBPT. In HH of John Pearson, age 54, Stage Driver, born in NH.
PEARSON, JABEZ, 27, M, Coal & Lumber Dealer, W, MA, 29, 35, NBPT*.
PEARSON, JAMES H., 24, M, Tin Plate Worker, W, MA, 285, 370, NBPT*. In HH of Joseph H. Dockum, age 27, Wood 7 Lumber D{ealer}, born in NH.

PEARSON, JOHN, 61, M, Baker, W, MA, 494, 737, NBPT.
PEARSON, JOHN, 54, M, Stage Driver, W, NH, 639, 926, NBPT.
PEARSON, JOHN, 52, M, Shoemaker, W, MA, 244, 353, NBPT.
PEARSON, JOHN, 4TH, 34, M, Clergyman, 2nd Adventist, W, NH, 285, 371, NBPT*.
PEARSON, JOSEPH, 30, M, Cabinetmaker, W, NH, 561, 834, NBPT. In HH of Mary Dorr, age 65, born in MA.
PEARSON, LEVI, 37, M, Watchman, W, MA, 770,1090, NBPT.
PEARSON, LINCOLN, 12, M, -, W, Maine, 285, 371, NBPT*. In HH of John Pearson, 4th, age 34, Clergyman, 2nd Advent., born in NH.
PEARSON, LUTHER, 45, M, Cordwainer, W, MA, 440, 583, NBPT*.
PEARSON, MARY A., 37, F, -, W, NH, 400, 523, NBPT*. In HH of Charles Pearson, age 40, House Carpenter, born in MA.
PEARSON, MARY ANN, 31, F, -, W, NH, 29, 35, NBPT*. In HH of Jabez Pearson, age 27, Coal and Lumber Dealer, born in MA.
PEARSON, MOODY, 63, M, Surveyor, W, MA, 27, 32, NBPT*.
PEARSON, NANCY, 52, F, -, W, Maine, 494, 737, NBPT. In HH of John Pearson, age 61, Baker, born in MA.
PEARSON, PAMELA B., 35, F, -, W, Maine, 285, 371, NBPT*. In HH of John Pearson, 4th, age 34, Clergyman, 2nd Advent., born in NH.
PEARSON, REBECCA B., 41, F, -, W, NH, 606, 886, NBPT. In HH of Amos Pearson, age 67, Carpenter, born in MA.

PEARSON, ROBERT H., 40, M, Master Mariner, W, MA, 337, 496, NBPT. In HH of Paul Simpson, age 76, Master Mariner, born in Maine.
PEARSON, SAMUEL P., 16, M, None, W, MA, 64, 92, NBPT. In HH of Ariel Pearson, age 55, Ropemaker, born in NH.
PEARSON, SAMUEL T., 21, M, Shoemaker, W, MA, 244, 353, NBPT. In HH of John Pearson, age 52, Shoemaker, born in MA.
PEARSON, SARAH J., 22, F, -, W, Maine, 212, 314, NBPT. In HH of Harris Pearson, age 33, Baker, born in NH.
PEARSON, SARAH R., 14, F, -, W, Maine, 494, 737, NBPT. In HH of John Pearson, age 61, Baker, born in MA.
PEARSON, SILAS, 47, M, Carpenter, W, MA, 759,1072, NBPT.
PEARSON, WILLIAM, 41, M, Soup Boiler, W, MA, 124, 181, NBPT.
PEARSON, WILLIAM N., 49, M, Wood & Lumber Dealer, W, MA, 351, 513, NBPT.
PEAVY, MARY J., 79, F, -, W, Maine, 431, 640, NBPT. In HH of Oliver P. Wiggin, age 44, Cooper, born in NH.
PEAVY, ROSILLA, 18, F, -, W, Maine, 431, 640, NBPT. In HH of Oliver P. Wiggin, age 44, Cooper, born in NH.
PEIRCE, BENJN., 56, M, Master Mariner, W, MA, 82, 119, NBPT.
PEIRCE, BENJN., 24, M, Tailor, W, MA, 310, 457, NBPT.
PEIRCE, PHILLIP H., 52, M, Grocer, W, Ireland, 86, 126, NBPT.
PENELL, SARAH, 65, F, -, W, Maine, 322, 476, NBPT. In HH of Nehamiah Sargent, age 50, Mariner, born in MA.

PENELL, SARAH, 22, F, -, W, Maine, 322, 476, NBPT. In HH of Nehamiah Sargent, age 50, Mariner, born in MA.

PENNEL, SARAH, 20, F, -, W, NH, 753,1061, NBPT. In HH of Martha Royers, age 57, born in MA.

PENTLAND, GEORGE, 46, M, Stretcher in Mill, W, England, 771,1091, NBPT.

PENTLAND, GEORGE, 8, M, -, W, England, 771,1091, NBPT. In HH of George Pentland, age 46, Stretcher in Mill, born in England.

PENTLAND, JAMES, 38, M, Overseer in Mill, W, England, 122, 179, NBPT.

PENTLAND, JAMES, 13, M, -, W, England, 771,1091, NBPT. In HH of George Pentland, age 46, Stretcher in Mill, born in England.

PENTLAND, JANE, 11, F, -, W, England, 771,1091, NBPT. In HH of George Pentland, age 46, Stretcher in Mill, born in England.

PENTLAND, JOHN, 15, M, -, W, England, 771,1091, NBPT. In HH of George Pentland, age 46, Stretcher in Mill, born in England.

PENTLAND, MARY, 45, F, -, W, England, 771,1091, NBPT. In HH of George Pentland, age 46, Stretcher in Mill, born in England.

PERCY, CATHARINE, 55, F, -, W, Ireland, 303, 446, NBPT. In HH of Patrick Crowley, age 26, Mariner, born in Ireland.

PERCY, JAMES, 40, M, Mariner, W, Ireland, 303, 446, NBPT. In HH of Patrick Crowley, age 26, Mariner, born in Ireland.

PERKERNY, PAUL R., 22, M, Carpenter, W, MA, 363, 534, NBPT. In HH of George N. Bartlett, age 29, Carpenter, born in NH.

PERKINGS, EUNICE, 41, F, -, W, Maine, 66, 95, NBPT. In HH of Josiah Perkings, age 45, Stone Mason, born in MA.

PERKINGS, JOSIAH, 45, M, Stone Mason, W, MA, 66, 95, NBPT.

PERKINS, CHARLES A., 19, M, Carpenter, W, MA, 486, 728, NBPT. In HH of Abby K. Livingston, age 53, born in MA.

PERKINS, ELIZABETH, 71, F, -, W, NH, 426, 631, NBPT. In HH of Thomas Perkins, age 77, Merchant, born in MA.

PERKINS, GEORGE, 43, M, Mariner, W, Maine, 169, 244, NBPT.

PERKINS, GEORGE, 17, M, Clerk, W, MA, 169, 244, NBPT. In HH of George Perkins, age 43, Mariner, born in Maine.

PERKINS, HENRY C., 45, M, Physician, W, MA, 587, 863, NBPT.

PERKINS, NATHANIEL, 51, M, Truck man, W, Maine, 533, 707, NBPT*.

PERKINS, THOMAS, 77, M, Merchant, W, MA, 426, 631, NBPT.

PERRY, ABIEL P., 48, M, Master Mariner, W, MA, 519, 773, NBPT. In HH of Samuel Wood, age 54, Blacksmith, born in Maine.

PERRY, AGNES A., 7, F, -, W, Nova Scotia, 588, 777, NBPT*. In HH of John N. Perry, age 33, Blacksmith, born in Nova Scotia.

PERRY, CHARLES, 52, M, Laborer, W, MA, 168, 201, NBPT*.

PERRY, CHARLES W., 1, M, -, W, NH, 330, 429, NBPT*. In HH of Rebekah Perry, age 27, born in NH.

PERRY, COOLEDGE, 23, M, Tailor, W, NH, 659, 949, NBPT. In HH of Rebecca Gardner, age 40, born in MA.

PERRY, FRANCES C., 4, F, -, W, NH, 330, 429, NBPT*. In HH of Rebekah Perry, age 27, born in NH.

PERRY, JOHN N., 33, M, Blacksmith, W, Nova Scotia, 588, 777, NBPT*.
PERRY, MARTHA, 76, F, -, W, DE, 350, 511, NBPT. In HH of David Wells, age 44, Laborer, born in MA.
PERRY, REBEKAH, 27, F, -, W, NH, 330, 429, NBPT*.
PERRY, SOPHIA A., 26, F, -, W, Nova Scotia, 588, 777, NBPT*. In HH of John N. Perry, age 33, Blacksmith, born in Nova Scotia.
PERRY, WILLIAM, 5, M, -, W, Nova Scotia, 588, 777, NBPT*. In HH of John N. Perry, age 33, Blacksmith, born in Nova Scotia.
PERSON, SARAH E., 29, F, -, W, NH, 646, 935, NBPT. In HH of Thomas Person, age 34, Operative, born in MA.
PERSON, THOMAS, 34, M, Operative, W, MA, 646, 935, NBPT.
PERVER, LOIS, 25, F, -, W, NH, 264, 333, NBPT*. In HH of Joseph Greenleaf, age 62, Sailmaker, born in MA.
PETERS, JAMES T., 35, M, Mariner, W, MA, 482, 641, NBPT*. In HH of John Evans, age 60, Croper, born in England.
PETERS, RICHARD, 54, M, Cooper, W, MA, 482, 641, NBPT*. In HH of John Evans, age 60, Croper, born in England.
PETERSON, ANN, 49, F, -, W, Maine, 66, 95, NBPT. In HH of Josiah Perkings, age 45, Stone Mason, born in MA.
PETTEGREW, MARY, 47, F, -, W, Ireland, 248, 359, NBPT. In HH of Mathew Pettegrew, age 40, Laborer, born in Ireland.
PETTEGREW, MATHEW, 40, M, Laborer, W, Ireland, 248, 359, NBPT.
PETTINGEL, BETSY, 21, F, -, W, Maine, 15, 19, NBPT*. In HH of William H. Pettingel, 30, House carpenter, born Maine.
PETTINGEL, WILLIAM H., 30, M, House Carpenter, W, Maine, 15, 19, NBPT*.
PETTINGELL, AMOS, 73, M, Rope Maker, W, MA, 31, 42, NBPT.
PETTINGELL, AMOS, 18, M, Boute {sic} Builder, W, MA, 88, 129, NBPT. In HH of Samuel Pettigell, age 44, Cooper, born in MA.
PETTINGELL, DAVID, 39, M, Mariner, W, MA, 203, 299, NBPT.
PETTINGELL, HENRY, 18, M, Shoemaker, W, MA, 5, 5, NBPT. In HH of John Pettingell, age 71, Rope Maker, born in MA.
PETTINGELL, JAMES S., 38, M, Cooper, W, MA, 318, 468, NBPT.
PETTINGELL, JOHN, 71, M, Rope Maker, W, MA, 5, 5, NBPT.
PETTINGELL, JOHN W., 44, M, Shoemaker, W, MA, 270, 397, NBPT.
PETTINGELL, JOSEPH W., 49, M, Mariner, W, MA, 262, 379, NBPT.
PETTINGELL, MARIA, 33, F, -, W, NH, 270, 397, NBPT. In HH of John W. Pettingell, age 44, Shoemaker, born in MA.
PETTINGELL, RICHARD, 23, M, Mariner, W, MA, 291, 426, NBPT.
PETTINGELL, RICHARD P., 17, M, Cooper, W, MA, 88, 129, NBPT. In HH of Samuel Pettigell, age 44, Cooper, born in MA.
PETTINGELL, SAMUEL, 44, M, Cooper, W, MA, 88, 129, NBPT.
PETTINGREW, JOSEPH G., 26, M, Mariner, W, Maine, 279, 357, NBPT*.
PHILBRICK, CAROLINE, 21, F, -, W, Maine, 733, 1035, NBPT. In HH of Stephen Downs, age 31, Mariner, born in MA.

PHILBRICK, ELIZA, 19, F, -, W, NH, 427, 633, NBPT. In HH of Walter Gould, age 49, Carpenter, born in Maine.
PHILBRICK, MEHITABLE, 25, F, -,W, Maine, 177, 256, NBPT. In HH of James N. Canney, age 41, Teamster, born in NH.
PHILBRICK, NATHANIEL E., 35, M, -, W, Unknown, 78, 87, NBPT*. In Jail. Convict.
PHILBRICK, SARAH, 23, F, -, W, Maine, 177, 256, NBPT. In HH of James N. Canney, age 41, Teamster, born in NH.
PHILBRICK, SUSAN, 19, F, -, W, Maine, 177, 256, NBPT. In HH of James N. Canney, age 41, Teamster, born in NH.
PHILBRICK, SYLVIA, 21, F, -, W, Maine, 177, 256, NBPT. In HH of James N. Canney, age 41, Teamster, born in NH.
PHILIP F., 23, M, Shoemaker, W, MA, 245, 355, NBPT.
PHILIPS, CATHERINE, 16, F, -, W, N.S., 627, 913, NBPT. In HH of William W. Eolls?, age 39, O.S. Presb. Clergyman, born in CT.
PHILLIPS, BRIDGET, 5, F, -, W, Newfoundland, 762,1075, NBPT. In HH of James Phillips, age 48, Mariner, born in England.
PHILLIPS, CATHERINE, 17, F, -, W, Newfoundland, 762,1075, NBPT. In HH of James Phillips, age 48, Mariner, born in England.
PHILLIPS, ELLEN, 8, F, -, W, Newfoundland, 762,1075, NBPT. In HH of James Phillips, age 48, Mariner, born in England.
PHILLIPS, JAMES, 48, M, Mariner, W, England, 762,1075, NBPT.
PHILLIPS, MARTIN, 3, M, -, W, Newfoundland, 762,1075, NBPT. In HH of James Phillips, age 48, Mariner, born in England.
PHILLIPS, MARY, 40, F, -, W, Ireland, 762,1075, NBPT. In HH of James Phillips, age 48, Mariner, born in England.
PHILLIPS, MARY A., 13, F, -, W, Newfoundland, 762,1075, NBPT. In HH of James Phillips, age 48, Mariner, born in England.
PHILLIPS, MICHAEL, 11, M, -, W, Newfoundland, 762,1075, NBPT. In HH of James Phillips, age 48, Mariner, born in England.
PHILLIPS, SAMUEL, 49, M, Attorney, W, MA, 586, 862, NBPT.
PHILLIPS, THOMAS, 19, M, -, W, Newfoundland, 762,1075, NBPT. In HH of James Phillips, age 48, Mariner, born in England.
PICKARD, ENOCH, 23, M, Porter, W, NH, 782,1108, NBPT. In HH of Enoch Tilton, age 45, Hotel Keeper, born in NH. In Hotel.
PICKERING, ANDREW J., 15, M, -, W, Maine, 479, 718, NBPT. In HH of Valentine Pickering, age 45, Carpenter, born in NH.
PICKERING, ELIZABETH P., 25, F, -, W, Maine, 479, 718, NBPT. In HH of Valentine Pickering, age 45, Carpenter, born in NH.
PICKERING, ELLEN L.R., 18, F, -, W, Maine, 479, 718, NBPT. In HH of Valentine Pickering, age 45, Carpenter, born in NH.
PICKERING, GEORGE W., 5, M, -, W, NH, 479, 718, NBPT. In HH of Valentine Pickering, age 45, Carpenter, born in NH.
PICKERING, JAMES M., 7, M, -, W, NH, 479, 718, NBPT. In HH of Valentine Pickering, age 45, Carpenter, born in NH.
PICKERING, JOHN A., 20, M, Farmer, W, NH, 479, 718, NBPT. In HH of Valentine Pickering, age 45, Carpenter, born in NH.

PICKERING, ROLLINS P., 22, M, Carpenter, W, NH, 479, 718, NBPT. In HH of Valentine Pickering, age 45, Carpenter, born in NH.
PICKERING, RUTH, 44, F, -, W, NH, 479, 718, NBPT. In HH of Valentine Pickering, age 45, Carpenter, born in NH.
PICKERING, RUTH M., 13, F, -, W, NH, 479, 718, NBPT. In HH of Valentine Pickering, age 45, Carpenter, born in NH.
PICKERING, VALENTINE, 45, M, Carpenter, W, NH, 479, 718, NBPT.
PICKERING, VALENTINE A., 23, M, Cabinetmaker, W, NH, 479, 718, NBPT. In HH of Valentine Pickering, age 45, Carpenter, born in NH.
PICKETT, JOSEPH, 35, M, Boat Builder, W, MA, 360, 530, NBPT.
PIERCE, AMANDA B., 18, F, -, W, Maine, 141, 207, NBPT. In HH of Joseph B. Landford, age 38, Overseer in Mill, born in MA.
PIERCE, CHARLOTTE, 18, F, -, W, Maine, 514, 685, NBPT*. In HH of Aaron Gardner, age 30, Carpenter, born in NH.
PIERCE, ENOCH, 26, M, Tailor, W, NH, 303, 395, NBPT*. In HH of James M. Cooper, age 39, House Joiner, born in MA.
PIERCE, NATHL. G., 24, M, Mariner, W, MA, 741,1047, NBPT. In HH of Gideon E. Leighton, age 50, Watchman, born in NH.
PIERCE, SEMANTHA, 18, F, -, W, Maine, 141, 207, NBPT. In HH of Joseph B. Landford, age 38, Overseer in Mill, born in MA.
PIERCE, THOMAS J., 35, M, Master Mariner, W, GAR {?}, 247, 357, NBPT. In HH of Robert Bayley, age 64, Merchant, born in MA.

PIKE, CHARLES S., 60, M, Merchant-Tailor, W, MA, 88, 103, NBPT*. In HH of Joseph T. Pike, age 64, born NH.
PIKE, DANIEL P., 35, M, Clergyman Chris., W, MA, 106, 126, NBPT*.
PIKE, EDMUND, 57, M, Master Mariner, W, MA, 17, 19, NBPT.
PIKE, EDMUND, 17, M, Pump & Block Maker, W, MA, 524, 781, NBPT. In HH of Elias Pike, age 66, Pump and Block Maker, born in MA.
PIKE, ELBRIDGE, 20, M, Shoemaker, W, MA, 509, 680, NBPT*. In HH of James Wilkinson, age 27, Farmer, born in Maine.
PIKE, ELIAS, 66, M, Pump & Block Maker, W, MA, 524, 781, NBPT.
PIKE, GEORGE A., 27, M, Pump and Block Maker, W, MA, 616, 898, NBPT. In HH of Mary A. Small, age 56, born in MA.
PIKE, J.W.C., 41, M, Painter and Glazier, W, MA, 423, 551, NBPT*.
PIKE, JOSEPH S., 69, M, Merchant, W, MA, 685, 977, NBPT.
PIKE, JOSEPH T., 64, M, None, W, NH, 88, 103, NBPT*.
PIKE, LABON, 47, M, None, W, MA, 509, 680, NBPT*. In HH of James Wilkinson, age 27, Farmer, born in Maine.
PIKE, LABON, 47, M, Truck man, W, Maine, 788,1114, NBPT. In Poor House.
PIKE, MARY, 27, F, -, W, Maine, 616, 898, NBPT. In HH of Mary A. Small, age 56, born in MA.
PIKE, SAMUEL B., 29, M, Master Mariner, W, MA, 304, 396, NBPT*. In HH of George W. Hill, age 50, Shoemaker, born in MA.
PIKE, SAMUEL M., 42, M, Mariner, W, MA, 382, 505, NBPT*

135

PIKE, STEPHEN S., 26, M, Ship Joiner, W, MA, 558, 741, NBPT*.

PIKE, WILLIAM, 30, M, Pump & Block Maker, W, MA, 524, 781, NBPT. In HH of Elias Pike, age 66, Pump and Block Maker, born in MA.

PIKE, WILLIAM, 16, M, Painter and Glazier, W, MA, 423, 551, NBPT*. In HH of J.W.C. Pike, age 41, Painter and Glazier, born in MA.

PIKE, WILLIAM C., 74, M, None, W, MA, 536, 713, NBPT*.

PIKE, WILLIAM C., 74, M, None, W, MA, 536, 713, NBPT*.

PILSBURY, ALFRED, 50, M, Clerk, W, MA, 307, 399, NBPT*.

PILSBURY, JOHN, 22, M, Shoemaker, W, NH, 200, 248, NBPT*. In HH of Edwin B. Bartlet, age 40, Shoemaker, born in NH.

PILSBURY, LYDIA, 74, F, -, W, Maine, 251, 315, NBPT*. In HH of Caroline Pilsbury, age 58, born in MA.

PILSBURY, OLIVER D., 31, M, Ship master, W, MA, 207, 258, NBPT*. In HH of Joseph W. Butler, age 31, Baker, born in MA.

PILSBURY, STEPHEN M., 24, M, Trader, W, MA, 307, 400, NBPT*.

PINGREY, ALFRED, 23, M, Grocer, W, MA, 556, 829, NBPT. In HH of Daniel Pingrey, age 48, Shoemaker.

PINGREY, ALFRED, 23, M, Grocer, W, MA, 556, 829, NBPT. In HH of Daniel Pingrey, age 48, Shoemaker, born in MA.

PIPER, ASENAH, 26, F, -, W, NH, 234, 341, NBPT. In HH of William Page, age 36, Master Mariner, born in MA.

PIPER, BENJAMIN, 33, M, Sailmaker, W, MA, 439, 581, NBPT*. In HH of William Jameson, age 48, Sailmaker, born in RI.

PIPER, CHARLES W., 25, M, Mason, W, MA, 37, 53, NBPT.

PIPER, FREDERICK, 16, M, Clerk, W, MA, 196, 287, NBPT. In HH of John Raynes, age 66, Master Mariner, born in Maine.

PIPER, HENRY L., 33, M, Mason, W, MA, 55, 81, NBPT.

PIPER, JAMES, 69, M, Rigger, W, MA, 152, 221, NBPT.

PIPER, JOHN E., 39, M, Hatter, W, MA, 443, 659, NBPT.

PIPER, JOHN P., 22, M, Engineer, W, MA, 273, 400, NBPT.

PIPER, JOSEPH, 44, M, Sailmaker, W, MA, 196, 287, NBPT. In HH of John Raynes, age 66, Master Mariner, born in Maine.

PIPER, JOSEPH L., 26, M, Boat Builder, W, MA, 152, 221, NBPT. In HH of James Piper, age 69, Rigger, born in MA.

PIPER, MARY, 49, F, -, W, D.C., 199, 292, NBPT. In HH of Walter Piper, age 78, Rigger, born in MA.

PIPER, NANCY, 33, F, -, W, Maine, 55, 81, NBPT. In HH of Henry L. Piper, age 33, Mason, born in MA.

PIPER, PHILLIP R., 47, M, Carpenter, W, MA, 786,1112, NBPT. In HH of Sarah Kimball, age 81, born in MA.

PIPER, ROBERT, 64, M, Rigger, W, MA, 333, 434, NBPT*.

PIPER, WALTER, 78, M, Rigger, W, MA, 199, 292, NBPT.

PIPER, WALTER J.H., 18, M, Mariner, W, MA, 199, 292, NBPT. In HH of Walter Piper, age 78, Rigger, born in MA.

PIPER, WILLIAM F., 33, M, Mariner, W, MA, 443, 659, NBPT. In HH of John E. Piper, age 39, Hatter, born in MA.

PLUMER, ALICE, 64, F, -, W,

Maine, 485, 726, NBPT. In HH of Nathan Plumer, age 66, Carpenter, born in MA.
PLUMER, ANN, 19, F, -, W, Maine, 204, 300, NBPT. In HH of William B. Cheney, age 35, Laborer, born in MA.
PLUMER, CHARLES, 19, M, Mariner, W, MA, 317, 466, NBPT.
PLUMER, CHARLES H., 33, M, Mariner, W, MA, 485, 727, NBPT.
PLUMER, DANIEL, 46, M, Saddle & Harness Maker, W, MA, 27, 37, NBPT. In HH of Mary Scott, age 81, born in MA.
PLUMER, EBENEZER, 73, M, Merchant, W, MA, 131, 193, NBPT.
PLUMER, ELIZABETH K., 28, F, -, W, NH, 87, 127, NBPT. In HH of Moses A. Plumer, age 33, Teamster, born in MA.
PLUMER, JERSULEE?, 70, F, -, W, Maine, 28, 38, NBPT. In HH of Moses Plumer, age 70, Carpenter, born in MA.
PLUMER, JOSEPH, 64, M, Merchant, W, MA, 251, 363, NBPT.
PLUMER, MARY, 36, F, -, W, NH, 349, 510, NBPT. In HH of Richard Plumer, age 36, Merchant, born in MA.
PLUMER, MOSES, 70, M, Carpenter, W, MA, 28, 38, NBPT.
PLUMER, MOSES A., 33, M, Teamster, W, MA, 87, 127, NBPT.
PLUMER, NATHAN, 66, M, Carpenter, W, MA, 485, 726, NBPT.
PLUMER, NATHAN D., 32, M, Mariner, W, MA, 384, 568, NBPT.
PLUMER, RICHARD, 36, M, Merchant, W, MA, 349, 510, NBPT.
PLUMER, SAMUEL S., 73, M, Grocer, W, MA, 361, 532, NBPT.
PLUMER, WILLIAM, 22, M, Ship Carpenter, W, MA, 592, 782, NBPT*.
PLUMER, WILLIAM P., 25, M, Stable Keeper, W, MA, 673, 965, NBPT.
PLUMMER, JONES, 16, M, Shoemaker, W, NH, 200, 248, NBPT*. In HH of Edwin B. Bartlet, age 40, Shoemaker, born in NH.
PLUMMER, THOMAS F., 17, M, Printer, W, MA, 263, 332, NBPT*. In HH of William H. Brewster, age 37, Printer and Publisher, born in NH.
PONDEN, JAMES, 16, M, Fishing, W, MA, 511, 682, NBPT*. In HH of John Ponden, age 51, Mariner, born in Ireland.
PONDEN, JOHN, 51, M, Mariner, W, Ireland, 511, 682, NBPT*.
POOLE, CHARLES, 29, M, Tailor, W, England, 44, 65, NBPT.
POOLE, JOHN, 27, M, Shoemaker, W, England, 522, 779, NBPT.
POOR, CHARLES, 25, M, None, W, NH, 166, 199, NBPT*. In Hotel run by Thomas Brown, age 49, born in MA.
POOR, CHARLES, 25, M, Carpenter, W, MA, 23, 30, NBPT.
POOR, DAVIS L., 32, M, Mariner, W, MA, 92, 135, NBPT. In HH of Elizabeth A. Poor, age 60, born in MA.
POOR, ISAAC, 25, M, Grocer, W, MA, 119, 175, NBPT.
POOR, JOHN, 38, M, Cabinet Maker, W, MA, 94, 137, NBPT.
POOR, NANCY, 35, F, -, W, Maine, 94, 137, NBPT. In HH of John Poor, age 38, Cabinet Maker, born in MA.
POOR, NATHAN, 40, M, Furniture Dealer, W, MA, 186, 270, NBPT.
POOR, THOMAS L., 34, M, Merchant, W, MA, 92, 135, NBPT.

In HH of Elizabeth A. Poor, age 60, born in MA.
PORTER, JOHN, 66, M, Merchant, W, MA, 249, 360, NBPT.
PORTER, SARAH, 74, F, -, W, MA, 788,1114, NBPT. In Poor House. .
PORTER, WILLIAM, 40, M, Teamster, W, MA, 535, 799, NBPT.
POST, ANN, 54, F, -, W, N.S., 493, 736, NBPT.
POST, CATHERINE, 15, F, -, W, N.S., 493, 736, NBPT. In HH of Ann Post, age 54, born in N.S. {Nova Scotia}.
POST, EBENEZER, 46, M, Master Mariner, W, Nova Scotia, 47, 70, NBPT.
POST, ELIZABETH, 20, F, -, W, N.S., 493, 736, NBPT. In HH of Ann Post, age 54, born in N.S. {Nova Scotia}.
POST, HANNAH, 22, F, -, W, N.S., 493, 736, NBPT. In HH of Ann Post, age 54, born in N.S. {Nova Scotia}.
POST, JAMES A., 44, M, Block Maker, W, MA, 103, 151, NBPT.
POST, JAMES O., 5, M, -, W, Maine, 493, 735, NBPT. In HH of John Post, age 24, Farmer, born in N.S. {Nova Scotia}.
POST, JOHN, 24, M, Farmer, W, N.S., 493, 735, NBPT.
POST, MARY, 17, F, -, W, N.S., 493, 736, NBPT. In HH of Ann Post, age 54, born in N.S. {Nova Scotia}.
POST, PHEBE A., 1, F, -, W, N.S., 493, 735, NBPT. In HH of John Post, age 24, Farmer, born in N.S. {Nova Scotia}.
POST, SAMUEL, 16, M, None, W, MA, 71, 102, NBPT. In HH of Elizabeth Post, age 44, born in MA.
POST, SARAH, 31, F, -, W, N.S., 493, 735, NBPT. In HH of John Post, age 24, Farmer, born in N.S. {Nova Scotia}.
POTTER, LEWIS, 33, M, Mariner, W, Maine, 87, 128, NBPT.
POWAS, CATHARINE, 20, F, -, W, Ireland, 601, 791, NBPT*. In HH of Patrick Kelly, age 23 Dealer in Wood, born in Ireland.
POWAS, ROGER, 23, M, Carpenter, W, Ireland, 601, 791, NBPT*. In HH of Patrick Kelly, age 23 Dealer in Wood, born in Ireland.
POWERS, BRIDGET, 40, F, -, W, Ireland, 231, 287, NBPT*. In HH of Margaret Sullivan, age 28, born in Ireland.
POWERS, BRIDGET, 3, F, W, 0, St. Johns, 171, 247, NBPT. In HH of James Powers, age 40, Laborer, born in Ireland.
POWERS, CATHARINE, 13, F, -, W, Ireland, 231, 285, NBPT*. In HH of Robert Powers, age 12, born in Ireland.
POWERS, ELIZA, 24, F, -, W, NH, 588, 865, NBPT. In HH of Stilman Simonds, age 43, Shoemaker, born in MA.
POWERS, ELLEN, 20, F, -, W, Maine, 140, 166, NBPT*. In HH of Hannah T. Marshall, age 39, Boarding House, born in MA.
POWERS, GEORGE, 20, M, Machinist, W, VT, 588, 865, NBPT. In HH of Stilman Simonds, age 43, Shoemaker, born in MA.
POWERS, JAMES, 7, M, - W, St. Johns, 171, 247, NBPT. In HH of James Powers, age 40, Laborer, born in Ireland.
POWERS, JANES, 40, M, Laborer, W, Ireland, 171, 247, NBPT.
POWERS, JOHN, 14, M, W, 0, Newfoundland, 171, 247, NBPT. In HH of James Powers, age 40, Laborer, born in Ireland.

POWERS, JOHN, 5, M, -, W, Ireland, 231, 285, NBPT*. In HH of Robert Powers, age 12, born in Ireland.
POWERS, JOHN, 5, M, -, W, Ireland, 231, 285, NBPT*. In HH of Robert Powers, age 12, born in Ireland.
POWERS, MARGARET, 35, M, -, W, Ireland, 171, 247, NBPT. In HH of James Powers, age 40, Laborer, born in Ireland.
POWERS, MARGARET, 9, F, -, W, St. Johns, 171, 247, NBPT. In HH of James Powers, age 40, Laborer, born in Ireland.
POWERS, MARY, 14, F, -, W, Ireland, 231, 285, NBPT*. In HH of Robert Powers, age 12, born in Ireland.
POWERS, MARY, 12, F, W, 0, Newfoundland, 171, 247, NBPT. In HH of James Powers, age 40, Laborer, born in Ireland.
POWERS, MICHAEL, 18, M, Fisherman, W, Ireland, 231, 285, NBPT*. In HH of Robert Powers, age 12, born in Ireland.
POWERS, ROBERT, 12, M, -, W, Ireland, 231, 285, NBPT*.
POWERS, THOMAS, 47, M, Brewer, W, Ireland, 449, 670, NBPT.
POWERS, THOMAS, 16, M, Brewer, W, MA, 449, 670, NBPT. In HH of Thomas Powers, age 47, Brewer, born in Ireland.
PRATT, BENJAMIN, 65, M, None, W, Maine, 716,1012, NBPT.
PRATT, BETSY, 57, F, -, W, Maine, 716,1012, NBPT. In HH of Benjamin Pratt, age 65, None, born in Maine.
PRATT, JOSEPH R., 17, M, None, W, Maine, 716,1012, NBPT. In HH of Benjamin Pratt, age 65, None, born in Maine.
PRESCOTT, HARRIET E., 15, F, -, W, Maine, 211, 262, NBPT*. In Boarding House.
PRESSEY, THOMAS E., 37, M, Carpenter, W, MA, 722,1021, NBPT.
PRESSY, LOUISA, 58, F, -, W, NH, 408, 533, NBPT*. In HH of Samuel H. Cobb, age 31, Mariner, born in Maine.
PRESSY, MARGARET, 35, F, -, W, NH, 509, 679, NBPT*. In HH of Nutter Brown, age 60, Farmer, born in NH.
PRICHARD, JOHN B., 29, M, Rigger, W, MA, 644, 932, NBPT.
PRINCE, WILLIAM N., 57, M, None, W, MA, 23, 28, NBPT. In HH of Jane Young, age 79, born in MA.
PRITCHARD, JAMES R., 16, M, Rigger, W, MA, 286, 417, NBPT. In HH of William Pritchard, age 49, Rigger, born in MA.
PRITCHARD, THOMAS, 79, M, Mariner, W, England, 198, 290, NBPT.
PRITCHARD, THOMAS, 70, M, Rigger, W, MA, 657, 947, NBPT.
PRITCHARD, WILLIAM, 49, M, Rigger, W, MA, 286, 417, NBPT.
PUTMAN, HANNAH, 39, F, -, W, MA, 788,1114, NBPT. In Poor House. .
PUTNAM, JOSEPH, 49, M, Blacksmith, W, MA, 175, 212, NBPT*.

- Q -

QUESTRONE, CHARLES P., 44, M, Shoemaker, W, MA, 269, 394, NBPT.
QUIMBY, DEBORAH P., 27, F, -, W, Maine, 484, 644, NBPT*. In

HH of Moses E. Quimby, age 27, House Carpenter, born in MA.
QUIMBY, MOSES, 50, M, Ship Joiner, W, MA, 476, 632, NBPT*.
QUIMBY, MOSES E., 27, M, House Carpenter, W, MA, 484, 644, NBPT*.
QUIN, ANN, 25, F, -, W, Ireland, 231, 286, NBPT*. In HH of Robert Quin, age 35, Fisherman, born in Ireland.
QUIN, ROBERT, 35, M, Fisherman, W, Ireland, 231, 286, NBPT*.
QUINN, DENNIS, 33, M, -, W, Ireland, 462, 613, NBPT*. In HH of Timothy Quinn, age 30, Operative, born in Ireland.
QUINN, JOANNA, 23, F, -, W, Ireland, 462, 613, NBPT*. In HH of Timothy Quinn, age 30, Operative, born in Ireland.
QUINN, TIMOTHY, 30, M, Operative, W, Ireland, 462, 613, NBPT*.

- R -

RACKLYEFT, EDMUND, 71, M, Baker, W, MA, 247, 311, NBPT*.
RACKLYEFT, OASLIMA C., 37, M, None, W, MA, 185, 227, NBPT*. In HH of Anna M. Emerson, age 49, born in MA.
RADCLIFFE, Aaron, 32, M, Machinist, W, England, 757, 1068, NBPT. In HH of John Holker, age 42, Operative, born in England.
RADCLIFFE, ISABELLA, 23, F, -, W, England, 757, 1068, NBPT. In HH of John Holker, age 42, Operative, born in England.
RAINS, MARY S., 48, F, -, W, Maine, 431, 641, NBPT.
RAMSDELL, JOHN C., 45, M, Master Mariner, W, MA, 159, 229, NBPT.
RAMSDELL, MARY, 24, F, -, W, Maine, 159, 229, NBPT. In HH of John C. Ramsdell, age 45, Master Mariner, born in MA.
RAND, CHARLES, 27, M, Mariner, W, MA, 101, 119, NBPT*.
RAND, DANIEL, 19, M, Mariner, W, MA, 553, 736, NBPT*. In HH of Daniel F. Rand, age 58, Laborer, born in MA.
RAND, DANIEL F., 58, M, Laborer, W, MA, 553, 736, NBPT*.
RAND, EDWARD, 22, M, Painter, W, MA, 553, 736, NBPT*. In HH of Daniel F. Rand, age 58, Laborer, born in MA.
RAND, EDWARD S., 65, M, Merchant, W, MA, 119, 142, NBPT*.
RAND, MIRIAM, 21, F, -, W, Maine, 101, 119, NBPT*. In HH of Charles Rand, age 27, Mariner, born in MA.
RANDALL, JOSEPH, 32, M, Shoemaker, W, MA, 21, 25, NBPT*.
RANDALL, MOSES D., 37, M, Teacher of Music, W, MA, 374, 491, NBPT*.
RARDON, CATHERINE, 20, F, -, W, Ireland, 664, 955, NBPT. In HH of Hannah Dole, age 62, born in MA.
RAYMOND, ANDREW, 50, M, Barber, M, MA, 600, 790, NBPT*.
RAYNES, JOHN, 66, M, Master Mariner, W, Maine, 196, 287, NBPT.
RAYTON, ELIZABETH D., 11, F, -, W, Maine, 616, 899, NBPT. In HH of Thomas Rayton, age 39, Master Mariner, born in Maine.
RAYTON, THOMAS, 39, M, Master Mariner, W, Maine, 616, 899, NBPT.
REACH, MARGARET, 23, F, -, W, Ireland, 13, 14, NBPT*. In HH

of Eunice Moody, age 62, female, born MA.
READ, ENOCH, M., 25, M, Trader, W, MA, 153, 183, NBPT*. In HH of William F. Stanwood, age 41, Shoe Business, born in MA.
REARDON, ELLEN, 11, F, -, W, Ireland, 142, 169, NBPT*. In HH of William C. Williams, age 53, Dealer in Lumber, born in MA.
REARDON, MARGARET, 38, F, -, W, Ireland, 142, 169, NBPT*. In HH of William C. Williams, age 53, Dealer in Lumber, born in MA.
REDMAN, ABBY A., 21, F, -, W, NH, 119, 142, NBPT*. In HH of Edward S. Rand, age 65, Merchant, born in MA.
REED, ABIGAIL, 23, F, -, W, England, 388, 511, NBPT*. In HH of James Folansbee, age 30, Operative, born in England.
REED, ALPHONZO, 11, M, -, W, NH, 118, 174, NBPT. In HH of Daniel Reed, age 35, Cabinet Maker, born in NH.
REED, ARABELLA, 25, F, -, W, Maine, 427, 555, NBPT*. In HH of James B. Reed, age 33, House Carpenter, born in MA.
REED, CATHARINE, 27, F, -, W, Ireland, 121, 144, NBPT*. In HH of David Wood, age 57, Ship master, born in MA.
REED, DANIEL, 35, M, Cabinet Maker, W, NH, 118, 174, NBPT.
REED, ELLEN A., 7, F, -, W, NH, 118, 174, NBPT. In HH of Daniel Reed, age 35, Cabinet Maker, born in NH.
REED, JAMES, 25, M, Baker, W, NH, 591, 868, NBPT. In HH of Samuel T. Payson, age 34, Baker, born in MA.
REED, JAMES B., 33, M, House Carpenter, W, MA, 427, 555, NBPT*.
REED, LEROY C., 6, M, -, W, NH, 118, 174, NBPT. In HH of Daniel Reed, age 35, Cabinet Maker, born in NH.
REED, MICAJAH S., 42, M, Shoemaker, W, MA, 399, 522, NBPT*.
REMICK, GEORGE W., 28, M, Machinist, W, MA, 234, 340, NBPT. In HH of Mary B. Remick, age 52, born in MA.
REMICK, JOHN E., 38, M, Stable Keeper, W, MA, 725,1024, NBPT. In HH of William S. Dodge, age 68, Carpenter, born in MA.
REMICK, PHILIP H., 39, M, Hatter, W, MA, 381, 562, NBPT.
RENDALE, WILLIAM A., 44, M, Grover, W, MA, 220, 326, NBPT.
RENNY, CHARLES, 19, M, Mariner, W, N.S., 493, 735, NBPT. In HH of John Post, age 24, Farmer, born in N.S. {Nova Scotia}.
RENNY, LOIS, 19, F, -, W, N.S., 493, 735, NBPT. In HH of John Post, age 24, Farmer, born in N.S. {Nova Scotia}.
REYES, JOHN S., 20, M, None, W, MA, 607, 887, NBPT. In HH of Eliza Reyes, age 48, born in MA.
REYNOLDS, CHARLES, 22, M, Blacksmith, W, Ireland, 325, 479, NBPT. In HH of Hugh McGlew, age 25, Blacksmith, born in MA.
RICHARDS, JAMES A., 23, M, Student, W, Sandwich Islands, 662, 953, NBPT. In HH of William B. Bannister, age 76, Gentleman, born in MA.
RICHARDSON, ANN, 70, F, -, W, MA, 788,1114, NBPT. In Poor House. .
RICHARDSON, ANNAH, 23, F, -, W, Maine, 158, 227, NBPT. In HH of Kesia Durham, age 54, born in Maine.
RICHARDSON, DAVID N., 15, M, Shoemaker, W, MA, 502, 670, NBPT*. In HH of Ponte

Richardson, age 41, Shoe Manufacturer, born in MA.
RICHARDSON, HANNAH M.B., 31, F, -, W, NH, 709,1004, NBPT. In HH of Jonathan C. Richardson, age 33, Carriage Maker, born in MA.
RICHARDSON, JOHN P., 63, M, Rigger, W, MA, 191, 278, NBPT.
RICHARDSON, JONATHAN C., 33, M, Carriage Maker, W, MA, 709,1004, NBPT.
RICHARDSON, JOSEPH, 21, M, Mariner, W, MA, 385, 569, NBPT. In HH of Betsy Richardson, age 62, born in MA.
RICHARDSON, MARY A., 23, F, -, W, Maine, 133, 197, NBPT. In HH of John Townsend, age 50, Shoemaker, born in Maine.
RICHARDSON, PONTE, 41, M, Shoe Manufacturer, W, MA, 502, 670, NBPT*.
RICKER, ABBY, 29, F, -, W, Maine, 631, 917, NBPT. In HH of Mary Ricker, age 61, born in Maine.
RICKER, BENJN. F., 25, M, Printer, W, Maine, 631, 917, NBPT. In HH of Mary Ricker, age 61, born in Maine.
RICKER, FREDERICK A., 20, M, Shoemaker, W, Maine, 631, 917, NBPT. In HH of Mary Ricker, age 61, born in Maine.
RICKER, LUCINDA, 31, F, -, W, Maine, 736,1041, NBPT. In HH of John L. Grindal, age 48, Grocer, born in Maine.
RICKER, MARY, 61, F, -, W, Maine, 631, 917, NBPT.
RICKER, MARY E., 23, F, -, W, Maine, 631, 917, NBPT. In HH of Mary Ricker, age 61, born in Maine.
RICKER, NOAH, 22, M, Operative, W, Maine, 736,1041, NBPT. In HH of John L. Grindal, age 48, Grocer, born in Maine.
RIDDER, WILLIAM, 32, M, Machinist, W, MA, 486, 728, NBPT. In HH of Abby K. Livingston, age 53, born in MA.
RIDGWAY, JOSEPH, 15, M, Student, W, MA, 44, 51, NBPT*. In HH of Josiah Bartlet, age 74, school teacher, born in MA.
RILEY, CATHARINE, 21, F, -, W, Ireland, 431, 564, NBPT*. In HH of Francis Riley, age 37, Farming, born in Ireland.
RILEY, FRANCIS, 37, M, Farming, W, Ireland, 431, 564, NBPT*.
RINES, JOHN, 44, M, Carpenter, W, NH, 588, 865, NBPT. In HH of Stilman Simonds, age 43, Shoemaker, born in MA.
RIPLEY, HEREKIAH, 27, M, Carpenter, W, Maine, 641, 928, NBPT.
RIPLEY, LOUISA S., 25, F, -, W, Maine, 641, 928, NBPT. In HH of Herekiah Ripley, age 27, Carpenter, born in Maine.
ROAF, ANDREW, 11, M, Operative, W, NH, 223, 277, NBPT*. In HH of Washington Roaf, age 21, Operative, born in NH.
ROAF, ELIZA, 20, F, -, W, NH, 223, 277, NBPT*. In HH of Washington Roaf, age 21, Operative, born in NH.
ROAF, OLIVE, 18, F, -, W, NH, 223, 277, NBPT*. In HH of Washington Roaf, age 21, Operative, born in NH.
ROAF, RACHEL, 55, F, -, W, Maine, 223, 277, NBPT*. In HH of Washington Roaf, age 21, Operative, born in NH.
ROAF, THOMAS, 55, M, Cooper, W, NH, 223, 277, NBPT*. In HH of Washington Roaf, age 21, Operative, born in NH.

ROAF, WASHINGTON, 21, M, Operative, W, NH, 223, 277, NBPT*. In HH of Stephen Fowle, age 33, Laborer, born in MA.
ROBBINS, AUGUSTA, 19, F, _, W, Maine, 31, 38, NBPT*. In HH of Albert Thompson, age 46, born NH.
ROBERTON, JOSHUA D., 21, M, Student, W, CT, 789,1115, NBPT. In HH of John M. Smith, age 34, Brick maker, born in MA.
ROBERTS, CATHARINE, 26, F, -, W, Maine, 515, 686, NBPT*. In HH of George P. Garland, age 65, Boarding House, born in NJ.
ROBERTS, GEORGE W., 16, M, Clerk, W, MA, 112, 166, NBPT. In HH of Soloman Roberts, age 54, Mariner, born in MA.
ROBERTS, HULD J., 17, F, -, W, Maine, 431, 641, NBPT. In HH of Mary L. Rains, age 48, born in Maine.
ROBERTS, JOSEPH, 42, M, Watchmaker, W, MA, 562, 748, NBPT*.
ROBERTS, MARY O., 42, F, -, W, Maine, 658, 948, NBPT. In HH of Parker Roberts, age 45, Merchant, born in MA.
ROBERTS, PARKER, 45, M, Merchant, W, MA, 658, 948, NBPT.
ROBERTS, SOLOMAN, 54, M, Mariner, W, MA, 112, 166, NBPT.
ROBERTS, WEALTHY, 17, F, -, W, Maine, 431, 641, NBPT. In HH of Mary L. Rains, age 48, born in Maine.
ROBERTS, WILLIAM, 17, M, Operative, W, Maine, 140, 166, NBPT*. In HH of Hannah T. Marshall, age 39, Boarding House, born in MA.
ROBINS, EBENEZER B., 40, M, Miller, W, MA, 40, 57, NBPT.
ROBINS, THOMAS B., 19, M, Shoemaker, W, MA, 40, 57, NBPT. In HH of Ebenezer B. Robins, age 40, Miller, born in MA.
ROBINSON, ADA, 10, F, -, W, Maine, 326, 481, NBPT. In HH of Benjn. Robinson, age 45, Shoemaker, born in Maine.
ROBINSON, ANN, 39, F, -, W, NH, 231, 337, NBPT. In HH of John L. Robinson, age 48, Grocer, born in NH.
ROBINSON, BENJN., 45, M, Shoemaker, W, Maine, 326, 481, NBPT.
ROBINSON, BENJN., 12, M, -, W, Maine, 326, 481, NBPT. In HH of Benjn. Robinson, age 45, Shoemaker, born in Maine.
ROBINSON, DAVID, 74, M, Trader, W, NH, 269, 345, NBPT*. In HH of Sarah Friend, age 54, born in MA.
ROBINSON, ELIZABETH, 15, F, -, W, Maine, 326, 481, NBPT. In HH of Benjn. Robinson, age 45, Shoemaker, born in Maine.
ROBINSON, GEORGE, 11, M, -, W, Maine, 326, 481, NBPT. In HH of Benjn. Robinson, age 45, Shoemaker, born in Maine.
ROBINSON, GEORGE A., 32, M, Shoemaker, W, MA, 500, 664, NBPT*.
ROBINSON, HARRIET N., 19, M, -, W, Maine, 326, 481, NBPT. In HH of Benjn. Robinson, age 45, Shoemaker, born in Maine.
ROBINSON, HARRIN S., 3, M, -, W, Maine, 326, 481, NBPT. In HH of Benjn. Robinson, age 45, Shoemaker, born in Maine.
ROBINSON, JOHN L., 48, M, Grocer, W, NH, 231, 337, NBPT.
ROBINSON, LANNA, 24, F, -, W, Maine, 177, 256, NBPT. In HH of James N. Canney, age 41, Teamster, born in NH.
ROBINSON, LUCY A., 16, F, -,

W, Maine, 326, 481, NBPT. In HH of Benjn. Robinson, age 45, Shoemaker, born in Maine.
ROBINSON, MARY E., 20, F, -, W, Maine, 503, 749, NBPT. In HH of Samuel Robinson, age 55, Shoemaker, born in Maine.
ROBINSON, MINDWELL, 53, F, -, W, Maine, 503, 749, NBPT. In HH of Samuel Robinson, age 55, Shoemaker, born in Maine.
ROBINSON, NANCY, 45, F, -, W, Maine, 326, 481, NBPT. In HH of Benjn. Robinson, age 45, Shoemaker, born in Maine.
ROBINSON, OLIVE C., 16, F, -, W, Maine, 503, 749, NBPT. In HH of Samuel Robinson, age 55, Shoemaker, born in Maine.
ROBINSON, PRISCILLA, 11, F, -, W, Maine, 503, 749, NBPT. In HH of Samuel Robinson, age 55, Shoemaker, born in Maine.
ROBINSON, ROBERT, 66, M, Shoe Dealer, W, Maine, 335, 437, NBPT*.
ROBINSON, ROBERT, 7, M, -, W, Maine, 326, 481, NBPT. In HH of Benjn. Robinson, age 45, Shoemaker, born in Maine.
ROBINSON, ROBERT JR., 44, M, Shoe Manufacturing, W, Maine, 577, 852, NBPT.
ROBINSON, ROBERT T., 18, M, Mariner, W, MA, 377, 494, NBPT*. In HH of William Robinson, age 37, Mariner, born in England.
ROBINSON, SAMUEL, 55, M, Shoemaker, W, Maine, 503, 749, NBPT.
ROBINSON, SAMUEL G., 40, M, Shoemaker, W, MA, 730,1029, NBPT.
ROBINSON, SARAH L., 17, F, -, W, NY, 577, 852, NBPT. In HH of Robert Robinson, Jr., age 44, Shoe Manufacturing, born in Maine.

ROBINSON, SYLVINA A., 18, F, -, W, Maine, 503, 749, NBPT. In HH of Samuel Robinson, age 55, Shoemaker, born in Maine.
ROBINSON, THOMAS, 35, M, Manufacturer, W, NH, 605, 795, NBPT*.
ROBINSON, WILLIAM, 37, M, Mariner, W, England, 377, 494, NBPT*.
ROFFE, EBENR., 33, M, Cabinetmaker, W, MA, 578, 853, NBPT.
ROGERS, EBENEZER, 67, M, Cabinet Maker, W, MA, 444, 587, NBPT*.
ROGERS, EDWARD, 38, M, Sailor, W, MA, 9, 9, NBPT.
ROGERS, GEORGE, 30, M, Shoemaker, W, MA, 431, 641, NBPT. In HH of Mary L. Rains, age 48, born in Maine.
ROGERS, GEORGE E., 23, M, Shoemaker, W, MA, 60, 66, NBPT*.
ROGERS, GEORGE L., 42, M, Master Mariner, W, MA, 683, 975, NBPT.
ROGERS, LUCY E., 19, F, -, W, LA, 683, 975, NBPT. In HH of George L. Rogers, age 42, Master Mariner, born in MA.
ROGERS, MARGARET, 23, F, -, W, Ireland, 60, 66, NBPT*. In HH or George E. Rogers, age 23, Shoemaker, born MA.
ROGERS, REBEKAH F., 60, F, -, W, MA, 175, 210, NBPT*. In HH of Silas Rogers, age 61, Cordwainer, born in MA.
ROGERS, REBEKAH F., 60, F, -, W, MA, 175, 210, NBPT*. In HH of Silas Rogers, age 61, Cordwainer, born in MA.
ROGERS, ROBERT, 37, M, Master Mariner, W, MA, 127, 187, NBPT.
ROGERS, SARAH, 50, F, -, W,

Ireland, 380, 560, NBPT. In HH of Elizabeth Storay, age 61, born in MA.
ROGERS, SILAS, 61, M, Cordwainer, W, MA, 175, 210, NBPT*.
ROLFE, GEORGE, 38, M, Boat Builder, W, MA, 581, 856, NBPT.
ROLLINS, RUTH, 19, F, -, W, Maine, 222, 276, NBPT*. In HH of Stephen Fowle, age 33, Laborer, born in MA.
ROLPH, MARY S., 19, F, -, W, Ireland, 18, 21, NBPT. In HH of George Currier, age 43, Mason, born in MA.
ROMAYNE/RONEYNE
ROMAYNE, CHARLOTTE, 17, F, -, W, Ireland, 330, 486, NBPT. In HH of Morris Romayne, age 58, Gentleman, born in Ireland.
ROMAYNE, GREEN, 19, M, Gentleman, W, Ireland, 330, 486, NBPT. In HH of Morris Romayne, age 58, Gentleman, born in Ireland.
ROMAYNE, MARY, 45, F, -, W, Ireland, 330, 486, NBPT. In HH of Morris Romayne, age 58, Gentleman, born in Ireland.
ROMAYNE, MARY, 22, F, -, W, Ireland, 330, 486, NBPT. In HH of Morris Romayne, age 58, Gentleman, born in Ireland.
ROMAYNE, MARY H., 13, F, -, W, Ireland, 330, 486, NBPT. In HH of Morris Romayne, age 58, Gentleman, born in Ireland.
ROMAYNE, MORRIS, 58, M, Gentleman, W, Ireland, 330, 486, NBPT.
ROMAYNE, WILLIAM H., 15, M, -, W, Ireland, 330, 486, NBPT. In HH of Morris Romayne, age 58, Gentleman, born in Ireland.
ROOT, ELLEN, 55, F, -, W, Nova Scotia, 439, 582, NBPT*.
ROSS, CHARLES H., 19, M, Shoemaker, W, MA, 436, 573,
NBPT*. In HH of Caroline Ross, age 51, born in MA.
ROSS, GAYTON O., 17, M, Shoemaker, W, MA, 436, 573, NBPT*. In HH of Caroline Ross, age 51, born in MA.
ROSS, LORENZO D., 40, M, Carpenter, W, MA, 457, 680, NBPT.
ROSS, MOSES M., 32, M, Grocer, W, MA, 436, 573, NBPT*. In HH of Caroline Ross, age 51, born in MA.
ROUNE, HENRY, 7, M, -, W, Ireland, 25, 33, NBPT. In HH of Rosanna Roune, age 54, born in Ireland.
ROUNE, MARY, 31, F, -, W, Ireland, 25, 33, NBPT. In HH of Rosanna Roune, age 54, born in Ireland.
ROUNE, MICHAEL, 17, M, Laborer, W, Ireland, 25, 33, NBPT. In HH of Rosanna Roune, age 54, born in Ireland.
ROUNE, ROSANNA, 54, F, -, W, Ireland, 25, 33, NBPT.
ROUX, MARGARET, 20, F, -, W, Maine, 431, 641, NBPT. In HH of Mary L. Rains, age 48, born in Maine.
ROWE, ANN, 24, F, -, W, VT, 573, 848, NBPT. In HH of Thomas Noyes, age 70, Shoemaker, born in MA.
ROWNAN, ELLEN, 34, F, -, W, Ireland, 93, 109, NBPT*. In HH of Thomas Rownan, age 35, Laborer, born in Ireland.
ROWNAN, THOMAS, 35, M, Laborer, W, Ireland, 93, 109, NBPT*.
ROYERS, GEORGE, 21, M, Shoemaker, W, MA, 753,1061, NBPT. In HH of Martha Royers, age 57, born in MA.
RUNDLETT, ADALIN, 24, M, Truck man, W, NH, 551, 823,

NBPT.
RUNDLETT, ALMIRA E.P., 30, F, -, W, Maine, 534, 797, NBPT. In HH of John N.B. Rundlett, age 29, Carpenter, born in NH.
RUNDLETT, CLOUSICA J., 38, F, -, W, NH, 508, 759, NBPT. In HH of Samuel H. Rundlett, age 41, Truck man, born in NH.
RUNDLETT, DAVIS S., 28, M, Machinist, W, NH, 604, 883, NBPT.
RUNDLETT, HARRIET A., 18, F, -, W, NH, 690, 982, NBPT. In HH of Thomas L. Rundlett, age 41, Agent Globe Mills, born in NH.
RUNDLETT, JOHN N.B., 29, M, Carpenter, W, NH, 534, 797, NBPT.
RUNDLETT, JOHNNA, 22, F, -, W, Maine, 551, 823, NBPT. In HH of Adalin Rundlett, age 24, Truck man, born in NH.
RUNDLETT, JONATHAN D., 40, M, Soap & Candle Manuf., W, NH, 600, 878, NBPT.
RUNDLETT, MARY O., 25, M, -, W, NH, 604, 883, NBPT. In HH of Davis S. Rundlett, age 28, Machinist, born in NH.
RUNDLETT, NARRISA B., 25, F, -, W, NH, 600, 878, NBPT. In HH of Jonathan D. Rundlett, age 40, Soap and Candle Manuf., born in NH.
RUNDLETT, OLIVER A., 30, M, Carpenter, W, NH, 521, 777, NBPT.
RUNDLETT, SAMUEL H., 41, M, Truck man, W, NH, 508, 759, NBPT.
RUNDLETT, THOMAS L., 41, M, Agent Globe Mills, W, NH, 690, 982, NBPT.
RUSSELL, ALBERT, 39, M, Iron Founder, W, Maine, 18, 22, NBPT*.
RUSSELL, CHARLES, 16, M, Carpenter, W, MA, 363, 534, NBPT. In HH of George N. Bartlett, age 29, Carpenter, born in NH.
RUSSELL, CHARLES A., 14, M, -, W, Maine, 220, 274, NBPT*. In HH of Martha L. Russell, age 25, born in Maine.
RUSSELL, HULDAH, 17, F, -, W, Maine, 264, 333, NBPT*. In HH of Joseph Greenleaf, age 62, Sailmaker, born in MA.
RUSSELL, JOSEPH, 80, M, Merchant, W, MA, 290, 424, NBPT.
RUSSELL, MARTHA L., 25, F, -, W, Maine, 220, 274, NBPT*.
RUSSELL, MARY A., 24, F, -, W, Maine, 461, 609, NBPT*. In HH of Timothy Hilliard, age 46, Shoe Store, born in NH.
RUSSELL, MARY M., 29, F, -, W, Maine, 18, 22, NBPT*. In HH of Albert Russell, age 39, Iron Founder, born Maine.
RUSSELL, PORTER, 66, M, Cabinetmaker, W, MA, 134, 159, NBPT*.
RUST, MARY, 24, F, -, W, NH, 610, 800, NBPT*. In HH of Edward W. Brown, age 31, Lab. Factory, born in NH.
RYAN, JANE, 30, F, -, W, Maine, 493, 735, NBPT. In HH of John Post, age 24, Farmer, born in N.S. {Nova Scotia}.
RYESON, JOHN, 32, M, Laborer, W, Denmark, 95, 139, NBPT.

- S -

SALLEY, MARY J., 23, F, -, W, Maine, 405, 529, NBPT*. In HH of Miriam James, age 50, born in NH.
SALTER, ABEL, 44, M, Barber, W, MA, 395, 585, NBPT.
SANBORN, FRANCES, 25, M,

Carpenter, W, NH, 452, 675, NBPT. In HH of Eveline Gunnison, age 46, born in Maine.

SANBORN, GEORGE A., 19, M, -, W, NH, 35, 49, NBPT. In HH of Mary C. Pike, age 36, born in MA.

SANBORN, JOHN W., 21, M, Spinner, W, NH, 35, 49, NBPT. In HH of Mary C. Pike, age 36, born in MA.

SANBORN, MARY A., 20, F, -, W, Maine, 35, 49, NBPT. In HH of Mary C. Pike, age 36, born in MA.

SANBORN, MELISSA A., W, F, -, W, Maine, 35, 49, NBPT. In HH of Mary C. Pike, age 36, born in MA. Melissa A. Sanborn listed as very old (check age in city Hall).

SANBORN, OLIVER, 29, M, Laborer, W, MA, 56, 62, NBPT*.

SANDERSON, HENRY M., 15, M, Clerk, W, MA, 489, 652, NBPT*. In HH of James S. Lattimer, age 42, Shoemaker, born in MA.

SARGENT, Aaron A., 23, M, Printer, W, MA, 730,1030, NBPT. In HH of Aaron P. Sargent, age 49, Sexton, born in MA.

SARGENT, Aaron P., 49, M, Sexton, W, MA, 730,1030, NBPT.

SARGENT, ABIGAIL, 37, M, -, W, NH, 364, 536, NBPT. In HH of Rufus Sargent, age 38, Architect, born in MA.

SARGENT, CHARLES R., 26, M, Machinist, W, NH, 172, 207, NBPT*.

SARGENT, CHARLOTTE, 20, F, -, W, NH, 259, 327, NBPT*. In HH of William J. Badger, age 39, Stage Agent, born in NH.

SARGENT, EBENR. P., 24, M, Overseer, W, MA, 735,1039, NBPT. In HH of John Sargent, age 59, Truck man, born in NH.

SARGENT, ELVIRA A., 43, F, -, W, NH, 480, 639, NBPT*. In HH of True W. Sargent, age 53, Trader, born in MA.

SARGENT, HANNAH, 31, F, -, W, VT, 284, 367, NBPT*. In HH of Horace Sargent, age 28, Stove Dealer, born in NH.

SARGENT, HENRY P., 29, M, Liver Stable, W, MA, 436, 572, NBPT*.

SARGENT, HORACE, 28, M, Stove Dealer, W, NH, 284, 367, NBPT*.

SARGENT, ISAAC, 21, M, Painter, W, MA, 735,1039, NBPT. In HH of John Sargent, age 59, Truck man, born in NH.

SARGENT, JAMES, 20, M, Stabler, W, MA, 436, 572, NBPT*. In HH of Henry P. Sargent, age 29, Livery Stable, born in MA.

SARGENT, JANE C., 28, F, -, W, NH, 284, 367, NBPT*. In HH of Horace Sargent, age 28, Stove Dealer, born in NH.

SARGENT, JOHN, 59, M, Truck man, W, NH, 735,1039, NBPT.

SARGENT, JOHN, 32, M, Watchman, W, MA, 156, 225, NBPT.

SARGENT, JOSIPHINE, 19, F, -, W, Maine, 177, 256, NBPT. In HH of James N. Canney, age 41, Teamster, born in NH.

SARGENT, KENDALL, 30, M, Operative, W, MA, 501, 747, NBPT.

SARGENT, MARY A., 39, F, -, W, NH, 501, 747, NBPT. In HH of Kendall Sargent, age 30, Operative, born in MA.

SARGENT, MOSES, 57, M, Boarding House, W, MA, 529, 789, NBPT.

SARGENT, MOSES, 26, M, Book Seller, W, MA, 300, 439, NBPT.

SARGENT, MRS., 27, F, -, W, NH, 529, 789, NBPT. In HH of Moses Sargent, age 47, Boarding

House, born in MA.
SARGENT, NATHANIEL, 53, M, Teamster, W, MA, 614, 806, NBPT*.
SARGENT, NEHAMIAH, 50, M, Mariner, W, MA, 322, 476, NBPT.
SARGENT, PRENTISS, 25, M, Stove Manufacturer, W, NH, 284, 367, NBPT*. In HH of Horace Sargent, age 28, Stove Dealer, born in NH.
SARGENT, ROBERT G., 19, M, Blacksmith, W, MA, 735,1039, NBPT. In HH of John Sargent, age 59, Truck man, born in NH.
SARGENT, RUFUS, 38, M, Architect, W, MA, 364, 536, NBPT.
SARGENT, RUFUS P., 14, M, -, W, Maine, 172, 207, NBPT*. In HH of Charles R. Sargent, age 26, Machinist, born in NH.
SARGENT, SAMUEL, 46, M, Laborer in Distiller, W, NH, 470, 623, NBPT*.
SARGENT, SARAH, 53, F, -, W, NH, 754,1062, NBPT. In HH of Charles Goodfrey, age 27, Mariner, born in MA.
SARGENT, SUSAN, 45, F, -, W, NH, 470, 623, NBPT*. In HH of Samuel Sargent, age 46, Laborer in Distillery, born in NH.
SARGENT, TRUE W., 53, M, Trader, W, MA, 480, 639, NBPT*.
SATTER, EBENEZER, 38, M, Tailor, W, MA, 334, 492, NBPT. In HH of Polly Satter, age 75, born in Maine.
SAUNDERS, ALBERT H., 18, M, Clerk, W, RI, 692, 984, NBPT. In HH of Benj. Saunders, age 40, Agent Ocean Mills, born in RI.
SAUNDERS, BENJ., 40, M, Agent Ocean Mills, W, RI, 692, 984, NBPT.
SAUNDERS, ELLEN H., 20, F, -, W, RI, 692, 984, NBPT. In HH of Benj. Saunders, age 40, Agent Ocean Mills, born in RI.
SAUNDERSON, SUSAN M., 27, F, -, W, Maine, 708,1003, NBPT. In HH of Sarah Easton, age 57, born in NH.
SAURIE, FRANKLIN, 22, M, Cord Stripper, W, MA, 177, 256, NBPT. In HH of James N. Canney, age 41, Teamster, born in NH.
SAWYER, ABBA, 35, F, -, W, Maine, 504, 672, NBPT*. In HH of Josiah Sawyer, age 36, Ship Joiner, born in MA.
SAWYER, JEREMIAH, 30, M, Physician, W, MA, 158, 190, NBPT*.
SAWYER, JOSIAH, 36, M, Ship Joiner, W, MA, 504, 672, NBPT*.
SAWYER, MEHETABLE, 37, F, -, W, NH, 518, 689, NBPT*. In HH of Charles Coffin, age 48, Ship Carpenter, born in MA.
SCALES, AUSTIN, 28, M, Laborer, W, Ireland, 472, 627, NBPT*.
SCALES, CATHARINE, 27, F, -, W, Ireland, 472, 627, NBPT*. In HH of Austin Scales, age 28, Laborer, born in Ireland.
SCALES, FRANCIS, 21, F, -, W, Ireland, 472, 627, NBPT*. In HH of Austin Scales, age 28, Laborer, born in Ireland.
SCALES, HANNAH, 19, F, -, W, Ireland, 472, 627, NBPT*. In HH of Austin Scales, age 28, Laborer, born in Ireland.
SCETES?, ELLEN, 16, F, -, W, Maine, 736,1041, NBPT. In HH of John L. Grindal, age 48, Grocer, born in Maine.
SCETES?, JANE, 24, F, -, W, Maine, 736,1041, NBPT. In HH of John L. Grindal, age 48, Grocer, born in Maine.
SCETES?, JOHN, 30, M, Carpenter, W, Maine, 736,1041,

NBPT. In HH of John L. Grindal, age 48, Grocer, born in Maine.
SCHAFF, HARRIET, 27, F, -, W, NH, 704, 999, NBPT. In HH of Robinson N. Schaff, age 30, Shoemaker, born in MA.
SCHAFF, ROBINSON N., 30, M, Shoemaker, W, MA, 704, 999, NBPT.
SCIDENBERG, HENRY, 42, M, Cabinet Maker, W, Bremen, 729,1028, NBPT.
SCRUTEN, CAROLINE F., 17, F, -, W, NH, 590, 779, NBPT*. In HH of Enoch Flanders, age 59, Caulker, born in MA.
SCULLY, CATHERINE, 13, F, -, W, Nova Scotia, 25, 34, NBPT. In HH of John Scully, age 36, Laborer, born in Ireland.
SCULLY, HANNAH, 14, F, -, W, Ireland, 25, 34, NBPT. In HH of John Scully, age 36, Laborer, born in Ireland.
SCULLY, JOHN, 36, M, Laborer, W, Ireland, 25, 34, NBPT.
SCULLY, JOHN, 6, M, -, W, Nova Scotia, 25, 34, NBPT. In HH of John Scully, age 36, Laborer, born in Ireland.
SCULLY, MARY, 38, F, -, W, Ireland, 25, 34, NBPT. In HH of John Scully, age 36, Laborer, born in Ireland.
SCULLY, PATRICK, 11, M, -, W, Nova Scotia, 25, 34, NBPT. In HH of John Scully, age 36, Laborer, born in Ireland.
SEALY, EDWARD P., 24, M, Mariner, W, MA, 111, 165, NBPT.
SEALY, MARY P., 24, F, -, W, Maine, 111, 165, NBPT. In HH of Edward P. Sealy, age 24, Mariner, born in MA.
SEARL, JOSEPH, 17, M, Carpenter, W, MA, 715,1011, NBPT. In HH of Philip Blumpey, age 75, Rigger, born in England.

SEDLEY, MARK W., 24, M, Laborer, W, NH, 155, 224, NBPT. In HH of Levi Dow, age 44, Fish Dealer, born in NH.
SEED, JAMES, 37, M, Operative, W, England, 776,1100, NBPT. In HH of Moses Winn, age 62, Laborer, born in MA.
SELBY, ELIZA A., 23, F, -, W, Maine, 326, 482, NBPT. In HH of Peter Fennimore, age 45, Shoemaker, born in MA.
SENNON, TIMOTHY, 30, M, Laborer, W, Ireland, 756,1066, NBPT.
SERGENT, HANNAH O., 24, F, -, W, Maine, 177, 256, NBPT. In HH of James N. Canney, age 41, Teamster, born in NH.
SEVERANCE, FLORENNA, 15, F, -, W, NH, 535, 711, NBPT*. In HH of Sarah Cheney, age 54, born in NH.
SEWARD, BETSY, 24, F, -, W, NH, 218, 324, NBPT. In HH of William Seward, age 24, Carpenter, born in MA.
SEWARD, JOHN B., 34, M, Harness Maker, W, MA, 622, 906, NBPT.
SEWARD, WILLIAM, 24, M, Carpenter, W, MA, 218, 324, NBPT.
SEWINN?, SAMUEL G., 30, M, Machinist, W, MA, 509, 762, NBPT.
SHACKFORD, DAVID, 23, M, Mariner, W, MA, 107, 159, NBPT. In HH of Henry Lunt, age 34, Mariner, born in MA.
SHACKFORD, SUSAN, 45, F, -, W, MA, 788,1114, NBPT. In Poor House. .
SHAFLISPH, ANN H., 49, F, -, W, NH, 551, 824, NBPT.
SHAIN, ANN, 15, F, -, W, Ireland, 778,1104, NBPT. In HH of Daniel Johnson, age 23, Grocer,

born in MA.

SHAIN, CATHERINE, 18, F, -, W, Ireland, 181, 262, NBPT. In HH of John Cogger, age 85?, Laborer, born in Ireland.

SHAIN, MARGARET, 13, F, -, W, Ireland, 181, 262, NBPT. In HH of John Cogger, age 85?, Laborer, born in Ireland.

SHAKFORD, JOSEPH, 50, M, Mariner, W, Ireland, 262, 380, NBPT.

SHAW, BARTHOLOMEW, 45, M, Laborer, W, Ireland, 207, 307, NBPT. In HH of David Comerford, age 63, Sailmaker, born in MA.

SHAW, ELIJAH M., 23, M, 2nd Overseer, W, NH, 461, 609, NBPT*. In HH of Timothy Hilliard, age 46, Shoe Store, born in NH.

SHAW, HARRIET L., 37, F, -, W, NH, 195, 239, NBPT*. In HH of Sarah J. Shaw, age 39, born in NH.

SHAW, MARIA, 30, F, -, W, CT, 233, 339, NBPT. In HH of William Shaw, age 39, Stable Keeper, born in MA.

SHAW, SAMUEL, 64, M, Coach Driver, W, MA, 611, 892, NBPT.

SHAW, SARAH J., 39, F, -, W, NH, 195, 239, NBPT*.

SHAW, WILLIAM, 39, M, Stable Keeper, W, MA, 233, 339, NBPT.

SHENNON, DAVID S., 23, M, Laborer, W, Ireland, 311, 459, NBPT.

SHENNON, ELLEN S., 25, F, -, W, Ireland, 311, 459, NBPT. In HH of David Shennon, age 23, Laborer, born in Ireland.

SHERMAN, AMANDA M., 6, F, -, W, RI, 11, 12, NBPT*. In HH of Stephen A. Sherman, age 29, 2nd Overseer OC, born RI.

SHERMAN, CHARLOTTE D., 31, F, -, W, RI, 11, 11, NBPT*. In HH of Silas E. Sherman, 34, Overseer Spinning Oc., born RI.

SHERMAN, EDWIN E., 8, M, -, W, RI, 11, 11, NBPT*. In HH of Silas E. Sherman, 34, Overseer Spinning Oc., born RI.

SHERMAN, EMELINE, 16, F, -, W, RI, 437, 576, NBPT*. In HH of Robert Sherman, age 28, Overseer Spinning, born in RI.

SHERMAN, FRANCES, 11, F, -, W, RI, 437, 576, NBPT*. In HH of Robert Sherman, age 28, Overseer Spinning, born in RI.

SHERMAN, MARY, 10, F, -, W, RI, 437, 576, NBPT*. In HH of Robert Sherman, age 28, Overseer Spinning, born in RI.

SHERMAN, MELISSA J., 4, F, -, W, RI, 11, 12, NBPT*. In HH of Stephen A. Sherman, age 29, 2nd Overseer OC, born RI.

SHERMAN, ROBERT, 28, M, Overseer Spinning, W, RI, 437, 576, NBPT*.

SHERMAN, ROBERT B., 6, M, -, W, RI, 11, 11, NBPT*. In HH of Silas E. Sherman, 34, Overseer Spinning Oc., born RI.

SHERMAN, SILAS E., 34, M, Overseer Spinning OC, W, RI, 11, 11, NBPT*.

SHERMAN, STEPHEN A., 29, M, 2nd Overseer. OC, W, RI, 11, 12, NBPT*.

SHERMAN, SUSAN, 36, F, -, W, RI, 437, 576, NBPT*. In HH of Robert Sherman, age 28, Overseer Spinning, born in RI.

SHERMAN, SUSAN, 20, F, -, W, RI, 437, 576, NBPT*. In HH of Robert Sherman, age 28, Overseer Spinning, born in RI.

SHERMAN, WILLIAM D., 9, M, -, W, RI, 11, 11, NBPT*. In HH of Silas E. Sherman, 34, Overseer Spinning Oc., born RI.

SHOOF, HENRY, 48, M, Ship master, W, Denmark, 129, 154, NBPT*.

SHOOF, HENRY, 48, M, Ship master, W, Denmark, 129, 154, NBPT*.
SHOOF, WILLIAM H., 16, M, Student, W, MA, 129, 154, NBPT*. In HH of Henry Shoof, age 48, Ship master, born in Denmark.
SHORT, JOSEPH, 16, M, None, W, MA, 510, 681, NBPT*. In HH of Mary A. Short, age 41, born in MA.
SHORT, MARY A.S., 30, F, -, W, Denmark, 502, 748, NBPT. William Stone, age 59, Merchant, born in MA.
SHORT, STEPHEN, 42, M, Cabinet Maker, W, MA, 143, 171, NBPT*.
SHURBUNE, CHARLES, 23, M, Tailor, W, MA, 626, 912, NBPT. In HH of Luther R. Chase, age 30, Carriage Maker, born in MA.
SHUTE, ELIZABETH, 64, F, -, W, NH, 606, 886, NBPT. In HH of Amos Pearson, age 67, Carpenter, born in MA.
SIDEBOTTOM, NATHAN, 34, M, -, W, England, 109, 162, NBPT. In HH of Margaret Hickman, age 58, born in MA.
SIDELINGER, CAROLINE A., 19, F, -, W, Maine, 641, 928, NBPT. In HH of Herekiah Ripley, age 27, Carpenter, born in Maine.
SILK, MARGARET, 24, F, -, W, Ireland, 474, 711, NBPT. In HH of Michael Murphy, age 48, Laborer, born in Ireland.
SILLEZ, EMILY, 16, F, -, W, NH, 173, 250, NBPT. In HH of George R. Sillez, age 28, Mariner, born in NH.
SILLEZ, GEORGE R., 28, M, Mariner, W, NH, 173, 250, NBPT.
SILLEZ, MARY, 32, F, -, W, Ireland, 173, 250, NBPT. In HH of George R. Sillez, age 28, Mariner, born in NH.

SILLOWAY, DANIEL, 35, M, Carpenter, W, MA, 3, 3, NBPT.
SILLOWAY, JAMES, 39, M, Baker, W, MA, 180, 220, NBPT*. In HH of Joseph Silloway, age 59, Cabinetmaker, born in MA.
SILLOWAY, JOHN R., 19, M, Mariner, W, MA, 164, 238, NBPT. In HH of Thomas Silloway, age 42, Coppersmith, born in MA.
SILLOWAY, JOSEPH, 61, M, Cabinetmaker, W, MA, 180, 220, NBPT*.
SILLOWAY, THOMAS, 42, M, Coppersmith, W, MA, 164, 238, NBPT.
SILLOWAY, THOMAS W., 21, M, Architect, W, MA, 164, 238, NBPT. In HH of Thomas Silloway, age 42, Coppersmith, born in MA.
SIMONDS, CAROLINE, 3, F, -, W, NH, 588, 865, NBPT. In HH of Stilman Simonds, age 43, Shoemaker, born in MA.
SIMONDS, ELECTA, 5, F, -, W, NH, 588, 865, NBPT. In HH of Stilman Simonds, age 43, Shoemaker, born in MA.
SIMONDS, ELLEN, 17, F, -, W, Maine, 588, 865, NBPT. In HH of Stilman Simonds, age 43, Shoemaker, born in MA.
SIMONDS, MARIETTA, 13, F, -, W, NH, 588, 865, NBPT. In HH of Stilman Simonds, age 43, Shoemaker, born in MA.
SIMONDS, OLIVE, 16, F, -, W, Maine, 588, 865, NBPT. In HH of Stilman Simonds, age 43, Shoemaker, born in MA.
SIMONDS, SCOTT, 10, M, -, W, NH, 588, 865, NBPT. In HH of Stilman Simonds, age 43, Shoemaker, born in MA.
SIMONDS, STILMAN, 43, M, Shoemaker, W, MA, 588, 865, NBPT.
SIMONDS, WARREN, 11, M, -,

W, VT, 588, 865, NBPT. In HH of Stilman Simonds, age 43, Shoemaker, born in MA.

SIMPSON, JOHN, 45, M, Master Mariner, W, MA, 350, 462, NBPT*.

SIMPSON, PAUL, 76, M, Master Mariner, W, Maine, 337, 496, NBPT.

SIMPSON, THOMAS, 30, M, Master Mariner, W, MA, 337, 496, NBPT. In HH of Paul Simpson, age 76, Master Mariner, born in Maine.

SISDOLL, REUBEN, 32, M, Engineer, W, MA, 126, 185, NBPT.

SKEELS, AMOS, 66, M, Tallow Chandler, W, VT, 455, 602, NBPT*.

SKEELS, WILLIAM, 25, M, Ship Carpenter, W, MA, 455, 602, NBPT*. In HH of Amos Skeels, age 66, Tallor Chandler, born in VT.

SKELLS, JOHN W., 24, M, Joiner, W, MA, 456, 603, NBPT*.

SKINNER, GEORGE W., 22, M, Physician, W, MA, 609, 889, NBPT.

SLATER, WILLIAM, 23, M, Weaver, W, England, 153, 222, NBPT. In HH of Martha A. Whright, age 86, born in England.

SMALL, BENJAMIN, 30, F, Mariner, W, MA, 119, 176, NBPT.

SMALL, BENJN., 32, M, Master Mariner, W, Maine, 616, 898, NBPT. In HH of Mary A. Small, age 56, born in MA.

SMALL, DENNIS W., 28, M, Master Mariner, W, Maine, 616, 898, NBPT. In HH of Mary A. Small, age 56, born in MA.

SMALL, ENOCH L., 16, M, Student, W, MA, 42, 60, NBPT. In HH of Thomas Small, age 54, Master Mariner, born in MA.

SMALL, HARRIET, 30, F, -, W, Maine, 616, 898, NBPT. In HH of Mary A. Small, age 56, born in MA.

SMALL, JOSEPH, 42, M, Master Mariner, W, MA, 79, 115, NBPT.

SMALL, THOMAS, 54, M, Master Mariner, W, MA, 42, 60, NBPT.

SMALL, THOMAS C., 21, M, Mariner, W, MA, 42, 60, NBPT. In HH of Thomas Small, age 54, Master Mariner, born in MA.

SMART, EMILY, 19, F, -, W, Maine, 15, 19, NBPT*. In HH of William H. Pettingel, 30, House carpenter, born Maine.

SMART, HARRISON H., 23, M, House Carpenter, W, NH, 15, 18, NBPT*. In HH of Milton Smart, age 47, Blacksmith, born Maine.

SMART, MARTHA, 43, F, -, W, NH, 15, 18, NBPT*. In HH of Milton Smart, age 47, Blacksmith, born Maine.

SMART, MILTON, 47, M, Blacksmith, W, Maine, 15, 18, NBPT*.

SMELL, ELIZABETH, 2, F, -, W, Maine, 331, 488, NBPT. In HH of William Smell, age 23, Operative, born in Maine.

SMELL, IRENA, 20, F, -, W, Maine, 331, 488, NBPT. In HH of William Smell, age 23, Operative, born in Maine.

SMELL, WILLIAM, 23, M, Operative, W, Maine, 331, 488, NBPT.

SMITH, AGNES, 40, F, -, W, Scotland, 765, 1080, NBPT. In HH of Thomas E. Smith, age 41, Spinner, born in England.

SMITH, BENJAMIN, 46, M, Painter, W, VT, 424, 552, NBPT*.

SMITH, CHARLES, 48, M, Gardner, W, MA, 32, 45, NBPT.

SMITH, CHARLES, 43, M, Master Mariner, W, MA, 537, 714, NBPT*.

SMITH, CHARLES A., 3, M, -,

W, MO, 120, 143, NBPT*. In HH of John Andrews, age 50, Cashier, born in MA.
SMITH, CHARLES F., 32, M, Master Mariner, W, NH, 395, 584, NBPT.
SMITH, CHARLES F., 17, M, Fisherman, W, MA, 537, 714, NBPT*. In HH of Charles Smith, age 43, Master Mariner, born in MA.
SMITH, DANIEL, 66, M, Carpenter, W, NH, 168, 243, NBPT.
SMITH, DANIEL, 62, M, Druggist, W, CT, 308, 454, NBPT.
SMITH, DANIEL A., 32, M, Carpenter, W, NH, 360, 529, NBPT.
SMITH, DANIEL H., 31, M, Machinist, W, MA, 114, 137, NBPT*.
SMITH, EDWARD W., 36, M, Mariner, W, MA, 401, 525, NBPT*.
SMITH, ELIZABETH N., 22, F, Merchant, W, Maine, 14, 16, NBPT. In HH of Enoch Smith, age 66, Mason, born in MA.
SMITH, ENOCH, 66, M, Mason, W, MA, 14, 16, NBPT.
SMITH, ENOCH W., 24, M, Merchant, W, MA, 14, 16, NBPT. In HH of Enoch Smith, age 66, Mason, born in MA.
SMITH, FOSTER W., 33, M, Dealer in Clothing, W, MA, 774,1094, NBPT.
SMITH, FOSTERE D., 59, M, Merchant, W, NH, 211, 312, NBPT.
SMITH, HARRIET S., 31, F, -, W, NH, 395, 584, NBPT. In HH of Charles F. Smith, age 32, Master Mariner, born in NH.
SMITH, ISABELLA N., 14, F, -, W, RI, 765,1080, NBPT. IN HH of Thomas E. Smith, age 41, Spinner, born in England.

SMITH, JAMES, 14, M, -, W, NH, 424, 552, NBPT*. In HH of Benjamin Smith, age 46, Painter, born in VT.
SMITH, JAMES T., 12, M, -, W, RI, 765,1080, NBPT. IN HH of Thomas E. Smith, age 41, Spinner, born in England.
SMITH, JHOR?. H., 30, M, Carpenter, W, MA, 151, 220, NBPT. In HH of Hannah White, age 45, born in Maine.
SMITH, JOHN M., 34, M, Brick maker, W, MA, 789,1115, NBPT.
SMITH, JOSEPH, 9, M, -, W, NY, 765,1080, NBPT. IN HH of Thomas E. Smith, age 41, Spinner, born in England.
SMITH, JUSTIN, 24, M, Tailor, W, MA, 211, 312, NBPT. In HH of Joster Smith, age 59, Merchant, born in NH.
SMITH, JUSTIN E., 23, M, Dentist, W, MA, 722,1021, NBPT. In HH of Thomas E. Pressey, age 37, Carpenter, born in MA.
SMITH, MARGARET R., 15, F, -, W, RI, 765,1080, NBPT. IN HH of Thomas E. Smith, age 41, Spinner, born in England.
SMITH, MARY, 21, F, -, W, Maine, 125, 182, NBPT. In HH of William Felch, age 31, Shoemaker, born in NH.
SMITH, MARY A.E., 27, F, -, W, England, 597, 875, NBPT. In HH of Mayo G. Smith, age 33, Dentist, born in MA.
SMITH, MARY G., 29, F, -, W, NH, 360, 529, NBPT. In HH of Daniel A. Smith, age 32, Carpenter, born in NH.
SMITH, MAYO G., 33, M, Dentist, W, MA, 597, 875, NBPT.
SMITH, MOREY S., 12, M, -,W, NH, 424, 552, NBPT*. In HH of Benjamin Smith, age 46, Painter, born in VT.

SMITH, NATHANIEL, 78, m, None, W, MA, 1, 1, NBPT*.
SMITH, NATHANIEL P., 33, M, None, W, MA, 1, 1, NBPT*. In HH of Nathaniel Smith, age 78 born MA.
SMITH, RUFUS, 34, M, Merchant, W, MA, 415, 618, NBPT.
SMITH, SUSAN G., 23, F, -, W, Maine, 326, 482, NBPT. In HH of Peter Fennimore, age 45, Shoemaker, born in MA.
SMITH, TERZAH, 49, F, -, W, NH, 424, 552, NBPT*. In HH of Benjamin Smith, age 46, Painter, born in VT.
SMITH, THOMAS E., 41, M, Spinner, W, England, 765,1080, NBPT.
SMITH, WORCESTER, 22, M, Printer, W, MA, 211, 312, NBPT. In HH of Joster Smith, age 59, Merchant, born in NH.
SNOW, JOHN, 48, M, Boarding House, W, Maine, 529, 788, NBPT.
SOLDAN, CHARLOTTE, 19, F, -, W, Denmark, 405, 604, NBPT. In HH of Joseph Ladd, age 33, Boat Builder, born in MA.
SOLDAN, MARY, 57, F, -, W, England, 405, 604, NBPT. In HH of Joseph Ladd, age 33, Boat Builder, born in MA.
SOMERBY, ABLERT, 28, M, Mariner, W, MA, 789,1115, NBPT. In HH of John M. Smith, age 34, Brick maker, born in MA.
SOMERBY, HENRY, 62, M, Carpenter, W, Maine, 788,1114, NBPT. In Poor House.
SOMERBY, JOSEPH A., 51, M, Branch Pilot, W, MA, 80, 117, NBPT.
SOMERBY, WILLIAM, 66, M, Printer, W, MA, 788,1114, NBPT. In Poor House.
SOUTHER, CATHARINE, 24, F, -, W, Ireland, 356, 470, NBPT*. In HH of John Souther, age 23, Mariner, born in NH.
SOUTHER, JACOB, 37, M, Mariner, W, Nova Scotia, 413, 540, NBPT*.
SOUTHER, JACOB, 37, M, Mariner, W, NH, 413, 540, NBPT*.
SOUTHER, JOHN, 23, M, Mariner, W, NH, 356, 470, NBPT*.
SOUTHER, NANCY, 35, F, W, 0, Ireland, 413, 540, NBPT*. In HH of Jacob Souther, age 37, Mariner, born in NH.
SOUTHER, SARAH, 10, F, -, W, NH, 413, 540, NBPT*. In HH of Jacob Souther, age 37, Mariner, born in NH.
SOUTHWELL, EMITY, 22, F, -, W, NH, 267, 342, NBPT*. In HH of Robert V. Southwell, age 21, Machinist, born in VT.
SOUTHWELL, MARY A., 19, F, -, W, VT, 267, 342, NBPT*. In HH of Robert V. Southwell, age 21, Machinist, born in VT.
SOUTHWELL, ROBERT V., 21, M, Machinist, W, VT, 267, 342, NBPT*.
SPALDING, ELIZABETH, 20, F, -, W, Nova Scotia, 298, 390, NBPT*. In HH of Prescott Spalding, age 70, None, born in MA.
SPALDING, OLIVER, 66, M, None, W, MA, 300, 392, NBPT*.
SPALDING, OLIVER B., 24, M, Trader, W, MA, 425, 553, NBPT*.
SPALDING, OLIVER P., 23, M, None, W, MA, 300, 392, NBPT*. In HH of Oliver Spalding, age 66, None, born in MA.
SPALDING, PRESCOTT, 70, M, None, W, MA, 298, 390, NBPT*.
SPATES, ANN, 46, F, -, W, Nova Scotia, 224, 330, NBPT. In HH of William A. Spates, age 44, Watchman, born in Nova Scotia.

SPATES, FRANCES A., 12, F, -, W, Nova Scotia, 224, 330, NBPT. In HH of William A. Spates, age 44, Watchman, born in Nova Scotia.

SPATES, JOHN E., 4, M, -, W, Nova Scotia, 224, 330, NBPT. In HH of William A. Spates, age 44, Watchman, born in Nova Scotia.

SPATES, JOSEPH G., 9, M, -, W, Nova Scotia, 224, 330, NBPT. In HH of William A. Spates, age 44, Watchman, born in Nova Scotia.

SPATES, MARIA E., 7, F, -, W, Nova Scotia, 224, 330, NBPT. In HH of William A. Spates, age 44, Watchman, born in Nova Scotia.

SPATES, MARTHA A., 19, F, -, W, Maine, 224, 330, NBPT. In HH of William A. Spates, age 44, Watchman, born in Nova Scotia.

SPATES, RICHARD N., 16, M, Operative, W, Maine, 224, 330, NBPT. In HH of William A. Spates, age 44, Watchman, born in Nova Scotia.

SPATES, WELTHA J., 14, F, -, W, Maine, 224, 330, NBPT. In HH of William A. Spates, age 44, Watchman, born in Nova Scotia.

SPATES, WILLIAM A., 44, M, Watchman, W, Nova Scotia, 224, 330, NBPT.

SPATES, WILLIAM H., 22, M, Watchman, W, Nova Scotia, 224, 330, NBPT. In HH of William A. Spates, age 44, Watchman, born in Nova Scotia.

SPEAD, EMMA R., 11, F, -, W, NH, 501, 747, NBPT. In HH of Kendall Sargent, age 30, Operative, born in MA.

SPEAKMAN, JOHN, 23, M, Overseer in Mill, W, England, 118, 174, NBPT. In HH of Daniel Reed, age 35, Cabinet Maker, born in NH.

SPENCER, ELIZABETH, 60, F, -, W, England, 107, 128, NBPT*. In HH of Sarah Marsh, age 65, born in MA.

SPILLER, ABIGAIL H., 44, F, -, W, Maine, 327, 483, NBPT. In HH of Henry Spiller, age 47, Tailor, born in MA.

SPILLER, HENRY, 47, M, Tailor, W, MA, 327, 483, NBPT.

SPILLER, WILLIAM H., 20, M, Clerk, W, MA, 327, 483, NBPT. In HH of Henry Spiller, age 47, Tailor, born in MA.

SPOFFORD, EDWIN F., 13, M, -, W, Maine, 647, 936, NBPT. In HH of John T. Spofford, age 55, Carpenter, born in MA.

SPOFFORD, ELIZABETH, 47, F, -, W, Maine, 647, 936, NBPT. In HH of John T. Spofford, age 55, Carpenter, born in MA.

SPOFFORD, JOHN T., 55, M, Carpenter, W, MA, 647, 936, NBPT.

SPOFFORD, RICHARD S., 17, M, Student, W, MA, 440, 654, NBPT. In HH of Richard S. Spofford, age 63, Physician, born in MA.

SPOFFORD, RICHARD T., 63, M, Physician, W, MA, 440, 654, NBPT.

SPOONER, HANNAH, 19, F, -, W, NH, 515, 686, NBPT*. In HH of George P. Garland, age 65, Boarding House, born in NJ.

SPRAWL, MERIA, 25, F, -, W, N.S., 493, 735, NBPT. In HH of John Post, age 24, Farmer, born in N.S. {Nova Scotia}.

SPRING, JOHN H., 49, M, Master Mariner, W, MA, 96, 113, NBPT*. In HH of John B. Swazey, age 31, Attorney at Law, born in Maine.

STACK, MORRIS, 22, M, Trader, W, Germany, 588, 865, NBPT. In HH of Stilman Simonds, age 43, Shoemaker, born in MA.

STANLEY, BENJAMIN F., 26,

M, Ship Carpenter, W, Maine, 496, 659, NBPT*.

STANLEY, JOHN C., 2, M, -, W, Maine, 496, 659, NBPT*. In HH of Benjamin F. Stanley, age 26, Ship Carpenter, born in Maine.

STANLEY, LUCY J., 22, F, -, W, Maine, 496, 659, NBPT*. In HH of Benjamin F. Stanley, age 26, Ship Carpenter, born in Maine.

STANWOOD, ALLEN A., 33, M, Shoemaker, W, MA, 154, 184, NBPT*. In HH of Peter Stanwood, age 69, Laborer, born in MA.

STANWOOD, ATKINSON, 49, M, Soap & Candle Manuf., W, MA, 565, 839, NBPT.

STANWOOD, BENJN., 66, M, Laborer, W, MA, 355, 518, NBPT.

STANWOOD, BETSY, 68, F, -, W, NH, 525, 697, NBPT*. In HH of William Stanwood, age 63, Harness Maker, born in MA.

STANWOOD, GEORGE W., 32, M, Shoemaker, W, MA, 355, 518, NBPT. In HH of Benjn. Stanwood, age 66, Laborer, born in MA.

STANWOOD, JOHN, 36, M, Sailor, W, Maine, 21, 26, NBPT. In HH of Lois Currier, age 65, born in Maine.

STANWOOD, JOSEPH, 53, M, Laborer, W, Maine, 788,1114, NBPT. In Poor House. .

STANWOOD, LOUISA M., 25, F, -, W, NH, 638, 925, NBPT. In HH of Merriam D. Gardner, age 48, born in NH.

STANWOOD, OTIS G., 28, M, Shoemaker, W, MA, 355, 518, NBPT. In HH of Benjn. Stanwood, age 66, Laborer, born in MA.

STANWOOD, PETER, 69, M, Laborer, W, MA, 154, 184, NBPT*.

STANWOOD, REBECCA, 49, F, -, W, Maine, 21, 26, NBPT. In HH of Lois Currier, age 65, born in Maine.

STANWOOD, SUSAN, 9, F, -, W, MA, 788,1114, NBPT. In Poor House. .

STANWOOD, THOMAS, 87, M, Caulker, W, Maine, 22, 27, NBPT.

STANWOOD, WILLIAM, 63, M, Harness Maker, W, MA, 525, 697, NBPT*.

STANWOOD, WILLIAM F., 41, M, Shoe Business, W, MA, 153, 183, NBPT*.

STAPLES, ABBY F., 30, F, -, W, Maine, 534, 798, NBPT. In HH of William S. Staples, age 26, Mastmaker, born in NH.

STAPLES, WILLIAM S., 26, M, Mastmaker, W, NH, 534, 798, NBPT.

STARR, ELIZABETH, 45, F, -, W, Ireland, 315, 408, NBPT*. In HH of William Adams, age 75, Merchant, born in MA.

STARRS, CATHARINE, 20, F, -, W, Ireland, 556, 739, NBPT*. In HH of Joseph B. Creasey, age 30, Painter, born in MA.

STARRS, MARGARET, 51, F, -, W, Ireland, 213, 264, NBPT*. In HH of Samuel Boardman, age 78, Ship Chandler, born in NH.

STEADMAN, EBENEZER, 71, M, Gentleman, B, MA, 354, 517, NBPT.

STEARNS, EDWIN, 26, M, Restorater, W, NH, 57, 63, NBPT*.

STEARNS, JOSEPH, 19, M, Carpenter, W, Maine, 452, 675, NBPT. In HH of Eveline Gunnison, age 46, born in Maine.

STEVENS, ABBA, 17, F, -, W, Maine, 507, 675, NBPT*. In HH of Moses Stevens, age 37, Ship Joiner, born in Maine.

STEVENS, ALBERT W., 16, M, Clerk, W, MA, 576, 851, NBPT. In HH of Samuel Stevens, age 57, Merchant, born in MA.

STEVENS, BENJAMIN, 17, M,

Harness Maker, W, MA, 500, 667, NBPT*. In HH of Lydia Stevens, age 39, born in MA.
STEVENS, CHARLES F., 47, M, Engineer, W, NH, 99, 146, NBPT.
STEVENS, CHARLES F., 20, M, Laborer, W, MA, 99, 146, NBPT. In HH of Charles F. Stevens, age 47, Engineer, born in NH.
STEVENS, DORATHA F., 22, F, -, W, NH, 84, 123, NBPT. In HH of Michael Stevens, age 28, Pilot, born in MA.
STEVENS, ELBRIDGE, 35, M, Barkeeper, W, MA, 166, 199, NBPT*. In Hotel run by Thomas Brown, age 49, born in MA.
STEVENS, ELIZA, 22, F, -, B, NH, 599, 789, NBPT*. In HH of William Coston, age 36, Mariner, Black, born in PA.
STEVENS, ELIZA J., 20, F, W, M, NH, 547, 818, NBPT. In HH of Richard Stevens, age 24, Mariner, Black, born in MD.
STEVENS, EMILY A., 13, F, -, W, Maine, 507, 675, NBPT*. In HH of Moses Stevens, age 37, Ship Joiner, born in Maine.
STEVENS, GRANVILLE A., 23, M, Machinist, W, NH, 384, 567, NBPT. In HH of William R. Wise, age 52, Laborer, born in MA.
STEVENS, ISAAC, 48, M, Tailor, W, MA, 527, 784, NBPT.
STEVENS, JOHN, 17, M, Ropemaker, W, MA, 96, 140, NBPT. In HH of Michael Stevens, age 63, Mariner, born in VT.
STEVENS, JOSEPH, 32, M, Mariner, W, MA, 96, 140, NBPT. In HH of Michael Stevens, age 63, Mariner, born in VT.
STEVENS, MICHAEL, 63, M, Mariner, W, VT, 96, 140, NBPT.
STEVENS, MICHAEL, 28, M, Pilot, W, MA, 84, 123, NBPT.
STEVENS, MOSES, 37, M, Ship Joiner, W, Maine, 507, 675, NBPT*.
STEVENS, RICHARD, 24, M, Mariner, B, NH, 599, 789, NBPT*. In HH of William Coston, age 36, Mariner, Black, born in PA.
STEVENS, RICHARD, 24, M, Mariner, B, MD, 547, 818, NBPT.
STEVENS, SAMUEL, 57, M, Merchant, W, MA, 576, 851, NBPT.
STEVENS, SAMUEL, 22, M, Mariner, W, MA, 96, 140, NBPT. In HH of Michael Stevens, age 63, Mariner, born in VT.
STEVENS, SAMUEL, JR., 24, M, Dry Goods Dealer, W, MA, 127, 152, NBPT*.
STEVENS, SARAH H., 45, F, -, W, Maine, 99, 146, NBPT. In HH of Charles F. Stevens, age 47, Engineer, born in NH.
STICKMAN, HENRY, 25, M, Mariner, W, MA, 110, 163, NBPT.
STICKNEY RUTH, 70, F, -, W, NH, 376, 556, NBPT. In HH of Mary Jones, age 80, born in MA.
STICKNEY, CALEB, 39, M, Pump and Block Maker, W, MA, 517, 770, NBPT.
STICKNEY, ENOCH P., 16, M, Clerk, W, MA, 416, 619, NBPT. In HH of Enoch P. Stickney, age 49, Tobacconist, born in MA.
STICKNEY, ESTHER B., 26, F, -, W, Maine, 467, 699, NBPT. In HH of William Stickney, age 56, Stable Keeper, born in MA.
STICKNEY, JACOB, 82, M, None, W, MA, 137, 163, NBPT*.
STICKNEY, JACOB, 76, M, Cabinetmaker, W, MA, 276, 406, NBPT.
STICKNEY, JOHN F., 49, M, Tobacconist, W, MA, 416, 619, NBPT.
STICKNEY, JOSEPH, 63, M, Laborer, W, MA, 538, 715, NBPT*.

STICKNEY, SALLY, 63, F, -, W, NH, 538, 715, NBPT*. In HH of Joseph Stickney, age 63, Laborer, born in MA.

STICKNEY, WILLIAM, 56, M, Stable Keeper, W, MA, 467, 699, NBPT.

STILES, GEORGE, 25, M, Overseer, W, MA, 140, 166, NBPT*. In HH of Hannah T. Marshall, age 39, Boarding House, born in MA.

STIMPLSON, EDWARD, 38, M, Insurance Agent, W, MA, 342, 502, NBPT.

STIMPLSON, ELIZABETH, 35, F, -, W, NH, 342, 502, NBPT. In HH of Edward Stimplson, age 38, Insurance Agent, born in MA.

STOCKMAN, CHARLES, 16, M, Pump & Block Maker, W, MA, 173, 208, NBPT*. In HH of Moses Stockman, age 42, Pumps & Block Maker, born in MA.

STOCKMAN, HANNAH, 30, F, -, W, NH, 278, 355, NBPT*. In HH of John T. Stockman, age 22, Operative, born in MA.

STOCKMAN, HENRY, 47, M, Block Maker, W, MA, 61, 68, NBPT*.

STOCKMAN, JOHN, 49, M, Tallow Chandler, W, MA, 281, 360, NBPT*.

STOCKMAN, JOHN, 22, M, Operative, W, MA, 278, 355, NBPT*.

STOCKMAN, JOSEPH H., 20, M, Block maker, W, MA, 61, 68, NBPT*. In HH of Henry Stockman, age 47, Block Maker, born MA.

STOCKMAN, MOSES, 42, M, Pump & Block Maker, W, MA, 173, 208, NBPT*.

STOCKNEY, ENOCH, 59, M, Grocer, W, MA, 425, 630, NBPT.

STONE, CHARLES E., 17, M, None, W, MA, 726,1025, NBPT. In HH of Giles P. Stone, age 51, Clerk, born in MA.

STONE, DEXTER E.M., 18, M, Mariner, W, Maine, 529, 788, NBPT. In Boarding House.

STONE, EBEN F., 28, M, Attorney at Law, W, MA, 684, 976, NBPT.

STONE, ELIZA A., 22, F, -, W, NH, 214, 266, NBPT*. In HH of John Q.A. Stone, age 23, Printer, born NH.

STONE, EUNICE, 78, F, -, W, MA, 174, 209, NBPT*. In HH of Hiram Tozer, age 41, Apothecary, born in Maine.

STONE, GILES P., 51, M, Clerk, W, MA, 726,1025, NBPT.

STONE, JOHN Q.A., 23, M, Printer, W, NH, 214, 266, NBPT*.

STONE, RICHARD, 50, M, Clerk Savings Inst., W, MA, 126, 151, NBPT*.

STONE, WILLIAM, 59, M, Merchant, W, MA, 502, 748, NBPT.

STORY, L. CATHARINE, 17, F, -, W, NY, 65, 74, NBPT*. In HH of Luther F. Dimmick, age 58, Cong. Clergyman, born VT.

STOVER, BETSEY C., 31, F, -, W, MA, 26, 31, NBPT*. In HH of George Stover, age 33, Trader, born in MA.

STOVER, HENRY, 55, M, House Carpenter, W, MA, 297, 389, NBPT*.

STOVER, JOSEPH, 46, M, None, W, MA, 147, 175, NBPT*. In HH of Sarah Stover, age 71, born in MA.

STOVER, NATHANIEL F., 21, M, Machinist, W, MA, 208, 259, NBPT*. In HH of William Stover, age 51, Clerk, born in MA.

STOVER, WILLIAM, 51, M, Clerk, W, MA, 208, 259, NBPT*.

STOVER, WILLIAM, 43, M,

House Carpenter, W, MA, 147, 175, NBPT*. In HH of Sarah Stover, age 71, born in MA.
STOVER, WILLIAM, 18, M, Clerk, W, MA, 243, 352, NBPT. In HH of Timothy Young, age 46, Master Mariner, born in Maine.
STOWE, LEONARD, 27, M, Baker/Grocer, W, NH, 430, 559, NBPT*.
STOWELL, JUSTARUS A., 50, M, Machinist, W, MA, 92, 108, NBPT*.
STOWELL, SALLY, 50, F, -, W, MA, 92, 108, NBPT*. In HH of Justarus A. Stowell, age 50, Machinist, born in MA.
STRAIN, JOHN, 22, M, Clerk, W, MA, 782,1108, NBPT. In HH of Enoch Tilton, age 45, Hotel Keeper, born in NH. In Hotel.
STRIMPSON, MARY, 24, F, -, W, Maine, 271, 398, NBPT. In HH of Horace Brown, age 52, Stage Agent, born in MA.
STROMBERY, FRANCIS C., 31, M, Gilder, W, Sweden, 288, 375, NBPT*. In HH of Ann Morrison, age 54, born in MA.
SUBRE, MARTIN, 40, M, None, W, Italy, 298, 435, NBPT. In HH of William A. Follansbee, age 35, Carpenter, born in MA.
SULLIVAN, ABBAS, 27, F, -, W, Ireland, 230, 284, NBPT*.
SULLIVAN, ANN, 7, F, -, W, Ireland, 230, 284, NBPT*. In HH of Abbas Sullivan, age 27, born in Ireland.
SULLIVAN, ARTHUR, 1, M, -, W, Ireland, 230, 284, NBPT*. In HH of Abbas Sullivan, age 27, born in Ireland.
SULLIVAN, CATHERINE, 35, F, -, W, Ireland, 347, 508, NBPT. In HH of Jeremiah Sullivan, age 40, Laborer, born in Ireland.
SULLIVAN, JAMES, 0, M, -, W, Ireland, 231, 287, NBPT*. In HH of Margaret Sullivan, age 28, born in Ireland. James, age 4 months.
SULLIVAN, JEREMIAH, 40, M, Laborer, W, Ireland, 347, 508, NBPT.
SULLIVAN, JEREMIAH, 4, M, -, W, Ireland, 230, 284, NBPT*. In HH of Abbas Sullivan, age 27, born in Ireland.
SULLIVAN, JULIA A., 6, F, -, W, NH, 161, 194, NBPT*. In HH of James Odell, age 40, Laborer, born in Ireland.
SULLIVAN, JULIA A., 5, F, -, W, NH, 330, 428, NBPT*. In HH of Elizabeth M. Danford, age 58, born in MA.
SULLIVAN, MARGARET, 28, F, -, W, Ireland, 231, 287, NBPT*.
SULLIVAN, MARY, 24, F, -, W, Ireland, 535, 799, NBPT. In HH of William Porter, age 40, Teamster, born in MA.
SULLIVAN, MARY, 4, F, -, W, Ireland, 347, 508, NBPT. In HH of Jeremiah Sullivan, age 40, Laborer, born in Ireland.
SULLIVAN, MARY E., 29, F, -, W, NH, 330, 428, NBPT*. In HH of Elizabeth M. Danford, age 58, born in MA.
SULLIVAN, MARY H., 40, F, -, W, NH, 161, 194, NBPT*. In HH of James Odell, age 40, Laborer, born in Ireland.
SULLIVAN, NANCY, 21, F, -, W, Ireland, 338, 441, NBPT*. In HH of George F. Granger, age 45, Lumber Dealer, born in MA.
SULLIVAN, STEPHEN, 2, M, -, W, England, 347, 508, NBPT. In HH of Jeremiah Sullivan, age 40, Laborer, born in Ireland.
SUMNER, EBENEZER, 30, M, Merchant, W, MA, 583, 859, NBPT.

SUMNER, JOHN, 23, M, Tinman, W, MA, 51, 57, NBPT*.
SWAIN, JOHN M., 23, M, Machinist, W, MA, 325, 420, NBPT*.
SWAN, ISAAC, 19, M, Mastmaker, W, MA, 625, 911, NBPT. In HH of Ester G. Swan, age 48, born in MA.
SWAP, BRADFUDD, 10, M, -, W, RI, 530, 790, NBPT. In HH of Almira Swap, age 42, born in MA.
SWAP, MINERVA, 29, F, -, W, CT, 530, 790, NBPT. In HH of Almira Swap, age 42, born in MA.
SWAP, WILLIAM H., 16, M, Laborer, W, CT, 530, 790, NBPT. In HH of Almira Swap, age 42, born in MA.
SWASEY, ANNA, 23, F, -, W, Maine, 601, 879, NBPT. In HH of Henry L. Swasey, age 60, Hatter, born in MA.
SWASEY, CHARLES K., 33, M, Restoration, W, MA, 34, 41, NBPT*.
SWASEY, CHARLES L., 23, M, Clerk, W, Maine, 601, 879, NBPT. In HH of Henry L. Swasey, age 60, Hatter, born in MA.
SWASEY, GEORGE B., 30, M, Master Mariner, W, Maine, 601, 879, NBPT. In HH of Henry L. Swasey, age 60, Hatter, born in MA.
SWASEY, HENRY L., 60, M, Hatter, W, MA, 601, 879, NBPT.
SWASEY, HENRY S., 12, M, -, W, LA, 601, 879, NBPT. In HH of Henry L. Swasey, age 60, Hatter, born in MA.
SWASEY, WILLIAM, 28, M, Trader, W, Maine, 601, 879, NBPT. In HH of Henry L. Swasey, age 60, Hatter, born in MA.
SWAZEY, ANN, 23, F, W, 0, England, 40, 47, NBPT*. In HH of Frances F. Monroe, age 32, female, Boarding House, born in Maine.
SWAZEY, JOHN B., 31, M, Attorney at Law, W, Maine, 96, 113, NBPT*.
SWEET, CHARLES E., 28, M, Mason, W, MA, 533, 708, NBPT*.
SWEET, EPHRAIM, 61, M, Shoemaker, W, MA, 43, 64, NBPT.
SWEETSER, FRANCIS, 15, M, Assistant Clothing, W, MA, 209, 260, NBPT*. In HH of Moses Sweetser, age 27, Clothing Store, born in MA.
SWEETSER, MOSES, 27, M, Clothing Store, W, MA, 209, 260, NBPT*.
SWEETSOR, EBENZ., 36, M, Merchant, W, MA, 428, 634, NBPT.
SYLVESTER, FRANCES, 25, M, Master Mariner, W, MA, 520, 774, NBPT. In HH of John Burnet, age 54, Laborer, born in N.S. {Nova Scotia}.
SYMES, EDWARD, 28, M, Wheelwright, W, Ireland, 709,1004, NBPT. In HH of Jonathan C. Richardson, age 33, Carriage Maker, born in MA.
SYMONDS, MARK, 59, M, Master Mariner, W, MA, 251, 362, NBPT.

- T -

TAFTS, NATHAN, 25, M, Tailor, W, MA, 626, 912, NBPT. In HH of Luther R. Chase, age 30, Carriage Maker, born in MA.
TALBOT, ANDREW, 7, M, -, W, Newfoundland, 462, 610, NBPT*. In HH of John Talbot, age 35, Laborer, born in Ireland.
TALBOT, HANNAH J., 20, F, -, W, Maine, 282, 361, NBPT*. In HH of Mary N. Talbot, age 41, born in

Maine.
TALBOT, JOANNA, 26, F, -, W, Newfoundland, 462, 610, NBPT*. In HH of John Talbot, age 35, Laborer, born in Ireland.
TALBOT, JOHN, 35, M, Laborer, W, Ireland, 462, 610, NBPT*.
TALBOT, JOHN E., 6, M, -, W, Newfoundland, 462, 610, NBPT*. In HH of John Talbot, age 35, Laborer, born in Ireland.
TALBOT, JOHN W., 18, M, Machinist, W, MA, 352, 464, NBPT*. In HH of John B. Tuttle, age 40, Grocer, born in NH.
TALBOT, MARY N., 41, F, -, W, Maine, 282, 361, NBPT*.
TALBOT, RICHARD S., 3, M, -, W, Newfoundland, 462, 610, NBPT*. In HH of John Talbot, age 35, Laborer, born in Ireland.
TALBOT, WILLIAM, 9, M, -, W, Newfoundland, 462, 610, NBPT*. In HH of John Talbot, age 35, Laborer, born in Ireland.
TALLYON, ELLEN, 25, F, -, W, Ireland, 122, 145, NBPT*. In HH of Enoch S. Williams, age 48, Merchant, born in MA.
TANER, CATHARINE, 20, F, -, W, Ireland, 8, 8, NBPT*. In HH of Samuel D. Goddard, 67, born MA.
TAPLEY, MARY E., 25, F, -, W, Maine, 708,1003, NBPT. In HH of Sarah Eaton, age 57, born in NH.
  Also see TOPPAN
TAPPAN, AMOS, 44, M, Dealer in Hardwood, W, MA, 411, 613, NBPT. In HH of Hannah Tappan, age 78, born in MA.
TAPPAN, EDWARD, 61, M, None, W, MA, 680, 972, NBPT.
TAPPAN, GEORGE T., 45, M, None, W, MA, 596, 873, NBPT. In HH of Ann Tappan {Toppan}, age 64, born in MA.
TAPPAN, JOSEPH, 29, M, Merchant, W, MA, 295, 430, NBPT.
TAPPAN, LAFAYETTE, 26, M, Trader, W, MA, 787,1113, NBPT. In HH of Elizabeth P. Currier, age 41, born in MA.
TAPPAN, SAMUEL B., 27, M, Auctioneer, W, MA, 296, 431, NBPT.
TAPPON, JOSEPH, 54, M, Auctioneer, W, MA, 283, 414, NBPT.
TARBOX, GEORGE R., 31, M, Overseer in Mill, W, Maine, 265, 388, NBPT.
TARBOX, MARY E., 22, F, -, W, Maine, 265, 388, NBPT. In HH of George R. Tarbox, age 31, Overseer in Mill, born in Maine.
TARBOX, MARY E., -, F, -, W, Maine, 265, 388, NBPT. In HH of George R. Tarbox, age 31, Overseer in Mill, born in Maine. Mary E. Tarbox, age 7 months.
TARITY, ELIZABETH, 27, F, -, W, Ireland, 391, 578, NBPT. In HH of Micheal Tarity, age 25, born in Ireland.
TARITY, MICHEAL, 25, M, None listed, W, Ireland, 391, 578, NBPT.
TATTLE, CLARA S., 2, F, -, W, ILL, 558, 831, NBPT. In HH of French Tattle, age, 29, Grocer, born in Maine.
TATTLE, FRENCH, 29, M, Grocer, W, Maine, 558, 831, NBPT.
TATTLE, REBECCA, 32, F, -, W, Maine, 558, 831, NBPT. In HH of French Tattle, age, 29, Grocer, born in Maine.
TAYLOR, CHARLES F., 22, M, Mariner, W, MA, 192, 281, NBPT. In HH of Hannah E. Taylor, age 69, born in MA.
TAYLOR, HANNAH, 22, F, -, W, Maine, 122, 179, NBPT. In HH of James Pentland, age 36, Overseer in Mill, born in England.

TAYLOR, MARGARET, 44, F, -, W, England, 160, 230, NBPT. In HH of Thomas Taylor, age 46, Weaver, born in England.
TAYLOR, MARY R., 20, F, -, W, NH, 163, 237, NBPT. In HH of Peter Taylor, age 21, Cord Grinder, born in England.
TAYLOR, PETER, 21, M, Cord Grinder, W, England, 163, 237, NBPT.
TAYLOR, POLLY, 65, F, -, W, NH, 693, 985, NBPT. In HH of Daniel Knight, age 44, Master Mariner, born in MA.
TAYLOR, ROSANA, 62, F, W, B, NH, 545, 816, NBPT. In HH of John Young, age 32, Barber, black, born in MA.
TAYLOR, THOMAS, 46, M, Weaver, W, England, 160, 230, NBPT.
TEEL, JOHN, 43, M, Sexton, W, MA, 349, 458, NBPT*.
TEEL, MOSES, 35, M, Machinist, W, NH, 64, 73, NBPT*.
TEEL, MOSES, JR., 6, M, -, W, Mis. Ter?, 64, 73, NBPT*. In HH os Moses Teel, age 35, Machinist, born NH.
TENNENT, MARY J., 26, F, -, W, NH, 211, 312, NBPT. In HH of Joster Smith, age 59, Merchant, born in NH.
TENNENT, THOMAS, 27, M, Math Instrument Make, W, PA, 211, 312, NBPT. In HH of Joster Smith, age 59, Merchant, born in NH.
TENNEY, ALMIRA, 25, F, -, W, Maine, 120, 143, NBPT*. In HH of John Andrews, age 50, Cashier, born in MA.
TENNEY, THOMAS, 30, M, Laborer, W, Ireland, 23, 27, NBPT*.
TENNEY, WINNIFRED, 29, F, -, W, Ireland, 23, 27, NBPT*. In HH of Thomas Tenney, age 30, Laborer, born Ireland.
TENNY, JAMES, 21, M, Carpenter, W, MA, 659, 949, NBPT. In HH of Rebecca Gardner, age 40, born in MA.
TEWKSBURY, GEORGE W., 19, M, Shoemaker, W, NH, 101, 118, NBPT*. In HH of Stephen Packer, age 49, Laborer, born in MA.
THOMAS, JOHN, 16, M, Painter, W, MA, 277, 354, NBPT*. In HH of John Burrill, age 50, Painter, born in MA.
THOMPSON, ALBERT, 46, M, None listed, W, NH, 31, 38, NBPT*.
THOMPSON, BENJAMIN P., 21, M, Operative, W, MA, 299, 436, NBPT. In HH of Erwena B. Thompson, age 49, born in MA.
THOMPSON, HELLEN V., 11, F, -, W, NH, 299, 436, NBPT. In HH of Erwena B. Thompson, age 49, born in MA.
THOMPSON, HELLEN V., 11, F, -, W, NH, 212, 313, NBPT. In HH of Theodore C. Bearson, age 31, Baker, born in NH.
THOMPSON, JOHN H., 14, M, -, W, NH, 299, 436, NBPT. In HH of Erwena B. Thompson, age 49, born in MA.
THOMPSON, MARY, 29, F, -, W, England, 104, 155, NBPT. In HH of Robert Thompson, age 28, Weaver, born in England.
THOMPSON, ROBERT, 28, M, Weaver, W, England, 104, 155, NBPT.
THOMPSON, THOMAS, 33, M, Master Mariner, W, Maine, 203, 298, NBPT.
THURLOW, Aaron, 22, M, Wheelwright, W, Maine, 460, 687, NBPT. In HH of Sewall Marden, age 55, Wheelwright, born in NH.
THURLOW, ADALINE, 22, F, -,

W, Maine, 73, 105, NBPT. In HH of Paul Thurlow, age 27, Master Mariner, born in MA.
THURLOW, JOSEPH R., 26, M, Mariner, W, MA, 102, 150, NBPT.
THURLOW, MOODY A., 58, M, Master Mariner, W, MA, 101, 148, NBPT. Note: Dwelling No. listed as 110, should be 101.
THURLOW, PAUL, 27, M, Master Mariner, W, MA, 73, 105, NBPT.
THURSTON, MARIA B., 7, F, -, W, Maine, 719,1018, NBPT. In HH of William Thurston, age 43, Dealer in Lumber, born in Maine.
THURSTON, MARY C., 11, F, -, W, Maine, 719,1018, NBPT. In HH of William Thurston, age 43, Dealer in Lumber, born in Maine.
THURSTON, WILLIAM, 43, M, Dealer in Lumber, W, Maine, 719,1018, NBPT.
TILTON, ABRAHAM W., 35, M, Machinist, W, NH, 513, 766, NBPT.
TILTON, DANIEL G., 33, M, Grocer, W, MA, 75, 109, NBPT.
TILTON, ELIZABETH E., 36, F, -, W, NH, 782,1108, NBPT. In HH of Enoch Tilton, age 45, Hotel Keeper, born in NH.
TILTON, ENOCH, 45, M, Hotel Keeper, W, NH, 782,1108, NBPT.
TILTON, HANNAH, 44, F, -, W, NH, 438, 577, NBPT*. In HH of Mary Tilton, age 63, born in NH.
TILTON, HANNAH, 30, F, -, W, NH, 513, 766, NBPT. In HH of Abraham W. Tilton, age 35, Machinist, born in NH.
TILTON, JACOB, 36, M, Machinist, W, NH, 438, 578, NBPT*.
TILTON, JANE, 31, F, -, W, NH, 438, 578, NBPT*. In HH of Jacob Tilton, age 36, Machinist, born in NH.

TILTON, JOHN E., 19, M, Clerk, W, MA, 436, 649, NBPT. In HH of John G. Tilton, age 50, Bookseller, born in MA.
TILTON, JOHN G., 50, M, Bookseller, W, MA, 436, 649, NBPT.
TILTON, JOHN G., 50, M, Bookseller, W, MA, 436, 649, NBPT.
TILTON, LUCY, 25, F, -, W, NH, 438, 577, NBPT*. In HH of Mary Tilton, age 63, born in NH.
TILTON, LYDIA, 38, F, -, W, NH, 355, 469, NBPT*. In HH of Nathaniel D. Tilton, age 35, Overseer, born in NH.
TILTON, MARY, 63, F, -, W, NH, 438, 577, NBPT*.
TILTON, NATHANIEL D., 35, M, Overseer, W, NH, 355, 469, NBPT*.
TILTON, STEPHEN W., 17, M, Clerk, W, MA, 436, 649, NBPT. In HH of John G. Tilton, age 50, Bookseller, born in MA.
TINDALE, WARREN, 34, M, Engineer, W, MA, 85, 125, NBPT. In HH of Cythia Tindale, age 60, born in MA.
TINEY, BENJAMIN P., 26, M, Iron Foundry, W, MA, 248, 312, NBPT*.
TINEY, JOHN, 65, M, Laborer, W, Maine, 788,1114, NBPT. In Poor House.
TINNEY, PERLEY, 76, M, Gentleman, W, MA, 669, 961, NBPT.
TITCOMB, BENAICHK, 35, M, Merchant, W, MA, 585, 861, NBPT. In HH of Emeline Chafin, age 40, born in MA.
TITCOMB, CHARLES R., 20, M, Merchant, W, MA, 425, 630, NBPT. In HH of Enoch Stickney, age 59, Grocer, born in MA.
TITCOMB, GEORGE, 62, M,

School Teacher, W, MA, 191, 235, NBPT*.
TITCOMB, GEORGE, 26, M, Mariner, W, MA, 191, 235, NBPT*. In HH of George Titcomb, age 62, School Teacher, born in MA.
TITCOMB, HENRY, 86, M, School Teacher, W, MA, 189, 231, NBPT* Occupation: "Last occupation - School Teacher".
TITCOMB, JEMINA, 60, F, -, W, England, 375, 555, NBPT. In HH of Michael Titcomb, age 69, Mast Maker, born in MA.
TITCOMB, JOHN W., 16, M, None, W, MA, 345, 506, NBPT. In HH of Joseph N. Titcomb, age 41, Merchant, born in MA.
TITCOMB, JOSEPH N., 41, M, Merchant, W, MA, 345, 506, NBPT.
TITCOMB, LUTHER, 62, M, Baker, W, MA, 788,1114, NBPT. In Poor House.
TITCOMB, MICHAEL, 69, M, Mast Maker, W, MA, 375, 555, NBPT.
TITCOMB, SOPHRONA, 33, F, -, W, Maine, 94, 137, NBPT. In HH of John Poor, age 38, Cabinetmaker, born in MA.
TITCOMB, ZEBULON, 62, M, Trader, W, MA, 454, 601, NBPT*.
TOBEY, JOSIAH, 56, M, Sailing Master, W, Maine, 554, 737, NBPT*. In HH of Martha Keyes, age 74, born in MA.
TOBEY, JULIA, 17, F, -, W, Maine, 554, 737, NBPT*. In HH of Martha Keyes, age 74, born in MA.
TOBEY, THOMAS, 13, M, -, W, Maine, 554, 737, NBPT*. In HH of Martha Keyes, age 74, born in MA.
TOBY, JAMES, 27, M, Operative, W, Maine, 22, 26, NBPT*.
TOBY, SOPHIA, 25, F, -, W, Maine, 22, 26, NBPT*. In HH of James Toby, age 27, Operative, born Maine.
TODD, FRANCIS, 71, M, Merchant, W, MA, 780,1106, NBPT.
TODD, JANE, 49, F, -, W, Maine, 452, 675, NBPT. In HH of Eveline Gunnison, age 46, born in Maine.
TODD, MARY A., 24, F, -, W, Maine, 334, 435, NBPT*. In HH of Samuel Todd, age 26, Machinist, born in Maine.
TODD, SAMUEL, 26, M, Machinist, W, Maine, 334, 435, NBPT*.
TODD, THOMAS G., 9, M, -, W, D.C., 594, 871, NBPT. In HH of Sophia Todd, age 64, born in MA.
TODY, JULIA, 16, F, -, W, Maine, 480, 639, NBPT*. In HH of True W. Sargent, age 53, Trader, born in MA.
TOGGERSON, ABBA, 16, F, -, W, Maine, 99, 116, NBPT*. In HH of Hannah Sargent, age 50, born in MA.
TOMPSON, HENRY, 23, M, Porter, W, Maine, 782,1108, NBPT. In HH of Enoch Tilton, age 45, Hotel Keeper, born in NH. In Hotel.
TOOD, ELILAS., 66, M, Pump and Block Maker, W, MA, 242, 351, NBPT.
TOOD, SAMUEL, 52, M, Painter, W, MA, 280, 410, NBPT.
Also see TAPPAN:
TOPPAN, ABRAHAM, 50, M, Clerk, W, MA, 552, 735, NBPT*.
TOPPAN, CHARLES, 25, M, Farmer, W, MA, 498, 661, NBPT*.
TOPPAN, CHARLES W., 17, M, Clerk, W, MA, 723,1022, NBPT. In HH of Henry Toppan, age 52, Grocer, born in MA.
TOPPAN, EDWARD JR., 54, M, Farmer, W, MA, 593, 783, NBPT*.
TOPPAN, EDWARD S., 28, M, Collector, W, MA, 70, 79, NBPT*.

TOPPAN, ENOCH C., 50, M, Master Mariner, W, MA, 788,1114, NBPT. In Poor House.
TOPPAN, ENOCH C., 16, M, Farming, W, MA, 489, 651, NBPT*. In HH of Rebekah H. Toppan, age 43, born in MA.
TOPPAN, HENRY, 52, M, Grocer, W, MA, 723,1022, NBPT.
TOPPAN, HENRY P., 27, M, Grocer, W, MA, 723,1022, NBPT. In HH of Henry Toppan, age 52, Grocer, born in MA.
TOPPAN, SYLVANIA, 24, F, -, W, NH, 498, 661, NBPT*. In HH of Charles Toppan, age 25, Farmer, born in MA.
TOPPAN, WILLIAM, 46, M, Mason, W, MA, 389, 512, NBPT*.
TOPPAN, WILLIAM H., 18, M, Mason, W, MA, 389, 512, NBPT*. In HH of William Toppan, age 46, Mason, born in MA.
TOPPANS, JOSEPH, 50, M, Mason, W, MA, 76, 85, NBPT*.
TORRY, MARY J., 19, F, -, W, Maine, 566, 840, NBPT. In HH of Lydia Cooley, age 39, born in MA.
TOWER, JOHN, 36, M, Laborer, W, MA, 486, 648, NBPT*. In HH of Betsy Tower, age 67, born in MA.
TOWLE, ABBA A., 22, F, -, W, NH, 461, 609, NBPT*. In HH of Timothy Hilliard, age 46, Shoe Store, born in NH.
TOWLE, ANTHONY F., 33, M, Silversmith, W, MA, 150, 178, NBPT*.
TOWLE, NATHAN, 35, M, Cordwainer, W, MA, 152, 182, NBPT*. In HH of Nathaniel Towle, age 67, No Occupation, born in NH.
TOWLE, NATHANIEL, 67, M, None, W, NH, 152, 182, NBPT*.
TOWLE, SAMUEL F., 35, M, House Joiner, W, MA, 150, 179, NBPT*.
TOWLE, THOMAS, 35, M, Cordwainer, W, MA, 151, 180, NBPT*.
TOWLES, GEORGE, 38, M, House Carpenter, W, MA, 146, 174, NBPT*.
TOWNSEND, CHARLES M., 20, M, None, W, Maine, 133, 197, NBPT. In HH of John Townsend, age 50, Shoemaker, born in Maine.
TOWNSEND, EMILY P., 12, F, -, W, Maine, 133, 197, NBPT. In HH of John Townsend, age 50, Shoemaker, born in Maine.
TOWNSEND, HARRIET M., 23, F, -, W, Maine, 133, 197, NBPT. In HH of John Townsend, age 50, Shoemaker, born in Maine.
TOWNSEND, JOHN, 50, M, Shoemaker, W, Maine, 133, 197, NBPT.
TOWNSEND, MARY W., 45, F, -, W, Maine, 133, 197, NBPT. In HH of John Townsend, age 50, Shoemaker, born in Maine.
TOWNSEND, OLIVER P., 12, M, -, W, Maine, 133, 197, NBPT. In HH of John Townsend, age 50, Shoemaker, born in Maine.
TOYS, HELEN S., 24, F, -, W, N.S., 663, 954, NBPT. In HH of Louisa L. Tracy, age 62, born in MA.
TOZER, HIRAM, 41, M, Apothecary, W, Maine, 174, 209, NBPT*.
TRACY, THOMAS, 69, M, Cong. Clergyman, W, MA, 210, 261, NBPT*.
TREFETHEN, CATHERINE A., 23, F, -, W, Maine, 553, 826, NBPT. In HH of George W. Trefethen, age 27, Mastmaker, born in Maine.
TREFETHEN, GEORGE W., 27, M, Mastmaker, W, Maine, 553, 826, NBPT.
TREFETHER, ALFRED, 36, M,

Keeps Bowling Alley, W, NH, 706,1001, NBPT.
TREFETHER, WILLIAM, 2, M, -, W, NH, 706,1001, NBPT. In HH of Alfred Trefether, age 36, Keeps Bowling Alley, born in NH.
TRUNDY, CORDELIA, 20, F, -, W, Maine, 162, 195, NBPT*. In Boarding House run by Hannah S. Davidson, 47, born in MA.
TUCKER, EBEN, 28, M, Carpenter, W, MA, 313, 462, NBPT. In HH of Elizabeth Tucker, age 63, born in MA.
TUCKER, JAMES, 62, M, None, W, MA, 358, 524, NBPT.
TUCKER, JOANNA G., 39, F, -, W, Maine, 21, 26, NBPT. In HH of Lois Currier, age 65, born in Maine.
TUCKER, JOSEPH E., 21, M, Clerk, W, MA, 21, 26, NBPT. In HH of Lois Currier, age 65, born in Maine.
TUCKER, WILLIAM, 38, M, Carpenter, W, MA, 313, 462, NBPT. In HH of Elizabeth Tucker, age 63, born in MA.
TUNNEY, SARAH, 30, F, -, W, Ireland, 405, 529, NBPT*. In HH of Miriam James, age 50, born in NH.
TUPLEY, WILLIAM, 53, M, Machinist, W, Maine, 35, 48, NBPT.
TURNER, BETSY B., 14, F, -, W, N.S., 754,1063, NBPT. In HH of Clarissa Turner, age 36, born in N.B. {New Brunswick}.
TURNER, CAROLINE, 16, F, -, W, Maine, 736,1041, NBPT. In HH of John L. Grindal, age 48, Grocer, born in Maine.
TURNER, CLARISSA, 36, F, -, W, N.B., 754,1063, NBPT.
TURNER, ELIZABETH, 24, F, -, W, Maine, 461, 609, NBPT*. In HH of Timothy Hilliard, age 46, Shoe Store, born in NH.
TURNER, EMELINE, 16, F, -, W, Maine, 736,1041, NBPT. In HH of John L. Grindal, age 48, Grocer, born in Maine.
TURNER, FANNY, 8, F, -, W, N.S., 754,1063, NBPT. In HH of Clarissa Turner, age 36, born in N.B. {New Brunswick}.
TURNER, HANNAH, 22, F, -, W, Ireland, 693, 985, NBPT. In HH of Daniel Knight, age 44, Master Mariner, born in MA.
TURNER, JOHN B., 6, M, -, W, N.S., 754,1063, NBPT. In HH of Clarissa Turner, age 36, born in N.B. {New Brunswick}.
TURNER, JOSHUA, 38, M, Master Mariner, W, NH, 195, 286, NBPT.
TURNER, OLIVE, 30, F, -, W, NH, 276, 406, NBPT. In HH of Jacob Stickney, age 76, Cabinetmaker, born in MA.
TUTTLE, FLORENCE, 32, F, -, W, NH, 23, 29, NBPT. In HH of Merari Tuttle, age 40, Factory Operative, born in NH.
TUTTLE, HARRIET N., 13, F, -, W, NH, 23, 29, NBPT. In HH of Merari Tuttle, age 40, Factory Operative, born in NH.
TUTTLE, HENRY M., 8, M, -, W, CT, 532, 706, NBPT*. In HH of Henry P. Tuttle, age 32, Blacksmith, born in Ct.
TUTTLE, HENRY P., 32, M, Blacksmith, W, CT, 532, 706, NBPT*.
TUTTLE, ISAAC, 26, M, Mariner, W, MA, 462, 611, NBPT*.
TUTTLE, JOHN B., 40, M, Grocer, W, NH, 352, 464, NBPT*.
TUTTLE, LUCY, 20, F, -, B, MA, 353, 516, NBPT. In HH of Samuel D. Ford, age 64, Hatter, born in MD.
TUTTLE, MARY C., 32, F, -, W, CT, 532, 706, NBPT*. In HH of Henry P. Tuttle, age 32,

Blacksmith, born in Ct.
TUTTLE, MERARI, 40, M, Factory Operative, W, NH, 23, 29, NBPT.
TYLER, JOHN, 50, M, Shoemaker, W, MA, 183, 265, NBPT.
TYLOR, ANN, 18, F, -, W, NH, 271, 398, NBPT. In HH of Horace Brown, age 52, Stage Agent, born in MA.

- V -

VANENBERRY, EMMA, 18, F, -, W, Nova Scotia, 283, 364, NBPT*. In HH of Gilbert Vanenberry, age 53, Ship Carpenter, born in Nova Scotia.
VANENBERRY, GILBERT, 53, M, Ship Carpenter, W, Nova Scotia, 283, 364, NBPT*.
VANENBERRY, RACHEL A., 15, F, -, W, Nova Scotia, 283, 364, NBPT*. In HH of Gilbert Vanenberry, age 53, Ship Carpenter, born in Nova Scotia.
VANENBERRY, WILLIAM A., 13, M, -, W, Nova Scotia, 283, 364, NBPT*. In HH of Gilbert VANENBERRY, age 53, Ship Carpenter, born in Nova Scotia.
VARINA, JOHN, 45, M, Mariner, W, MA, 486, 648, NBPT*. In HH of Betsy Tower, age 67, born in MA.
VARNUM, WILLIAM, 30, M, Grocer, W, Vet {sic}, 315, 464, NBPT. In HH of William E. Goover, age 24, Operative, born in Maine.
VERINA, JULIET C., 7, F, -, W, Maine, 511, 764, NBPT. In HH of Nicholas Verina, age 36, Master Mariner, born in MA.
VERINA, NICHOLAS, 36, M, Master Mariner, W, MA, 511, 764, NBPT.
VERINA, WILLIAM C., 38, M, Master Mariner, W, MA, 510, 763, NBPT.
VERMILE, THOMAS E., 1, M, -, W, NY, 214, 316, NBPT. In HH of Ashbell G. Vermilye, age 27, O.S. Presbyterian Clergyman, born in NJ.
VERMILYE, ASHBELL G., 27, M, Clergyman, O.S. Pres, W, NJ, 214, 316, NBPT.
VERMILYE, HELEN L., 22, F, -, W, NJ, 214, 316, NBPT. In HH of Ashbell G. Vermilye, age 27, O.S. Presbyterian Clergyman, born in NJ.
VERRELL, JOSEPH, 26, M, Watchman, W, NH, 461, 609, NBPT*. In HH of Timothy Hilliard, age 46, Shoe Store, born in NH.
VERRILL, DAVIS, 25, M, Carpenter, W, Maine, 490, 732, NBPT.
VERRILL, HENRY J., 29, M, Machinist, W, NH, 391, 514, NBPT*. In HH of Freeman O. Willey, age 37, Machinist, born in NH.
VERRILL, MARY J., 18, F, -, W, NH, 391, 514, NBPT*. In HH of Freeman O. Willey, age 37, Machinist, born in NH.
VERRILL, PHEBE N., 23, F, -, W, Maine, 490, 732, NBPT. In HH of Davis Verrill, age 25, Carpenter, born in Maine.
VING, JAMES, 30, M, Operative, W, MA, 446, 592, NBPT*.
VINOX, FRANCES, 7, F, -, W, New Brunswick, 500, 666, NBPT*. In HH of William Vinox, age 30, Ship Carpenter, born in New Brunswick.
VINOX, MARGARET, 28, F, -, W, New Brunswick, 500, 666, NBPT*. In HH of William Vinox,

age 30, Ship Carpenter, born in New Brunswick.
VINOX, WILLIAM, 30, M, Ship Carpenter, W, New Brunswick, 500, 666, NBPT*.
VONMALL, AUGUSTINE, 29, M, Cabinetmaker, W, France, 445, 665, NBPT.
VONMALL, HANNAH, 28, F, -, W, St. Johns N.B., 445, 665, NBPT. In HH of Augustine VonMall, age 29, Cabinetmaker, born in France.
VONMALL, JOHN H., 3, M, -, W, St. Johns N.B., 445, 665, NBPT. In HH of Augustine VonMall, age 29, Cabinetmaker, born in France.
VREEN, GEORGE A., 17, M, Carpenter, W, MA, 48, 71, NBPT. In HH of Lydia A. Vrccn?, age 39, born in MA.

- W -

WAIT, CHARSE E., 19, F, -, W, RI, 367, 541, NBPT. In HH of Loyd A. Wait, age 39, Agent of James Mill, born in RI.
WAIT, LOYD A., 39, M, Agent of James Mill, W, RI, 367, 541, NBPT.
WAIT, LYDIA, 38, F, -, W, Maine, 158, 191, NBPT*. In HH of Isaac Bradley, age 40, "Telaphonemaker", born in NH.
WAIT, ROWANA K., 28, F, -, W, Maine, 367, 541, NBPT. In HH of Loyd A. Wait, age 39, Agent of James Mill, born in RI.
WALDRON, CATHERINE, 54, F, -, W, Maine, 787,1113, NBPT. In HH of Elizabeth P. Currier, age 41, born in MA.
WALDRON, ELIZA, 24, F, -, W, Maine, 392, 515, NBPT*. In HH of Moses Flanders, age 36, Blacksmith, born in NH.
WALEN, JOANNA, 22, F, -, W, Ireland, 197, 244, NBPT*. In HH of Stephen Frothingham, age 81, Merchant, born in MA.
WALKE, SOPHIA, 64, F, -, W, Sweden, 282, 413, NBPT.
WALKER, DEXTER M., 34, M, Overseer at OC Mills, W, MA, 9, 9, NBPT*.
WALKER, ELEAZER, 51, M, Iron Founder, W, MA, 225, 279, NBPT*.
WALKER, EUNICE W., 19, F, -, W, Maine, 175, 211, NBPT*. In HH of Francis M. Walker, age 22, Iron Founder, born in MA.
WALKER, EUNICE W., 19, F, -, W, Maine, 175, 211, NBPT*. In HH of Francis M. Walker, age 22, Iron Founder, born in MA.
WALKER, FORDYE?, 18, M, Clerk, W, MA, 789,1115, NBPT. In HH of John M. Smith, age 34, Brick maker, born in MA.
WALKER, FRANCIS M., 22, M, Iron Founder, W, MA, 175, 211, NBPT*.
WALKER, HORACE J., 24, M, Manufacturing, W, NH, 38, 45, NBPT*.
WALKER, JOSEPH J., 27, M, Overseer Carding, W, NH, 535, 712, NBPT*.
WALKER, LUCINDA H., 57, F, -, W, Maine, 9, 9, NBPT*. In HH of Dexter M. Walker, Overseer at OC Mills, born in MA.
WALKER, LUCINDA H., 57, F, -, W, Maine, 9, 9, NBPT*. In HH of Dexter M. Walker, Overseer at OC Mills, born in MA.
WALKER, MARTHA A., 29, F, -, W, NH, 535, 712, NBPT*. In HH of Joseph J. Walker, age 27, Overseer Carding, born in NH.
WALKER, NAOMI, 23, F, -, W, Maine, 88, 129, NBPT. In HH of Samuel Pettigell, age 44, Cooper,

born in MA.
WALKER, STACY G., 23, M, Clerk, W, NH, 461, 609, NBPT*. In HH of Timothy Hilliard, age 46, Shoe Store, born in NH.
WALLIS, LYDIA, 27, F, -, W, NH, 382, 504, NBPT*. In HH of Harriet B. Ash, age 24, born in Maine.
WALSAH, EDWARD, 13, M, -, W, Newfoundland, 540, 810, NBPT. In HH of John Walsah, age 52, Laborer, born in Newfoundland.
WALSAH, JAMES, 8, M, -, W, Newfoundland, 540, 810, NBPT. In HH of John Walsah, age 52, Laborer, born in Newfoundland.
WALSAH, JOANNA, 5, F, -, W, Newfoundland, 540, 810, NBPT. In HH of John Walsah, age 52, Laborer, born in Newfoundland.
WALSAH, JOHN, 52, M, Laborer, W, Newfoundland, 540, 810, NBPT.
WALSAH, MARGARET, 10, F, -, W, Newfoundland, 540, 810, NBPT. In HH of John Walsah, age 52, Laborer, born in Newfoundland.
WALSAH, MARY, 39, F, -, W, Newfoundland, 540, 810, NBPT. In HH of John Walsah, age 52, Laborer, born in Newfoundland.
WALSAH, MARY, 12, F, -, W, Newfoundland, 540, 810, NBPT. In HH of John Walsah, age 52, Laborer, born in Newfoundland.
WALTON, JAMES K., 40, M, Carpenter, W, MA, 362, 533, NBPT.
WALTON, JOHN, 34, M, Painter, W, MA, 146, 214, NBPT.
WALTON, JOSEPH H., 17, M, Clerk, W, MA, 366, 540, NBPT. In HH of Samuel Walton, age 45, Master mariner, born in MA.
WALTON, SAMUEL, 45, M, Master Mariner, W, MA, 366, 540, NBPT.

WALTON, SAMUEL, 23, M, Carpenter, W, MA, 366, 540, NBPT. In HH of Samuel Walton, age 45, Master mariner, born in MA.
WALTON, TALIE?, 73, M, None, W, England, 280, 359, NBPT*.
WARD, ELIZABETH, 27, F, -, W, England, 160, 231, NBPT. In HH of Thomas Ward, age 26, Weaver, born in England.
WARD, GEORGE W., 24, M, Wheelwright, W, Maine, 337, 439, NBPT*.
WARD, PHEBE R., 35, F, -, W, Maine, 337, 439, NBPT*. In HH of George W. Ward, age 24, Wheelwright, born in Maine.
WARD, THOMAS, 26, M, Weaver, W, England, 160, 231, NBPT.
WARREN, EDWARD, 26, M, Engineer, W, Maine, 40, 47, NBPT*. In HH of Frances F. Monroe, age 32, female, Boarding House, born in Maine.
WARREN, ELIZABETH, 64, F, -, W, NH, 354, 468, NBPT*. In HH of Caroline H. Frothingham, age 37, born in NH.
WARTERMAN, WILLIAM, 19, M, Clerk, W, NH, 736,1041, NBPT. In HH of John L. Grindal, age 48, Grocer, born in Maine.
WASHBURN, EDWARD A., 31, M, Ep. Clergyman, W, MA, 211, 262, NBPT*. In Boarding House.
WATERMAN, ESTHER, 20, F, -, W, Maine, 467, 620, NBPT*. In HH of Freeman Greenough, age 47, Laborer, born in Maine.
WATERS, CATHARINE, 28, F, -, W, Ireland, 224, 278, NBPT*. In HH of Ann Mahaffy, age 32, born in Ireland.
WATERS, FRANCIS, 34, M, Umbrella Vender, W, Ireland, 224, 278, NBPT*. In HH of Ann

Mahaffy, age 32, born in Ireland.
WATSON, WILLIAM M., 19, M, Operative, W, VT, 354, 468, NBPT*. In HH of Caroline H. Frothingham, age 37, born in NH.
WATTS, GEORGE, 9, M, -, B, MA, 599, 789, NBPT*. In HH of William Coston, age 36, Mariner, Black, born in PA.
WATTS, ISAIAH, 12, M, -, B, Maine, 599, 789, NBPT*. In HH of William Coston, age 36, Mariner, Black, born in PA.
WATTS, LEONARD, 6, M, -, B, MA, 599, 789, NBPT*. In HH of William Coston, age 36, Mariner, Black, born in PA.
WAY, JOSEPH, 33, M, None, W, NH, 244, 307, NBPT*. In HH of Susanna Marden, age 55, born in NH.
WAY, NATHANIEL G., 33, M, Confectioner, W, NH, 244, 307, NBPT*. In HH of Susanna Marden, age 55, born in NH.
WAYLAND, HONORA, 22, F, -, W, Ireland, 668, 959, NBPT. In HH of John N. Cushing, age 30, Merchant, born in MA.
WAYLAND, MARGARET, 24, F, -, W, Ireland, 377, 557, NBPT. In HH of Nicholas Johnson, age 22, Merchant, born in MA.
WEARE, SARAH W., 23, F, -, W, Maine, 117, 140, NBPT*. In HH of Eli G. Kelly, age 37, Physician, born in NH.
WEAVER, ANDREW, 28, M, Shoemaker, W, Maine, 431, 641, NBPT. In HH of Mary L. Rains, age 48, born in Maine.
WEBBER, CHARLES, 26, M, Shoemaker, W, MA, 607, 797, NBPT*. In HH of Sarah B. Goodwin, age 45, born in MA.
WEBBER, CHARLES, 18, M, Operative, W, Maine, 140, 166, NBPT*. In HH of Hannah T. Marshall, age 39, Boarding House, born in MA.
WEBSTER, JAMES, 68, M, Shoemaker, W, MA, 135, 160, NBPT*.
WEBSTER, JAMES, 68, M, Shoemaker, W, MA, 135, 160, NBPT*.
WEBSTER, SUSAN, 60, F, -, W, NH, 351, 463, NBPT*. In HH of John O.W. Brown, age 58, Trader, born in NH.
WEEKS, FREDERICK W., 33, M, Mariner, W, MA, 543, 813, NBPT. In HH of John Weeks, age 60, Laborer, born in NH.
WEEKS, JOHN, 60, M, Laborer, W, NH, 543, 813, NBPT.
WEEKS, JOSEPH, 18, M, Mariner, W, MA, 543, 813, NBPT. In HH of John Weeks, age 60, Laborer, born in NH.
WELCH, BETSY, 70, F, -, W, NH, 316, 410, NBPT*.
WELCH, CHARLES F.W., 16, M, Mariner, W, Maine, 614, 896, NBPT. In HH of Eunice W. Welch, age 48, born in Maine.
WELCH, EUNICE, 48, F, -, W, Maine, 614, 896, NBPT.
WELCH, FRANCIS A., 42, M, Master Mariner, W, MA, 290, 379, NBPT*.
WELCH, HANNAH, 17, F, -, W, Maine, 64, 93, NBPT. In HH of George Pearson, age 28, Ropemaker, born in MA.
WELCH, JAMES W., 29, M, Shoemaker, W, MA, 193, 237, NBPT*. In HH of Stephen E. Cutter, age 47, Sexton, born in MA.
WELCH, JOHN, 23, M, Laborer, W, Nova Scotia, 178, 257, NBPT. In HH of Patrick Holland, age 26, Laborer, born in Ireland.
WELCH, MARY, 20, F, -, W, Nova Scotia, 14, 17, NBPT*. In HH of Edwin Lawrence, age 36,

Newspaper Publisher born in MA.
WELCH, MARY, 19, F, W, 0, Nova Scotia, 178, 257, NBPT. In HH of Patrick Holland, age 26, Laborer, born in Ireland.
WELCH, MORRIS, 27, M, Laborer, W, Ireland, 227, 333, NBPT.
WELCH, PETER, 18, M, Mariner, W, Nova Scotia, 178, 257, NBPT. In HH of Patrick Holland, age 26, Laborer, born in Ireland.
WELCH, RICHARD, 70, M, Trader, W, MA, 62, 69, NBPT*.
WELCH, RICHARD, JR., 42, M, Tailor, W, MA, 71, 80, NBPT*.
WELCH, RICHARD, JR., 42, M, Tailor, W, MA, 71, 80, NBPT*.
WELCH, SARAH L., 41, F, -, W, Maine, 290, 379, NBPT*. In HH of Francis A. Welch, age 42, Master Mariner, born in MA.
WELCH, WILLIAM T., 24, M, Painter, W, Maine, 614, 896, NBPT. In HH of Eunice W. Welch, age 48, born in Maine.
WELDON, ALBERT, 10, M, -, W, RI, 290, 425, NBPT. In HH of Prince Weldon, age 46, Machinist, born in RI.
WELDON, CAROLINE C., 12, F, -, W, RI, 290, 425, NBPT. In HH of Prince Weldon, age 46, Machinist, born in RI.
WELDON, CELIA, 44, F, -, W, RI, 290, 425, NBPT. In HH of Prince Weldon, age 46, Machinist, born in RI.
WELDON, HENRIETTA, 18, F, -, W, RI, 290, 425, NBPT. In HH of Prince Weldon, age 46, Machinist, born in RI.
WELDON, HENRY, 7, M, -, W, RI, 290, 425, NBPT. In HH of Prince Weldon, age 46, Machinist, born in RI.
WELDON, LYDIA A., 16, F, -, W, RI, 290, 425, NBPT. In HH of Prince Weldon, age 46, Machinist, born in RI.
WELDON, PRINCE, 46, M, Machinist, W, RI, 290, 425, NBPT.
WELDON, SARAH J., 14, F, -, W, RI, 290, 425, NBPT. In HH of Prince Weldon, age 46, Machinist, born in RI.
WELLS, AMBROSE H., 23, M, Grocer, W, VT, 417, 621, NBPT. In HH of Daniel Wells, age 47, Grocer, born in VT.
WELLS, ANN, 48, F, -, W, VA, 350, 511, NBPT. In HH of David Wells, age 44, Laborer, born in MA.
WELLS, ANN N.S., 20, F, -, W, Maine, 417, 621, NBPT. In HH of Daniel Wells, age 47, Grocer, born in VT.
WELLS, ANNA, 21, F, -, W, NY, 665, 956, NBPT. In HH of William Wells, age 25, Merchant, born in MA.
WELLS, ARTEMESSA, 17, F, -, W, East Canada, 417, 621, NBPT. In HH of Daniel Wells, age 47, Grocer, born in VT.
WELLS, CATHERINE, 42, F, -, W, VT, 417, 621, NBPT. In HH of Daniel Wells, age 47, Grocer, born in VT.
WELLS, CATHERINE M., 12, F, -, W, East Canada, 417, 621, NBPT. In HH of Daniel Wells, age 47, Grocer, born in VT.
WELLS, DANIEL, 47, M, Grocer, W, VT, 417, 621, NBPT.
WELLS, DANIEL W., 14, M, -, W, East Canada, 417, 621, NBPT. In HH of Daniel Wells, age 47, Grocer, born in VT.
WELLS, DAVID, 44, M, Laborer, W, MA, 350, 511, NBPT.
WELLS, DAVID R., 25, M, Grocer, W, NH, 193, 283, NBPT. In HH of William Lecraw, age 28, Master Mariner, born in MA.
WELLS, HARRIET C., 16, F, -,

W, East Canada, 417, 621, NBPT.
In HH of Daniel Wells, age 47,
Grocer, born in VT.
WELLS, JOHN., 77, M,
Tollgatherer, W, MA, 433, 569,
NBPT*.
WELLS, ORLEND L., 13, F, -,
W, East Canada, 417, 621, NBPT.
In HH of Daniel Wells, age 47,
Grocer, born in VT.
WELLS, SIMEON B., 20, M,
Operative, W, VT, 417, 621, NBPT.
In HH of Daniel Wells, age 47,
Grocer, born in VT.
WELLS, WILLIAM, 60, M,
None, W, MA, 209, 260, NBPT*.
In HH of Moses Sweetser, age 27,
Clothing Store, born in MA.
WELLS, WILLIAM, 25, M,
Merchant, W, MA, 665, 956,
NBPT.
WELLS, WILLIAM C. W., 32, M,
Joiner, W, MA, 433, 569, NBPT*.
In HH of John Wells, age 77,
Tollgatherer, born in MA.
WELLS, WILLIAM H., 38, M,
School Teacher, W, CT, 595, 872,
NBPT.
WESCOTT, ABIGAIL, 64, F, -,
W, NH, 319, 414, NBPT*. In HH of
Charles Wescott, age 63, Mariner,
born in MA.
WESCOTT, CHARLES, 43, M,
Mariner, W, MA, 319, 414,
NBPT*.
WESTON, BETSY, 55, F, -, W,
NH, 424, 552, NBPT*. In HH of
Benjamin Smith, age 46, Painter,
born in VT.
WESTWORTH, ELISABETH,
23, F, -, W, NH, 56, 62, NBPT*. In
HH of Oliver Sanborn, age 29,
Laborer, born MA.
WESTWORTH, MARY, 25, F, -,
W, NH, 56, 62, NBPT*. In HH of
Oliver Sanborn, age 29, Laborer,
born MA.
WESTWORTH, SARAH A., 21,
F, -, W, NH, 56, 62, NBPT*. In HH
of Oliver Sanborn, age 29, Laborer,
born MA.
WEYMOUTH, ABBA, 49, F, -,
W, Maine, 13, 15, NBPT*. In HH
of Mary Chase, age 77, born in MA.
WHEATLAND, ALLICE, 14, F, -,
W, Ireland, 25, 33, NBPT. In HH of
Rosanna Roune, age 54, born in
Ireland.
WHEATLAND, ELLEN, 60, F, -,
W, Ireland, 25, 33, NBPT. In HH of
Rosanna Roune, age 54, born in
Ireland.
WHEATLAND, PATRICK, 18,
M, None, W, Ireland, 25, 33,
NBPT. In HH of Rosanna Roune,
age 54, born in Ireland.
WHEELER, ALFRED, 35, M,
Shoemaker, W, NH, 387, 572,
NBPT.
WHEELER, ALFRED, 35, M,
Shoemaker, W, NH, 387, 572,
NBPT.
WHEELER, GEORGE, 22, M,
Shoemaker, W, MA, 607, 797,
NBPT*. In HH of Sarah B.
Goodwin, age 45, born in MA.
WHEELER, JOSEPH, 47, M,
Shoe Cutter, W, NH, 526, 698,
NBPT*.
WHEELER, LEMUEL, 35, M,
Blacksmith, W, Maine, 775,1097,
NBPT.
WHEELER, MARTHA, 13, F, -,
W, Maine, 775,1097, NBPT. In HH
of Lemuel Wheeler, age 35,
Blacksmith, born in Maine.
WHEELER, MARY S., 45, F, -,
W, NH, 526, 698, NBPT*. In HH of
Joseph Wheeler, age 47, Shoe
Cutter, born in NH.
WHEELER, MOSES B., 30, M,
Resterator, W, MA, 504, 751,
NBPT.
WHEELER, NANCY W., 33, F, -,
W, Maine, 775,1097, NBPT. In HH
of Lemuel Wheeler, age 35,

Blacksmith, born in Maine.
WHEELER, SILAS, 66, M, Stone Mason, W, MA, 347, 456, NBPT*.
WHEELWRIGHT, ABRAHAM, 92, M, Merchant, W, MA, 430, 637, NBPT.
WHEELWRIGHT, ELIZA, 18, F, -, W, NY, 339, 498, NBPT. In HH of Ann Wheelwright, age 54, born in MA.
WHEELWRIGHT, ELLEN, 11, F, -, W, NY, 339, 498, NBPT. In HH of Ann Wheelwright, age 54, born in MA.
WHEELWRIGHT, MARY, 70, F, -, W, MA, 788,1114, NBPT. In Poor House. .
WHEELWRIGHT, SAMUEL, 16, M, Clerk, W, NY, 339, 498, NBPT. In HH of Ann Wheelwright, age 54, born in MA.
WHEELWRIGHT, SARAH, 13, F, -, W, NY, 339, 498, NBPT. In HH of Ann Wheelwright, age 54, born in MA.
WHIDDEN, JOSEPH, 39, M, Mariner, W, MA, 78, 114, NBPT. In HH of Sarah Potter, age 64, born in MA.
WHIPPLE, CHARLES, 69, M, Bookseller, W, MA, 599, 877, NBPT.
WHITE, ABBY, 19, F, -, W, Maine, 151, 220, NBPT. In HH of Hannah White, age 45, born in Maine.
WHITE, ANN M., 16, F, -, W, Maine, 151, 220, NBPT. In HH of Hannah White, age 45, born in Maine.
WHITE, BRIDGET, 27, F, -, W, Ireland, 648, 938, NBPT. In HH of Anthony Cogger, age 37, Laborer, born in Ireland.
WHITE, CAROLINE, 12, F, -, W, Maine, 151, 220, NBPT. In HH of Hannah White, age 45, born in Maine.
WHITE, DENNIS, 32, M, Laborer, W, Ireland, 648, 938, NBPT. In HH of Anthony Cogger, age 37, Laborer, born in Ireland.
WHITE, ELIZABETH, 26, F, -, W, Maine, 151, 220, NBPT. In HH of Hannah White, age 45, born in Maine.
WHITE, ELIZABETH T., 6, F, -, W, CT, 671, 963, NBPT. In HH of William Asby, age 29, Farmer, born in MA.
WHITE, GEORGE E., 16, M, Student, W, MA, 44, 51, NBPT*. In HH of Josiah Bartlet, age 74, school teacher, born in MA.
WHITE, HANNAH, 45, F, -, W, Maine, 151, 220, NBPT.
WHITE, HARRIET S. {SIC}, 20, M, -, W, Maine, 204, 301, NBPT. In HH of Lavina Johnson, age 41, born in MA.
WHITE, JOHN, 5, M, -, W, Ireland, 648, 938, NBPT. In HH of Anthony Cogger, age 37, Laborer, born in Ireland.
WHITE, JOHN H., 39, M, Master Mariner, W, England, 195, 285, NBPT.
WHITE, MARY A., 8, F, -, W, Maine, 151, 220, NBPT. In HH of Hannah White, age 45, born in Maine.
WHITE, WILLIAM B., 24, M, House Joiner, W, NH, 513, 684, NBPT*.
WHITTEN, AMOS, 44, M, Express man, W, Maine, 717,1013, NBPT.
WHITTEN, HANNAH, 41, F, -, W, Maine, 717,1013, NBPT. In HH of Amos Whitten, age 44, Express man, born in Maine.
WHITTEN, JOHN, 48, M, Mariner, W, England, 232, 338, NBPT.
WHITTER, CHARLES, 33, M, Mason, W, England, 230, 336,

NBPT.
WHITTER, PHEBE C., 33, F, -, W, Maine, 230, 336, NBPT. In HH of Charles Whitter, age 33, Mason, born in England.
WHITTIER, ALEXANDER, 30, M, Carriage Maker, W, NH, 422, 550, NBPT*.
WHITTIER, EZEKIEL G., 39, M, Shoemaker, W, MA, 448, 594, NBPT*.
WHITTY, JOHN, 48, M, Calker, W, Ireland, 200, 295, NBPT.
WHITTY, MARGARET, 47, F, -, W, Newfoundland, 200, 295, NBPT. In HH of John Whitty, age 48, Calker, born in Ireland.
WHRIGHT, GEORGE E., 12, M, -, W, NB, 153, 222, NBPT. In HH of Martha A. Whright, age 86, born in England. NB most likely New Brunswick.
WHRIGHT, HENRY J., 7, M, -, W, Maine, 153, 222, NBPT. In HH of Martha A. Whright, age 86, born in England.
WHRIGHT, LUCES A., 9, F, -, W, NB, 153, 222, NBPT. In HH of Martha A. Whright, age 86, born in England. NB most likely New Brunswick.
WHRIGHT, MARTHA A., 86, F, -, W, England, 153, 222, NBPT.
WIGGEN, DOLLY F., 30, F, -, W, NH, 702, 995, NBPT. In HH of Isiah Wiggen, age 28, Overseer, born in NH.
WIGGEN, ISIAH, 28, M, Overseer, W, NH, 702, 995, NBPT.
WIGGIN, ALBERT P., 9, M, -, W, NH, 431, 640, NBPT. In HH of Oliver P. Wiggin, age 44, Cooper, born in NH.
WIGGIN, ALVAN S., 8, M, -, W, NH, 501, 668, NBPT*. In HH of Edwin Wittin, age 34, Ship Joiner, born in NH.
WIGGIN, EDWIN, 34, M, Ship Joiner, W, NH, 501, 668, NBPT*.
WIGGIN, MARY A.B., 23, F, -, W, NH, 501, 668, NBPT*. In HH of Edwin Wittin, age 34, Ship Joiner, born in NH.
WIGGIN, MARY B., 42, F, -, W, NH, 431, 640, NBPT. In HH of Oliver P. Wiggin, age 44, Cooper, born in NH.
WIGGIN, OLIVER P., 44, M, Cooper, W, NH, 431, 640, NBPT.
WIGGIN, PLINY N., 13, M, -, W, NH, 431, 640, NBPT. In HH of Oliver P. Wiggin, age 44, Cooper, born in NH.
WIGGLEWORTH, JOHN H., 32, M, Carpenter, W, MA, 147, 216, NBPT.
WILBUR, HERVEY, 64, M, Cong. Clergyman, W, MA, 7, 7, NBPT*.
WILDES, HENRY, 24, M, Engineer, W, MA, 787,1113, NBPT. In HH of Elizabeth P. Currier, age 41, born in MA.
WILDS, ASA W., 66, M, Barrister, W, MA, 410, 611, NBPT.
WILEY, HIRAM., 43, M, Machinist, W, NH, 456, 679, NBPT. In HH of Sarah Bradstreet, age 42, born in MA.
WILKINS, GEORGE, 31, M, -, W, Unknown, 78, 87, NBPT*. In Jail. Convict.
WILKINS, GEORGE, 31, M, -, W, Ireland, 78, 87, NBPT*. In Jail. Convict.
WILKINSON, JAMES, 27, M, Farmer, W, Maine, 509, 680, NBPT*.
WILKINSON, MARY W., 20, F, -, W, NH, 509, 680, NBPT*. In HH of James Wilkinson, age 27, Farmer, born in Maine.
WILLEY, ELIZABETH V., 29, F, -, W, NH, 391, 514, NBPT*. In HH of Freeman O. Willey, age 37, Machinist, born in NH.

WILLEY, FANNY M., 6, F, -, W, NH, 391, 514, NBPT*. In HH of Freeman O. Willey, age 37, Machinist, born in NH.

WILLEY, FREEMAN O., 37, M, Machinist, W, NH, 391, 514, NBPT*.

WILLEY, HANNAH, 8, F, -, W, NH, 391, 514, NBPT*. In HH of Freeman O. Willey, age 37, Machinist, born in NH.

WILLIAMS, ABRAHAM, 62, M, Merchant, W, MA, 326, 423, NBPT*.

WILLIAMS, ENOCH S., 48, M, Merchant, W, MA, 122, 145, NBPT*.

WILLIAMS, FRANKLIN, 23, M, -, W, Portugal, 78, 87, NBPT*. In Jail. Convict.

WILLIAMS, JAMES C., 32, M, Mariner, W, Denmark, 165, 239, NBPT. In HH of Joseph Janverin, age 38, Master Mariner, born in MA.

WILLIAMS, JOHN, 36, M, Clerk, W, NY, 165, 198, NBPT*. In HH of Betsy Page, age 45, born in MA.

WILLIAMS, JOSEPH, 64, M, None, W, MA, 490, 653, NBPT*.

WILLIAMS, JOSEPH JR., 17, M, Clerk, W, MA, 490, 653, NBPT*. In HH of Joseph Williams, age 64, None, born in MA.

WILLIAMS, MARY, 24, F, -, W, Maine, 476, 713, NBPT. In HH of James Freeman, age 54, Mariner, born in MA.

WILLIAMS, MARY, 20, F, -, W, Nova Scotia, 563, 749, NBPT*. In HH of Samuel Haines, age 45, Ship Carpenter, born in England.

WILLIAMS, ROSWELL S., 31, M, Painter, W, VT, 439, 581, NBPT*. In HH of William Jameson, age 48, Sailmaker, born in RI.

WILLIAMS, ST. HELENA {SIC}, 46, M, Mariner, W, St. Helinna, 537, 803, NBPT. In HH of Peter Dodd, age 47, Mariner, born in Newfoundland.

WILLIAMS, WILLIAM C., 53, M, Dealer in Lumber, W, MA, 142, 169, NBPT*.

WILLIAMS, WILLIAM L., 16, M, Student, W, MA, 142, 169, NBPT*. In HH of William C. Williams, age 53, Dealer in Lumber, born in MA.

WILLIAMSON, HARRIET, 20, F, -, W, Maine, 265, 335, NBPT*. In HH of Chester A. Greenleaf, age 23, 2nd Overseer, born in MA.

WILLIAMSON, MARY, 18, F, -, W, Maine, 265, 335, NBPT*. In HH of Chester A. Greenleaf, age 23, 2nd Overseer, born in MA.

WILLMAN, CLEMENTINE, 17, F, -, W, Maine, 631, 917, NBPT. In HH of Mary Ricker, age 61, born in Maine.

WILLMAN, SARAH E., 23, F, -, W, Maine, 631, 917, NBPT. In HH of Mary Ricker, age 61, born in Maine.

WILLS, HORACE G., 16, M, Student, W, MA, 44, 51, NBPT*. In HH of Josiah Bartlet, age 74, school teacher, born in MA.

WILLS, RUFUS, 35, M, Merchant, W, MA, 429, 635, NBPT.

WILSON, ALBERT, 22, M, Carver, W, MA, 308, 401, NBPT*. In HH of Joseph Wilson, age 71, Carver, born in Maine.

WILSON, CHARLES, 50, F, Laborer, B, MA, 598, 788, NBPT*.

WILSON, ELIZABETH, 68, F, -, W, NH, 308, 401, NBPT*. In HH of Joseph Wilson, age 71, Carver, born in Maine.

WILSON, HANNAH, 58, F, Laborer, B, MA, 598, 788, NBPT*. In HH of Charles Wilson, age 50,

Laborer, Black, born in MA.
WILSON, JOSEPH, 71, M, Carver, W, Maine, 308, 401, NBPT*.
WILSON, LAVINA, 22, F, -, W, Maine, 385, 569, NBPT. In HH of Betsy Richardson, age 62, born in MA.
WILSON, THOMAS H., 16, M, None, W, MA, 390, 575, NBPT. In HH of Elizabeth Wilson, age 46, born in MA.
WILSON, THOMAS H., 16, M, None, W, MA, 390, 575, NBPT. In HH of Elizabeth Wilson, age 46, born in MA.
WILSON, WILLIAM, 18, M, Clerk, W, MA, 308, 401, NBPT*. In HH of Joseph Wilson, age 71, Carver, born in Maine.
WINCHESTER, ALVAN, 50, M, Mariner, W, MA, 788,1114, NBPT. In Poor House.
WINGATE, EBENEZER, 83, M, None, W, NH, 135, 161, NBPT*. In HH of Sarah Mace, age 54, born in MA.
WINGATE, JEREMY C., 47, M, Milkman, W, NH, 125, 149, NBPT*.
WINKLE, BRIDGET, 6, F, -, W, Ireland, 112, 133, NBPT*. In HH of John Winkle, age 31, Laborer, born in France.
WINKLE, ELLEN, 30, F, -, W, Ireland, 112, 133, NBPT*. In HH of John Winkle, age 31, Laborer, born in France.
WINKLE, HARRY, 8, M, -, W, Ireland, 112, 133, NBPT*. In HH of John Winkle, age 31, Laborer, born in France.
WINKLE, JOHN, 31, M, Laborer, W, France, 112, 133, NBPT*.
WINN, JEREMIAH G., 28, M, Bootmaker, W, Maine, 459, 686, NBPT.
WINN, JOHN, 26, M, Overseer Weaving, W, Maine, 31, 37, NBPT*.
WINN, MARY, 59, F, -, W, NH, 776,1100, NBPT. In HH of Moses Winn, age 62, Laborer, born in MA.
WINN, MARY C., 23, F, -, W, Maine, 459, 686, NBPT. In HH of Jeremiah G. Winn, age 28, Bootmaker, born in Maine.
WINN, MOSES, 62, M, Laborer, W, MA, 776,1100, NBPT.
WINN, WILLIAM L., 38, M, -, W, Unknown, 78, 87, NBPT*. In Jail. For Trial.
WINSLOW, MARY J., 20, F, -, W, NH, 271, 398, NBPT. In HH of Horace Brown, age 52, Stage Agent, born in MA.
WISE, ALBERT, 38, M, Tin Plate Worker, W, MA, 269, 395, NBPT.
WISE, CATHERINE, 37, F, -, W, Ireland, 359, 528, NBPT. In HH of Mathew Wise, age 31, Blacksmith, born in Ireland.
WISE, GEORGE H., 25, M, Carpenter, W, MA, 384, 567, NBPT. In HH of William R. Wise, age 52, Laborer, born in MA.
WISE, MATHEW, 31, M, Blacksmith, W, Ireland, 359, 528, NBPT.
WISE, THOMAS S., 16, M, Operative, W, MA, 384, 567, NBPT. In HH of William R. Wise, age 52, Laborer, born in MA.
WISE, WILLIAM R., 52, M, Laborer, W, MA, 384, 567, NBPT.
WISE, WILLIAM R., 18, M, Operative, W, MA, 384, 567, NBPT. In HH of William R. Wise, age 52, Laborer, born in MA.
WITCHER, BENJN., 33, M, Teamster, W, NH, 450, 672, NBPT.
WITCHER, ELIZABETH, 10, F, -, W, NH, 450, 672, NBPT. In HH of Benjn. Witcher, age 33, Teamster, born in NH.
WITCHER, HANNAH, 32, F, -,

W, NH, 450, 672, NBPT. In HH of Benjn. Witcher, age 33, Teamster, born in NH.

WITHERILL, JOSHUA, 25, M, Spinner, W, RI, 102, 149, NBPT. In HH of William S. Evans, age 44, Ropemaker, born in MA.

WITHERILL, MARY, 23, F, -, W, CT, 102, 149, NBPT. In HH of William S. Evans, age 44, Ropemaker, born in MA.

WOART, RICHARD W., 16, M, Student, W, MA, 182, 223, NBPT*. In HH of Mary Woart, age 74, born in MA.

WOLLING, ELIZABETH, 26, F, -, W, Maine, 235, 342, NBPT. In HH of Nathaniel Hodge, age 57, Shoemaker, born in MA.

WOOD, AMOS, 54, M, Ship Carpenter, W, MA, 565, 751, NBPT*.

WOOD, CHARLES D., 25, M, Truck man, W, MA, 521, 778, NBPT.

WOOD, CHARLES J., 1, M, -, W, Maine, 521, 778, NBPT. In HH of Charles D. Wood, age 25, Truck man, born in MA.

WOOD, CHARLES N., 12, M, -, W, NH, 386, 571, NBPT. In HH of William W. Wood, age 40, Rigger, born in MA.

WOOD, DAVID, 57, M, Ship master, W, MA, 121, 144, NBPT*.

WOOD, EBEN F., 22, M, Blacksmith, W, MA, 519, 773, NBPT. In HH of Samuel Wood, age 54, Blacksmith, born in Maine.

WOOD, EDWIN A., 9, M, -, W, NH, 386, 571, NBPT. In HH of William W. Wood, age 40, Rigger, born in MA.

WOOD, ELIZA, 24, F, -, W, NH, 386, 571, NBPT. In HH of William W. Wood, age 40, Rigger, born in MA.

WOOD, ELIZABETH A., 0, F, -, W, NH, 386, 571, NBPT. In HH of William W. Wood, age 40, Rigger, born in MA. Elizabeth age 8 months.

WOOD, FRANK O., 3, M, -, W, NH, 386, 571, NBPT. In HH of William W. Wood, age 40, Rigger, born in MA.

WOOD, GEORGE, 30, M, Shoemaker, W, MA, 478, 635, NBPT*.

WOOD, GEORGE, 17, M, Ship Carpenter, W, MA, 565, 751, NBPT*. In HH of Amos Wood, age 54, Ship Carpenter, born in MA.

WOOD, GEORGE L., 17, M, Mariner, W, NH, 386, 571, NBPT. In HH of William W. Wood, age 40, Rigger, born in MA.

WOOD, GEORGE W., 30, M, Shoemaker, W, MA, 479, 637, NBPT*.

WOOD, JOHN, 75, M, Merchant, W, Maine, 66, 75, NBPT*.

WOOD, MARY W., 8, F, -, W, NY, 182, 223, NBPT*. In HH of Mary Woart, age 74, born in MA.

WOOD, PAMELIA G., 25, F, -, W, Maine, 521, 778, NBPT. In HH of charles D. Wood, age 25, Truck man, born in MA.

WOOD, PHEBE, 37, F, -, W, Maine, 736,1041, NBPT. In HH of John L. Grindal, age 48, Grocer, born in Maine.

WOOD, SAMUEL, 54, M, Blacksmith, W, Maine, 519, 773, NBPT.

WOOD, WILLIAM H., 19, M, Laborer, W, NH, 386, 571, NBPT. In HH of William W. Wood, age 40, Rigger, born in MA.

WOOD, WILLIAM W., 19, M, Rigger, W, MA, 386, 571, NBPT.

WOODBURN, GEORGE F., 10, M, -, W, RI, 525, 782, NBPT. In HH of John Woodburn, age 37, Weaver, born in England.

WOODBURN, JOHN, 37, M, Weaver, W, England, 525, 782, NBPT.

WOODBURN, MARGARET, 56, F, -, W, England, 526, 783, NBPT. In HH of Mathew Woodburn, age 62, Confectioner, born in England.

WOODBURN, MARY E., 15, F, -, W, RI, 526, 783, NBPT. In HH of Mathew Woodburn, age 62, Confectioner, born in England.

WOODBURN, MARY E., 13, F, -, W, NY, 525, 782, NBPT. In HH of John Woodburn, age 37, Weaver, born in England.

WOODBURN, MATHEW, 62, M, Confectioner, W, England, 526, 783, NBPT.

WOODBURN, NANCY, 37, F, -, W, England, 525, 782, NBPT. In HH of John Woodburn, age 37, Weaver, born in England.

WOODBURN, WILLIAM T., 29, M, Confectioner, W, England, 527, 784, NBPT. In HH of Isaac Stevens, age 48, Tailor, born in MA.

WOODBURY, CHARLES, 17, M, Shoemaker, W, MA, 371, 488, NBPT*. In HH of Samuel Woodbury, age 40, Watchman, born in MA.

WOODBURY, NANCY, 69, F, -, W, NH, 395, 518, NBPT*. In HH of John Bailey, Jr., age 37, House Carpenter, born in MA.

WOODBURY, PHILIP O., 7, M, -, W, AL, 492, 734, NBPT. In HH of Philip Johnson, age 58, Merchant, born in MA.

WOODBURY, SAMUEL, 40, M, Watchman, W, MA, 371, 488, NBPT*.

WOODMAN, ALBERT L., 23, M, Carpenter, W, MA, 26, 36, NBPT. In HH of John Woodman, age 52, Shoemaker, born in MA.

WOODMAN, ALFRED, 16, M, Tailor, W, MA, 285, 416, NBPT. In HH of Daniel Woodman, age 50, Painter, born in MA.

WOODMAN, DANIEL, 50, M, Painter, W, MA, 285, 416, NBPT.

WOODMAN, HENRY A., 26, M, Clergyman, Congrational, W, MA, 273, 350, NBPT*.

WOODMAN, JAMES M., 44, M, Engineer, W, MA, 603, 881, NBPT.

WOODMAN, JOHN, 52, M, Shoemaker, W, MA, 26, 36, NBPT.

WOODMAN, JOSEPH, 56, M, Cooper, W, MA, 202, 252, NBPT*.

WOODMAN, NATHAL., 64, M, Carpenter, W, MA, 619, 902, NBPT.

WOODMAN, NATHAN, 22, M, Blacksmith, W, NH, 145, 173, NBPT*. In HH of Hiram Canney, age 42, Blacksmith, born in NH.

WOODMAN, SALLY, 70, F, -, W, MA, 788,1114, NBPT. In Poor House. .

WOODMAN, SARAH, 51, F, -, W, NH, 285, 416, NBPT. In HH of Daniel Woodman, age 50, Painter, born in MA.

WOODS, ASAHEL D., 23, M, Laborer, W, Maine, 764,1078, NBPT. In HH of Jonathan Lovering, age 33, Hotel Keeper, born in NH.

WOODWELL, JACOB A., 25, M, Machinist, W, MA, 319, 414, NBPT*. In HH of charles Wescott, age 63, Mariner, born in MA.

WOODWELL, SARAH, 60, F, -, W, NH, 319, 414, NBPT*. In HH of Charles Wescott, age 63, Mariner, born in MA.

WORK, JOSEPH W., 27, M, Operative in Mill, W, MA, 142, 209, NBPT.

WYATT, JOSEPH, 55, M, Laborer, W, MA, 788,1114, NBPT. In Poor House.

WYATT, JOSEPH, 54, M,

Carpenter, W, MA, 761,1074, NBPT.
WYMAN, SAMUEL, 19, M, Student, W, MA, 791,1119, NBPT. In HH of Richard Adams, age 28, Carpenter, born in MA.
WYMAN, SAMUEL W., 47, M, Physician, W, MA, 414, 617, NBPT.

- Y -

YORK, ELIZABETH, 21, F, -, W, NH, 566, 840, NBPT. In HH of Lydia Cooley, age 39, born in MA.
YORK, ISIAH, 52, M, Laborer, W, NH, 610, 891, NBPT.
YORK, JULIA A., 11, F, -, W, NH, 610, 891, NBPT. In HH of Isiah York, age 52, Laborer, born in NH.
YORK, LUCY A., 25, F, -, W, NH, 396, 586, NBPT. In HH of Jacob R. Folonsby, age 27, Weaver, born in NH.
YORK, MARY A., 25, F, -, W, NH, 612, 893, NBPT. In HH of William Hills, age 70, None, born in MA.
YORK, MARY G., 47, F, -, W, NH, 610, 891, NBPT. In HH of Isiah York, age 52, Laborer, born in NH.
YORK, SAMUEL A., 16, M, Mariner, W, NH, 610, 891, NBPT. In HH of Isiah York, age 52, Laborer, born in NH.
YOUNG, ANN, 38, F, -, W, NH, 242, 304, NBPT*. In HH of Charles Hezeltine, age 48, Dry Goods Dealer, born in VT.
YOUNG, CHARLES H., 13, M, -, B, MA, 545, 816, NBPT. In HH of John Young, age 32, Barber, black, born in MA.
YOUNG, FRANCIS H., 15, M, -, B, MA, 545, 816, NBPT. In HH of John Young, age 32, Barber, black, born in MA.
YOUNG, GEORGE E., 29, M, Mast Maker, W, Maine, 514, 767, NBPT.
YOUNG, GEORGE N., 29, M, Teamster, W, MA, 644, 932, NBPT. In HH of John B. Prichard, age 29, Rigger, born in MA.
YOUNG, GEORGE W., 35, M, Ropemaker, W, MA, 506, 755, NBPT.
YOUNG, JACOB H., 42, M, Grocer, W, MA, 316, 465, NBPT.
YOUNG, JAMES, 19, M, Farm Hand, W, MA, 593, 783, NBPT*. In HH of Edward Toppan, Jr. age 54, Farmer, born in MA.
YOUNG, JAMES, 55, M, Grocer, W, MA, 340, 499, NBPT.
YOUNG, JANE MCP?., 23, F, -, W, Scotland, 313, 406, NBPT*. In HH of Josiah Bradlee, age 49, Merchant, born in MA.
YOUNG, JOHN, 32, M, Barber, B, MA, 545, 816, NBPT.
YOUNG, JOHN H., 8, M, -, B, MA, 545, 816, NBPT. In HH of John Young, age 32, Barber, black, born in MA.
YOUNG, JOSEPH A., 5, M, -, B, MA, 545, 816, NBPT. In HH of John Young, age 32, Barber, black, born in MA.
YOUNG, LOUISA H., 38, F, -, B, MD, 545, 816, NBPT. In HH of John Young, age 32, Barber, black, born in MA.
YOUNG, MARY J., 30, F, -, W, Maine, 514, 767, NBPT. In HH of George E. Young, age 29, Mast Maker, born in Maine.
YOUNG, THOMAS, 17, M, Engineer, W, MA, 243, 352, NBPT. In HH of Timothy Young, age 46, Master Mariner, born in Maine.
YOUNG, TIMOTHY, 46, M, Master Mariner, W, Maine, 243, 352, NBPT.

APPENDIX: GONE TO CALIFORNIA

The 1850 Newburyport City Directory listed the following people as in California. Each name was marked in the directory with an *.

In the *History of Newburyport From The Earliest Settlement of the County to the Present Time* by Mrs. E. Vale Smith, published in 1854; Boston, Press of Damrell and Moore. On pages 236-237 it is stated "that in the fall and winter of 1848-1849, the excitement consequent on the discovery of gold in California, produced similar effects here in what it wrought in other portions of the country. Probably a larger proportion of young men left Newburyport for the gold regions, than from many other towns of the same size, perhaps from the hereditary habit of emigrations. Quite a number of vessels were put up here for the Pacific coast, while by far the larger proportion of adventurerers from Newburyport sailed from Boston or New York."

"The first vessel which left our wharves for California was the brig 'Ark'... It not only carried off a large number of active and enterprising young men, most of whom carried all their property with them, but it unsettled the character of many who remained....The effect of the gold *higera* on Newburyport has proved by no means beneficial. Of those who have, none have added largely to the taxable property of the place."

ALEXANDER, E. CHARLES, House-joiner, Boards 50 Federal St.

ASH, CHARLES, Truck man, House 21 Kent St.

BABSON, SETH, Firm of Babson & Teel, Occupation: Firm of Babson & Teel, sash and blind factory, 4 Carter St., H 11 Broad St.

BALCH, LEONIDAS, Clerk, Boards 20 Green St.

BARTLETT, WILLIAM, Captain, House 41 Middle St.

BARTLETT, WILLIAM JR., Merchant, Boards 3 Market St.

BAYLEY, JOHN T., Captain, House 2 Beck St.

BAYLEY, ORRIN, None listed, Board 80 Federal St.

BRAY, NEHEMIAH A, Captain, House 10 Elm St.

BRICHER, GEORGE S., Machinist, Boards 10 Essex St.

BRICHER, WALTER, Machinist, Boards 10 Essex St.

BUNTIN, CHARLES, Captain, House 119 High St.

CARR, HENRY, None listed, Boards 16 Temple St.

CATE, S.P., Stage proprietor, House 1 Park St.

CHEEVER, BENJ H., Joiner, Boards 4 Salem St.

COLBY, ROBERT C., None listed, Boards 13 Beck St.

COLMAN, DAVID E., House carpenter. House 12 Congress St.
CONCH, JOHN H., Captain, House, 2 Court St.
COOK, RUFUS, Confectionery and variety store, 107 Water St.
CURRIER, CHARLES H., Pump & block maker, Boards 18 Beck St.
CURRIER, GEORGE JR., Mason, House, 35 Ocean St.
CURRIER, GORHAM, Sail maker, Cushing's Wharf. House 21 Lime St.
CURRIER, SAMUEL JR., Mason, House, 68 Middle St.
DARIAH, WILLIAM, House joiner, House 5 Allen St.
DAVIS, CHARLES W., House joiner, 60 Lime St.
DAVIS, WILLIAM E., None listed, 33 Pleasant St., House 35 Green St.
ELLSWORTH, WILLIAM N., Cordwainer, House 7 Orange St.
HALE, CHARLES H., House joiner, House 6 Allen St.
HALE, MOSES E., Merchant, House 24 Green St.
HERVEY, JOSEPH R., Merchant, House 109 High St.
HODGE, CHARLES JR., Druggist, 3 Pleasant St., Boards 67 State St.
HUNT, JOSEPH, Printer, House 6 Tremont Place.
HUSE, WILLIAM, Clerk, House 12 Tremont Place.
JAQUES, AMOS T., None listed, House 16 Warren St.
JOHNSON, JOSIAH, Carpenter, House 19 Carter St.
JONES, OLIVER, Captain, House 63 Lime St.
KEZER, SAMUEL, House joiner, House 1 Independent St.
KIDDER, WILLIAM, None listed, Boards 20 Federal St.

KILBORN, WARREN, House joiner, House 49 Middle St.
KITCHING, WILLIAM, Captain, House 5 Ann St.
KNAPP, ANTHONY JR., House joiner, Boards 7 Parsons St.
LE CRAW, WILLIAM, Captain, House 4 Parsons St.
LE CRAW, WILLIAM JR., Mariner, Boards 38 Lime St.
LEIGHTON, JONATHAN, None listed, House 9 Boardman St.
MARSHALL, CHARLES, Captain, Boards 72 High St.
MOODY, GARDINER, House joiner, Boards 51 Middle St.
MYRICK, FREDERIC W., Captain, Boards 24 Fair St.
NASON, CHARLES, Publisher and Proprietor Daily and Weekly Union, (firm of Nason, Bragdon & Co.) 3 and 36 State St., House High St.
NELSON, THOMAS, Grocer, 43 Federal St. Boards 11 Fair St.
NOYES, JACOB JR., Mariner, Board 70 Federal St.
NOYES, SEWALL B., Mason, House 8 Ship St.
PAGE, JOHN H., Joiner, House 28 Boardman St.
PATTEN, ALFRED, Painter, House 7 Roberts St.
PATTEN, HENRY, Joiner, Boards 1 Orange St.
PEABODY, JAMES C., Editor of the Weekly Union. Boards E.S. Nason, High St.
PERRY, CHARLES W., Seaman, House 18 Merrill St.
PETTINGELL, RICHARD, Seaman, Boards 20 Middle St.
PLUMER, DANIEL, None listed, House 83 Lime St.
PLUMER, NATHANIEL D., Operative, House 64 Federal St.
PORTER, JOHN P., House joiner, House 5 Broad St.

RAYNES, JOHN, Captain, House 2 Court St.
ROGERS, DANIEL, Soap Chandler. Boards 15 Middle St.
ROSSITER, JOSEPH, Captain, House 134 Merrimac St.
RUST, FREDERICK, None listed, House 22 Olive St.
SABINE, HILLARD, Engineer Globe Mills, House 5 Spring St.
SARGENT, ELBRIDGE A., Clerk, Boards 15 North St.
SMITH, D.H., Machinist, House 91 High St.
SMITH, JUSTIN, None listed, Boards 5 Smith St.
SMITH, WOOSTER, None listed, 11 Water St. House 8 Smith's Avenue.
SPRING, JOHN, Captain, House 74 High St.
STEVENS, CHARLES B., Mariner, Boards 36 Middle St.
STEWART, JAMES F., None listed, House 23 Warren St.
STICKNEY, JACOB, 3RD, Grocer, 44 and 46 Water St.
STICKNEY, WILLIAM W., Printer, Boards 3 Spring St.
SWASEY, CHARLES, Clerk , Boards 30 Fair St.
SWASEY, GEORGE B., Captain, Boards 30 Fair St.
TEEL, WILLIAM, Firm B & T, (Firm of B{Babson} & T{Teel}, Carter St. Boards 222 Merrimac St.
TENNENT, THOMAS, None listed, 4 Smith's Avenue.
VARNEY, D.G., Dentist, 62 State St. Board Washington House.
VARNEY, NICHOLAS, Captain, House 9 Pike St.
VARNEY, WILLIAM, Captain, House 8 Fair St.
WALTON, SAMUEL, Captain, House 7 Tremont St.
WALTON, SAMUEL JR., Captain, Boards 7 Tremont St.
WATKINS, JOSEPH, None listed, 46 Pleasant St.
WELLINGTON, GEORGE, Rigger, House 15 Charles St.
WILCOMB, NEWELL, House carpenter, House 10 Charles St.
WOOD, EBEN, Blacksmith, Boards 70 Federal St.

Surname Index

A

Adams: Ann A., 2; Harriet, 1; Joel, 1; Joseph C., 125; Margaret H., 60; Paul S., 2; Richard, 20, 179; William, 156
Akerman: Joseph, 94
Alexander: E. Charles, 180; Hannah, 2
Ambrose: David N., 3
Ames: Ebenezer, 3
Andrews: John, 153, 162
Anright: James, 4
Appleton: Ann, 4
Araften?: John, 38
Armitage: George, 4
Asby/Ashby: William, 33, 99, 173
Ash: Charles, 180; Harriet B., 169
Atkinson: Elisa A., 30; John, 4, 126
Aynwant: Michael, 38, 110

B

Babson: Sarah E., 5; Seth, 180
Badger: William J., 147
Bagley: Abner, 60
Bailey, Jr.: John, 178
Balch: John, 126; Leonidas, 180; William, 110; William C., 6, 78
Ballou: Joseph W., 71
Bannister: William B., 103, 105, 141

Barrett: James, 61
Bartlet: Edwin B., 136, 137; Josiah, 142, 173, 175
Bartlett: Edmund, 105; Franklin, 56; George N., 44, 115, 123, 132; William, 180
Bartlett, Jr.: William, 180
Bass: Rhoda, 10
Batchelder: Sarah, 10; Thomas L., 45
Batiss: George W., 56
Bayle: Bridget, 11; George, 11
Bayley: Charles M., 39; John T., 180; Orrin, 180; Robert, 22, 25, 135
Bean: Alonzo, 27; Hiram, 11
Bearson: Theodore C., 162
Bell: William, 87
Bent: Dennis, 13
Berdge: Rhoda, 13
Bickford: Horace, 13, 17; Jonathan, 10
Blacks/Mulattos, 40, 54, 90, 92, 99, 100, 102, 105, 126, 127, 128, 140, 156, 157, 162, 166, 170, 175, 176, 179
Blaidsdell: Charles H., 14
Bliss: Terence, 14, 119
Blumpey: Philip, 16, 149
Boardman: Greenleaf, 22; Isaac H., 113; Rebecca, 123
Bowman: John, 91, 92
Bradlee: Josiah, 63, 179
Bradley: Isaac, 168
Bradstreet: Sarah, 17, 69, 174
Bragdon: Samuel, 38; William, 19
Bray: Nehemiah A., 180
Brewer: William H., 31
Brewster: William H., 79, 137
Bricher: George S., 180; Walter, 180
Brickett: Joseph, 18
Brown: Abel D., 21, 78; Alban, 27; Alexander, 19; Charles, 20; Charles H., 19; David, 18; Edward W., 76, 146; Hannah, 78; Horace, 1, 7, 25, 48, 81, 159, 167, 176; Jenness, 21; John O.W., 19, 21, 170; Lyman, 19; Mary L., 20; Merch, 19; Mercy, 21; Nathan B., 19; Nutter, 19, 20, 22, 139; Sarah, 20; Thomas, 44, 88, 96, 100, 137
Buntin: Charles, 23, 180; Thomas, 64
Burnet: John, 40, 160
Burrill: Edward, 24; John, 23, 162
Butler: Joseph W., 136
Butman: Elizabeth, 39
Butts: Moses, 1, 24

C

Caldwell/Caldwill: John, 27, William W., 64, 95
Campbell: Anna, 25; Randloph, 59

Caney: Michael, 101
Cannery: Thomas F., 26
Canney: Catherine, 26; James N., 13(2), 49, 61, 69, 87, 121, 122, 134, 143, 147, 148, 149
Canning: Samuel C., 26
Carpenter: Rebekah, 5, 24
Carr: Hannah, 27; Henry, 180
Carry: James, 53
Case: Moses P., 14
Cassman: James, 79
Casson: John W., 28
Cate: S.P., 180; William, 29
Chafin: Emeline, 163
Chase: Bailey, 30; Hannah, 30; Luther R., 65, 86, 151, 160; Tristram, 18
Cheever: Benj. H., 180
Cheney: James, 77; Sarah, 149; William B., 137
Choate: True, 11, 31
Chute: Dorothy, 6, 55, 78
Cilley, Jr.: James, 97
Clanin: Mary, 32
Clarkson: Sophia, 32
Clement: Amos C., 10
Cobb: Samuel H., 139
Coffin: Charles, 12, 48; Charles, 148; Emery, 35; George, 35; Isaac S., 28, 35(2); Mary, 1; Nathaniel, 32, 119; Theodore A., 34
Cogger: Anthony, 4, 5, 173; John, 36, 61, 150
Colby: Robert C., 180
Collins: Eliza, 126; Sarah 37
Colman: David E., 181; Jeremiah, 111
Comerford: David, 150
Conch: John H., 181
Conners: Patrick, 117, 118
Cook: Abigail, 38, 39; Hannah, 38; Jeremiah, 38; Moody D., 38; Phebe, 86; Rufus, 181
Cook, Jr.: Samuel, 14
Cooley: Lydia, 95, 103, 119, 165, 179
Coombs: John, 7; Philip, 34
Cooper: Harriet, 39; James M., 135; John, 40
Coran: Martin, 40, 126
Corey: Robert, 40

Coston: William, 40, 157, 170
Coswell: Michael, 40
Couillard: Richard, 122
Creasey: Joseph B., 156; Phebe A., 41; William, 41; William J., 1
Crofoot: Hosea Y., 32, 108
Cross: Enoch, 59
Crowley: John, 56; Patrick, 132
Currier: Albert, 95; Charles H., 181; Elizabeth, 35, 43, 64, 114; Elizabeth P., 19, 161, 168, 174; George, Jr. 181; Lois, 36, 156, 166; Samuel, 43; Thomas, 90, 118
Curtis: Susan, 44
Cushing: John N., 170; William, 106, 119
Cutter: Stephen E., 170; Thomas H., 128

D

Dairy: Michael, 45, 64
Danford: Elizabeth M., 159
Danforth: Rufus, 59
Darathy: Bridget R., 47, 110, 126
Dariah: William, 181
Davenport: Moses, 113
Davidson: Hannah, 11; Hannah S., 75, 166
Davis: Charles W., 181; Luther, 34; Thomas, 43; William, 34; William E., 181
Dean: John, 67; William W., 93
Delap: Jemmina, 55
Delill: Judith, 98
Dennean: Patrick, 18
Dessinette: Sally, 118
Devereau: John, 20
Devine: William, 49
Dimmick: Luther F., 116, 158
Dixon: Margaret, 51
Dockum: Joseph H., 130
Dodd: Peter, 58, 175
Dodge: Dana, 29; John, 22, 36, 37; Samuel, 51; William S., 141
Dole: Hannah, 140; Parker D., 92; Parker M., 78, 105
Donahue: Michael, 52

Door: Mary, 89, 122
Dorr: Mary, 6, 18, 65, 131
Dow: Levi, 149
Downs: Abby F., 37; Stephen, 5, 9, 12, 57, 133
Drown: Richard W., 103
Durham: Kesia, 54, 141

E

Easton: Forest, 56; Sarah, 64, 105
Eaton: Jabez, 56; Jebez, 55, 56; Sarah, 161
Edes: Lois P., 56
Edgecombe: Elexzane, 53
Elliot: Hannah P., 56
Elliott: Hannah P., 9
Ellsworth: William N., 181
Emerson: Anna M., 66, 140
Emery: David, 65; Mary, 56
Eolls?: William W., 134
Evans: David, 58; John, 133; William S., 57, 177

F

Farwell: Perlis?, 58
Felch: William, 72, 123, 153
Felcher: Furver, 46
Fennimore/Finnimore: Peter, 149, 154; Samuel, 32
Flanders: Enoch, 149; Moses, 22, 168; Samuel, 69, 95
Fogg: George W., 6, 121; Jeremiah W., 47
Folansbee/Follansbee: James, 141; Love, 61; William A., 159
Folonsby: Jacob R., 179
Foote: Harriet, 39; Lewis, 29, 96
Ford: Samuel D., 166
Foss: Joseph N., 62
Fowle: Stephen, 37, 76, 120, 122, 143, 145
Freeman: James, 84, 175
French: Edson G., 65; Lewis, 65
Friend: Sarah, 143

Front: David, 90
Frost: George, 66; Samuel 66
Frothingham: Caroline H., 21, 34, 169, 170; Henry, 59; Joseph A., 56; Stephen, 168
Fullington: Lois, 41, 70, 81, 97, 118

G

Gaddis: Joseph, 67
Gardner, 62: Aaron, 3, 135; Merriam D., 156; Rebecca, 49, 108, 132, 162
Garland: Elizabeth, 14, 17, 21, 85, 90; George P., 29, 45, 56, 58, 68, 87, 143, 155
Gaskill: John, 7
George: Edward N., 76
Gerrish: Orwin B., 68, 69
Gilland: Francis, 69
Gilman: John S., 111
Goff: George W., 19
Goodfrey: Charles, 148
Goodhue: Thomas, 19
Goodwin: Benjamin, 96; Catherine, 41; Sarah B., 170, 172
Goover: William E., 70, 167
Gould: Ann, 71; Walter, 5, 12, 134
Granger: George F., 71, 159
Graves: Alexander, 97
Graves, Jr.: William, 40
Greenleaf: Cheater A., 175; Chester A., 50; George, 71; Joseph, 32, 77, 117, 133, 146
Greenough: Freeman, 169
Griffith: Nancy, 74, 75
Grindal: John L., 1, 21, 27, 28, 69, 85, 115; John L, 120; John L., 142, 148, 166, 169
Gunnison: Eveline, 36, 98, 156, 164
Gunnson: Eveline, 147

H

Hackett: James, 76
Hadley: Josiah, 13
Haines: Samuel, 58, 76, 175

Hale: Austin J., 68, 77; Charles, 1; Charles H., 181; Moses E., 181; Sarah, 95, 128
Hall: James, 78; Nancy, 122
Hardy: Dudley, 79; Mary J., 91, 95, 97
Harris: William L., 79, 80
Hatch: Hannah, 81
Hayden: Otis, 38
Hedden: John, 82
Hervey/Hervy: Joseph R., 181; William, 89
Hezeltine: Charles, 179
Hickman: Margaret, 89, 151
Hildreth: Dexter, 23, 79
Hill: George W., 135; John, 6; Louisa H., 83; Widow of Joshua Hills, 84
Hillard: Timothy, 150
Hilliard: Timothy, 2, 13, 59, 83, 146, 165, 166, 167, 169
Hills: William, 62, 100, 122 (2), 179
Hodgdon: Adriel H., 16, 24, 28, 76, 88; Moses, 14
Hodge: Charles Jr. 181; Nathaniel, 84, 177
Holker: John, 140
Holland: Patrick, 23, 28, 69, 71, 170, 171
Hollister: Jacob, 90
Hooke: Sarah, 1, 86
Hopkinson: Julia A., 86, 117
Horton: Daniel, 70; Jacob, 45, 64, John Jr., 89
Hougue: Sarah, 2
Hoyt: Jemima, 87; Joseph C., 87
Hudson: Charles H., 4
Huggett: Sarah, 91, 104, 105
Hunt: Joseph, 181
Huse: Joseph, 85, 88; Mary Y., 24, 77; William, 95, 181

J

Jack: Andrew, 102
James: Miram, 71; Miriam, 30, 98, 121, 146, 166
Jameson: William, 17, 175
Janverin: Joseph, 175
Jaques: Amos T., 181

Jenkins: Mary, 110
Johnson: Daniel, 149; Harrison J.O., 91; Henry, 3; Jonathan G., 91; Josiah, 181; Lavina, 173; Nicholas, 170; Patrick, 46, 91; Paul, 96; Philip, 91, 178; Samuel O., 80; William, 91
Jones: Mary, 157; Oliver, 181
Jordan: Simon, 22
Joy: Richard, 93, 98; Walter, 17, 106

K

Kavanagh: John, 16
Kelly: Eli G., 170; Patrick, 138
Kerman: Ruth A., 73
Keyes: Martha, 164
Kezer: Francis M., 48; Samuel, 181
Kidder: William, 181
Kilborn: George, 96; John C., 96; Warren, 181
Kimball: Harriet N., 33; Joseph D., 97; Michjah B., 71, 93; Sarah, 136
Kitching: William, 181
Knapp, Jr.: Anthony, 181
Knight: Daniel, 162, 166; George, 78
Kyes: William, 96

L

Ladd: Joseph, 154
Landford: Joseph B., 135
Lang: David, 127
Lattimer: James S., 147
Lawrence: Edwin, 170
Le Craw: William, 171, 181
Le Craw, Jr.: William, 181
Leighton: Gideon E., 101, 135; Jonathan, 181; Sarah, 78, 100
Lenlar: Henry, 71
Litch: James, 23
Littlefield: Solomon, 63, 101
Livingston: Abby K., 64, 102, 132, 142
Lory: Daniel O., 29, 53, 103
Loud: Sarah, 103
Lovering: Jonathan, 78, 178
Lucy: Catharine, 102, 104; Cornelius,

Lunt: Benjamin, 59; Daniel, 105; Ezra, 105; George, 113; Henry, 29, 149; Joseph C., 105; Moody, 60; Samuel, 28, 92; Sarah B., 104
Lurvey: David, 55, 72

M

Mace: Sarah, 105, 176
Mahaffy: Ann, 71, 169
Malchi: Jeremiah, 53, 54
Maloney: James, 6, 11, 12, 15, 29, 34, 38, 44, 53, 54, 73, 87, 99, 100, 109, 119, 126, 130, 138
Malony: Patrick, 106
Mansfield: Albert F., 108; David, 108
March: Enoch C., 108
Marden: Ira, 122; Sewall, 162; Susanna, 100, 103, 170
Marr: Margareat (sic), 108
Marsh: Sarah, 155
Marshall: Charles, 181; Hannah T., 63, 76, 93, 106, 138, 143, 158, 170
Marston: Stephen W., 103
Martin: Bartholomew, 110; Grating, 32
Maxswell: Dorcas, 110
McCarter: John, 110, 111
McCoffery: Catherine, 110, 126
McGimley: Edward, 112
McGlew: Hugh, 141
McGray: Thomas, 45, 112, 114
McGrull: James, 113
McManney: Barnard, 114
McPhee: John, 16
McQuillen: Robert, 80, 95
Medbury: Nicholas, 63, 87
Merchant: C.S., 30, 72, 94
Merrill: Asa, 117; Elizabeth A., 116; Hannah, 18; Jacob, 117; John, 117; Joseph, 28; Nathaniel J., 116; William H., 116
Mills: Bartlett, 23
Mincham: Margaret, 125
Monroe: Frances F., 74, 81, 103, 105, 160, 169
Moody: Gardiner, 181; Henry, 125; Patrick, 119
Mooney: A.W., 20, 78
Morrison: Ann, 159; Thomas, 63; William, 119
Moseley: Ebenezer, 33, 55, 106; Edward S., 34, 94, 120
Mott: Rebekah, 119
Munroe: George, 110
Murphy: David, 117; Ephraim, 122; Michael, 151
Myrick: Frederic W., 181

N

Nash: Rebekah, 122
Nason: Charles, 181
Nelson: Elizabeth S., 54; John B., 122; Mary, 81, 113; Thomas, 181
Newman: Sarah, 34
Nichols: William, 77
Noble: Benjamin, 7, 124, 129
Norman: George W., 6, 124
Noyes: Jacob, 14; Jacob Jr., 181; Margaret F., 75; Samuel, 125; Sewall B., 181; Thomas, 41, 42, 56, 100, 123, 145

O

O'Conner: Michael, 126
Odell: James, 159
Osgood: Nathl., 118; Rebecca, 127; Walter, 55, 56, 108
Owens: Ellen, 106

P

Packer: Stephen, 40, 162
Page: Betsy, 175; John, 129; John H., 181
Paker: William B., 105
Parker: Phineas, 81
Parsons: Sarah, 129
Patten: Alfred, 181; Henry, 181
Payson: Samuel, 18; Samuel T., 2, 64,

86, 141
Peabody: Charles, 79; James C., 181; Lucinda, 22; Lucinda G., 79
Pearson: Amos, 131, 151; Ariel, 131; Charles, 131; George, 170; Jabez, 131; John, 13, 99; John IV, 130; John, 130 (2); Levi, 21, 28, 42, 45, 53, 54, 60, 63, 73, 99; Luther, 126; Michael, 130
Peirce: Sarah, 87
Pentland: George, 10, 50; James, 87, 161
Perkings: Josiah, 133
Perkins: Elizabeth C., 67, 91; Henry C., 56; Nathaniel, 95
Perry: Charles W., 181; John N., 132, 133; Rebekah, 132
Pettigel/ll: Mary, 18; Richard 181; Samuel, 168; William H., 152
Phillips: Samuel, 105
Pickering: Valentine, 134
Pickman: Nancy, 87
Pike: Elias, 136; J.W.C., 136; Joseph S., 67; Mary C., 147
Pilsbury: Caroline, 136
Pingrey: Daniel, 136
Piper: Charles W., 47; Robert, 95
Plumer: Daniel, 181; Ebenezer, 1; Nathaniel D., 181
Poor: Elizabeth A., 137, 138; John, 164
Porter: John, 20, 25, 52; John P., 181; William, 159
Post: Ann, 114; Elizabeth, 138; John, 18, 37, 119, 141, 146, 155
Powers: James, 139; Robert, 138
Pratt: Benjamin, 30
Pressey: Thomas E., 107
Prichard: John B., 179
Prince: Polly, 75

R

Rains: Mary L., 14, 16, 72, 143, 144, 145, 170
Rand: Edward S., 28, 102, 141
Raymond: Andrew, 90
Raynes: John, 136
Rebecca, 62

Reed: Daniel, 155
Remick: Mary B., 141
Rendall: Lydia, 124
Reyes: Eliza, 129(2), 141
Richardson: Betsy, 142, 176; Jonathan C., 8, 57, 160; Sophia, 45, 78
Ricker: Mary, 142, 175
Ripley: Herekiah, 73, 118, 151
Ritching: William H., 52
Roaf: Washington, 68, 142
Roberts: Parker, 111, 118
Robinson: Benjn., 101, 144; Robert, 46, 109; William, 121
Rogers: Daniel, 182; Edward, 55; George L., 81; Silas, 144
Rolfe: George, 33
Romayne: Morris, 52, 120
Ross: Caroline, 145
Rossiter: Joseph, 182
Roune: Rosanna, 124, 172
Royers: Martha, 77, 78, 132, 145
Rundlett: Adalin, 146; Samuel H., 62
Rust: Frederick, 182
Rynes: John, 182

S

Sabine: Hillard, 182
Samrt: Milton, 98
Sanborn: Oliver, 99, 110, 172
Sargent: Charles R., 148; Elbridge A., 182; Hannah, 15, 49, 64, 129, 164; Horace, 41; John, 148; Kendall, 155; Nehamiah, 131, 132; True W., 164
Satter: Polly, 148
Scidenberg: Henry, 119
Sennon: Timothy, 100
Seward: John B., 7
Shaflish: Ann H., 98
Shakford: Joseph, 114
Shaw: William, 53
Shennon: David, 123
Shoof: Henry, 6
Short: Mary A., 151
Sillez: George R., 100
Simonds: Stilman, 31, 33, 102, 138, 142, 155

Simpson: Paul, 29, 54, 131
Skeels: Amos, 50, 51
Small: Mary A., 135, 152
Smart: Milton, 8, 36
Smith: Benjamin, 32, 42, 67, 109, 153, 154, 172; D.H., 182; Daniel, 23; John M., 36, 154, 168; Joster, 162; Justin, 182; Mayo G., 110; Thomas E., 152, 153; Wooster, 182
Somerby: Joseph A., 98
Souther: Jacob, 111; John, 113
Spates: William A., 154
Spofford: Richard S., 121
Spring: John, 182
Stanwood: William 45; William F., 141
Steven/s: Betsy, 11; Charles B., 182; Isaac, 178; Lydia, 157; Moses, 156; Samuel Jr., 109; Samuel, 156
Stewart: James F., 182
Stickney: Enoch, 163; Jacob, 45, 56, 65, 88, 166; Jacob, 3rd, 182; Joseph, 158; William, 157; William W., 182
Stone: Eben F., 83; Giles P., 66; Richard, 23
Storay: Elizabeth, 145
Stover: Sarah, 158, 159; Willilam, 158
Stowell: Justarus A., 123
Sullivan: Margaret, 24, 138
Swan: Ester G., 160
Swap: Almira, 99, 100, 129
Swasey/Swazey: Charles, 182; John B., 119, 155
Sweet: Charles E., 82
Sweetser: Moses, 172
Symonds: Mark, 112

T

Talbot: Mary N., 14, 93
Tappan: See Toppon: Hannah, 111, 161; Sarah, 75
Tarbox: George R., 20
Taylor: Hannah E., 161; Thomas, 7, 57
Teel: William, 182
Tennet: Thomas, 182
Thompson: Albert, 46, 143; Erwena, 162
Thurlow: Paul, 162

Thurston: William, 111
Tilton: Enoch, 3, 5, 6, 7, 13, 14, 15, 16, 37, 54, 55, 69, 80, 82, 101, 134, 159, 164; Jacob, 46; Mary, 93
Tindale: Cythia, 163
Todd: Sophia, 113, 164
Toppan: Charles, 165; Edward Jr, 179; Henry, 164; Rebekah H., 116, 165
Tower: Betsy, 167
Towles: George, 69
Townsend: John, 13, 142
Tozer: Hiram, 158
Tracy: Louisa L., 165; Thomas, 123
Trefather/Trefether: Alfred, 37, 166
Tucker: Elizabeth, 166
Turner: Clarissa, 28
Tuttle: Henry P., 109; John B., 71

V

Varney: D.G., 182; William, 182
Vermilye: Ashbell G., 50, 93
Verrill: Davis, 82
Vinox: William, 167
Vreen: Lydia A., 168

W

Walton: Samuel, 182; Samuel Jr., 182
Ward: George W., 22
Watkins: Joseph, 182
Weeks: John, 170
Welch: Eunice W., 11, 12, 13, 18, 171; Francis A., 171; Morris, 37, 52
Wellington: George, 182
Well/s: David, 133; Daniel, 172; William, 52, 171; William H., 125
Wescott: Charles, 172, 178
Wheelwright: Abraham, 94; Ann, 53, 173
White: Hannah, 89, 98, 123, 153; John H., 105
Whright: Martha A., 15, 56, 115, 126, 152
Wiggin/s: Oliver P., 10, 29, 84, 88, 131
Wilbur: Hervey, 26
Wilcomb: Newell, 182

Wilkinson: James, 135
Willey: Freeman O., 167, 174
Williams: Abraham, 82; Enoch S., 34, 78, 161; William C., 43, 141
Wilson: Abigail, 89, 117; Elizabeth, 176; Joseph, 175
Wingate: Jeremy C., 73
Winn: Moses, 32, 70, 98, 149
Wise: Albert, 29; William R., 157
Woart: Mary, 105, 177
Wood: Charles D., 177; David, 141; Eben, 182; Samuel, 132
Woodburn: John, 127
Woodman: Ann G., 18, 37, 124; Sally, 91

Y

Young: George W., 38; Jane, 44, 139; John, 92, 100, 162, 179; Timothy, 159

Occupation Index

A

Accountant, 80
Agent, 7
Agent Globe Mills, 146
Agent Ocean Mills, 148
Agent of James Mill, 168
Agt. Ploughshuvil?, 128
Apothecary, 25, 84(3), 116, 165
Apprentice Blacksmith, 76
Architect, 148, 151
Architect & Builder, 34
Artist, 111
Assist. In Clothing, 160
Assist. in Shoe Store, 86
Attached to Railroad, 79
Attorney, 109, 134, 158, 160
Auctioneer, 119, 161(2)

B

Babson & Teel, 180, 182
Baggage Master, 69
Baker, 2, 12, 13, 24(3), 32, 44, 64, 79, 86, 105, 125, 129, 130, 131, 140, 141, 151, 164
Baker/Grocer, 159
Baptist Clergyman, 1, 115
Barber, 28(2), 70, 105, 127, 140, 146, 179
Bar Keeper, 54
Barkeeper, 157
Barrister, 174
Beer Manufacturer, 65
Blacksmith, 1, 6, 19, 26, 31, 36, 56, 58, 60, 64, 68(6), 70, 76, 83, 87, 91, 92, 93, 102, 103, 112(4), 115, 118(3), 122, 123, 127, 128, 133, 139, 141, 148, 152, 166, 172, 176, 177(2), 178, 182
Block Maker, 43, 44, 138, 158(2)
Boarding House, 47, 67, 109, 118, 147, 154
Boat Builder, 82(2), 98, 120, 126, 133, 135, 136, 145
Book Agent, 5, 33
Bookbinder, 42
Bookseller, 25, 147, 163(2), 173
Boot & Shoemaker, 61
Boot/Shoe/Clothing, 73
Bootmaker, 44, 86, 176
Boots Shoe Dealer, 86
Bow Manufacturer, 19, 20
Branch Pilot, 104, 154
Brewer, 101, 102, 139(2)
Brick Maker, 153
Broker, 51, 66
Butcher, 24

C

Cabinetmaker, 11, 20, 32, 80, 115, 118, 119, 129, 131, 135, 137, 141, 144(2), 146, 149, 151(2), 157, 168
Captain, 180(4), 181(6), 182(8)
Carder, 10
Carpenter, 1, 2(2), 5, 9(3), 10, 13, 14(2), 19, 24, 31, 36, 38, 39(2), 40, 41(2), 48(2), 51, 52(2), 53, 55, 58, 62, 64, 65(2), 67, 68, 69, 71, 73, 75, 77(2), 80, 82, 84, 85, 88, 89(2), 90, 91, 96(2), 97, 98(2), 99, 105, 106, 114, 115, 116, 117(2), 120(2), 122, 123, 124(3), 125, 129(2), 130, 131, 132(2), 135, 136, 137(3), 138, 142(2) 145, 146(4), 148, 149(2), 152, 153(4), 154, 155, 156, 162, 166(2), 167(2), 168, 169(2), 174, 176, 177, 178, 179, 181
Carriage Maker, 30, 81(3), 129, 142, 174

Carver, 175, 176

Cashier, 3, 121

Caulder, 120

Caulker, 60(2), 73, 97, 123, 156

Chaise Maker, 8(2)

Chandler, 51

Clergyman, 131

Clergyman Chris., 135

Clergyman, Congregational, 25. 39, 50, 56, 123, 169, 174, 178

Clergyman, Epis., 169

Clergyman, Methodist, 37, 117

Clergyman, O.S. Presb., 57, 167

Clergyman, R.C., 100

Clerk, 1, 3, 5, 6, 19, 20(2), 21

Clerk, Bartlet Mills, 23

Clerk, 25, 30(2), 33, 37, 39, 41, 42, 45, 46, 47, 50, 56, 59, 60, 63(2), 70(2), 71, 75(2), 80, 83, 84, 86, 89, 91, 92(2), 100(3), 111, 120, 124(2), 129, 132, 136(2), 143, 147, 156, 158(2), 159, 160, 163, 164(2), 166, 168, 169(3), 173, 175, 176, 180, 181, 182(2)

Clerk Savins Inst., 158

Clothing Dealer, 75

Clothing Store, 7, 74, 75, 160

Coach Driver, 5(2), 10, 67(2), 103, 150

Coach Maker, 75

Coachman, 103

Coal and Lumber Dealer, 130

Coal Dealer, 63(2)

Coaster, 41

Collector, 164

Collector of Taxes, 39

Combmaker, 81

Conductor, 28, 99

Confectioner, 28, 45, 48, 55, 103, 121, 122, 170, 178(2)

Confectionery & Variety Store, 181

Constable, 28, 51

Conveyances, 116

Cooper, 2, 3(4), 18, 31, 32, 60, 70(4), 118, 129(4), 133(3), 142, 174, 178

Coppersmith, 151

Corder in Mill, 42

Cord Stripper, 87, 148

Cordwainer, 59, 60, 86(2), 131, 145, 165(2), 181

Cotton Spinner, 62

Counselor, 121

Counselor & Attorney, 14, 97

Crockery Dealer, 10

Custom House Weigher, 84

D

Daguerrotypist, 13, 25

Dancing Master, 128

Dealer in Clothing, 153

Dealer in Coal, 35

Dealer in Fish, 7

Dealer in Hardwood, 161

Dealer in Junk, 36

Dealer in Lumber, 163, 175

Dealer in Wood, 95

Dentist, 95, 121, 153(2), 182

Depot Master, 98

Dept. Collector, 23

Deputy Sheriff, 2, 73

Distiller, 25(2)

Drayman, 84, 102, 103, 109

Dresser, 61

Dresser in Mill, 104

Druggist, 44, 48, 93, 153, 181

Dry Goods Dealer, 22, 25, 66, 74, 83, 157

E

Editor, 181

Engineer, 19, 48, 74, 90, 91, 105, 117, 136, 157, 163, 169, 174, 178, 179

Engineer, 182

Express Agent, 37

Express Driver, 54

Expressman, 92. 173

F

Factory Agent, 6

Factory Operative, 167

Fancy Goods, 77

Farmer, 4(2), 6, 10, 19, 21, 35, 37(2), 48, 51, 52, 80, 101(2), 102(2), 113(3), 114, 119, 122, 134, 138, 164(2)

Farm Hand, 179

Farming, 99, 142, 165

Fireman, 25, 27, 58, 70, 90(2)

Fish Dealer, 53

Fisherman, 7(2), 16, 32, 35, 41, 68, 80(3), 100, 108(2), 117(3), 139, 140(2), 153

Fishing, 137

Fish Monger, 49

Fruit Dealer, 92

Fruit Seller, 33

Furniture Dealer, 137

G

Gardener, 8, 9, 47, 60, 63, 103

Gentleman, 7, 52, 129, 145(2), 156, 163

Gilder, 159

Goldsmith, 30, 45, 62, 86(2), 124

Grainer, 105

Grinder, 162

Grocer, 2, 4, 15, 19, 21, 38, 39(2), 56, 62, 73, 75, 80, 91, 92, 104, 116, 131, 136(2), 137(2), 141, 143, 145, 158, 161, 163, 164, 165(2), 166, 167, 171(3), 179, 181, 182

Grocer/Baker, 159

H

Hackman, 7, 71

Harness Maker, 4, 7, 50, 59, 75, 93, 98, 149, 156, 157

Hatter, 4, 62, 68, 80, 85(2), 86(2), 129, 136, 141, 160

Hermetical Sealer, 25

Hostler, 44

Hotel Keeper, 103, 163

House Carpenter, 6, 36, 40(2), 52(2), 56, 59, 70, 82, 102, 128(3), 130, 133, 140, 141, 152, 158, 159, 165, 181, 182

House Joiner, 10, 18, 19, 39(2), 65, 122, 165, 173, 180, 181(6)

Housewright, 59

I

In Charge of Bridge, 93

In Charge of R.R. Bridge, 93

In Jail, 27, 32, 37, 54, 56, 67, 77(2), 90(2), 106, 134, 174(2), 175, 176

Innholder (Hotel), 21

In Poor House, 6, 11, 12, 15, 34, 37, 38, 39, 44, 53(2), 54(2), 64, 70, 73(2), 87, 90(2), 92(2), 94, 99, 100(3), 103, 105, 106, 109, 111, 119(2), 121, 122, 124, 126, 127, 178, 179

Insurance Agent, 158

Iron Founder, 70. 83, 146, 168 (2)

Iron Foundry, 71, 74, 84, 118, 163

193

Iron Molder, 31(2)

J

Jeweler, 63, 85

Jeweler/Silversmith, 63(2) Also See Silversmith and Goldsmith

Joiner, 34, 39, 64, 69, 81, 82, 117, 152, 172, 180, 181(2)

Judge Police Court, 109

K

Keeps Bowling Alley, 165

L

Lab Factory, 19

Laborer, 2, 4(4), 5, 6, 7, 8(2), 9, 13, 14, 15(2), 18, 26(2), 27(5), 28(2), 30, 31(2), 33, 35(2), 36(2), 37, 38(2), 39, 40, 42, 45(2), 49(2), 50(2), 51, 53, 54, 57, 58(2), 59, 60(2), 61(2), 62(2), 63(4), 66, 69(2), 72, 74(2), 76(2), 78(2), 79(2), 80, 82, 83, 85(2), 86(2), 87, 90, 94(2), 95, 96, 98(2), 99(3), 100(2), 101, 102(2), 103, 105, 106(2), 107(3), 108, 110(4), 111(2), 112(2), 113(2), 114(5), 115, 117, 118, 119, 120, 121, 122, 123, 124(3), 125(4), 126, 127(2), 128, 132, 133, 138, 140, 145(2), 146, 148, 149(3), 150(2), 156(3), 157, 159, 160, 162, 163, 165, 169(2), 170, 171(2), 173, 175(2), 176(3), 177, 178(2), 179

Laborer Dye House, 29

Laborer in Distiller, 148

Laborer in Foundry, 46

Laborer in Mill, 24

Livery Stable, 147

Lumber Dealer/Merchant, 71, 72, 96(2)

M

Machine Shop, 90

Machinist, 6, 8, 11, 12, 17, 19, 21, 29(2), 31, 32, 33, 45, 49, 54, 58, 60, 66, 68, 74, 89(4), 99, 100, 108(2), 109, 115(2), 116, 124, 127, 138, 140, 141, 142, 146, 147, 149, 153, 154, 157, 158, 159, 160, 161, 162, 163, 164, 166, 167, 171, 174, 175, 178, 180(2), 182

Manufacturer, 144

Manufacturing, 168

Marble Worker, 48(2)

Mariner, 1, 2(2), 5(3), 6, 7(2), 9(2), 10, 11, 16(2), 17, 18, 19, 20(2), 22(3), 24(3), 26(3), 28, 29, 30(2), 31, 32(2), 34(2), 37, 38(6), 39, 40, 43, 45, 46, 48, 50(2), 51, 52, 54(3), 55(5), 56(3), 59, 60, 62, 63(2), 64(2), 69(4), 71(3), 72, 73, 74, 77(4), 79(3), 80, 81(4), 84, 88(2), 89, 90, 91(3), 92(4), 94(5), 96, 97(4), 98, 99(3), 100(4), 102(4), 103, 104(3), 105(2), 107, 109, 110(3), 114, 118, 119, 120, 121, 122, 124(3), 125(2), 126, 129(4), 132(3), 133(5), 134, 135(2), 136(2), 137(5), 138, 139, 140(3), 141, 142, 143, 144, 148, 149(2), 150, 151, 152(3), 153, 154(3), 157(6), 158, 163, 164, 166, 170(3), 172, 173(3), 175(2), 176, 177, 179, 181(2), 182

Mason, 3, 4, 7, 43(2), 44(6), 45, 47, 51(5), 70(2), 73, 89, 97, 104, 105, 119, 120, 125, 136, 153, 160, 165(3), 173, 181(3)

Master Mariner, 5, 9, 11, 14, 17, 20, 21, 22, 29, 30(2), 31, 34(2), 39(3), 43, 50(2), 53, 59, 60, 64, 72(4), 74, 77, 80, 87(3), 90, 92, 93, 95, 97(5), 98, 99, 100, 103(2), 104(2), 105, 108, 119, 121(2), 122, 127, 128(2), 130, 131(2), 135(3), 138, 140(2), 144(2), 152(6), 153, 155, 160(3), 162, 163, 164, 166, 167(2), 169, 170, 179

Master of Steamer, 114

Mast Maker, 39(2), 104(2), 156, 165, 179

194

Mate, 30

Math Instrument Maker, 35, 47(2), 162

Merchant, 1, 2, 4, 5, 7(2), 11(2), 13, 14, 15(2), 17(2), 20, 22(2), 25(3), 30, 34(3), 35, 37, 39(2), 44, 45(2), 47(3), 57, 64, 66, 70, 80, 85, 86, 89, 92(5), 96, 97(2), 102(2), 109, 121, 123, 124, 132, 135, 137(4), 138, 140, 143, 146, 153(3), 154, 157, 158, 159, 160, 163(2), 164(2), 172, 175(2), 177, 180, 181(2)

Merchant Tailor, 16, 31, 135

Milkman, 176

Miller, 143

Millwright, 114

Morocco Dresser, 89

Mule Spinner, 16

Music Instrument Maker, 104

N

Newspaper Publisher, 99

Notary Public, 17, 39

O

Operative, 3, 10, 11(2), 12(2), 17, 21(3), 22, 27, 28, 29, 31, 37, 40, 44, 46(2), 50(2), 51, 53, 54, 57(2), 61, 62(2), 63, 67(4), 70, 73, 74(2), 75(3), 76(2), 78(4), 79, 80, 82, 85, 86, 87, 91, 92(2), 94, 95, 97(3), 100, 103, 105, 111, 118(3), 121, 123, 124, 127, 129, 130, 133, 142(2), 143(2), 149, 152, 155, 158, 162, 167, 170(2), 172, 176(2), 181

Operative in Mill, 20, 81(2), 110, 178

Organ Builder, 2(2)

Ostler, 22, 81

Overseer, 1, 7, 20, 27, 31, 44(2), 49, 57(2), 60, 69(2), 73, 98, 99, 100, 108, 123, 147, 150(2), 158, 174

Overseer at OC Mills, 168

Overseer Card, 36

Overseer Carding, 168

Overseer Harness, 85

Overseer in Mill, 17, 21, 37, 55, 85, 90, 94, 98(3), 132, 155, 161

Overseer Spinning, 150(2)

Overseer Weaving, 98

P

Painter, 1, 14, 17, 21, 22(3), 23, 24(3), 30(2), 32, 38, 41(2), 42, 44, 45(2), 51, 52, 54, 65, 71, 73, 75, 76, 78, 81, 85, 86, 88(5), 89, 90(2), 91(2), 92, 93, 100, 102(2), 103, 107, 109(2), 110, 118, 124, 129, 130(2), 140, 147, 152, 164, 169, 171, 175, 178, 181

Painter and Glazer, 135, 136

Paymaster in Mill, 18

Peddler, 46, 88

Periodical Book Store, 5

Physician, 5, 42, 50, 92, 95(2), 116, 132, 148, 155, 179

Pilot, 3

Plater, 127

Plate Worker, 72

Porter, 82(2), 134, 164

President Savings Bank, 80

Printer, 17, 31, 32, 69, 75, 89(2), 120, 129, 137, 142, 147, 154(2), 158, 181, 182

Printer & Publisher, 18

Probate Agent, 48

Publisher, 181

Pump and Block Maker, 100, 135(2), 136, 157, 158(2), 164, 181

R

Reading Room Keeper, 87

Restoration, 160

Restorator, 22, 46, 55, 99, 156, 172

Rigger, 15, 18(2), 32, 95, 136(3), 139(4), 142, 177, 182

Roll Coverer, 73, 118

Rope Maker, 2, 57(2), 58(2), 130(2), 133, 157, 179

S

Saddle and Harness Maker, 137

Sailing Master, 164

Sailmaker, 26, 34, 37, 43, 47(2), 48, 70, 73, 76, 77(2), 90(2), 120, 136(2), 181

Sailor, 66, 121, 144, 156

School Teacher, 2, 8, 28, 29, 64, 121, 163, 164, 172

Seaman, 4, 181(2)

Servant/Attends School, 33

Sexton, 45(2), 53, 147, 162

Shipbuilder, 121

Ship Carpenter, 20, 21, 23, 34(4), 48, 55, 72(2), 82(2), 85, 88(2), 89, 101, 102, 117(2), 119, 137, 156, 167, 168

Ship Chandler, 15

Ship Joiner, 5, 22, 31(2), 32(5), 58(2), 136, 140, 148, 157, 174

Ship Master, 6, 41, 68, 88, 92, 104, 136, 150, 151, 177

Ship Master "Late", 120

Shipwright, 68

Shoe Cutter, 117

Shoe Dealer, 41, 47, 130, 144

Shoemaker, 2(4), 3, 4(2), 5, 8(3), 9 (2), 10(2), 12(2), 13(2), 14, 16, 18, 24(2), 28, 29(2), 30, 32(2), 33, 36(2), 39(2), 41, 42(3), 43(2), 44(2), 46(2), 47(3), 48, 49, 53, 55, 56, 58, 59(2), 61(4), 62, 64(3), 70(2), 71, 72(3), 73(2), 74, 75, 77, 78(2), 83(3), 84(2), 86, 87, 92(2), 93(2), 95(2), 96(2), 97, 98, 99, 100, 101(2), 102(2), 107, 108, 109, 116, 117(3), 119, 120(6), 121, 123(2), 124(3), 125, 129, 130(3), 131(2), 133(3), 134, 136, 137(2), 139, 140, 141(2), 142, 143(2), 144(4), 145(3), 149, 151, 156(3), 160, 162, 165, 167, 170(5), 172(2), 174, 177(2), 178(2)

Shoe Manufacturer, 8, 109, 142. 144

Shoe Store, 84

Shop Carpenter, 26

Silk Dyer, 51

Silversmith, 93, 165 See Jeweler

Soap and Candle Manufacturer, 146, 156

Soap Boiler, 51, 131

Soap Chandler, 182

Spinner, 4, 41, 43, 66, 70, 74(2), 147, 154, 177

Sportsman, 41

Stable Keeper, 37, 53, 104, 137, 141, 150, 158

Stabler, 147

Stage Agent, 5, 20

Stage Driver, 1, 2, 115, 131

Stageman, 54

Stair Builder, 37

State Proprietor, 180

Stevedore, 7

Stone Cutter, 90, 172

Stone Mason, 96, 132, 173

Stove Dealer, 29, 77, 95, 147

Stove Manufacturer, 77, 148

Stretcher in Mill, 132

Student, 6, 14, 49, 52, 54, 58, 63, 72, 77(2), 87, 105, 115, 141, 142, 143, 151, 152, 155, 173, 175(2), 177, 179

Student Putnam School, 15, 39, 49

Superintendent of Poor House, 25

Surveyor, 131

Surveyor of Lumber, 123
Surveyor of the Port, 90

T

Tailor, 2, 39, 43, 45, 96, 115, 123(2), 132, 135, 137, 148, 151, 153, 155, 160, 171(2), 178

Tallow Chandler, 107, 108, 152, 158

Teacher of Music, 140

Teacher of Navigation, 124

Teamster, 2, 26, 48, 70, 81, 85, 126, 137, 138, 148, 176

Telaphonemaker (sic), 17

Telegraph Agent, 81

Tinman, 86, 160

Tinner, 86, 130

Tin Plate Worker, 29(2), 39, 52, 80, 83, 87, 97, 115, 130, 176

Tobacco Manufacturer, 88

Tobacconist, 88, 89, 90, 116, 157

Tollgatherer, 172

Town Crier, 81

Trader, 4, 5, 6, 7, 11, 14, 17, 19, 20, 27, 64, 66, 81, 86, 91, 111, 116, 119, 123, 136, 141, 143, 148, 160, 161, 164, 171

Traller?, 86

Treasurer R.R., 48

Truck driver, 103

Truckman, 8, 9, 36(2), 38, 65, 80, 90, 95, 101, 102, 104, 120, 132, 135, 145, 146, 147, 177, 180

U

U.S. Army, 115(2)
Umbrella Vender, 169

V

Victualer, 2(2), 14, 28(3), 116, 119

W

Watchmaker, 6, 54(2), 63, 74, 103, 143

Watchman, 18, 19(2), 52, 54, 100, 131, 147, 155(2), 167, 178

Weaver, 11, 12, 23(2), 43, 47, 77, 97, 104, 110, 126, 152, 162(2), 169

Wharfinger, 129

Wheelwright, 8, 53, 57, 77, 108, 109(2), 116, 119, 160, 162, 169

Wood and Lumber Dealer, 51. 131

Wool Business, 116

Wool Puller, 81

Work in Distillery, 74

Birth Place Index:

A

AL, 178

B

Breman, 149

C

Canada, 5(2), 6(2), 9(3), 24, 33, 64(6), 65(2), 66(6), 88, 90(2)
CT, 7, 18, 20, 30, 36, 37(3), 42, 48, 53, 54, 57(2), 81, 100, 115, 121, 128, 129, 143, 150, 153, 160(2), 166(3), 172, 173, 177

D

D. C. (District of Columbia), 69, 136
DEL, 99, 133
Denmark, 98, 146, 150, 151(2), 154, 175

E

East Canada, 171(3), 172(2)
England, 3(3), 4, 7, 10(2), 12(7), 15(6), 16(2), 24, 28(2), 30, 31, 35(2), 43(6), 44, 45, 47(2), 48, 50(4), 51, 56(2), 57(5), 61(7), 62(4), 64, 66(4), 67(2), 73(2), 76(4), 77(5), 78(10), 80, 85(7), 86(2), 88, 90(2), 91(3), 92(4), 95, 98, 99, 103(2), 105, 113(2), 118(4), 120, 121(6), 123(4), 124, 129, 130, 132(7), 134, 137(2), 140, 141, 144, 149, 151, 152, 153, 154(2), 155(3), 159, 160, 162(5), 164, 169(3), 173(3), 174, 178(5)
Enlance?, 72

F

France, 60, 80, 81, 91, 168, 176

G

GA, 115(2)
GAR?, 135
Germany, 4, 13, 14, 15, 103, 155

H

Halifax, 122
Holland, 86

I

ILL, 42(2), 161
Ireland, 2, 3(8), 8(7), 10, 11(5), 13, 14(4), 15(2), 17(2), 18, 22(4), 23(10), 24(2), 25(3), 26(6), 27(14), 28(5), 29(4), 33(2), 34, 35(5), 36, 37(4), 38(17), 39, 40(14), 41, 42(10), 43(3), 45(7), 46(11), 47(6), 49(7), 50(6), 51(3), 52(14), 53(5), 54(5), 55(2), 57(3), 58(9), 59(4), 60(3), 61(6), 62(2), 64(2), 66, 67(2), 69(5), 70, 71(8), 72(2), 76(8), 77, 78(4), 79(3), 80, 81(3), 82(6), 83(7), 85(4), 86(4), 87(7), 88(2), 90(3), 91(2), 92(2), 93(2), 94(11), 95(5), 97(2), 98(2), 99(8), 100(2), 101(2), 102(8), 103(10), 104(6), 105(8), 106(17), 107(8), 108(2), 109(4), 110(15), 111(20), 112(12), 113(14), 114(17), 115(6), 117(3), 118(3), 119(10), 121(4), 122(5), 123(5), 124(2), 125(10), 126(16), 127, 128(8), 130, 131, 132(2), 133(2), 134, 137, 138(5), 139(7), 140(6), 141(4), 142(2), 144(2), 145(14), 148(4), 149(4), 150(6), 151, 154(2), 156(3), 159(8), 160, 161(4), 162(2), 166(2), 168(2), 169(3), 170(2), 171, 172(3), 173(3), 174(2), 176(5)
Italy, 71, 128(3), 159

J

Jamaca, 80

L

LA, 81(2), 144, 160

M

MA, 1(8), 2(14), 3(8), 4(7), 5(12), 6(12), 7(14), 8(7), 9(10), 10(8), 12(13), 13(2), 14, 15(7), 16(4), 17(8), 18(7), 19(10), 20(11), 21(10), 22(10), 23(3), 24(8), 25(13), 26(3), 27(5), 28(6), 29(10), 30(13), 31(10), 32(13), 34(13), 35(7), 36(3), 37(9), 38(6), 39(24), 40(2), 41(8), 42(6), 43(7), 44(19), 45(10), 46(2), 47(11), 48(11), 49(6), 50(4), 51(13), 52(10), 53(5), 54(5), 56(10), 57(5), 58(9), 59(7), 60(8), 61(2), 62(4), 63(15), 64(5), 65(4), 66(3), 67, 68(10), 69(7), 70(17), 71(6), 72(10), 73(14), 74(9), 75(14), 76(2), 77(16), 78(3), 79(5), 80(16), 81(14), 82(7), 83(4), 84(6), 85(7), 86(12), 87(6), 88(9), 89(12), 90(11), 91(12), 92(20), 93(6), 94(4), 95(7), 96(6), 97(13), 98(8), 99(10), 100(15), 101, 102(9), 103(7), 104(15), 105(8), 107, 108(5), 109(12), 110(3), 111, 112, 115(6), 116(8), 117(9), 118(4), 119(8), 120(16), 121(8), 122(4), 123(5), 124(9), 125(4), 126(3), 127(11), 128(11), 129(18), 130(14), 131(13), 132(8), 133(14), 134, 135(14), 136(24), 137(21), 138(5), 139(9), 140(11), 141(8), 142(6), 143(6), 144(10), 145(9), 146(4), 147(12), 148(9), 149(7), 150(2), 151(10), 152(13), 153(11), 154(11), 155(6), 156(11), 157(15), 158(22), 159(6), 160(13), 161(9), 162(4), 163(13), 164(16), 165(13), 166(7), 167(5), 168(5), 169(5), 170(8), 171(4), 172(7), 173(6), 174(5), 175(11), 176(10), 177(8), 178(14), 179(14)

Maine, 1(3), 2(2), 3, 4(4), 5(4), 6(5), 7, 9(3), 10(4), 12, 13(2), 14(6), 15(4), 16(2), 17(5), 18, 19(3), 20(2), 21(3), 22(4), 23(2), 24(5), 25(2), 27(7), 28(3), 29(6), 30(5), 31(4), 32(8), 33, 34(4), 35(3), 36(6), 37(3), 38, 39(3), 40(3), 41(2), 42(3), 44, 45(2), 46(2), 47(4), 48(8), 49(4), 50(2), 51(2), 52(3), 53(3), 54(6), 55(9), 56(5), 57(4), 58, 59(3), 61(3), 62(5), 63(7), 64(2), 65(6), 66(5), 67(5), 68(3), 69(3), 70(5), 71(5), 72(6), 73(4), 74(9), 75(7), 76(3), 77(2), 78(2), 79(9), 80(3), 81, 82(3), 83(6), 84(8), 85(5), 86(4), 87(6), 88(7), 89(8), 90(3), 93(2), 95(2), 96(12), 97(2), 98(8), 99, 100(2), 101(5), 102(10), 103(2), 105(7), 107(5), 108(3), 109, 111(2), 112, 116(4), 117, 118(8), 119(2), 120(6), 121(5), 122(4), 123(6), 124(3), 126, 127(3), 128, 129(2), 130(3), 131(8), 132(4), 133(5), 134(7), 135(4), 136(2), 137(4), 138(3), 139(4), 140(5), 141(2), 142(11), 143(15), 144(10), 145, 146(8), 147(3), 148(6), 149(2), 151(3), 152(9), 153(2), 154(3), 155(6), 156(9), 157(4), 158, 159, 160(6), 161(6), 162(4), 163(4), 164(12), 165(9), 166(6), 167(2), 168(9), 169(4), 170(7), 171(3), 172(5), 173(10), 174(2), 175(5), 176(5), 177(6), 178, 179(3)

MD, 157, 179
Mississippi Territory, 162
MO, 153
Montividon, 29

N

N.S., 2(6), 7, 141(2)
NC, 57
New Brunswick, 15, 16, 18 41(6), 43(6), 46(4), 49, 57, 68, 72(4), 80, 81, 90, 107, 111(2), 112(2), 114, 115(3), 123(3), 166, 167(2), 168, 174(2)
Newfoundland, 4, 16(7), 18(4), 24, 38, 46(2), 47, 51(2), 64, 70(2), 71, 72, 79(3), 83(2), 91(5), 93(8), 94(3), 106, 110(2), 112(6), 125(5), 126(5), 134(7), 138, 139, 160, 161(4), 169(7), 174

NH, 1(6), 2(7), 4(7), 5, 8(6), 9, 10(7), 12(17), 13(5), 14(10), 15(2), 17, 18(3), 19(9), 20(12), 21(13), 22(3), 24(2), 25(2), 26(4), 27(2), 28(4), 29(2), 30(3), 31(8), 32(2), 33(18), 34(2), 35(2), 36(7), 38(2), 39(4), 40(3), 41(5), 42(2), 43, 44(3), 45(4), 46(5), 47(3), 48(6), 49(6), 51(6), 53(10), 54(8), 55(8), 56(11), 57(3), 58, 59(9), 60(9), 61(7), 62(8), 63(4), 64(3), 65(2), 66(2), 67(9), 68(4), 69(8), 70(3), 71(2), 72(2), 73(5), 74, 75(5), 76(3), 77(4), 78(6), 79(2), 80(3), 81(2), 83(3), 84(9), 85(?), 86, 87(3), 88(6), 89, 90(3), 91(3), 92, 93(8), 95(9), 96(3), 98(4), 99(3), 100(3), 102(2), 103(4), 104, 105(3), 106, 108(12), 109(6), 110(2), 111, 114, 115, 116(10), 117(6), 118(3), 119(4), 120(4), 121(3), 122(8), 124(5), 125, 126, 127(9), 129(6), 130(9), 131(5), 132(5), 133(3), 134(5), 135(7), 136(2), 137(4), 138, 139(2), 141(6), 142(6), 143(3), 145, 146(12), 147(10), 148(4), 149(6), 150(2), 151(7), 152(2), 153(8), 154(5), 155(2), 156(4), 157(6), 158(5), 159(5), 162(10), 163(9), 165(4), 166(6), 167(5), 168(3), 169(6), 170(5), 171, 172(8), 173, 174(13), 175(4), 176(6), 177(8), 178(4), 179(8)

NJ, 25, 67, 76, 96, 167(2)

Norway, 18

Nova Scotia, 2(6), 7, 13(8), 18, (2), 22, 23(9), 24, 26(9), 28, 35(2), 40, 41(2), 43(2), 44(4), 49(4), 51, 54, 58, 64, 65(9), 66(2), 68(8), 71(3), 72, 74(5), 76(3), 79(2), 81, 86, 94(6), 101(14), 102(4), 106(4), 107(9), 109(2), 112, 113(5), 114(4), 115, 116(3), 117(4), 118(4), 119(2), 125(3), 133(3), 134, 138(9), 149(3), 154(4), 155(6), 165, 166(3), 167(5), 170(2), 171(2), 175

NY, 5, 6, 30, 31, 33, 42, 50(2), 57, 58(3), 65, 74, 79, 87(2), 99(2), 109(2), 115, 123, 144(2), 158, 167, 171, 173(4), 175, 177, 178

P

PA, 40, 50, 96, 115, 162
Portugal, 100, 175
Pr. Edward Island, 24(3), 60(4), 82(6), 117, 121(2)
Prussia, 98

R

RI, 10, 18, 19, 32, 37(4), 45(2), 50(3), 51, 58, 73, 86, 87, 89(2), 90(2), 97, 109, 118, 122, 127, 148(3), 150(14), 153(3), 160, 168(2), 171(8), 177(2), 178

S

Sandwich Islands, 141
Scotland, 26, 31, 50(2), 57, 67(5), 94, 97(3), 152, 179
St. Johns, 138(2), 139, 168 (2)
Surnam, 100
Sweden, 90, 91, 159, 168

U

Unknown, 134, 174, 176

V

VA, 84, 117, 128, 171
VETsic, 167
VT, 4, 5(2), 6(2), 7, 8, 9(6), 13, 17(5), 18, 22(2), 28(2), 34, 41, 50, 55, 59(3), 65, 83, 84(3), 95(2), 100(4), 108, 110, 127, 138, 145, 147, 152(3), 154(2), 157, 170, 171(3), 172(2), 175

W

West Indies, 105

www.ingramcontent.com/pod-product-compliance
Lightning Source LLC
Chambersburg PA
CBHW050148170426
43197CB00011B/2003